MW01625277

THE DANCE OF ASTROLOGY

From Clockwork to Quantum, and Beyond:

Meditations and Speculations

Douglas C. Egan

ISBN-13: 978-0692596340

ISBN-10: 0692596348

R1616

Dedications:

To my friend Julio Bello, without whose influence this book would likely not have come into being;

To certain other friends as well, who not only gave me the gift of life, but taught me how to use it;

And to my wife Margaret, who completes my Circle.

"Cycles ferried my cradle, rowing and rowing like cheerful boatmen."

—Walt Whitman

"Things are not as they appear to be;

nor are they otherwise."

—Lankavatara Sutra

TABLE OF CONTENTS

Introduction

I am an alcoholic. That may seem to be a strange sentence with which to open a book that primarily concerns itself with astrology, physics, and consciousness; but there are reasons for this. One is simply to acknowledge that, had I not been blessed with a certain moment of clarity at a particular point in the past that has led to continued sobriety, I would probably not have been around to pen this book that you are holding. The second (and more significant) reason is that my personal journey into sobriety has paralleled in many ways the journey of thought and learning that this book has required, and most importantly has provided me the supreme gift of becoming more open-minded and receptive to new ideas and new ways of seeing. Through opening our eyes, the world also opens up. In saving my own life, I've not had the luxury of hanging onto old ideas. Receptivity was forced upon me; but in allowing others to storm the ramparts of my beliefs, I was able to let my guard down enough to find out, with much relief, that the invaders were not only benign but beneficial. Seemingly unimportant and unrecognized at the time, this more persuadable position has ultimately led to the many exploratory essays contained herein.

Early in sobriety I discovered, to my amazement, that everything that I thought I knew about drinking and alcoholism was wrong—completely, 100% wrong. That simple but earth-shaking revelation led me to subsequently question what else about my assumptions, or regarding life, I might be wrong about. What *other* things did I "know" to be true that were also inaccurate? There turned out to be many. What a joy it has been to explore the various truths that had never previously existed, at least for me. The journey started there, and it has never ended.

This is not a book of answers; it is a book of questions. The really good things that we stumble across lurk not at the end of a pat answer, but at the end of a searching question. You will be invited to ponder things on your own and in tandem with the ideas presented here: human consciousness and knowledge evolve in connection with other minds, not in a vacuum. The I Ching, in its wisdom states, "In this way learning becomes many-sided and takes on a cheerful lightness, whereas there is always something ponderous and one-sided about the learning of the self-taught."

The primary audience for this book is likely to be those interested in astrology, but it is hoped that it may also provide something of appeal to those interested in subjects as varied as physics, consciousness, synchronicity, and metaphysics, or spirituality. In fact, those are exactly the section titles in the book. They are to be seen as components of a larger picture, petals of an awakening and more comprehensive flower that will continue to open up as time goes on. The march of human understanding and knowledge is ever-flowing. This is a moment in time, as Jung pointed out, and as such it has and contains the characteristics of this moment in time. This particular moment will not come again. It will be supplanted by other moments, no doubt shedding additional light on many of the inquiries presented herein. The book is primarily a series of meditations or short essays; it is not necessarily a programmed journey building from one section to the next, somehow leading to a prearranged conclusion. Theoretically, one could jump into any section and hopefully enjoy it as is, but there probably *is* something to be said for starting at the beginning and working one's way through in order.

There are five main sections to the book. It starts with physics and ends with metaphysics, but it could nearly as easily be read in reverse order, because one of the points of the book is to examine the relationship between the physical and the non-physical world, and to question whether everything *can* ultimately be reduced to physics, chemistry, and other associated disciplines that form our current scientific paradigm. You will notice a caveat near the beginning of the physics section. That's because this area may not be the first interest for those who are attracted to this material for other reasons. If you can, hang in there. It will ultimately add to the overall experience. Astrology, and especially synchronicity, will eventually show up as a bridge between the various sections.

The chapters are parts making up a greater whole. The whole is the realm of human experience and knowledge, and how these two interact with our own brief journeys here on earth. The physical world, consciousness, synchronicity, astrology, and metaphysics: if one assigns emotion to synchronicity (which is actually the subject of a later contemplation), those familiar with horoscopic study will be able to see that these ultimately break down into the familiar four "elements" of astrology: earth, air, water, and fire. These historic elements of life may seem anachronistic to the modern mindset, but they have an undeniable and powerful history spanning multiple human cultures in vastly different times and locales. A fifth element was also added at times in antiquity, but seems upon analysis somewhat redundant; its function easily assigned to that of fire. The Indians and the Greeks spring to mind most immediately here as associated with these elements. For even the skeptic, however, they may have value, if one is open-minded. It may be noted that the composing principles of our own lives seem to boil down to the physical world, consciousness and intellect, emotion, and the spiritual—whatever one may envision that to be. Into these four "buckets," then, may be placed all of human life and experience in its vast variety.

This is not an astrology textbook, nor is it an attempt to teach astrology to the uninitiated. There are no celebrity charts with accompanying analysis. There are a plethora of excellent astrological "cookbooks" out there that do a great job of explaining astrology to the curious or to the newcomer. ("Cookbooks" use the format of explaining the various astrological factors—for example, "Moon in Sagittarius"—in a very programmed and logical fashion: it is then up to the "cook," the astrologer, to put these factors into a stew and come up with a tasty dish, or overall picture.) This book attempts instead to examine some of the philosophical underpinnings of astrology, and indeed of life itself. The book *is* about astrology, although it comes at it from an oblique angle. It does assume that the reader will have some working knowledge of that discipline; it is not a beginner's book. It may be found by some to have a surprisingly little amount of actual astrology in it, if one is expecting techniques or similar approaches. That is not in error. The goal here is to look at the larger picture of life, which includes, but may or may not be dominated by, astrology. That in itself is up for debate, as is nearly everything else in this book. And the book is finally hopeful that astrology may yet again have its day in the sun; the discipline was shut out of the club at the very beginning of the Enlightenment because it had no easy fit in the new scientific materialism, but it refuses to die. Too many people find something there. Defying certain stereotypes, its supporters include many highly educated and deeply thoughtful seekers. And, perhaps unconsciously anticipating a future compatibility, the scientific worldview itself has been steadily moving in the direction of a more holistic and connected model of the world: astrology may finally (as examined in this book) not be so far from the possibilities shown by the new physics that is emerging from old paradigms.

This book wants you to "question everything." That is the subject of a bumper sticker that has appealed to youth for generations, but it is also a good motto for life. What *do* we know for sure? *Are* we sure? Where do new things come from? How can we accept new ideas? Is everything known? Then how do we find out what's not known? Philosophical assumptions should be questioned, and so should physics, and so should astrology. Everything should be on the table.

There are two core concepts to be mentioned in this context that will reappear frequently throughout this book. They are generalized notions, applying equally well to science, astrology, work, relationships, personal happiness, and almost anything else one could name. One may be set forth by a simple formula: R=K+1. For those rusty with math, here we are letting R represent Reality, and K represent human Knowledge. Thus, regardless of what new things we may discover or know, reality itself will always be one step ahead of us, one mystery beyond. More knowledge gives us a better picture of reality, but it stimulates new questions, which further require new knowledge, and so on. It is an endless cycle. In fact, we don't even know where we stand in this process of discovery: are we near the beginning, or near the end? Since it *always* feels like we're just around the corner from everything being tidied up and known, this subjective perception is a poor gauge. Cavemen discovering how to control fire likely felt that they were a pretty clever bunch, pretty close to knowing everything there was to know.

R=K+1, then, seems to be one of the great principles of the universe, and has implications in our own personal lives as well. As above, so below. The laws that apply to the universe are good for us, too. The formula indicates that there will *always* be something else left to know, that our understanding will never be complete. The +1 is the unknown factor, ever needing to be added onto our misguided feeling of being able to describe reality at any given point in time pretty well through our current knowledge. That delusion *must* be shattered, as it is simply not true.

Our history on this planet has been a continual series of misconceptions that we have it all mostly figured out, with only a nagging question or two left to fill in the blanks on, using whatever tools we have at the moment. Lord Kelvin, who in the 19th century did significant work with electricity, thermodynamics, and physics, is reputed to have said around 1900 that "there is nothing new to be discovered in physics now, all that remains is more and more precise measurement." (He also called the then-new discovery of x-rays a "hoax.") And yet he was one of the most brilliant men of his generation. Prince or pauper, genius or not so much, we are all prone to falling into this fallacy, into forgetting the +1. The word hubris was coined more than two thousand years ago for just such errors in thinking. We have always been proved either wrong, or more commonly incomplete; there has always been more to know.

Reality is out there, but the journey to understanding it is akin to a mathematical asymptote: we approach closer and closer, but we never quite get there. So we must remain ever humble, whether physicists, housewives, businessmen, or astrologers. Over and over, the human march towards knowledge is one of false starts, delusions, setbacks, rethinkings, aha! moments, and eating humble pie. Heliocentrism and plate tectonics were speculated centuries before they were accepted or proved to be true; those favoring them early were ridiculed—or worse, persecuted. It is often thankless to be walking outside of the current structure, but the larger message is one of an ongoing process of construction and certainty, deconstruction, clearer thinking, and reconstruction. We balk at the deconstruction, as it seems like wasted work, too much trouble, and fear and discouragement set in. But the +1 is the good stuff, ever lingering out there beyond the settled K. That's Reality.

A story here in brief that has been told numerous times, but that encapsulates the above principle, is that of the blind men and the elephant:

There were six blind men who lived together in a village. One day, an elephant trader came through and, finding out that they had never heard of such a creature, gave them all a chance to experience the pachyderm. The first man touched his leg and exclaimed, "Oh, an elephant is like a pillar!" The second, who was touching the tail, countered, "No, an elephant is more like a piece of rope." The third, touching his trunk, said, "No, I think an elephant is best compared to a large tree branch." The fourth, grabbing the ear, said, "You are all inaccurate—an elephant is just like a fan." The fifth, touching the elephant's side, noted, "I think maybe it's more like a big wall." The sixth, holding on to the tusk, said, "You others are incorrect. Anyone can tell that an elephant is very similar to a smooth pipe."

Of course they were all of them wrong, and all of them right. Reality is never simple, although simple principles may guide its explorations, chief among them the traits of being open, receptive, questioning, and humble. Our personal visions are always biased and limited. There is always more to know about anything, and about everything. R = K+1.

***

The other core concept and related companion to the equation above that will appear in various incarnations throughout the book is the simple phrase, "believing is seeing." Everyone has heard that "seeing is believing," but few have considered its corollary. "Believing is seeing" recognizes not only the power of our consciousness in determining our reality, but also its limitations. We see the world not as it is, but as it is colored *by us* through our perceptions, egos, values, beliefs, prejudices, preferences, errors in thinking, errors in feeling, preconceptions, doubts, fears, hopes, and dreams. We project our own beliefs out onto the world, and not surprisingly, they are reflected back to us. *None* of us see things entirely clearly. Here is another asymptote: we can, with effort, make an approach towards clarity of personal thought, but we can never finally arrive. Our beliefs about the way things are guide our seeking, and skew our selective perceptions towards finding confirmation for these biases in the world around us. The real *problem* is that most of us don't recognize this. We assume, erroneously, that we do see things clearly. This is where all the problems of the world begin.

Because of this blind spot, most of us do not seek out new ways of looking at things, as we are secure and complacent in our entrenched views. We then blissfully try to paste our limited understandings onto others, assuming that they, too, must see things in the same way that we do, or at least that they *should*. They don't. Why would they? They are living in their own beliefs. After all, we reason, isn't there an "objective" reality out there? And are we not just the ones to perceive it most clearly, untainted by the fuzzy vision that others possess?

So a big point to be made in this book is to simply recognize that idea, and to remind ourselves that we all are no more than fleshy bags of consciousness, all existing with the same human limitations. The journey, then, is to find out how our own selves might fit in with other selves, and with whatever larger reality is out there—to join together in seeking clarity. The quest, as it has been throughout man's history, is to find out how it all works. The quest is indeed how to find out *how* to find out how it all works, and what the meaning of it all is. By breaking free of our unconscious distortions and biases, we can start to relax and embrace the idea that, for ourselves as well as others, believing is indeed seeing. It's OK. We just need to be aware of that, and to acknowledge that we are all creating our own realities out of limited and distorted information. Our version of reality is personalized and egocentric, and bears only varying degrees of congruence with a more independent level of reality that is larger than ourselves. However, as we shall see, the story of even that reality is a bit more complicated than it may seem.

(It is also always easy to come down with a case of the "shoulds." From an astrological perspective, if we are Air signs, then the world should be a logical and communicative place. If we are primarily Earth, then people should be more practical. If we are mainly Water, then people should be emotionally sensitive and compassionate. And if we are mostly Fire, then people should of course take an open, energetic, and vibrant approach to life. No "wet blankets" needed or tolerated! And this idea can easily be extended through various permutations and combinations of the above. For example, if one is primarily Earth and Air, then people should be practical, responsible, analytically oriented, and logical. If one is primarily Water and Earth, then people should be practical and yet emotionally sensitive to others, etc. It takes a lot of effort to maintain a larger vision, to realize that people can be quite different from us, and still find the tolerance to accept that fact and be OK with it.)

An old African folktale goes:

There was an elderly farmer on the outskirts of a village who was tilling his field. One hot afternoon, he stood up to say hello to a traveler that he noticed passing his way along the road towards his town. The traveler said, "There's been a terrible fire in my village miles away, and everyone has to find a new place to live. Can you tell me, what are the people like in the village that's on up ahead?"

The farmer thought for a minute and, instead of answering directly, asked the traveler, "Tell me first, what were the people like in the village that you have just left?"

"Oh, they were kind of terrible, actually. A lot of backbiting, small-minded people who wouldn't lift a finger to help each other. I'm actually not sad to be leaving."

The farmer leaned on his hoe and thought for a minute. "Well, I'm sorry to tell you, but you'll likely find the same sort of people in the village on up ahead." Disappointed, the traveler said goodbye and resolved to keep looking for better circumstances.

A short while later, another traveler was passing by in the same fashion, and again the ancient farmer stood up slowly to talk with the man. Again he heard the story of the fire, and again the new traveler asked, "What can you tell me about the people in the village up ahead?"

Again, the farmer asked "What sort of people were in your village? What were they like?"

"I miss them already," the traveler said with a tear. "They were some of the best people you could ever have known. They were my friends: helpful, caring—they'd give you the shirt off their back if you were in need."

The farmer brightened and wiped a drop of sweat from his brow. "Rest assured, my friend, you will find the same sort of people on up ahead. Welcome."

The great Goethe said, "A man sees in the world what he carries in his heart."

Isaac Asimov expressed a parallel sentiment when he noted, "Your assumptions are your windows on the world. Scrub them off every once in a while, or the light won't come in." We need always to keep our assumptional windows clean, and our minds open. We need to examine our beliefs as they relate to the correctness of our world picture. There are plenty of scientists who are as dogmatic and fundamentalist about their theories and beliefs as others may be about religion, and there are plenty of astrologers who are equally close-minded about ideas that don't sit well with their own particular pet interpretations. What's not good for the goose is also not good for the gander. In fact, in light of how difficult it is to overcome our own personally limited or defective paradigms, it is perhaps no surprise to see the troubles that have been encountered in the changing of culture-wide paradigms.

To take as an example a common belief that many people "know," skepticism of the main subject of this book: many have noted that people who "don't believe in astrology" generally don't "believe" (which is completely the wrong word) for one of two reasons. Either they haven't developed the proper awareness to see it in action (i.e. they haven't had an *experience* of it, usually because they haven't tried and aren't interested), or they simply write it off a priori because they can't think of any physical way that it could work. The second seems much more common. We will address both of these in this book. It doesn't surprise any physicist that some people are better at math than other people. They also might reluctantly agree that intelligence may possibly include those who are better at verbal, social, conceptual, or linguistic skills than they are at math. Why, then, should it seem so strange that some folks might be better at emotions, or synchronicity, or intuition, or astrology? And yet we all assume that others are just like us, or at least that they *should* be (only of course lacking a bit in whatever our own personal favorite quality is).

There is a quote (often incorrectly attributed to Herbert Spencer, per Wikipedia) by the Rev. William H. Poole (after an earlier quote by William Paley), that might serve as general good advice for anyone involved in investigations towards the truth. He states: "There is a principle which is a bar against all information, which is proof against all argument, and which cannot fail to keep a man in everlasting ignorance. This principle is: contempt prior to examination."

***

Ultimately, we are *not* only our personal and fleshy selves; ultimately, we are interconnected and a part of larger structures. We are the universe and the universe is us. This book, then, finally assumes this as fact: that there exists a comprehensive, interconnected and overriding, holistic structure to the universe that lies beyond, and yet within us. This Whole includes, but is not limited to, the visible and seemingly separate and dualistic world that we see around us. Both modern science and spirituality confirm this, which gives hope perhaps for one day finding peace between the two; the very idea of wholeness in fact presumes that. Astrology and physics may be read from the Whole, and the Whole may be read from astrology and physics. Astrology has recognized this interconnected and unbroken continuity since its inception. The dance of astrology is our swirling and intertwined movement through life in tandem with the planetary ballet. Our cycles exist side by side. The question of connection is the only item of contention. That will be addressed in the pages ahead. Astronomy provides the math and astrology provides the meaning. The exact link is not yet known, but several possibilities will be examined.

***

In regards to the discovery of our own identities, getting to know ourselves: nothing outside of astrology has done a better job in laying out our personal "believing is seeing" templates, our patterns of needs, desires, hopes, and fears that we project onto the world around us. As humans, all of us see the world through rose-colored, or other-colored, glasses. We see the world as red or blue or yellow depending on our proclivities and temperaments, and the world in turn sees us painted in these hues. It is astrology that shows us where these colors come from, what tint they are, and where their origins lie. But how does astrology *itself* work? The examination of that mystery is what ties together the five-petaled flower investigated here.

The purpose of this book, as mentioned above, is not to delineate or interpret the colored glasses through which we all have our faulty views of the world—there are other books for that. The purpose here is to examine the substrate, to search from whence those glasses may arise, and to discover if they arise from an existing paradigm involving an entirely materialistic universe, or from something else only hinted at, but as yet unknown. (It is important here to understand that when a "materialistic universe" is mentioned, that term is meant to include existing and known forms of *energy* as well, since Einstein showed their equivalence. We know that matter *is* energy; they are two sides of a single coin. Thus, saying that "the materialistic world is illusory, everything is energy" does not really address the issues brought up here. We are looking beyond this conventional thought on the pair, and beyond conventional energies.) Discovering how physics and astrology might peacefully coexist is just one example of the search for an underlying connectedness. This book assumes the idea of Wholeness, the idea that ultimately everything is connected. But *how* is it connected? What might be the mechanism or glue?

For that matter, if everything is One, then what *is* that One? Again, we will be asking more questions than we will be providing answers. We will be inviting you, the reader, to use all of this as a springboard for your own speculations and understandings. This is simply a distillation of many varied threads of thought. If there is anything here that seems original, it is only because the roots are not evident.

We have at all times everything that we need to figure the world out right in front of us; some of it only seems hidden or mysterious because we haven't yet recognized it, acknowledged it, or put a name to it. Relativity and atomic energy did not need Einstein to exist, but it took that great man to recognize them and show them to the rest of us. They were right there in front of us all along. Eventually, to borrow an idea from Pierre Teilhard de Chardin, "everything that rises must converge." Higher ideas are often simpler, and yet at the same time they may paradoxically contain more of reality. In this way new knowledge, new wisdom, and new insights move us forward as a species trying to decipher the nature of the world around us.

> "The task is not so much to see what no one has yet seen; but to think what nobody has yet thought, about that which everybody sees."—Erwin Schrödinger

***

Some housekeeping: the book does not intend to be chauvinistic or to emphasize one gender over another. The word "man" is occasionally used, but is intended to represent all of us together, men and women equally, as has been the tradition when talking about our species. "Human" is not much of a fix, as it simply adds a couple of letters. More politically correct solutions to this ancient wording have often proved unwieldy and awkward. Let it be known that the Whole is an inclusive union of opposites, a denial of false dualistic thinking. It is composed equally of male and female energy as shown in the popular yin-yang symbol. Our culture, it is true, often glorifies the masculine, the analytical over the intuitive, and is often much the poorer for it. We will attempt to move beyond that.

In regard to citations: there are no footnotes—this is not a scholarly paper, but a simple collection of ideas. When a quote or attributable concept that is specific to a particular person arises, it is dealt with in the text; the goal is to honor those whose ideas have contributed. For similar reasons, the addition of an index would have proved onerous; therefore, one will find instead blank pages for notes at the end.

For those not familiar with astrology: The planets, sun, and moon in astrology represent symbolic archetypes as well as physical bodies. Thus, when talking about the sun or moon as an astronomical object, it is not capitalized. However, when talking about the astrological *archetype* involved, it *is* capitalized: the Sun. (One will also typically find in astrology books the sun and moon lumped in with the planets. The better term might be "bodies," but that sounds awkward. Astrologers know that the sun and moon are not planets; this is just a form of shorthand, a way of not continually having to say "the planets and the sun and the moon." One says "the planets are doing this or that," and that is normally understood to include the sun and moon.) Signs are always capitalized (Leo, Virgo), as they also stand for archetypal energies. Archetypes are *very important* in the symbolic world, of which astrology is a part. Other terms such as "consciousness" may also be capitalized when the emphasis is on a larger principle or archetype: "It came into my consciousness that a larger Consciousness seemed to pervade the situation."

The creation of the book has required frequent forays to Wikipedia and other internet sites for fact-checking, which has also synergistically generated some new ideas or directions at times. When a quote, idea, or section is taken as a whole from Wikipedia, it is noted as such. Wikipedia certainly has its flaws, but this author is in thrall with the whole concept: in terms of the dissemination of human knowledge, Wikipedia is right up there with Gutenberg and the internet itself. A grateful acknowledgement must be given here to Tim Berners-Lee, the inventor of the World Wide Web (www...), and both Jimmy Wales and Larry Sanger, who started Wikipedia. All three of these men rose above the motivation for profit to donate to humanity two of the three advances just mentioned. (I guess a shout-out to Gutenberg may as well be in order, too.) Thank you, guys. And finally, thanks to Michelle Dotter and Sage Kalmus, who assisted in all of these musings with their proofreading and editing skills. Three heads are always better than one.

The book is a series of mini essays that fall roughly into the named sections or categories. However, the fit is far from perfect. Many could just as easily have been placed into another category. It was often difficult to choose their home, as they were written in no particular order; again, the book is not meant to be a programmed and linear exposition, but a collection. Astrologers may recognize that the book was written during a period when Saturn was in aspect to Neptune in the sky.

In addition, each section opens with a personal synchronistic anecdote that was written down at the time, and has traveled with me through my life to date. There are indeed many more, though perhaps less striking ones. It is to these odd occurrences that I have turned in order to stay curious and seeking when the temptation to question the ideas presented herein has loomed larger than it should have. All of the ideas presented here are works in progress: we've not reached the end of our explorations yet, and these various concepts are open-ended projects for ongoing discussions.

One of my own great joys has been that of being a lifelong and avid reader; first of many, many books, starting in childhood, and lately of many, many articles on the internet. It is difficult to convey the delight that I have experienced in being exposed to countless ideas from the astrological, the scientific, and the spiritual communities. I have, in addition, learned even more from listening to and conversing with others in "real time." There is no substitute for that. My hope is that this book will add a moment or two of pleasure or inspiration to someone else through simply passing along ideas or concepts that were freely provided to me. We're all in this together. They say that books, ideas, and indeed all other forms of shared knowledge are "food for thought." Let's eat.

PHYSICS

A Curious Thing

In 1976, I was young and restless, in my mid-twenties, and already an alcoholic; although like most young alcoholics, I had not yet realized that. My time was taken up blunting my potential and chasing after the sensual pleasures of life. Although I had already been exposed to many spiritual traditions (besides my parents' Christianity), such as Buddhism, Hinduism, and astrology, I was unable to put any of these teachings into practice. I was spiritually curious, but unevolved; intellectually curious, but unwilling to do the work to progress. Consistently, I chose those paths that led to gratification of the ego and of the flesh. It was a time of confusion and alternation between feeling either less than others or better than others, but never feeling equal to or part of. A time of being mystified by and out of sync with the larger flow of life, of humanity; a time of being an outsider in my own skin. A difficult time.

I had been decently educated but was working as a self-employed house painter, the better to be able to drink as I wanted. I was a binge drinker, and therefore had some small control over the timing of my drinking, but never over the amount. I had the compulsion to get blindly intoxicated several times a week, and it was always experienced as both an irresistible urge and a gateway into excitement and the unknown. The "boring" life of productivity and responsibility was not for me. Early experiments with mind-expanding psychedelics and other drugs had ultimately left me with inexpensive beer as my drug of choice. Being self-employed allowed me the freedom that I craved: "I'm sorry, Mrs. Jones," (I would say, so hung over that I was vibrating and feeling as though poison were running through my veins), "but I won't be able to make it over to finish your job today. Something has come up."

In this context, in the spring of 1976, a certain increasing aura began to surround my daily experiences. They seemed to become more electric and charged; coincidences appeared more frequently. Sudden events, seemingly both good and bad, appeared at random, and there was a distinct whiff of danger in the air—which I mistakenly interpreted as erotic possibility. (For those interested in this sort of thing, the transiting planet Uranus was nearly exactly conjunct my natal Mars.) At the time, I was driving a 1967 VW Microbus, the original "hippie van," fleshed out with a bed, sink, and stove. In it, I had traveled to many places around the US, with a special fondness for the mountains of Colorado. Two incidents stand out involving the van at that time, which, looking back, should have signaled a certain sense of the ominous, although that subtlety blew past me.

One was driving along River Road in New Orleans while following a truck pulling a cement mixer. Suddenly, the cement mixer somehow became detached from the truck and dropped off behind, heading right towards me. I narrowly avoided being hit by swerving off the road, frightened and disconcerted. About a week later, a real accident occurred.

Good alcoholic that I was, I used my money for booze rather than for the necessities of life. My van had, for about a month, been showing increasing difficulty with the essential skill of stopping in a reasonable amount of time. I had traced this to a leak in the hydraulic brake system, which was dripping fluid onto the brake drums, not allowing them to grip effectively. Later, when I "had the money," I would fix them. Later seemed to drag on. I could stop, it just took a while, and I had to plan ahead.

One day, while driving to a painting job, a car stopped suddenly in front of me. I mashed the brakes as hard as I could, only to watch in horror as my van seemingly ignored the request, and slid effortlessly into the car ahead. Bam! There was minimal damage, however, mostly a bent bumper on my own vehicle, and the other driver took pity and allowed me to carry on without calling the police.

Around this time, I had moved into a new apartment in Uptown New Orleans, several miles from the famous French Quarter. One night shortly after the above incident (and with the brakes still not repaired), I drove down to the French Quarter on a Friday night to "party," which is of course the universal euphemism for getting wasted. Driving drunk was never something I had even given a thought to. Of course I would have to drive drunk—I always did. I didn't have the money for cabs. Alcoholics do not think very clearly, and do not think of others too deeply, I'm afraid.

I was a loner at that time, and my alcoholic forays into the Quarter usually involved attempts to meet women. (I'm simply being honest here. There was no question of being "evolved" at that time—my level of consciousness was somewhere more physical than spiritual, I'm afraid.) A key technique that I used was to attempt to guess, and then talk with women about, their zodiac sign and associated factors, always with an agenda in mind. I had at this time already been studying astrology for five or six years and knew most of the basics, although obviously the more subtle and ethereal aspects of it eluded me. But I was pretty fired up on the subject, and in fact had attempted to put together an astrologically based dating service in New York, but in the days prior to the internet and personal computers this was doomed to failure.

So after chatting up and failing to impress a particular woman one evening, I became quite depressed, and sitting in a bar called the Jimani (which is still there, on Chartres St.), I continued to drink more heavily. Uranus at this time was exact to the degree on my Mars. There is a bit of hazy memory involved with the rest of the night, but apparently, at around four o'clock in the morning of March 20th (New Orleans is a very late-night city), I was attempting to drive home to my new apartment and ran smack into the back of a parked truck on Magazine St., outside of the French Quarter. In a fortunate twist of fate, the truck involved was parked in front of a twenty-four-hour fire station, and those good folks were out within seconds to see this young drunk pinned in his VW van, steel and steering wheel crumpled and forced into the meager cabin. I had struck the truck (which was on the other side of the street) such that the driver's side of my vehicle took the full, head-on brunt of the crash. It apparently looked as if I had aimed for the truck, which was of course unoccupied at that hour. Later, they found a half-empty bottle of booze behind the front seat. Whether this was an impulsive suicide attempt, I'll never know. I've never since had anything resembling a suicidal interest or impulse, but this question for a while stayed in my mind with a certain suspicion and uncomfortable flavor after reading an article about intoxicated one-car crashes and impulsive suicide attempts.

At any rate, a 1967 Volkswagen microbus was a marvelous and classic machine, but it had a few drawbacks. One was that the only thing separating the driver from the outside world was about an eighth of an inch of sheet metal. When the firemen got to me after the crash, I was completely pinned in the driver's seat by the crumpled front panel and steering wheel. They had to cut me out of the van with a torch, and I was taken to Charity Hospital in New Orleans, unconscious. I had snapped my left femur in half, dislocated my hip, broken many of the bones in my left foot, shattered my kneecap, and sustained a concussion. But I was alive. And for that, I am forever grateful.

To say that this was the biggest event of my life up until that time is a large understatement, and it's difficult to convey the intense emotionality of it in print. I fully appreciated how close I had come to death, and I resolved to change my life. While, amazingly, no one in my family or at the hospital had talked to me about my drinking (this was New Orleans, after all), I realized this had become a huge problem. I resolved to stay sober, which I did for about six months—my longest period of sobriety until I got sober for good much later. I also made a decision to let my obsession with astrology go: not that I had identified any way in which that *interest* was a factor in the accident (although I was well aware of the Uranus/Mars transit), but it was just that I wanted to change *everything* in my life. Whatever I had been before, I wanted to be something different. Top to bottom, inside out. I wanted to be a new person. I wanted a new life, and I wanted to appreciate that life, unencumbered by old thought patterns or habits. I wanted a fresh start. Many things had to go; astrology was one of them.

So I began my recuperation at my parents' house for the next eight months, after having been in the hospital for a full four weeks. I had a couple of surgeries, which left a metal rod in my left femur that poked into the muscles of my buttocks, reminding me constantly of my recent incident. It was very noticeable to me, and uncomfortable. Many scars, many thoughts of this event provided daily companionship. I was on crutches, with limited movement. But I was alive, and I was optimistic and hopeful: this new life was mine, and I was going to change. I began after a couple of months to look for work of some sort and took a job supervising paperboys for a local weekly newspaper, which was perfect for my reduced mobility. One of the paperboys had an older sister named Pat, and we began to date.

Pat and I were compatible. She was easygoing and adaptable, and we had many good times, as she helped me to get back into the stream of life. In fact, as in all good relationships, new opportunities for growth began to appear, and life at the time seemed full of promise, partly from letting go of some of my former preconceived notions and biases. I had made a deal with myself that, where in the past I had micro-analyzed my relationships through an astrological lens, this time I was going to start clean, unencumbered by old baggage, and let Pat be who she was. I was not going to project my views of astrological traits onto her. I was not going to ask her when her birthday was. I was just going to let her be herself, and appreciate her for that, and let things develop as they might.

So they did develop over the course of several months, and although we ultimately did not end up together, it was a good relationship, and one that felt appropriate and right at that moment in time. The relationship seemed almost as if it were part of a package that included the traumatic event and the mental and internal changes associated with it. That should be all there is to say about it. However, after a couple of months of dating, and even though things were going well with my new plan to avoid astrology, I became more and more antsy and curious, and finally I couldn't stand it any longer. I asked her when her birthday was.

It was March 20th at 4:10 a.m. I have a photocopy of her birth certificate.

The Physical World

We live in a physical world. Our world may be more than physical, but the physical world is the one that we interact with every day, and so it's a great place to start our explorations. It's the chair you're perhaps sitting in, it's the dust particles in the shaft of light coming through the Venetian blinds. It's the spheres of rock and gas flying around our sun that are the basis for both astrology and astronomy. It's the extent of the cosmos billions of light years in every direction, and it's the elusive electron orbiting the nucleus of the iron atoms that lie at the core of our very own ball in space, the earth. It's the hormones that rage in our adolescence, and it's the wrinkled skin and clouded eyes in old age. It's taste, smell, touch, hearing, and sight. It's the force that stubs our toe, and it's the force that destroyed Hiroshima. The study of the physical world begins appropriately with the discipline known as physics, which underlies all of the other "hard" sciences (chemistry, biology, etc.).

We start with the physical world, because that's where we live. Ultimately, we will use the physical world as a springboard for our further explorations. As an early hint towards these explorations, we may simply make note at this time of the odd dichotomy that, while modern physics is busily trying to deny anything other than the measurable material world (materialism), the very findings of this same discipline are turning much of what we've known about the solidity and predictability of that world into pixie dust.

Note: The following is difficult material. It's difficult because, as we've investigated further and further into the intricacies of our material world, things have gotten stranger and stranger, and therefore more difficult to understand, even for the rarified people who are coming up with these ideas. If you are not up for the ride, feel free to skip past the following segments, although please do stop and read the very brief "Recap" section at the end. It would be a shame to get discouraged and put the book down simply because it starts with the most difficult of the five sections. Please hang in there: there's lots of good, and more accessible, stuff ahead!

If this sort of thing *does* appeal to you, please know that you are not going to "learn physics" in the following pages. This is simply an overview. If you want to follow along, it would be *extremely* helpful to keep the internet at hand, and spend much time on Wikipedia and YouTube striving to clarify things. Diagrams and videos are of the utmost help here; words can only go so far. There are plenty of explanations out there that do not depend on math to make their point. The "Additional Reading" section at the end of the book also provides many possibilities for exploration. Modern physics is an incredible and fascinating world unto itself, aside from its possible interactions with other studies and disciplines. Buckle up... here we go!

The Double Slit

> "We choose to examine a phenomenon which is impossible, absolutely impossible, to explain in any classical way, and which has in it the heart of quantum mechanics. In reality, it contains the only mystery." —Richard Feynman

Suppose that you were invited to a party. Now suppose that when you got there, you were confronted with two doors at the entrance to the party. Suppose that when you opened one door, there would be but a single person sitting there, perhaps looking uncomfortable and forlorn with a party hat on, apologetic but welcoming. Now suppose that if you opened the other door the party would be full of people laughing and having fun, music playing and cake in sight. It is the same room. Does this seem strange? Does it seem strange that using one door or the other could actually determine different realities? Let's talk.

Is light a particle or a wave? What *is* a particle or a wave? A particle seems to be a definite "object" with boundaries, some solidity or substance, and the ability to interact with other particles or forces. A particle may be thought of, for example, as being similar to a billiard ball. It may be measured as to position, mass or weight, size, and trajectory or movement. It has the ability to knock into other billiard balls, to knock them into other paths, and thereby to also knock itself into a new path. The laws of how billiard balls do this are in the realm of the "classical" (Newtonian) physics that Feynman noted we are moving away from.

What are waves? Waves are "traveling disturbances moving through a medium." They are not localized, but spread out. That medium may be the vacuum of space (electromagnetic waves), air (sound waves), or a peaceful and glassy lake (water waves). For a simple example, let's use the lake. A placid lake has a smooth surface; if we drop a pebble into it, waves will spread out from the impact point in a circular fashion. If the pebble is dropped at the shoreline, a half-moon splay of waves will be visible moving away from us. Now, if we drop in two pebbles simultaneously and near each other at the shoreline, there will be two half-moon semicircles of waves moving away.

However, this complicates the picture. As the waves expand outwards, the two sets of waves interact and form what is known as an *interference pattern*. This has a very predictable visual form, and is characteristic of *all* waves of any type. The interference pattern may have areas where two waves "hit" each other, which produces a summation, an even larger wave (a greater amplitude), while in other areas the troughs intersect, producing a lowered effect. The reader is *strongly encouraged* here to look online for visual demonstrations of the double slit experiment, as it is very difficult to understand without diagrams or videos, and it is the centerpiece in understanding just how odd modern physics really is.

***

The debate over whether light is of a wave or a particle nature goes way back to the Greeks, although we will pick it up with Newton. Isaac Newton speculated that light was a stream of particles, which he called "corpuscles." His rival, Christiaan Huygens, thought instead that light traveled in waves. Mainly due to Newton's stature and eminence, the particle theory became the more popular for a couple of hundred years. The debate never went away, however; each side could produce good arguments in its favor, but none seemed definitive. Finally, in 1801, Thomas Young produced the first version of what became known as the double slit experiment, one of the iconic touchstones of modern science.

The double slit experiment is of a very simple design: two flat plates are set upright on end. The further plate is the "receiver" plate on which light will fall and be observed. The nearer plate is an intermediate plate, which contains two rectangular slits piercing it, side by side. A light is shone against the first (intermediate) plate, and travels through the two slits, hitting the receiver plate a short distance away. One would expect that perhaps there would be two rectangular spots of light on the second plate, one for each slit. But no: when the receiver plate is observed, it shows *several alternating* bands of dark and light, spread out rather than localized; a figure that could only have come from a wave type of interaction producing an *interference pattern*, similar to that noted on the pond above. What is going on here?

To Young, it was clear that light must indeed be a wave; only waves act like that. Particles may bump into each other, but they don't "interfere" with each other in the predictable spectrum-like way that waves do. A few years of easy convincing later, and the scientific establishment was on board: light was finally and forever a wave. (Or at least until the dawn of the 20th century.) The wave nature of light was further solidified by James Maxwell's work with electromagnetic waves in the 1800s, and his demonstration that light was simply another part of what came to be known as the electromagnetic spectrum. You can see an amazing demonstration of Young's original experiment, now featuring bystanders on a beach, by searching on YouTube for "The Original Double Slit Experiment by Veritasium." He demonstrates all of the above ideas, including the interference interactions using water waves. You may also search for Young's original drawings of light's interference patterns, and compare them to the water waves. It's really amazing that something this profound could be so simple. Science's secrets indeed are often "hidden in plain sight." (There is another recommended YouTube video towards the bottom here that better explains the additional material to follow. There are basically two versions of the double slit: the original, and the more modern ones.)

In fact, the name "Original Double Slit Experiment" is an apt title, for it turns out that the experiment from 1801 had some life left in it yet in the modern world, and some secrets to reveal. Let's fast forward a bit. A hundred years after Young, Einstein, in 1905, was simultaneously working on relativity (which treated light as a wave), and the "photoelectric effect" (explained later), which hinted that the old idea of light as a particle might not be quite dead yet. In the photoelectric experiments, light behaved as if it were indeed a particle, banging into things and scattering the debris, just like a billiard ball might. Einstein himself never really attempted to reconcile these opposing points of view at the time; it would be others who would move these concepts forward in the years ahead.

***

It was beginning to seem, in the early 20th century, that light was acting as both a particle *and* a wave, although it could never be caught being both at the same time. Niels Bohr coined the term "complementarity" to explain this idea that two completely different facets of something could be seen as not being incompatible (as they seemed to be), but complementary in forming the whole of that thing (whatever that thing might be.) If one did an experiment which looked for the wave nature of light (such as using a prism), light behaved as a wave. If one then did an experiment (involving the newly named photons, or light particles) which looked for particle type of interactions from light, one found that light obliged, and then acted as a particle. Amazing! (Keep in mind here that particles and waves truly *are indeed* completely different things. It's kind of like fuzzy stuffed bunnies and transmission gears: things should be either fuzzy stuffed bunnies or transmission gears, *but not both.*)

The double slit experiment in the 20th century was pressed back into service, but with some new sophistication, and some new twists. (These are all in videos online. It's helpful either through videos or diagrams to see what's really going on here.) As we move on, it's important to remember that waves can go through both slits at the same time (just as water waves would be able to) and then interfere with each other after the slits, while particles must either go through one slit or the other, just as a billiard ball would have to.

There is, in addition, a certain randomness involved as we fire particles or beams at the slits: we can never know in advance exactly where an *individual* photon or billiard ball will go in the double slit experiment (which slit it will go through); only after the fact can we find out where it actually *did* go. The chain of cause and effect and its associated predictability has disappeared. The results are always a statistical distribution. We find, during this process, that the transition from a state of probability and uncertainty to the actual final concrete manifestation of the event is connected to what is known as the "collapse the wave function," which will be explained later.

Also, as if things weren't strange enough already, it was discovered by Louis de Broglie in 1924 that not only was light able to demonstrate both particle and wave-like properties, but so were electrons and then atoms; which meant that *matter itself* was both a particle and a wave. Let that sink in for a moment. The term "matter wave" came into use. In the double slit, new and unheard of things were taking place.

***

If one fired atoms at a single slit, they would form a single line on the far side consistent with particle behavior. Nothing very exciting there. However, if one fired atoms at a double slit (side by side), an interference pattern would then magically appear, meaning that the atoms were demonstrating wave, rather than particle, behavior. (A sort of "locator screen" was used to receive the atoms after the slits, and indicate their position.) However, it was discovered that if one used a detector at the slits to discover *which* slit each atom went through individually, the atoms suddenly stopped "performing" their wave trick, and went back to being simply particles: the final plate now showed only two vertical bars instead of the interference pattern. (*Please* look online!) This was easily reversible, and endlessly reproducible: track or monitor the atoms, and they acted like particles; leave them alone and they acted like waves. *Somehow, the experimenter's observation, measurement, or interaction itself was causing them to switch from particles to waves and back*. Somehow, they "knew" when someone was "watching" them, and changed their behavior. Bizarre!

But it got even stranger. An interference pattern is "built up" by thousands of hits (atoms fired at the twin slits), that eventually reveal themselves to be the familiar pattern. But perhaps somehow the various atoms, as they went through one slit or the other just happened to interact in such a way that produced the pattern. What would happen if the atoms were sent *one at a time* through the slits to see what picture formed? Good idea! So experiments were designed to do this. It was found that if each singly-fired atom were checked (observed) as to which of the two slits it ended up going through, the discrete "particle" or two-bar picture formed. But if no one was looking, and the atoms were left to themselves, *even firing them one at a time*, they miraculously produced the interference pattern. They were somehow "interfering" with *themselves*: even a single atom was forming an interference wave pattern. The only conclusion that could be drawn from this was that single atoms, matter, were somehow *going through both slits at the same time*: the characteristic of a wave. (The atoms weren't actually going through as particles: the point here is that their alternate-self *waves* were going through, and then showing up as particles when they hit the screen. But observation or monitoring caused them to remain particles the whole time and choose one slit or the other.)

For a great animated explanation of this phenomena, as it developed more fully, search for the "Dr. Quantum Double Slit" video on YouTube. It is recommended for its simple and straightforward explanation, although it comes from a movie that was highly controversial (and not unjustifiably so). The actual process that is producing all of these odd effects is, again, associated with the concept of "collapsing" the wave function, which will be explained more fully in the segment titled "More Concepts" coming up, under the "Wave Function" and "Copenhagen Interpretation" headings. For now, it may be noted that the wave function is an equation that describes all quantum systems prior to objective manifestation.

(What *are* light waves, anyway? In a sense, they are simply waves of potentiality: waves of where the particle component of light or matter may be eventually found or manifested. The ephemeral wave at this point, which is not yet matter, is then governed by the wave equation. The transition from matter or light being a wave into being a particle when it hits the locator screen is governed by the wave function, or equation. Prior to the "collapse" of the wave function, matter and light exist only as potentialities, not actualities. When we measure them prior to the locator screen, we are collapsing their potentials prematurely, and forcing them to act like particles earlier than if we had left them alone. That explains the two different patterns found on the locator screens above. Again, in the double slit, it must be stressed that it is our own meddling that does this, that is associated with these effects.)

It's also important to keep in mind that it is not advanced physics, or current theories, that are so strange: it is *nature itself* which is this strange. Physics simply attempts to describe nature and to glean its secrets. And more secrets are revealed year by year. R=K+1. Not only is matter actually "frozen" energy, and not only is matter both a particle and a wave; but the nature of matter, and thus the nature of reality itself, may be determined by our interactions with it, and even by our consciousness. If this intrigues you, read on.

> "A paradox is not a conflict within reality. It is a conflict between reality and your feeling of what reality should be like." —Richard Feynman

In the Beginning

The word physics itself stems from the Greek word "physis," simply meaning nature. Indeed, the discipline grew out of a larger study of the world that originally fell under the term "natural philosophy" until the period of the Enlightenment. It found its earliest flowering amongst the Greeks; Plato and his student Aristotle are most commonly mentioned here. Although primitive peoples across the globe had no doubt made experiments and inquiries into the way things were since man first chipped flint and mastered fire, the Greeks were the first major group in the West to systematically pursue these studies and, more importantly for history, to write them down. (Less well documented were their debts to India and the Middle East.) Of note is that, regarding some of these seminal figures, in simpler times it was not inconceivable that a particularly bright person could know pretty much all there was to know about the world—an obvious impossibility in today's complex scientific environment.

Today's scientific investigations of the world are most commonly associated with *inductive* reasoning: that is, conclusions are drawn from an assortment of observations and the repetition of these observations. This is part of the vaunted "scientific method," and it has served us quite well. It additionally leaves room for constant change and improvement: if a particular observation turns out different from previous ones, then the conclusions at the end must be scrapped, and new theories proposed to explain the changed observations. Theories, conclusions, and predictions are thus always works in progress. The sun has come up for thousands of years, but there is no guarantee that it will come up tomorrow: it is only highly likely, and subject to ongoing observations. In contrast, many early investigations of the world used more *deductive* reasoning: this was Plato's method, and it is in fact interesting that Plato's student, Aristotle, is considered the "first scientist" in large part because he moved from Plato's more philosophical and deductive reasoning methods, towards a more inductive and experimental approach.

In deductive reasoning, one *starts* with a particular premise and then reaches certain conclusions by deduction. Deductive reasoning is top down, whereas inductive reasoning is bottom up. Although in practice science is a complex interplay of inductive and deductive reasoning, we are separating them here for the sake of simplicity. Deductive reasoning can also be powerful, and is used by everyone every day, but it has a weakness in that if the initial premise is flawed, then the results will be flawed also. "GIGO," as they say in the computer world. (Garbage in, garbage out.) Plato (as have many others) started with a vision of the ideal world, and then attempted to deduce how things would manifest in accordance with this ideal. An example is his idea of the "music of the spheres," which he shared in conjunction with Pythagoras and others. The idea of spheres being perfect (and the world being perfect), in fact, set astronomy back for centuries until Kepler finally established that the planetary orbits were actually elliptical.

Many of these early premises of deductive reasoning were either so intuitively obvious (everything in the sky rotated around the earth) or so firmly entrenched and culturally reinforced (God had created Eve, women, out of a rib removed from Adam) that it took quite a while for modern science to gain a foothold. The clash of the Enlightenment and its associated scientific revolutions at the end of the Middle Ages with religious orthodoxy may actually be thought of as a clash between these two ways of investigating the world. Were people from that time on to find out more about the world through unencumbered observation of natural processes, or were we to find out more about the world by trying to divine God's plan—obsessively interpreting the lines in the Bible, contradictory though many of them were? Interestingly, this is, in fact, a conflict that continues to this day: the ideal, the preconceived premise, vs. observed facts. Sometimes they coincide, and sometimes they don't. There are large implications here for astrology, as well as for science.

But man by nature has a curious and experimental mind, and so it was inevitable that a more scientific approach would eventually become prominent, if not exclusive. The breakthroughs came largely as the result of Kepler, Copernicus, Galileo, and Newton; although a parallel philosophical tract was occurring along with the scientific one. Kepler showed that the spheres weren't perfect. Copernicus and Galileo showed that we were *not* the center of the universe, but just another ball hurtling through space. Giordano Bruno went even further than these two in his visionary speculations, but was perhaps less politically savvy, and was burned at the stake for his efforts.

But it was Newton who really solidified the scientific and mathematical approach. It was one thing to know that the earth was traveling, along with the other planets, around the sun in an elliptical orbit; it was quite another to be able to know how all of that worked, to know the laws of motion and gravity that glued the universe together. And for bonus points, Newton had developed a whole new branch of mathematics, calculus, in order to figure all of this out. It's no wonder that Alexander Pope, newly emboldened by a more lax attitude towards irreverence, penned: "Nature and Nature's laws lay hid in night: God said, Let Newton be! and all was light."

Newton was such a towering figure, and had moved the pieces so far down the board at once, that it is no wonder there was a strong feeling in the following centuries amongst many, that pretty much everything had been figured out about physics and how the world worked. It was now just a matter of details, tidying up, and applying this knowledge in the field of engineering to produce an amazing new, technological, and more secular society: the Industrial Revolution had arrived! Movement, mass, gravity, acceleration: all of the things that made trains run, steam engines turn waterwheels, and cotton gins work—all were now easily understood. God had not disappeared, but He had seemingly become just a bit less necessary on a day to day basis.

Besides this practical effect, wherein man seemed now to be able to understand his world without divine intervention, there was an accompanying philosophical change that was perhaps even more important. This new way of looking at things became known as the "clockwork universe." If the laws of nature could be understood, and if the laws of movement and causation were laid down by mathematical formulae, then this meant that ultimately everything could be predicted.

It's probably difficult to imagine today what an amazing concept this must have been back at that time. Up until then, things happened, but quite often no one really knew why. Humans had tried incantations and appealing to divine intervention since their tails had disappeared, but the results had been, to say the least, a bit spotty. Rain either came or it didn't. Crops thrived or withered. Children lived or died. It was difficult to discern the will of the gods, or of God. But now! If the movements of Venus or Mars could be understood, then maybe someday one might be able to understand what makes the rain itself come, to predict it and control it. A new optimism in man's ability to control his world, based on prediction, swept through history. Religion never disappeared, but it began to answer different needs in people; its power as an explanatory force began to wane.

So tightly integrated were the new mathematical and scientific discoveries, and so prolific the new society-changing inventions and ideas, that it is no surprise that people quite naturally concluded that the universe must ultimately be a giant clockwork. It had perhaps been set in motion by God, but since then had been ticking away, the precise gears turning like an elegant Swiss mechanism, moving along with a beauty inspired by its very knowability. If one could only know all of the variables for a given situation, why then, one could predict *anything*: one could predict the very motion of the cosmos and everything in it! Astronomy benefited most from this new excitement, but astrology did, too: if everything was a clockwork, then of course it stood to reason that our lives were synchronized with the ticking of the pendulum, and moving forward according to the gears of the horoscope. Like everything else, if one could just find the magic key, the right formula, the hidden equation, then all would be predictable and certain.

It was not to be.

It's All Relative

Physics may be thought of as having five major historical divisions. First, there was the primitive or archaic: this included early man's explorations and experiments, illuminated with mainly deductive reasoning. Here we find Plato and the shamans, trying to discover the world through a series of philosophically-derived principles, along with tentative empirical forays. Second was the period ushered in by Newton, Galileo, and their contemporaries: true and rigorous experimentation and observation combined with more open-mindedness, and now featuring mathematical underpinnings for theories with increased predictability. Modern science had been born. Third was the bridge between Newton and the modern world, occupied by perhaps the greatest scientific visionary mind of all time, Albert Einstein, with whom this section will be concerned. Fourth was the overthrow of Einstein's lingering attachment to the clockwork universe by quantum theory in all of its weirdness. And fifth will be whatever comes next. To say that there will be no next, that we have it all figured out, that there are no major surprises lurking in the wings, is to ignore the lessons of history. We then might as well be back tending a steam engine, and being amazed that Newton had figured out everything there was to know about the universe. The universe is deeper and more sly than that; it's not giving up all of its secrets quite that easily. And if what comes next is not shocking and worldview-changing, we will also have missed the lessons of the past. Physics was not complete, and did not end with Aristotle, Newton, Einstein, or Bohr; and it won't end with the current paradigm or generation. As Carl Sagan put it:

> "It is hopelessly narrow-minded... to imagine that all significant laws of physics have been discovered at the moment our generation begins contemplating the problem. There would be a twenty-first century physics and a twenty-second

> century physics, and even a fourth millennium physics."

***

So on to Einstein. Galileo, in 1632, in his *Dialogue Concerning the Two Chief World Systems* (which concerned the comparison between Copernicus's heliocentric version of the solar system and Plato's geocentric system), pointed out that if one were a sailor in a ship, below decks and sailing on a smooth sea, it would be impossible to tell if the ship were moving or not: to the sailor's frame of reference in the hold, the two situations would feel to be, and appear to be, the same. Only if he came up on deck could he discern if in fact the ship were anchored or moving.

Newton then moved this idea forward a bit by stating that the laws of physics for an inertial frame of reference (the sailor down below) were the same *within his frame of reference* as for a different observer in another frame of reference (for example another sailor up on deck who can see that the ship is moving, or his wife waving goodbye from the shore). However, Newton's ideas were ultimately hampered by his view that there was an unvarying, constant and universal time in which this could all take place. Newton was also unable to effectively use information discovered during his lifetime, in 1676, by Ole Rømer (a Danish astronomer) that the speed of light wasn't, as had been previously thought, instantaneous, but in fact had a definite speed. (Rømer, incredibly, did a halfway accurate ballpark measurement of the speed of light at the time by using the moons of Jupiter.)

So the idea of relativity was not necessarily new; it just had not been fleshed out and put into mathematical formula yet, a daunting task in itself. At the same time, during the burgeoning Scientific Revolution, people had begun to become increasingly interested in both magnetism (which had been known about for quite a long time), and electricity. The latter was a more recent fascination, and there was much investigation taking place. Into this milieu stepped James Maxwell.

James Clerk Maxwell was a towering figure in physics history, and the subject of one of only two portraits that Einstein had hanging on his wall in admiration. A Scotsman born in 1831, Maxwell built on ideas produced by others (including Ørsted, who had noticed in 1820 that an electric current could deflect a compass needle) to realize that electricity and magnetism ultimately were two components of a single entity: the electromagnetic force (or EM). This was one of the most important discoveries in the history of physics, and without it modern science would likely have been delayed for a much longer time. He also showed that the two were not only connected and part of a single system, but that the system traveled in waves just as light did, and in fact traveled at the exact same speed that light did. These EM waves also behaved in equations just as light did. This of course gave hints that light itself was likely part of what became known as the electromagnetic spectrum, and threw the debate as to whether light was a particle (as Newton and others had thought) or a wave over to the wave camp. Shortly after this, in 1887, the Michelson-Morley experiments (which were initially attempts to prove aether as a medium that permeated the universe) unexpectedly showed that the speed of light was constant no matter what its orientation, path, direction, or relation to frames of reference. How could that be? Things were moving into new and unknown territory.

Maxwell had generated a series of equations which governed the behavior of his new electromagnetic spectrum; work had been going on in this area feverishly since his breakthrough discoveries. However, the discovery that the speed of light was a constant was creating havoc. Around 1892, Dutch physicist Hendrik Lorentz, along with others, worked out equations which sought to unify these difficulties, and to allow a means to "transform" certain constants in the equations according to relative motion involving the speed of light. It was found that objects in motion were predicted to contract in length, and that time as a constant was subject to variance as well. French physicist Jules Henri Poincaré burnished these new equations and gave them the title "The Lorenz Transformations" in honor of Lorenz. They are still used today.

***

It is a frequently repeated tale that Albert Einstein did poorly in school. There is some basis for this, but the underlying reason seems more that he was somewhat dreamy and disengaged from the tight rules of school, and simply "marched to his own drummer." (He was born March 14, 1879.) At any rate, he did not fit in well enough with the established academic lineage to obtain a more prestigious position after graduation from the Polytechnic Institute in Zurich, and ended up, famously, working at the Swiss patent office. It was here, in 1905, that Einstein's (and physics' in many ways) most amazing year began. He had just received his PhD. and was 26 years old. He published four short papers back to back in that year that quite simply turned physics and Newton's former preeminence on its head. It is mentioned in science history as Einstein's Annus Mirabilis, or "miracle year."

Let's look at his four papers in no particular order. Although physicists at that time didn't really know what matter was "made of," the existence of atoms as some sort of tiny and indivisible component of things was strongly suspected (in part due to earlier work by the chemist Dalton), and they had been postulated as far back as ancient Greece and India. There was no universal agreement, however, and not much was known about them. Einstein in 1905 took up an examination of what is known as Brownian motion (for example, the behavior of dust particles on the surface of a liquid), and through his analysis of this effect not only convincingly demonstrated the existence of atoms, but allowed French physicist Jean Perrin to experimentally determine the actual mass and dimensions of these atoms using Einstein's work. Einstein, then, did not "discover" atoms, but moved them into mainstream acceptance. Not bad for starters.

Upping the ante, Einstein published a paper titled "On the Electrodynamics of Moving Bodies." Here, he paid tribute in mentioning past research done by Newton, Maxwell, Lorentz, Hertz, and Doppler, and then quickly kicked things into overdrive. He solidified the idea that the speed of light is a constant, and thus is independent of any moving reference frame. He came to this insight in a visionary fashion, by imagining himself to be sitting on a beam of light, and asking himself what his relation to the world around him might be. He further concluded, moving beyond Newton for good, that there is no such thing as an ultimate and fixed frame of reference. *Everything* in the entire universe is relative. All we really have are an endless series of different observers' frames of reference, all valid, and all of which have the same speed of light tying them together as a constant.

For good measure, Einstein added time into the relativity equation, something that hadn't really been done before. Even with early experiments on relativity, it had mostly been assumed that time was a fixed and eternal parameter. Now that, too, was gone. Finally, he used the Lorenz transformations and his own new ideas and native gifts for explanation to demonstrate, for example, why someone traveling near the speed of light would become compressed in size, in addition to aging more slowly than a stationary brother. All pretty amazing concepts, and ones that are easy to imagine turned the physics world on its head.

Einstein's ideas have been verified experimentally over and over, and are even part of such mundane calculations as adjusting GPS systems to take time relativity into account on a daily basis. He wrapped all of this up by calling it the "Special Theory of Relativity"; later he will add gravity, inertia, and mass into the equations to produce a "General Theory of Relativity." This book is far too much of an overview to go into the fascinating details and explanations of Einstein's relativity, but if you have a scientific and curious mind, there are numerous and excellent books out there that explain it well. Look for one with lots of pictures and diagrams, which are a necessity in grasping these difficult concepts. The core philosophical take-away is this: nothing after the publication of this paper was fixed, stable, and eternal any more, but was only relative to everything else around it, and to a particular observer's point of view.

OK. Atoms. Relativity. Not enough for you? How about this simple equation: $E=mc^2$. You've probably heard of that one; it is hands-down the most famous equation in history, and its beauty is in its simplicity. It basically states that matter and energy *are the same thing*. There is no independent difference, and only a simple multiplier separates them. One can be converted into the other, and vice versa. So there you have it: we are all basically energy that is walking, talking, and thinking. Don't wonder if it's true, there's proof. Matter is nothing more than a special type of energy: "solidified," slowed down, or stored energy, so to speak. Crystallized. Matter contains a *lot* of energy, too: that "c" component of the equation is the speed of light squared, a rather large number. That's why an atomic bomb, such as seen in the pictures of the bombing of Hiroshima, can produce so much energy from a little bit of matter. The A-bomb that destroyed Hiroshima was a fission bomb; today's nuclear weapons are H-bombs, driven by fusion (which also drives the sun), that are 1,000 times more powerful than the old A-bombs. Each one. All over the world. Let that sink in for a minute. 1,000 times more powerful than the weapon that destroyed Hiroshima. Each bomb. That's a lot of $E=mc^2$.

Einstein casually dropped this "bomb" on the physics community in a paper titled "Does the Inertia of a Body Depend Upon Its Energy Content?" Again, he drew upon Maxwell and Hertz, and then added his own recent relativity. But ultimately, it was his pure visionary genius that allowed this equation to emerge from his mind, and out into the world. His towering reputation as the greatest physicist/scientist of all time is well deserved. So many things in science turn out to be simple and right in front of us: it takes an Einstein to recognize them. For good or bad then, the world changed in that particular moment. Needless to say, although Einstein had no direct role in the creation of the atomic bomb, it was his equations and work which had made the bomb a realistic possibility, and Einstein, a pacifist, had very mixed emotions about that. In his later life, he made great pleas for peace in the world.

For astrologers, there is additional synchronistic meaning in the fact that Pluto, the ruler of darkness, explosions, and transformations was discovered in 1930, just when all of this was taking place. Pluto, on discovery, was in Cancer, and exactly conjunct the United States horoscope's Mars. A couple of years later, the important concept of the nuclear chain reaction occurred to Leó Szilárd while he was walking across a street in London, and he quickly invented the atomic bomb, patenting it in 1934. (British patent number 630,726.) The whole fabric of the 20th century hadn't changed yet, but it would shortly. Duck and cover! (As an interesting aside to all this, if one could convert matter into energy perfectly, the average adult male would have the energy equivalence of about 80 times the largest nuclear explosion ever detonated.)

Atoms, Relativity, Energy/Matter equivalence. (Remember, these are not in order.) What could possibly remain for our busy boy *in the single year in which he had also received his PhD.*? Whew! Well, he threw out one more paper (which he later expanded on in other writings) titled "On a Heuristic Viewpoint Concerning the Production and Transformation of Light." Physicists for a while had been intrigued by what was known as the "black body radiation problem" or the "ultraviolet catastrophe," a later term. Basically, calculations at the time of how much radiation (light and heat) a warming body such as a stove put out as it went from black to red to white-hot didn't make sense; they showed that at some point a body would be putting out an infinite amount of radiation, which obviously wasn't possible. Something had to be wrong with the calculations, or with the physics. Amazingly, it was this seemingly simple little problem that ultimately ended up moving physics into the quantum age.

Prior to Einstein, Max Planck in 1900 had temporarily solved the problem, at least as to the calculations, by simply inserting a made-up number that seemed to make things work. That number, "h," became known as Planck's constant. Although derived almost intuitively, it turned out to be right on target, and in fact is used heavily in physics to this day. At the same time, Planck had realized that he could only make sense of the calculations if the radiation energy was not emitted from the black body in an analog, continuous fashion, but only if it were emitted in discrete, intermittent packets. He called these packets "quantas" of energy: quantum physics had been born, but no one knew it yet. The key concept here is that analog energy (like radio and old-fashioned TV waves) is continuous, and varies infinitely and continuously, while quantum energy is carried by discontinuous, discrete packets, and varies only in either/or jumps, similar to a digital computer. It was thought that the heating of a stove was smooth and continuous, but at the nuclear level it turned out to be digital and jumpy.

***

In parallel with all of this, Einstein was intrigued with what was called the "photoelectric effect." Here, light was shone on a metal plate, and sometimes electrons struck by the light were "kicked off" of the plate, and sometimes they weren't. It was found that even with a very strong light, if the wavelength was low, no electrons were ejected; conversely, even a less strong light with a higher wavelength would eject electrons. These effects, tying in with Planck's discoveries, seemed to only occur in a "stepped" fashion that couldn't be reconciled with a smooth curve, but could be attributed to staggered and discrete quantas of energy. Here, after having previously left Newton behind, Einstein also now left Maxwell behind. Maxwell's theories had been based on fluid, continuous versions of electromagnetic radiation, but here was evidence that this radiation was now exhibiting more packet/quanta-like characteristics. (We will recall here that radiant heat, visible light, microwaves, x-rays, television and radio waves are all the same thing: simply different parts of the electromagnetic spectrum, varying only in their frequencies/wavelengths.) Maxwell had moved light from its former particle status (Newton) towards a more wavelike picture; now Einstein was moving it back to a more discrete and particle-like one.

Niels Bohr, the later dean of quantum mechanics, initially doubted the meaning of these results, in his first of several disagreements with Einstein. However, and ironically, this is exactly the effect that helped Bohr to develop his model of the atom, and his version of quantum theory, while Einstein later distanced himself from the quantum revolution that he had helped to usher in (because of Heisenberg, as we shall see), even though it was specifically his work on the photoelectric effect which was mentioned in his later Nobel Prize. Einstein could have, at this point, conceivably taken the lead in the development of quantum mechanics, but fate seemingly had other plans. Perhaps Einstein had been given too many gifts already, and it was time to share the wealth.

***

Einstein, although again probably the most significant single person in the history of physics, was also somewhat in the position of being a bridge figure between Newton and today's investigators. Although discovering the photoelectric effect, which helped lead to quantum mechanics, he later disavowed much of what QM was pursuing, and like Newton, ultimately wanted to believe that the universe was constant, predictable, determinable, and fixed. His was an updated clockwork universe in a sense, where things could bend and distort, but were still subject to definite concrete predictions, and unequivocal answers from equations. Things moved not in some random fashion, but in a well-oiled gear form. But the movement was actually illusory in some sense. With his own discoveries involving time, he himself leaned towards an idea that was first put forth by the Greek philosopher Parmenides, and later became known as the "block universe": that when one added in time as a dimension to the other three dimensions, one was left with a sort of spacetime block where nothing actually did move, nothing was indeterminate, and all was fixed like flies in amber. Things could seem to yaw and warp in accordance with the principles of relativity, but that distortion was an illusion, contained within equations, and in truth, there was no real movement.

In the increasingly prevalent view of the universe as being composed primarily of energy, with its associated movement and dynamism, this static interpretation began to seem somewhat anachronistic. In fact, in his critique of this idea, Karl Popper (a prominent philosopher of science) teasingly called Einstein himself "Parmenides." (A Greek who had similar ideas.) All was One, but in a very static fashion. Time and space here were one composite thing, and any seeming movement was already built into, and explained by, the way that the block was viewed.

An analogy that has been used by some is that of a loaf of raisin bread, dissected into slices, but still in its block form. During our lives, in a journey from one end of the loaf to another, we encounter various raisins (events). They are there waiting for us, and we simply come across them as we move along our fixed timeline through the loaf. Except that there really isn't any movement; the "me" five years from now already exists further on "ahead" in the loaf. The me that is existing now will stay here in this location. I may even look back in the loaf at the me of five years past. We all exist together in the loaf: fixed, frozen, and unchangeable. There is a lack of movement and dynamism, but all is predictable.

Theoretically, if one had some sort of key linking one part of the loaf to another, prediction of the future would be easy. This is a vision that may appeal to many astrologers who want definite answers and fool-proof predictions. But since, in this scenario, time *as movement* is actually a misconception, illusion, or fallacy, the events that seem ordered in time are actually all existing at once, and in some sense we are experiencing them all at once. Everything is a clock, but the clock has stopped. All of the various "ages" of ourselves exist at once.

Unfortunately, one problem with this model is that there have been no good ideas as to why I only experience the present moment, or why I experience the flow of time through the loaf in one direction only. Why *do* I have the experience of a conscious self-moving through the flow of time, and why are my remembrances only of the past, and not of the future? Much debate and discussion has been put into these ideas (of a block type universe) over the years, but at this point, due to quantum advances, they are not in the mainstream of current physics theories. Or more accurately, they are incompatible with half or more of today's physics. More on that later. They may again perhaps do a bit better with some astrologers, or those strongly attracted to the idea of a 100% fated universe. Although they cannot be proved or disproved, the (illusory or not) timeline of physics has moved on.

So ultimately, Einstein clung to the older, classical clockwork model, even going so far as to come up at one point with a "cosmological constant" to add to equations and hold things still, which he later regretted. This was a fudge factor designed to eliminate the empirical evidence of a changing universe. He had changed the world, and yet had difficulty accepting the changes that he himself had put into motion.

The changes, however, were here.

Moving On

Niels Bohr was probably the most prominent name in quantum physics for most of his lifetime. He was born Oct 7, 1885, and was concerned enough with balance in life that he eventually had the well-known taijitu (yin-yang symbol) from Taoism made into a family coat-of-arms along with the words "Contraria Sunt Complementia" (Opposites Are Complementary). He was only 20 years old during Einstein's annus mirabilis, barely behind the great man himself. He did not quite match Einstein's influence, but regularly appears in the "top 5 physicists of all time" lists in his own right, and, like Einstein, became a father figure, mentor, and moral force in his later years. He was second only to Einstein in influence during the amazing Golden Age of modern physics that occupied the first half of the 20th century. They had much respect for each other and were not enemies or rivals, but some of their famous disagreements shed much light on the transition of physics from Newton to Einstein to quantum, where we are today. Who knows where we'll be tomorrow?

It was Bohr who most fully recognized the implications of Planck's and Einstein's puzzling experiments that showed that, rather than being continuous as Maxwell had believed, electromagnetic (EM) radiation instead operated in a jagged, stepped, and discrete form. It was Bohr who gave us the model of the atom (now outdated, but still prevalent in the popular imagination) as that of a nucleus with electrons orbiting around it, the pre-modern "planetary" model. Rutherford had pioneered this picture, but Bohr added quantum calculations and the idea of stepped energy shells, which then made the whole thing work. Others had given us hints and calculations, but it was Bohr who laid the atom out in all its glory for our perusal. It was Bohr that allowed physicists to finally make sense of the Periodic Table of the Elements which had existed in several forms prior to this, but which had never been understood. Scientists had noted that certain elements formed into natural groupings, but had never understood why that was. Bohr's new ideas explained why, and thus chemistry as much as physics benefited from his concepts. His model also allowed scientists to make sense of spectrography, which had first been used in 1876, and remains one of the most important tools in astronomy and chemistry to this day. It was Bohr who really began the branch of physics known as quantum mechanics, although he was far from the only important contributor.

Like relativity, there are many good popular books out there that explain the basic tenets and principles of quantum mechanics, depending on the reader's interest. It should be noted that the generic term "quantum mechanics" covers quite a lot of ground, and that many, many ideas that have been developed by different theorists now dovetail together to form what might just as easily be called "modern physics." It is obviously a field that is known to be difficult to study, but the basics begin with the idea that, as previously mentioned, energy is organized, transmitted, and distributed, not in a continuous fashion, but in packets, or quanta. There are continuous exchanges of energy between the various atoms that make up our world and the universe. Matter itself, in fact, is held together by these energy exchanges or bonds between atoms and molecules. The main mechanisms for the distribution and exchange of energy are photons, which are known primarily as the carriers of light, although they carry energy exchanges for the entire electromagnetic spectrum. Photons carry energy from one atom to another.

1927

In 1927, Charles Lindbergh becomes a hero in America by becoming the first person to fly an airplane (the "Spirit of St. Louis") solo across the Atlantic; at about the same time, the first transatlantic telephone call is made. Work on Mt. Rushmore begins in South Dakota. Stalin takes over the Communist party from Trotsky, and in China, the Communists declare war on Chiang Kai-shek. Back in the U.S., The Great Mississippi Flood destroys much of its lower Delta, flooding 27,000 square miles and prompting the creation of the extensive levee system existing today. Louis Armstrong provides a new music, jazz, to flappers in urban America, and Blind Willie McTell and Bessie Smith begin to popularize blues music to rural blacks. Bessie writes a moving song, "Backwater Blues," about the Mississippi flood. Hitler holds his first Nazi meeting in Berlin. The era of "talking pictures" begins with Al Jolson's "The Jazz Singer" (in blackface). Gandhi writes his autobiography to that date titled *The Story of My Experiments With Truth*, as he prepares to lead India to independence. He buys the entire first edition printing, in order to ensure that it will be reprinted. And in Brussels, the Fifth Solvay Conference takes place, consolidating what has been the most amazing quarter century in the history of physics.

The conference is a meeting of the minds of an incredible group of physicists: out of the 29 attendees, 17 ultimately will receive Nobel prizes. The conference is taking place in Brussels. Ernest Solvay, a wealthy industrialist, started the conferences in 1912, and since then the intermittent get-togethers have attracted the cream of the crop in the world of physics. The very first conference, in 1912, had featured as its theme the question of classical physics vs. the new and emerging quantum ideas. The fifth is also dedicated to quantum, and the level of excitement and discovery amongst the attendees is palpable. In the few years leading up to the conference, nearly unbelievable advances in the discipline have taken place so quickly that they can hardly be kept up with:

1900 - Max Planck postulates that energy is distributed through "quanta."

1905 - We have already talked about Einstein's amazing year and discoveries: the atom, relativity, early quantum, and mass/energy equivalence.

1908 - Hermann Minkowski builds on Einstein (who was his former student), and puts into place the idea of time being a 4th dimension, coining the term "spacetime."

1913 - Niels Bohr comes up with the planetary atomic model with electron shells.

1916 - Einstein adds gravity (inertia) and mass, and comes up with his General Theory of Relativity, building on his earlier Special Theory. He is already uncomfortable with the new quantum thinking. He initially doesn't like Bohr's atom, and then comes to accept it.

It takes a few years for these advances to sink in, and then things leap forward again:

1924 - Louis de Broglie shows that not only light, but matter itself is also a wave, in addition to its particle nature. Wow.

1925 - Werner Heisenberg comes up with the first mathematical theory of quantum mechanics, which he calls "matrix mechanics."

1926 - Erwin Schrödinger comes up with his own version, which he calls "wave mechanics." They are ultimately shown to be the same thing, but Schrödinger's version is simpler to work with and wins out. Schrödinger's famous "wave function" calculation becomes likely the most famous equation in physics after Einstein's $E=mc^2$. It shows that matter is not something firm and definite, but simply a wave of potentiality that "collapses," or solidifies into what we know as the physical world under certain circumstances. The interpretation of this new and bizarre concept gives physicists material for endless disagreements as to what it all means. Max Born cements in the idea that the new discipline of quantum mechanics, as shown in the wave equation, is probabilistic rather than deterministic. It is in this year, and in relation to this, that Einstein famously states "God does not play dice with the universe," to which Bohr replies "Einstein, stop telling God what to do." Newton is gone, and Einstein is hanging on to his coattails. Gilbert Lewis names the new and intensively examined light particle the photon.

1927 - The biggest names in physics at this time are Einstein, Bohr, Heisenberg, Schrödinger, Wolfang Pauli, and Paul Dirac. In the same year as the Solvay conference, Heisenberg comes up with his important uncertainty principle, and his mentor Bohr has his own contribution with the idea of complementarity. Together, they ensure that the quantum view of the world will forever have no fixity to it, but will permanently remain fluid, strange, and deal in probability and possibility rather than definite determination. (More will be said about these in the next section.) Together, Bohr and Heisenberg put in place what will become known as the Copenhagen interpretation of quantum mechanics, which is still the most popular version to this very day. Later, Bohr will have a falling out with his student Heisenberg regarding the latter's continuing to work in Germany during WWII. Also in 1927, Dirac comes up with equations incorporating Einstein's relativity into quantum mechanics; in 1930 he will publish *Principles of Quantum Mechanics*, which, amazingly, is still in use academically at this time. In astronomy in 1927, the Belgian Georges Lemaître (an unusual combination of a priest, an astronomer, and a professor of physics) first proposes that the universe is not static but expanding, throwing a bombshell into astronomy and cosmology nearly as big as the one that quantum was lobbing into physics. Edwin Hubble (for whom the well-known telescope is named) later confirms this.

In addition, Lemaitre realizes that if this is the case, our universe must have had a "point" beginning, and postulates the Big Bang (although that term came into use later). It was quite a year! (See elsewhere in this book the interesting tale of how horror writer Edgar Allan Poe intersects with all of this.)

The conference goes well, the participants return to their countries, and their research. Here are a few highlights from the ensuing years:

1928 - Dirac builds on an idea of Wolfgang Pauli and postulates spin, a measure of angular velocity, as a property of particles. This will be valuable for its use in many quantum physics experiments in the future.

1935 - The Einstein/Bohr disagreements are in full swing. Einstein cannot accept probability or entanglement (see later explanation), and with two others comes up with a very famous thought experiment: the EPR paradox, which he hopes will finally dismiss both of these. (By the way, none of this is to diminish Einstein: he remains the largest and most important figure in the history of physics: if nothing else, his difficulty in embracing the changes that came along in his beloved branch of science simply makes him more human.) Bohr gently refutes each point that Einstein makes and successfully defends the new quantum model. For those with a technical mind, a wonderful narrative of this episode in physics history, in his own words, appears in Bohr's small book *Atomic Physics and Human Knowledge*. Quantum has thus withstood the last major assault by Einstein, although the great man, in between his increasing humanitarian and philosophical concerns, never gave up hope in trying to unseat the new upstart in physics for the next 20 years, until his death in 1955. It was in response to the EPR experiment that Schrödinger invented his famous cat, to add to the speculations and discussions. It must have been a heady time to be a physicist!

1964 - In the particle field, Murray Gell-Mann and George Zweig both predict a further category of sub-atomic particles that they called quarks. These are smaller than, and make up, the previously "smallest" particles: protons, neutrons, etc. At first just theoretical, quarks are found in 1968. They form, along with leptons and bosons, what is today called the "Standard Model" in physics, which was more or less solidified in the mid-1970's. It explains the roots of matter, yet is still a work in progress. The recently discovered Higgs is a Very Famous Boson.

1965 - 30 years after the EPR experiment, physicist John Bell writes a paper titled "On the Einstein Podolsky Rosen Paradox" (EPR), which features a brilliant new analysis leading to Bell's Theorem, which is based on Bell's Inequalities, a series of tests. In it, he even more completely refutes Einstein's arguments against quantum and entanglement: that some sort of "hidden variables" might save classical physics. Bell proved conclusively that it was *mathematically impossible* for any theory of hidden variables to in fact produce the verified predictions of quantum mechanics, and so this idea couldn't reverse these new discoveries. Quantum was real, and entanglement was real. Entanglement has not really been talked about yet, but is one of the most bizarre ideas in quantum mechanics. (It will be explained in a following section.) Berkeley particle physicist Henry Stapp has flatly declared: "Bell's Theorem is the most profound discovery of science." The implications are immense, and haven't really been fully explored yet. As a taste, entanglement is the basis for the new and rapidly growing field of quantum computing. Bell's ideas were verified experimentally several times, most notably by Alain Aspect in 1982.

1980 - Alan Guth and others come up with the idea of Cosmic Inflation: the idea that, in the expanding universe, it is not that the galaxies are all moving away from each other as seemed to be observed; rather, the real story is that *space itself* is expanding, and carrying the galaxies along with it. Wow.

1998 - Not only are the galaxies expanding away from us, but they are doing so *at an ever-increasing rate of speed*. It begins to look as if the evolution of the universe, which was once predicted to slow and then collapse in on itself due to the force of gravity (into the "Big Crunch") may just keep expanding forever. There is, it must be said, much speculation as to what the fate of the universe may be, however. This is definitely a work in progress.

2012 - To much fanfare, the Higgs boson, the so-called "God Particle" (although that is a completely media-driven misnomer) was declared to be found by the CERN particle accelerator in Geneva. It acquired that nickname partially because it is predicted to be omnipresent in the universe, and also because it is the carrier or creator of mass. A pretty hefty responsibility! This was the Holy Grail of current physics, and goes a long way towards completing the Standard Model. There are some, however, who would like more verification, and now that the Large Hadron Collider (CERN) is up and running again at twice the power, perhaps that will happen.

There have been many, many more advances in physics over the years, and many, many more in recent years; progress in this field, while perhaps not matching the first half of the 20th century, continues apace at a dizzying speed. Here we have tried to concentrate on those findings that may be most applicable for the reader in reading through the rest of this particular book. Physics is an exciting field, and one with never-ending surprises. Our book starts with the physical, but that is just a start. The universe itself hints at many more secrets ahead. The following sections contain some discussions on the various theories and discoveries that were presented in the brief history above.

More Concepts

It's difficult to exaggerate just how far modern physics has moved from classical Newtonian physics, with its clockwork universe. One hears of strings, alternative universes, zero point energy, and hundreds of other terms and concepts which surely would have had ol' Isaac scratching his head. Anything seems possible, and indeed, anything pretty much *is* possible. It is truly a "Brave New World." The very proliferation of ideas in recent decades has forced the scientific community to be more attentive to alternative potentialities. Anything, it would seem, is feasible: except, of course, astrology.

MORE CONCEPTS IN MODERN PHYSICS: The double slit experiment is only one of the many strange, and often counter-intuitive, concepts of modern physics. Here is a list of some of those other ideas, in no particular order, with notes and speculations. Many, if not most, provide much food for thought of a philosophical nature as well.

THE DOUBLE SLIT: To recap: this experiment demonstrates that light is at the same time a wave and a particle (as is matter), and also shows (according to some interpretations) that consciousness can affect the physical world. The weirdness doesn't stop there.

COMPLEMENTARITY: To recap: Bohr saw the wave/particle nature of light (and matter) as an example of complementarity: objects could exhibit incompatible but complementary properties; there were thus questions as to how accurately we could know the whole. For example, light is likely "something" that may act as a particle at times or as a wave at times, depending on how we are measuring it. But what *is* it? That something seems to be beyond duality, and beyond our current conceptions or visualizations of things. It remains a core mystery: we have learned to measure it, but its essence remains unknown. This may be similar to lightning before electricity was discovered: we could see it, but what *was* it? It likely points at deeper, and as yet undiscovered, levels of reality.

RELATIVITY: To recap: The only absolute constant that we know of in the material world is the speed of light. No known energy or matter can go faster than the speed of light. Relativity becomes a function of this idea, and leads to all sorts of strange phenomena, such as one twin traveling near the speed of light and aging more slowly than another twin left behind; matter becoming shorter in length as it approaches the speed of light, in addition to becoming heavier; and many other oddities. Philosophically, the idea that there is ultimately no fixed frame of reference in either time or space shook the world's sense of stability in a way that hadn't happened since Copernicus. This is Einstein's *Special Theory of Relativity*.

GENERAL THEORY OF RELATIVITY: This is our current best thinking about how gravity works, and is very difficult to understand and visualize. Its nature may be put into perspective by its alternate title, the *Geometric Theory of Gravitation*. Einstein says that things are not pulled together because of some sort of "gravitational attraction," but that things moving in space (angular or linear momentum) are drawn together passively by the geometry involved. Mass (what we often erroneously call weight) creates a distortion in spacetime similar to a bowling ball sitting on a bed. If one were to roll a marble nearby, the marble would "fall into" the bowling ball because of the distortion (indentation) on the bed. That's geometry, not what we commonly think of as gravity. Similarly, our moon wants to "fall into" the distortion in spacetime created by the earth, and is prevented from doing so only by its opposing inertial force that is trying to get it to fly away. Too much General Relativity (gravity) and the Moon would fall into the earth as meteorites do every day. Too much opposing inertial force, and the moon would fly off into space as our own rockets do (which is obviously intentional). In early 2016, scientists announced that they had found evidence of gravitational waves, considered an incontrovertible confirmation of the theory. The General Theory of Relativity is also one stumbling block for a Theory of Everything (see below). Of note is that, although this is the currently accepted explanation for masses being attracted to each other, since it is so complicated and difficult to visualize, even scientists themselves continue to casually refer to "gravity" most of the time when they are explaining those attractions. This is understood to be standing in for the more correct geometric explanation.

MATTER/ENERGY EQUIVALENCE: To recap: energy is matter and matter is energy. They are different forms of the same thing. One can be converted into the other: $E=mc^2$. Generally, that one thing is thought to be energy, and matter is seen as a subset of energy. But the equation can go in either direction. Conceivably, they could be complementary components (as in wave/particle duality) of something we really can't name yet.

PAULI EXCLUSION PRINCIPLE: Wolfgang Pauli, a fellow alcoholic who played out Josef von Sternberg's movie *The Blue Angel* in real life by marrying a cabaret singer with unfortunate results, produced in 1925 his "exclusion principle," which states basically that electrons can't be of the same configuration or in the same place at the same time. Along with Bohr's electron shells, this is the reason that, even though matter is really 99.999% empty space, we experience it as solid and substantial. These two concepts also demonstrated that matter (electrons) could instantaneously change energies and locations without any intermediary path or transitional state (although this is somewhat illusory when the wave nature is taken into account). This is completely contrary to classical mechanics, and added to the developing bizarreness of reputation that was enveloping quantum mechanics. In addition (as Planck had done with his constant), Pauli came up with the elementary particle known as the neutrino using pure intuition and speculation in 1930; the neutrino was later verified to be real. Since it is of nearly infinitesimal mass with no electric charge, trillions of them are actually passing through your body right now, undetected, as you read this. There's a lot going on in that vast empty space of matter! Neutrinos are also a wild-card candidate in the search for dark matter. Finally, Pauli collaborated with the psychotherapist Carl Jung in looking at how consciousness might interact with matter, and was instrumental in helping Jung move towards his concept of synchronicity, the subject of a later section.

PROBABILITY: Max Born won the Nobel prize for his work demonstrating that, in quantum mechanics (i.e. modern physics), everything is governed solely by probability. The old days of Newton's predictability and determinism are gone. The clock of the clockwork universe has stopped. Or rather, it may continue to tick, but we can only speculate where the hands may be at a given moment by using a probability distribution curve. Here, the statistics of large groups and averages come into play. We have statistical truths and forecasts rather than individual predictions. Physics has become like sociology. That is, if we have a million clocks, the vast majority will likely all show 3 o'clock at this moment; but there is always room for outliers that may read something different. This is not because of some shoddy clock mechanism, but *because possibility and probability are baked into the fabric of the cosmos*. They are "laws," just like the laws of motion and gravity. We can no longer say that if we hit ball B with mallet A, that it will go in direction C. We can only specify the probability of it doing so. This prompted Einstein's "God does not play dice with the universe" comment. But it's here to stay. The implications for life in general are large. We live in a probabilistic world, not a deterministic one. Micromanagers everywhere are wringing their hands.

THE UNCERTAINTY PRINCIPLE: First introduced by Heisenberg in 1927, it is often confused by non-physicists with the probability component of quantum above, since probability seems "uncertain." They are, however, in fact two somewhat similar, related, and yet different concepts. The uncertainty principle states simply, that in any physical system with two paired variables or properties (known as conjugate variables), the more accurately one measures a particular one, the less that can be known about the other. There are a number of different situations in which this might manifest; the most common example given is usually for the two variables of position and momentum (which can be thought of as direction). So, for example, the more accurately we measure the exact position of an electron (or a baseball in flight), the less able we are to successfully predict exactly where it's heading. Conversely, the more accurately we are able to see the path (momentum) of an electron or a baseball, the less able we are to measure exactly where it is at this moment. If you are mathematically minded, look up Heisenberg's equation. It is nearly as simple and elegant as Einstein's, and requires minimal understanding to grasp. It is straightforward, it is verifiable, and thus uncertainty also has become a part of our view of the universe. The practical, real-world take home here is that we can't know everything about anything. There is a certain fuzziness and imprecision built into how accurately we may perceive the world. It may even be thought of as philosophic companion to R=K+1.

THE ELECTRON CLOUD: Probability coupled with the Uncertainty Principle led to the conclusion that the Bohr's "planetary" model of the atom, with its neat nucleus of protons and neutrons circled by electrons looking like little balls was (although still used, and still in the public imagination) inaccurate and inadequate for representing what was really going on. It was superseded by a model that featured, instead of the discrete and easily visualized electron "orbits," electron *clouds*, which are somewhat confusingly also called "orbitals." The visual form of these (look them up online) took one of several shapes, typically looking like a 3-dimensional "cloud" surrounding the nucleus. They are, in fact, nothing more than a 3D graph of mathematical functions describing the probabilities of where the electron *might* be found. They are a probability distribution. This is an important concept. Until we actually measure where the electron *is* (and thereby of course lose our opportunity for an accurate momentum), it might be anywhere: its position is literally nothing more than a possibility, a probability. The cloud is a visual concept of that probability.

THE WAVE FUNCTION: The wave function (or wavefunction) is similar to the above: it is a mathematical formulation which describes the *quantum state* of a particle or system, and includes all of our favorites: probability, the uncertainty principle, and other quantum parameters. It is most commonly expressed through Schrödinger's equation, which he came up with in 1926. Schrödinger's equation describes the evolution of the wave function over time, and introduces the notion of "superposition." Here, the electron in the example above is considered to be nowhere and everywhere at the same time, in all possible positions and states until some measurement of it takes place. It's in superposition. It's a smear of possibilities and probabilities. It's a ghost. Mathematics takes precedence here, since we can never know where the electron *is* prior to measurement: its state and position exist as pure potentiality. It is, then, some sort of measurement, or interaction of the quantum system with the "outside," that "collapses" the wave function into actual measurable and concrete parameters in a classical sense. This is not like "well, it's somewhere, we just don't know where it is"; this is like "no, it *really is* nowhere—and everywhere—until we interact with it." This has all been verified experimentally and mathematically: welcome to the new quantum world!

The state of anything in the universe (at least in the micro world), then, prior to observation and measurement, is one of superposition: upon measurement or observation, the probability wave function collapses, and manifests as energy or matter in a particular position and configuration. The concept of the "collapse" of the superposition wave function is very important and central to quantum mechanics, and will be revisited more than once in this book. To repeat: everything exists as energy, as mere unrealized potentialities, possibilities and probabilities, until something causes these to collapse into a single tangible actuality, which produces the world as we know it.

> "Collapse is the crystallizing of the possibilities of the quantum realm into the concrete actualities of the spacetime realm. So, collapse is not something that happens anywhere in spacetime. It is the creation of spacetime itself."—Physicist Ruth E. Kastner

THE COPENHAGEN INTERPRETATION: Quantum physics is so counterintuitive and bizarre that there is currently no universally accepted way to interpret the findings and calculations involved. What do they mean? How does it all work? The "Copenhagen interpretation" is an informal grouping of agreements and attitudes about how to interpret quantum results, first formulated by Bohr and Heisenberg around 1927. (Bohr worked in Copenhagen.) Since then, for getting close to a century now, it has remained by a notable margin the most popular version of quantum interpretation, although it is a somewhat loose assemblage of principles. Generally, it includes the ideas of probability and the uncertainty principle along with the idea that things are described by the wave function, which operates in a domain known as "configuration space" (where superposition exists) that is beyond, different from, and separate from ordinary physical spacetime. It is primarily mathematical. It is the collapse of the indeterminate wave function that turns possibilities into actualities and brings them into being in the ordinary physical world. The collapse of the wave function is caused by interaction with the "classical" (everyday) world: primarily through measurement or observation. This happens continuously and everywhere, which is why we see the world as we do. Generally, the idea of causation is taken away. More philosophical or mystical versions (the Von Neumann–Wigner interpretation, for example) would say that things don't even exist at all in time and space until they are observed (on which all versions agree, via measurement), but go further in that the collapse may ultimately be traced back to consciousness itself, which is seen as being behind and responsible for the observation or measurement. If there were no consciousness involved, no one to read the measurement, then the material world would simply remain waves of energy and possibilities. Measurement and observation here presuppose the existence and interaction of a consciousness which drives the train.

These more exotic Copenhagen interpretations are generally the approach used in this book when physics is talked about, simply because one of the themes of the book *is* how consciousness may interact with matter to produce such odd effects as synchronicity, psi, and astrology. We *want* to be broad-minded here, as we are searching for answers to seemingly strange phenomena flying under the accepted radar. We are travelling the side alleys; but of course, it is often the side alleys where the breakthroughs for new things are found. One can never produce new models using old thinking or templates. New things always require new thinking.

Thus, it is important to emphasize that, while Copenhagen in general remains the dominant interpretation of quantum mechanics, these more speculative versions do not; they are considered "fringe" by the mainstream. However, it is also important to understand that, although consciousness as a possible interpretation was never very popular with physicists, and is probably even less so today, that doesn't knock it out of the ring as a contender. We *still* don't know what this is ultimately all about. The book is still being written. It's also important to note that the consciousness implied here is that connected with *measurement*, although in its larger context, of course, measurement simply means "interaction with." As several theorists have pointed out, measurement is not the same as pure consciousness, however: the double slit experiment may not be affected by "staring at it," as some have put it, but only through consciousness somehow physically interacting with the quantum subject. Measurement, physical interaction, is the intermediary between consciousness and matter; although the above mentioned subjects such as synchronicity and psi may question even that concrete connection. The world, we are finding out, is very odd. The overall suggestion here is that what we currently know of traditional matter/energy rules of the game may not be adequate to fully explain reality, especially the cracks in the accepted paradigm that are visible over in the corners, and on the edges.

Physicists, by the way, hate it when people "go macro" (the scale that involves the world around us) regarding these collapses, as their experiments and evidence remain largely at the micro (quantum, subatomic) scale. They caution that the idea that consciousness may be involved in the collapsing of wave functions (whether necessary or merely possible) is purely speculative at this time; and even if that were the case, there is a lot of distance between causing an electron to manifest as either a wave or a particle, and manifesting a BMW in the driveway. This is behind much of the dismissive "quantum flapdoodle" charges that are levied at various New Age figures. But if things are not discrete and separate, but are a connected Whole—then the micro is attached to, and in fact makes up and determines the macro; the division is ultimately false, and a connection between the two may be traced (see the parallel idea of decoherence below). The collapse of endless wave functions is finally what *does* make up the solid matter of the world around us. More will be revealed here.

(At this time, there is a tremendous push going on in the scientific world towards quantum computers, for which entanglement—see below—is a key functioning component. Seemingly every week, larger and more macro scale objects are being entangled. Recently, two diamonds a millimeter in size were able to be linked together like this. These are visible objects in our everyday world, not electrons or quarks. This is important, because there is a direct relationship between entanglement and the delayed and controllable collapse of the wave function in a computer. We *are* moving up into the macro world here, and into exciting new territory.)

ALTERNATE INTERPRETATIONS: A survey of 33 physicists at a high-level conference in 2013 revealed that, after Copenhagen, the most popular interpretations of quantum were *informational* interpretations. The seminal figure in these was John Archibald Wheeler. Besides championing Einstein's general relativity, he coined the terms quantum foam and wormholes, and popularized the new (at that time) idea of black holes—in addition to working on the Manhattan Project, which produced the A-bomb. Quite a busy man! Wheeler was generally not in the group of physicists prone to mysticism, and yet, according to Wikipedia, "Wheeler speculated that reality is created by observers in the universe." A pretty heady thought, that, and very similar to the Copenhagen interpretation.

Some interpretations can be quite different. Several of them have been proposed by folks who are *really* bothered by the probability thing, and wish to maintain Newton's and Einstein's predictable universe. The block universe was mentioned earlier, although that isn't really considered a quantum interpretation; it pretty much just sidesteps or ignores quantum calculations completely and produces a vision of the logical consequence of an Einsteinian spacetime system. This goes back again to the heart of what Einstein and Bohr argued about. More true alternative interpretations that actually use the quantum calculations, but attempt to minimize probability, are those of David Bohm (pilot wave theory, built by extending ideas first put forth by de Broglie), and the "many worlds" theory. Bohm's ideas fall into what is known as the "hidden variables" group. That is, according to this camp, quantum mechanics only *appears* to be probabilistic; that mistake is simply because there are some "hidden variables" somewhere that will be discovered, and will make everything deterministic again in a classical way. Einstein was in this group. (See the EPR discussion.) Bohm speaks of an "implicate order" underlying the cosmos as we know it, which then becomes the "explicate order" that we see. Although Bohm clung to determinism, he tried to bridge the gap to quantum, and this was his solution. For this book, the positive component of Bohm's ideas is that the hidden implicate order could conceivably (which Bohm himself acknowledged) include consciousness, and thus might point the way to synchronicity or similar things. Bohm is not well supported today by the mainstream, but his ideas are intriguing.

The "many worlds" or "multiverse" theories are currently enjoying some time in the sun. In fact, while none of the 33 physicists mentioned above chose Bohm's ideas, many worlds came in third after Copenhagen and informational (Bohm has a connection with informational systems also). Many worlds or the multiverse gets around probability and indeterminacy by stating that every time a wave function collapses, *all possible outcomes are actually manifested*. It's not a probability of just one out of many possibilities manifesting, as with other interpretations: here, *all possibilities are actually manifested for a given situation*. Conveniently, however, they create other universes in which to manifest, which we can't see or verify. Here, Schrödinger's cat is alive in one universe, and dead in another. (See below.)

This idea captures not only scientists', but the public's imagination, and has been the subject of science fiction films, popular science documentaries, etc. It's a quite glamorous notion. There may be another version of me out there who really gets that girl I've been pining after, even though this takes place in some other universe that I can never know about. In another universe, I won't have a boss who picks on me. In another universe, peace prevails and humans are wise, hyper-intelligent, and advanced. (We humans are so ego-centric!) The popular idea of the multiverse seems always to come back to maybe just one other universe, which seems focused on me and my little struggles in life. And things are never worse, they always seem to be better. (It is perhaps no coincidence that this is starting to sound remarkably like many religions' idea of heaven: the hope that there is a possibility for a better life *somewhere*.)

But that's not really what the theory implies. The theory implies that for every two possibilities (for example), instead of life or quantum choosing one or the other to manifest, *each* will manifest, creating in the process another entire universe to manifest in. And it's not just me: every time an electron (for example) is found in a particular place, it might just as well have been found in another place (using only an electron and two possibilities for simplicity). Most quantum theories would force it to "choose" one or the other, and that would be the end of the story. But for many worlds, since *all* possible positions must manifest, a new universe must be created so that the electron is found, not in either place, but in both places, one in each universe. Just in the space of typing this, the electrons in my fingers have probably created millions of new universes. Anywhere, anytime (even at the subatomic level) that two competing possibilities exist, a new universe must be created. Quite a task, but in MW it seems so easy. One can see how this could get unwieldy very quickly: basically it would almost instantaneously produce an exponentially increasing infinite number of universes. Perhaps that's the case, but in science as well as life, the simpler explanation is often better. This is the principle known as Occam's Razor. Infinitely proliferating universes does not seem simple. (David Chalmers and others have another variation of this known as the multiple minds theory.)

There are other theories that attempt to explain the transition from quantum weirdness to concrete, classical reality. Another is *quantum decoherence*, which sidesteps the whole idea of the collapse of the wave function in lieu of the idea that quantum objects, in coming into contact with other quantum objects or with classical objects,simply "decohere"; i.e., lose their "quantumness" and join the classical world. It's as if the quantum objects were being "contaminated" by contacts outside themselves, and then solidifying. A visualization might be that of water starting to freeze, and watching an ice crystal form and then rapidly extend across the surface in beautiful and connecting crystals. This also happens everywhere, and in a continual fashion. It poses a difficulty in designing quantum computers.

But until someone *really* disproves it, we're looking at Copenhagen as remaining the dominant force in quantum interpretation.

SCHRÖDINGER'S CAT: Erwin Schrödinger was born August 12th. His wife was born December 3rd. She must have been a very tolerant woman, because Schrödinger apparently considered himself quite the ladies' man, and had endless affairs during the course of their marriage. Nonetheless, he found time to come up with his famous wave equation, which became the centerpiece of quantum mechanics. However, Schrödinger himself was never comfortable with many of the interpretations of quantum mechanics, and satirically came up with his cat paradox to accent the bizarreness of it all. Here is the experiment in his own words:

"One can even set up quite ridiculous cases. A cat is penned up in a steel chamber, along with the following device (which must be secured against direct interference by the cat): in a Geiger counter, there is a tiny bit of radioactive substance, so small, that perhaps in the course of the hour one of the atoms decays, but also, with equal probability, perhaps none; if it happens, the counter tube discharges and through a relay releases a hammer that shatters a small flask of hydrocyanic acid. If one has left this entire system to itself for an hour, one would say that the cat still lives if meanwhile no atom has decayed. The psi-function of the entire system would express this by having in it the living and dead cat (pardon the expression) mixed or smeared out in equal parts."

This is a very famous thought experiment, and many wonderful visual representations may be found online. Basically, Schrödinger is saying that according (especially) to the Copenhagen interpretation: if a cat has a 50% chance of being alive and a 50% chance of being dead when a sealed box is opened after an hour (during which poison gas may or may not have been released), and according to quantum theory things as specified by the wave equation are in a superposition until observed, then what state is the cat in prior to opening the box? Is it alive? Is it dead? One can find endless disagreements over this with a little research. Many quantum interpretations would argue that the cat is both alive and dead, or neither alive nor dead, but exists in the box prior to opening as simply the *potential* for either one; it is the opening and observation that forces the wave function to collapse, and chooses one of those two states to manifest as concrete reality.

ENTANGLEMENT: This is another item which appalled Einstein, and which he derisively called "spooky action at a distance." Wikipedia explains it best: "Quantum entanglement is a physical phenomenon that occurs when pairs or groups of particles are generated or interact in ways such that the quantum state of each particle cannot be described independently—instead, a quantum state may be given for the system as a whole." Far-reaching speculations may be generated from this peculiar phenomenon. It means that physical objects can be connected, can be considered as one thing, regardless of having separate positions in space. As an example, consider two electrons which are entangled (electrons may be "put into entanglement"—this is the heart of upcoming quantum computers). Normally, with separate quantum states, if we measure an electron's spin—a measurement of angular momentum—for example, we may find (subject to the usual probability and wave function collapse) its spin to be up. A nearby electron may be measured to be either spin up or spin down; there would only be a random correlation between the two. However, if two electrons are "entangled," they then share the same quantum state and function *together*, and are linked. Distance is no barrier, and actually has nothing to do with it. Let's suppose that one electron (electron B) is taken across the universe from its entangled mate, electron A. If we then measure electron A to have a down spin, we are assured that electron B will have an up spin (entangled electrons always have complementary spins). If we had measured electron A to have an up spin, then electron B would have had a down spin. Each "knows" what the other one is up to, billions of light years away. It's important to note that, prior to measurement, neither electron A nor B even *has* a particular spin: the spin is a 50/50 probability that only is determined at the moment of measurement. But once electron A's spin is known, electron B's will also be immediately fixed and determined, even though it is across the universe.

To present it another way: Observer A is looking at electron A but hasn't measured it yet. Observer B, who is across the universe, is looking at electron B but hasn't measured it yet. Each electron may be either spin up or spin down. If the electrons are *not* entangled, then when Observer A measures his electron and discovers it to be spin up, it has no bearing whatsoever on Observer B's electron. Observer B's electron may be found to be either spin up or spin down on measuring it. However, if the electrons are entangled (and usually they will have had to be close together to become entangled prior to moving across the universe), then if Observer A finds his electron to be spin down, Observer B will *always* find his electron to be spin up, and *instantaneously* so. The information *seemingly* does not obey the normal rules of spacetime, or the speed of light limit, but that's only due to an incorrect understanding of what's going on.

It's important to note that the reason this phenomenon looks as it does is not because some "signal" is being sent across the universe (which would have to obey the speed of light), but because the electrons are in *quantum superposition* together: that is what entanglement *is*. They are in superposition together, they share a *common wave function*, they are part of the same equation, and they collapse together. Collapsing one collapses the other. It is the same collapse. (If we wanted to actually send confirmation of the position of B back to observer A, we would have to send the information by the old speed of light route.) Because of quantum possibility rules, electron A may have *either* spin up or spin down—this isn't discovered (or "collapsed") until it is measured. But *whatever* spin the collapse reveals, electron B on the other side of the universe will "know" this and adjust itself accordingly to have the opposite spin.

What is really happening is that the collapsing quantum state of one is taking the other along with it, since they are entangled; a single wave function describes both: that is the key. They are inseparably connected by sharing a wave function. We can also note that, although researchers have only been able to entangle very small objects at this time, the wave function does not necessarily have to be on an atomic scale, but may theoretically be as large as the universe. Wave functions in practice never get that size, because they typically have contact with the macro or classical world while they are still at the atomic scale. The wave function is then collapsed, and fixed concrete reality takes over. Finally, we may also note that the process is not one of *causation* (which is what threw Einstein), but one of *correlations*, resulting from the entangled quantum states.

THE EPR PARADOX: Closely connected with what are known as the Einstein/Bohr debates, this was Einstein's last and greatest stand in trying to disprove quantum. With two colleagues, he attempted to prove, through a thought experiment, that the quantum theory of physics was "not complete," and therefore invalid as it stood: that the wave function was not a complete description of reality. In fact, the paper, written in 1935, was called "Can Quantum-Mechanical Description of Physical Reality Be Considered Complete?" Again, Einstein disliked both uncertainty and entanglement; this thought experiment went after both. By "not complete," Einstein primarily meant that he felt there might be hidden variables lurking out there somewhere that would bring reality back to a predictable, deterministic basis. The results of this very public foray in front of the physics community at large must have disappointed him, as well as his co-authors Boris Podolsky and Nathan Rosen, who made up the rest of the "EPR." (That said, again, Einstein remained a premier physicist until his death, and actually made other contributions that were used and absorbed by the quantum camp.)

At the 1927 Solvay Conference, Born and Heisenberg had declared: "While we consider ... a quantum mechanical treatment of the electromagnetic field ... as not yet finished, we consider quantum mechanics to be a closed theory, whose fundamental physical and mathematical assumptions are no longer susceptible of any modification. ... On the question of the 'validity of the law of causality' we have this opinion: as long as one takes into account only experiments that lie in the domain of our currently acquired physical and quantum mechanical experience, the assumption of indeterminism in principle, here taken as fundamental, agrees with experience." In other words, "we know it may need some fine tuning, but quantum is basically complete in its major tenets, and describes reality as we can currently know it." That has held true to this day. In response, Einstein replied: "Quantum mechanics is very worthy of regard. But an inner voice tells me that this is not yet the right track. The theory yields much, but it hardly brings us closer to the Old One's secrets. I, in any case, am convinced that He does not play dice." Believing is seeing, it would seem, even for great physicists. It was a full eight years later that Einstein finally came up with the EPR thought experiment, and presented it to his colleagues. Each point was carefully and successfully countered by Bohr, and in the end quantum, uncertainty, and entanglement were victorious. Determinism had died earlier in the century, and now it remained dead.

BELL'S THEOREM: EPR was a thought experiment only, although a thoroughly examined and vetted one. So were the results *really, really* valid in the real world, or was it just fancy thinking? In 1964, further examinations by Irish physicist John Bell added to EPR when he demonstrated that, not only were the original conclusions about EPR correct, but that it *was in fact a mathematical impossibility* to achieve the results of quantum mechanics (quantum itself had already been verified experimentally) through any use of “hidden variables.” It appeared that quantum did indeed describe the world. Subsequently, Alain Aspect and several others have demonstrated entanglement and non-locality in the real world through many experiments focusing specifically on EPR issues. As mentioned above, these experiments underlie much of the research going on towards the production of a quantum computer. Spooky action at a distance is real, and God apparently *does* play dice with the universe.

ENTROPY: This is another big principle in physics. It is associated with the second law of thermodynamics, and basically states that, without additional energy input, the disorder in a closed system will always increase over time. Without new effort or energy, things will always get more disorganized, never more organized, on their own. I like it because it explains why my house always seems to need cleaning. It has great implications for everything from weather patterns to relationships. It is featured frequently in discussions about time. Ever since Einstein, time itself has been a big topic of conversation, with the biggest question being why time seems to always move in one direction only (the so-called “arrow of time”). This law figures heavily into those discussions. (There are also some who propose that time doesn’t even exist at all, that it’s simply an illusion, or an emergent property of our world, dependent on other factors.)

THE OBSERVER EFFECT: This has become somewhat of a catch-all term with some confusion attached to it. In physics, it more strictly refers to the idea that the actual physical act of observation (or measurement) changes what is being observed. For example, to observe an electron, we must fire a photon (light particle) at it. However, in doing so, we “bump,” and thus change, the trajectory of the electron. A more mundane example would be this: you are trying to measure the temperature inside a closed box. To measure it, you must put a thermometer in the box. However, the very introduction of the thermometer changes the temperature slightly. Our observation is connected with, and changes reality. There is a similar case in the double slit experiment, when our observation produces different results under different circumstances. It is often confused with the Uncertainty Principle, which simply states that uncertainty is a built-in mathematical function of any system with wave-like properties. This is separate from interaction, as it is "baked into" the system *prior to* any interaction, although interaction bears it out. Since that includes all matter and energy, it's pretty prevalent. Einstein tried to get around this and demonstrate "local realism," the idea that things have a definite value for complementary variables prior to measurement, but his attempts failed. Speaking of Einstein, the observer effect is also frequently confused with what is more correctly thought of simply as different frames of reference when talking about relativity.

QUANTUM ZENO EFFECT: Try figuring this one out through classical physics. Radioactive atoms often "decay" into other similar (or dissimilar) atoms, giving off energy. Their "half-life" is the time it takes, on average, for half of the atoms in a given bunch to decay. This is the basis for nuclear power. It is probabilistic; there is no way to tell when a particular, individual atom will decay. (See cat, Schrödinger's.) We are back to an aggregate statistical system. However, the quantum Zeno effect states that if we actually *watch* a particular atom, it will *never* decay. A "watched pot never boils" is a metaphor, but a Zeno atom is a real phenomenon of physics. The effect has been experimentally verified. It includes not only atomic decay, but also such things as spin; any changeable or unstable state in the quantum world will "suspend" if we are monitoring it. It again hints at the mysterious and possible power of the observer's consciousness. We can actually control whether an atom decays or not. *Why* does watching the little atom cause it to freeze?

STANDARD MODEL: The currently accepted best-guess version of how matter is put together, and how the universe works. The Standard Model is the crowning achievement (thus far) of particle physics. It is underlain by quantum theory. The Higgs Boson a couple of years ago generated great excitement, as it confirmed expectations of that particle being part of the Standard Model. These are the type of investigations that are currently taking place at The Large Hadron Collider associated with CERN in Geneva, Switzerland. It is exciting work for modern physicists. The Standard Model, for example, states that matter is made up of, and force carried by, quarks, leptons, and bosons. Quarks and leptons make up the group known as fermions, which constitute matter. The bosons carry force, the most prominent example being the photon. The best known lepton is the electron. Together, all of these make up what is colloquially known as the "particle zoo." Physicists readily admit, however, that the Standard Model is very much a work in progress. One weakness at this point is a failure in being able to integrate it (and quantum) with Einstein's theory of general relativity, which spells out the modern theory of gravity. The Holy Grail in physics is the so-called Theory of Everything (TOE), which would integrate all of the various ill-fitting parts into a seamless and elegant uber-theory that (theoretically!) would explain everything.

DARK MATTER: If one needs an example, Standard Model notwithstanding, that things are not quite as tightly figured out as they seem, one need only to examine the ideas of dark matter and dark energy. Dutch astronomer Jan Oort (for whom the Oort cloud is named) in 1932 was the first person to notice that the large scale composition and movement of the universe on a galactic level could not be explained by the known visible matter: stars, planets, gas, galaxies, etc. It appeared as if something invisible, but with large gravitational effects, was moving objects in the universe around. Things were predictable, but only if one hypothesized this mysterious "dark matter" that couldn't be seen. In addition, there is also an even more mysterious dark energy, which is hypothesized to be what is causing the accelerating expansion of the universe. As it turns out, dark energy makes up about 68% of the universe, and dark matter makes up about 27%. If you do the math here, you will find that the things we can actually see and measure (the aforementioned stars, planets, gasses, and galaxies so wonderfully brought to us in the Hubble telescope photos) make up only about 5% of the entire universe around us. Yes, that's right. *Everything* that we can currently see is only about 5% of what's actually out there in the universe, interacting and affecting things. What is this stuff? Where is this stuff? Why can't we see it? We simply don't have any idea yet what's going on with the 95% that's right here with us, surrounding us, and yet invisible. Well, we do have some ideas, but no one really knows yet. The take-home from *this* astounding discovery? If we can't find 95% of the universe, and if we didn't even know that it existed, so that we couldn't find it, until 1932; then what else might exist that we're unaware of? A humbling thought.

BLACK HOLES: Black holes are another staple of science fiction, and are not to be confused with wormholes, which are a different item. Black holes were predicted by Einstein's general theory of relativity, although, like quantum, Einstein himself was unable to accept that they existed. They had, in fact, been speculated about as early as 1783 by clergyman and amateur scientist John Michell. The premier researcher investigating black holes in contemporary science is well-known astrophysicist Stephen Hawking. Black holes have been shown to be an important part of the structure of the universe. It is thought that most galaxies in fact contain black holes at their center, although these do not have enough mass to attract the entire galaxy; other forces must be at work. Perhaps the black holes have acted as "seeds" for galactic formation, in the same way that a speck of sand in an oyster acts as a seed for a large pearl. The other galactic matter could then aggregate together with other complex and distributed gravitational patterns, and use rotational motion to produce the results that we see.

Black holes occur when enough matter collapses into itself (for example during the death of a star) that a super-dense and super-massive object, with almost no actual size, has a gravitational field so strong that even light is unable to escape. The popular image is that everything nearby is "sucked into" a black hole, and there is certainly an element of truth to this image, although the gravitational effects do not extend as far outward as one might think. Hawking has recently proposed with some controversy, and some acceptance, that, due to quantum effects, black holes are not, in fact, black, but have a slight glow to them. In addition, he proposes at the same time that black holes eventually "evaporate" into nothingness, through quantum probability processes. The edge of a black hole is known as the "event horizon," and conceals the "singularity" within. The singularity (meaning a point which is singular or exceptional to normal things) is an area where all normal laws of physics break down, and become meaningless. The Big Bang is suspected to have started with such a singularity.

FASTER THAN THE SPEED OF LIGHT: There is currently some thinking that, not only is the rate of expansion of the universe speeding up; it may actually be expanding faster than the speed of light. If that were the case, then there would be stars and galaxies forming on the other side of the universe that we would simply never be aware of, because they would be moving away from us faster than light (information about them) could ever reach us. Kind of sad, in a way! How is this possible? It is true that nothing can move faster than the speed of light in our known spacetime; Einstein's laws hold true. However, what would make this possible comes from what is already known about the expansion of the universe: it's not that the galaxies are moving away from each other through existing space; it's the far stranger case, accepted as scientific fact, that *space itself is expanding*. And the expansion of space may not be subject to the laws of the spacetime being created.

ZERO-POINT ENERGY: Also known as vacuum energy, this is a pretty heady concept. Because quantum mechanics posits that there is at least a remote possibility of *anything* happening, this means that even a "pure" vacuum is not inert and lifeless, but contains the *potential* for energy (and thus mass) to "pop out of nothingness," to manifest from pure mathematical possibility. This has been experimentally verified by the Casimir Effect, and has great implications for space and the universe at large. What we think of as "empty space" thus becomes more correctly, a teeming stew of as yet unrealized possibilities. (In addition, and besides the quantum effects, the average cubic inch of "empty" space may contain a half to a dozen hydrogen atoms and a dust grain or two.) There is some current speculation that our universe itself may have actually appeared out of "nothingness" through sheer quantum possibility. Wow.

AND ON INTO THE FUTURE: These fields are moving fast. Currently in the news is the rapid advance of quantum computers, based on entanglement. In addition, investigators have now entangled macro scale objects, showing that the quantum basis of reality holds as we move up the size scale; we just have to understand *how*. String theory has been in fashion a bit in recent years, but seems to be waning. A picture on the internet purports to show light acting as a particle and a wave simultaneously. Quantum teleportation has been successfully demonstrated (again at the quantum scale and in conjunction with entanglement), although we have a long way to go for Star Trek-like convenience. Quantum tunneling is actually being used in real world applications, and consists of objects seemingly going through or across real physical walls or barriers from one side to the other, *simply because of quantum probability waves*, because the chance that they could do so is never zero. This is similar to zero-point energy above.

The history and development of physics is a large and complicated subject. Many weighty books have been written trying to cover these topics. For those interested, it can be an extremely rewarding subject, even for the layman, so feel free to browse further. Most concepts of physics can actually be explained in ways that those with basic physical and mathematical instincts can grasp or visualize. Einstein himself said, "If you can't explain it to a six year old, you don't understand it yourself." (Of course, he may have been a rather exceptional six year old.) He also said, "Everything should be made as simple as possible, but not simpler." As Carl Sagan noted above, it would be hubristic to fancy that, at exactly *our* particular moment in time, we have mostly figured it all out except for a few details. That's never been true, and probably never will be. For forward thinkers, the great thing about where quantum physics is today is that no one really *knows* what it describes, once you get past the calculations. The future is wide open. The choices range from consciousness, through various other possibilities, to infinitely produced universes. Take your pick: you can't be wrong, if no one knows what the answer is. The jury is still out. All options are still on the table, although many researchers are loathe to admit that. Stay tuned.

One take-away from all of this for *anyone* is that quantum, relativity, and current astrophysics are just plain *weird.* And, since these disciplines do nothing more than attempt to describe the universe as it is, then it is really the *universe itself* which is so strange, and holding on to so many secrets. The most imaginative among us have fallen short in trying to compete with the various revelations about the world that keep popping up like quantum foam bubbles. The way that modern science looks at the universe bears little resemblance to the orderly model that many of us learned as kids. And the take-away from *that* is: if the universe is as strange as described here, then why couldn't it get stranger? Where are the boundaries that say what we *can* discover, or are "supposed" to discover? Who says? Quantum itself accepts *all* possibilities. What will we find next?

For those who are *really* into all of this, and want to follow some of the philosophical speculations that can arise, there are a lot of great books listed in the back of this one, and there is a wonderful series of essays on all things quantum done by Thomas J. McFarlane at http://www.integralscience.org/tom/. A particular one which addresses many of the issues brought up in this book is the one titled "Consciousness and Quantum Mechanics." They are very well written, but very deep and intense.

"My own suspicion is that the Universe is not only queerer than we suppose, but queerer than we CAN suppose."—J.B.S. Haldane

It is certainly looking that way.

Recap

It's OK if your head is spinning. Physics has gone through some amazing changes over the last hundred years or so. If this sort of thing appeals to you, there are a large number of books out there ready, willing, and able to explain "physics for the layperson." It can be quite a rewarding journey.

If, however, you are not so inclined and are just plain confused, don't feel alone—it's pretty daunting stuff. If you've skipped over much of the last few sections, here is a quick and dirty recap of the major ideas, which form some of the philosophical underpinnings for the rest of this book:

Early physics involved trying to shoehorn reality into various idealistic ideas of how things *should* be (Plato). His student, Aristotle, moved things from idealism to a more experimental basis, anticipating modern science. The greatest name for nearly the next 2,000 years or so was that of Newton, who laid out the laws of gravity, motion, and optics. Finally, the movements of the solar system could be explained!

Newton, however, based his concepts on the idea that there were *fixed frames of reference*, especially of time. In other words, there was a universal and unchanging space and time in the universe that everyone could agree upon, and that was the same for everyone everywhere. Because of the predictability and seeming infallibility of his laws, he also wound up the spring on what is known as the "clockwork universe," the idea that everything has a traceable cause, that everything is determined, and by extension, that if one could accurately know all of the variables surrounding a particular situation, one could exactly predict the outcome or evolution of that situation. Much of astrology still lingers in that space.

In 1905, Einstein blew all of that away by showing that both space and time were *relative* rather than fixed, and measurements held true only for each observer's particular frame of reference. Space could be wide or compressed, time could be long or short *compared to another person's frame of reference*. GPS systems today, including our cell phones, actually self-correct based on the calculations required for this relativity. The immutability of time and space was gone. Einstein also demonstrated that, amazingly, matter and energy were actually the same thing: matter was just another form of energy. Matter could be turned into energy, and energy into matter. His equation for this, $E=mc^2$, is easily the most famous in history. Einstein, however, still clung to the Newtonian idea of an orderly, predictable world with definite answers. He was a clock kind of guy. Spacetime was a monolithic block, unchangeable. Like Newton, if one knew all of the variables, one could predict any occurrence or situation.

That lasted about 10 minutes. As if the world was not shocked and confounded enough by Einstein's bombshells, the quantum physics guys (Bohr, Schrödinger, Heisenberg, Pauli, Born, Dirac, and many others) followed on Einstein's heels with revelation after revelation: the universe was *not* predictable, but only probabilistic: with all of the finest information that one could muster, the best that one could ever hope for was a statistical probability curve that something *might* happen. Unexpected rogue results were always a possibility. Strict causation was gone. Not only that, but it was *mathematically impossible* to know everything about a particular thing despite our best efforts; a fuzzy world of mystery surrounded all things in the universe. And to top it off, it was proven repeatedly that, if not everything in the universe was connected (those theories are still being worked on), some things certainly were, and an object millions of miles away could *instantaneously* affect something here in the lab, appearing to (but not really) violate the previous speed of light limit. In actuality, the effect was produced by the two (or more) things being inseparably connected in the first place. Reading one was, in effect, reading the other. This is known as entanglement. And speaking of light, it became known that light was simultaneously two completely different and seemingly incompatible things: it was both a particle and a wave at the same time. Oh, and by the way, so was *matter*. Whew.

The most popular version of quantum mechanics, the Copenhagen interpretation, further states that objects in the universe at the quantum level (meaning really small, although this may have larger implications) *do not exist in any particular state at all* until they are measured or observed, or until they interact with other matter—or rather they exist in the potential for all states simultaneously. This is the implication of the double slit experiment, the centerpiece of quantum strangeness. Everything exists only as a wave of potentialities until observation or measurement takes place. In a sense, it is observation (through interaction or measurement) that creates physical reality as we know it. That's a pretty intense thought. If you've read the previous sections, Schrödinger's Cat is then both alive and dead until its box is opened.

Meow.

Consciousness

A Curious Thing

About two weeks before I had the tremendous auto accident mentioned at the beginning of this book, I had been killing time browsing some antique stores on Magazine St. in New Orleans. I found, in the St. Vincent de Paul thrift store—a cavernous trove of all things interesting, run by the Catholic Church—a life-size statue of a Catholic monk or saint, very stereotypical with a bald head, ring of hair, and brown robes with prayer beads hanging from his waist. He was in the pose of walking and staring ahead, while holding a staff. The craftsmanship and paint were superb. He seemed friendly and wise. He was not St. Francis, I was told, but I can't recall who it was, or if they even knew. He was from a church that had been retired and demolished. I made several circles around the dim and dusty store, disinterestedly turning over various other items, but kept returning to the statue. He was high up on a large shelf, staring out into space. I asked how much, and the deal was done. I decided to name him St. Vitus, in the idea that I would have a housewarming party for my new apartment, and call it the "St. Vitus Dance." My irreverence here was obvious. I wondered later whether my irreverence had anything to do with my accident. I occupied the apartment for only one month. There were no dances, no warming of the house.

At the time, I was still marginally dating a woman named Joanne, whom I had dated for the last year or so of college. She had a poster over the bed in her apartment that showed a photograph of a young man holding a beer, with the caption: "If You Drink a Lot of Beer, You Drink a Lot." Hmmm. I completely ignored this. We see what we want to see. She was from Atlanta, and at the time of my purchase, she was back visiting her parents there, while I was in New Orleans. She was probably trying to figure out what to do about me, as she had a strong drive to settle down and have kids, and I was showing little aptitude in that direction. And she did have good intuition. I called her up that night and said: "You'll never guess what I bought today."

Now, I ask the reader to stop here; please just stop for a moment, step back, and think about this statement very carefully. Suppose I (or name a friend, relative, or significant other) had called you up last evening and said, "you'll never guess what I bought today." What would you say? How would you know what to say? How would you guess? There are probably hundreds of thousands of things in this world that would qualify for "you'll never guess what I bought today," some of them quite obscure. What do you think the odds would be of guessing even something that *wasn't* obscure? Try it with others, and see how often you or they get this question correct.

So I asked her this in our conversation, and there was a small pause on the other end of the line for a few seconds. Then she said "A life-size statue." Exact words, no kidding. Just completely matter-of-fact, with only the slightest questioning lilt at the end of the phrase. "A life-size statue."

Now it may be true that a gang of monkeys with word processors and an infinite amount of time could indeed manage, at some point, to come up with the works of William Shakespeare through random pecking. That considered, what do you think the odds are here? For the skeptical, or those who fall back on "coincidences happen all the time": what do you *really* think the odds are here? Not just "a statue," but "a life-size statue."

As the monkeys typed, they would eventually come up with this particular quote from the Bard: "There are more things in heaven and earth, Horatio, than are dreamt of in your philosophy."

Indeed.

Is There a Generally Accepted Theory of Consciousness?

Nope. It's wide open. Have at it.

What's It Like to Be a Bat?

There are two themes within the consciousness research community that have found their way, in recent times, towards icon status. One is David Chalmers' "The Hard Problem" (of consciousness), and the other is Thomas Nagel's "What's it Like to be a Bat?" Both point to the ineffable quality of consciousness, and to how difficult it is to even talk about the subject in a language that everyone can agree on and understand. Before we touch on the latter theme, let's look at the former for a second. The phrase "The Hard Problem" has caught on, largely because it encapsulates what the debate about the nature of consciousness is all about. It was formerly known in the mists of philosophical history as the Mind/Body Problem, but has received some rejuvenation with the new name. The Hard Problem is in juxtaposition to what Chalmers terms the "easy problems" of consciousness. The easy problems are, of course, easy only in a relative sense; nothing that exists or comes from between our ears is simple by anyone's reckoning. But the easy problems are the ones that can conceivably be, through current knowledge and science, investigated by conventional means: those might include visual or auditory perception and processing, some sorts of problem solving, instinctual behavior, memory, etc. Many of the parameters, in short, that might be taken over one day by artificial intelligence.

In the parallel A.I. community, the famed Turing Test was hypothetically designed to differentiate the degree of success for an A.I. system in attempting to replicate human intelligence and consciousness, and it may certainly be the case that one day computers will be able to take in information, analyze it, and act on it in a fashion that seems eerily similar to humans. But they're *not* human. John Searle's Chinese Room thought experiment is designed to demonstrate this from a reasoning or linguistic perspective. More importantly, however, and left out of the computer's algorithms (and forever unreachable by any machine), is the very *essence* of consciousness: The *subjective* feeling of *what things are like*. To a computer, does the DOS operating system feel any different than the IOS one? To us as users it certainly does!

Subjective experiences are known as "qualia." A computer can do a spectrum analysis, and tell us that what we are looking at is what we label the color red; but what does that *mean* to the computer? Where is the *experience* of that? To return to our physicists for a moment, Erwin Schrödinger has said: "The *sensation* (the author's emphasis) of color cannot be accounted for by the physicist's objective picture of light-waves. Could the physiologist account for it, if he had fuller knowledge than he has of the processes in the retina and the nervous processes set up by them in the optical nerve bundles and in the brain? I do not think so." This is what Chalmers is getting at with his simple dual differentiating concepts. In contrast to "easy" and predictable biological processes, he's asking what it's like for us to *see* red, to experience it, to be aware of how it ties in with other experiences, memories, smells, and associations. The totality of the *experience*, the qualia, and how it may or may not tie into the more mundane and material parts of the brain is the Hard Problem.

The power of this question is reflected in Thomas Nagel's famous (and earlier) question of "what's it like to be a bat?" Nagel fights against the current paradigm of reductionism in consciousness studies, the urge for materialist-trained scientists to want to "reduce" consciousness to simple biochemistry. Similar to Schrödinger above, Nagel muses: suppose we can dissect a bat's brain, and make great strides in physiology and functioning, in mapping pathways and tracks, in knowing about axons and dendrites and conceptual frameworks and neural connections. That's all well and good, but if we can do all of that, then in the end the central question will still remain: what's it like to *be* a bat?" What's it like to be a human? What's it like to be a dog, an ape? Each of these have a *subjective* experience of what it's like to be them; experiences which go beyond analysis, and experiences which are unique to them, which can never be shared by others. We can speculate, but we can never know what it's like to be a bat. (By the way, did you know that bats are not only not blind, but that many can see better than humans? You're not alone: neither did Neil deGrasse Tyson, in a news item that posted recently. Neither did this author. At all times, we have to continually check the things that we think we "know.")

The Hard Problem has remained hard for a very long time. One might say that it is in fact *the* central philosophical problem of the ages. The Greeks, the Indians, the Chinese, the Japanese, and the Europeans have all attempted to scale the wall. In the West, Descartes was the most visible person asking this question for several centuries. In addition to being a towering force in mathematics, he is known as the father of modern philosophy. He is, of course, most famous for his axiom "I think, therefore I am," which has ultimately been turned into a t-shirt cliché. He came to this idea during a process of trying to eliminate anything from his consciousness that might be false, that he might be able to doubt. In the end, he was left with only his simple precept. Descartes was a *dualist*, believing that the mind and the body were two separate things; that the mental, although interactive with, was somehow independent from the physical: a view which has had the edge in Western thought until modern times. He placed consciousness in primacy over matter, although the interactions went both ways synergistically. The body was warm, squishy, messy, and subject to the laws of the physical universe, including time and space. The mind was something else, difficult to define, difficult to know. It was pure thought, independent of physical laws, and had the power of free will. As to just how the thinking mind and the physical body interacted: that remained a mystery, although there have been many theories put down through the years, by Descartes and others.

Although there are many variations and gradations on all sides of the consciousness debate such as physicalism, idealism, epiphenomenalism, and many others, the primary rival to dualism has been *monism*. In the last hundred years, monism has supplanted dualism amongst the scientific community, precisely because it lends itself well to reductionism. With monism as it is most commonly understood, there is no separate "something" that is consciousness, but only the material universe: consciousness is somehow a physical process, although we may not understand how that is so yet. This coincides with the rise of both materialism and scientism, and is a tempting view in the modern world. But there are many holdouts, David Chalmers among them. (Among non-funded-research parties, there are many, *many* holdouts.) It also lends itself to larger philosophical views and discussions. According to dualism, the world is more than a monistic sameness of whatever current version of physics and biology is in place; there is room for other "stuff" in the universe, perhaps undiscovered—consciousness being among whatever may lurk out there. According to monism, the universe is made up of only one stuff, and that stuff is physical (or physical energy, its doppelganger; the two are interchangeable). Materialists talk about the "ghost in the machine" to emphasize the (to them) illusory nature of consciousness as something separate. For them, the machine is primary.

Note (confusedly) that this may seem to be the opposite of most science vs. spirituality discussions, where spirituality is more closely allied with Oneness, while science speaks more to separateness, analysis, and differentiation. That's because here the oneness (conscious monism) that science is talking about is a purely physical one, while the Oneness that spirituality talks about includes both the physical, the spiritual, consciousness, and whatever else there may be. Spirituality's version of Oneness may thus be seen to be a higher order or vision of oneness. Paradoxically, for our discussion here, it includes the *consciousness* version of dualism, which adds something more to base physicality. Science's oneness contains only the physical and physical energy, while spirituality's Oneness adds both an independent consciousness, and spirit (which the scientists disavow). An example of a Oneness that includes both the physical world and consciousness as separate and yet connected (sort of like light's wave/particle duality) is that which is proposed by the Eastern religions, especially Hinduism, which is sort of the "mother religion" for most of the other Eastern schools of thought.

So, "alternative" views of *consciousness* are usually *dualistic*, because they allow for more than the physical in the world; but they are often seen in tandem with *spiritual* traditions that are *non-dualistic* because they assume that the ultimate One contains more than just material energy, and that *all* is connected. Much of materialism, and all of "Western" religious tradition is dualistic, because it specifies that everything and everyone is separate and disconnected. (In other words, my mind couldn't be connected in any way to your mind.) Whew! It *is* confusing, and this discourse is obviously not going to end any time soon.

A notable early attempt to resist the growing materialism, while adding in some ideas of Oneness in a Western version of Eastern thought, was *idealism*, whose early proponent was George Berkeley, for whom the University of California at Berkeley is named. (No wonder it has such an alternative reputation!) Berkeley was also known as the Bishop of Cloyne, and continued a tradition of educated Catholic clergy occasionally lapsing into philosophy. He was also a contemporary of Isaac Newton, and could probably see where this whole materialism thing was going. He called his philosophy "immaterialism," and posited that the only things that really existed were Spirit and Consciousness. Matter was an illusion of consciousness and perception. Spirit of course, coming from the Christian tradition, was God. But this idea is remarkably similar to what has been taught in the East for thousands of years.

Although one might not think so today, Berkeley was tremendously influential, and in fact David Papineau, in his wonderfully concise book *Introducing Consciousness*, states that "nearly every significant philosopher from the late 18th century to the early 20th century has been a paid-up idealist." It is a reflection of our times that the pendulum has swung so far in the other direction towards materialism in the modern world; many people simply can't recall or understand any other way of looking at things. It is easy to assume, since materialism has proved so successful in the scientific and technological realms, that that there really isn't any other valid way to look at the world. But there is. One problem with the idealist type of philosophies, however, continues to linger in the modern world, and affects more than one current philosophical system, including the more outré interpretations of quantum mechanics. Idealism posits that reality is created by our own mind, and "radical" idealism (Berkeley) states that indeed there *is* no actual material world, but only the experiences of our mind. The problem then is how to account for shared experiences, if each of our private consciousnesses is creating its own reality; and how to perhaps keep some of these ideas viable, or at least contributory, without deteriorating into solipsism.

***

The subject of consciousness is complicated. What *is* it? What role *does* our brain play? It's obvious that if there is some sort of dualism (independent consciousness), the more transcendent portion of consciousness interacts constantly with the lower level physical brain functions, eyesight being but one example. Perhaps it may be that the brain is necessary but not sufficient for consciousness. There is even a position called *mysterianism* which states that we will never be able to figure consciousness out, that it's simply beyond our ability to do so. Perhaps, as in Flatland, (a book soon to be mentioned), our consciousness is in dimension "x," while the solution to how our consciousness works is in dimension "x+1" that we are not privy to. Most philosophers, however, don't give in to the despair of mysterianism.

What is consciousness? What is lack of consciousness? What about dreams? Are we "conscious" during dreams? Dreams involve memory, imagery, problem-solving, creativity, and all of the things that are normally associated with consciousness; and yet most people would say that we are not conscious during our dreams. Certainly we are less *aware* of the outside world. Real-world physical perception seems, in fact, to be the only thing that's actually missing from dreams. Qualia are there: the phenomenal experiences of "what something is like." Dreams, in fact, can be frighteningly "real." What's it like to be chased down the street by aliens, naked? If the difference between dreams and waking life is only that daylight perception and awareness are missing from dreams, then what is the difference between consciousness and awareness? Awareness is what the materialists often mistake for consciousness, but consciousness goes beyond simple awareness. It includes the awareness of *being* aware.

Perhaps dreams are some sort of a holographic version of consciousness: a lower consciousness "dimension" that still contains all of the normal consciousness information. Freud, of course, talked about the "unconscious," ushering in the idea of different levels of consciousness. Freud himself stopped with the unconscious, but his student Jung seemed to feel that if there were different lower levels of consciousness, then perhaps there might also exist higher levels as well: perhaps even some sorts of states of "super-consciousness." Freud's idea was that dreams contain information from a lower subset of consciousness, the unconscious. Jung, however, looked instead for messages from this superconscious, which he termed the collective unconscious. Is the unconscious, then, part of consciousness, or are they two separate things? Certain modern experiments such as those involving "blind sight" have helped blur the distinction. Are possible states of super-consciousness, such as the collective unconscious, or spiritual awareness, part of personal consciousness?

A famous Taoist story: The great master Chuang Tzu once dreamt that he was a beautiful butterfly fluttering about here and there. In the dream he had no awareness of his identity as a person, he was only a butterfly. But suddenly, he awoke and found himself lying there, a human named Chuang Tzu. He then thought to himself, "was I before a man who dreamt about being a butterfly, or am I now a butterfly who dreams about being Chuang Tzu?" Consciousness and its relation to reality, and to our own unconscious, or superconscious, remains ever mysterious.

Who can be conscious? Humans obviously can. But what about bats? Dogs? Gorillas? Computers? Amoebas? Bacteria? Thermostats? This has great implications for the interpretations of quantum mechanics that incorporate consciousness. In Schrödinger's cat experiment, who is collapsing the wave function?

The human who is opening the box? Might the cat itself be collapsing the wave function? What "level" of consciousness would be required to collapse a wave function? David Gross has talked about the onset of consciousness in infants as being possibly akin to a "phase transition," similar to when water turns into ice or vice versa. *Something* is there initially, but at some point it becomes something else that is the same, but different. Could this be true? What about cats? And what about the implications of the Wigner's friend variation of Shrodinger's thought experiment? Things get complicated pretty quickly.

If consciousness is just a physical function, then it's easy to explain that there are gradations of consciousness, according to the level of evolutionary development: dogs being "more conscious" than amoebas, for example. But this line of thinking actually seems more about intelligence than about consciousness, and the two are different. A smart animal may be able to solve problems, but may not recognize itself in the mirror (the well-known "mirror test"), leading us to speculate that its sense of self, and experiencing of self, is somehow different from our rich version. A computer may be far superior to us in solving problems, but likely has no qualia, no experiences. An animal has experiences, and learns from experiences: how, then, is its consciousness similar to, or different from a computer, or from us? Is an educated person "more conscious" than a less educated one? Monism leaves more room for various Darwinian degrees of consciousness up through humans, while to dualists it would seem that human consciousness is human consciousness, having more of an on/off character, and it may be intelligence, moral character, spiritual awareness, or something else that explains the further variations. In addition, we often talk about one person as being of a "higher consciousness" or more "evolved" than another person. What does that mean? Is that possible? (It certainly seems so.) And if intelligent people, from a Darwinian perspective, may be "more conscious," then why the heck don't they agree with us more? Or if consciousness is more than just a physical function, then what does that mean for amoebas, or for that matter, rocks? Does consciousness permeate everything (panpsychism), with only ourselves, the more highly developed forms, able to recognize it, and take advantage of it? Astrology itself gives yet another dimension to consciousness, as it shows *where* we put our conscious energy, of what type it is, and thus where and how our consciousness may actually evolve within the limitations of horoscopic ease or difficulty.

***

Idealism gets rid of the problem of duality: it is the mirror image of material monism—everything is now again a product of only one thing, but it is consciousness this time, instead of physicality. Most people in the modern world, however, find this much too weird and fuzzy-headed, and thus prefer to drag consciousness along with them on the contemporary march into materialism. However, the physicalists have to perform such odd gyrations of explanations in order to bring together the mysterious world of consciousness with the physical, that many people are suspicious of that as well, even though it's currently the dominant paradigm. It seems unlikely to many that the full spectrum, spread, and glory of human consciousness can arise simply from a few pounds of blubbery gray flesh.

A sort of intermediary *scientific* ground then is *functionalism*, which theorizes that consciousness consists of a group of amorphous *functions* which exist nowhere but in their organizing capacities and processes. Evolution has led to these functions, and they in turn produce what we call consciousness. The idea is somewhat akin to Plato's Forms, or that of archetypes. This again, however, fails to explain the direct experience that most of us have of being a conscious being "looking out" through our eyes at the world, inaccurate analogy though that may be. Functionalism does lend itself to the popular modern analogy of the brain as computer, with the physical brain being the "hardware," and the functions of consciousness being the "software." However, it doesn't really explain why the smell of a rose is the smell of a rose, as an experience beyond that of simple olfactory perception. A computer may have artificial olfactory receptors, but it has no experience of a rose. The *qualia* is missing.

The popularity of David Chalmers lets us know that there is still life in the dualist perspective. Chalmers, however, has a rather confusing and convoluted version, attempting to marry the modern love for biochemical processes (a sort of "lower consciousness") with a more mysterious "higher consciousness"—one that can experience a rose in a self-aware way, in all its ramifications and glory. Chalmers uses information as the bridge, which sort of makes sense (and is more compatible with modern physics), but which also leads to some strange implications, such as thermostats having consciousness because they carry information. Chalmers does deserve much credit for his attempts to bridge the gap between physical monism and traditional dualism. Chalmers views his own version of dualism, not as a rejection of science, but as a rejection of the *current state of science*. This, of course, ties in well with one of the general themes of this book, that science as currently stated is simply not complete, and that there yet may be some very odd discoveries ahead.

Another attempt at marrying physicality to something more nebulous is what has historically been known as *property dualism* (which is where David Chalmers leans): the original Descartes dualism was *substance dualism*, meaning that the physical world, and the mind, were of two completely different substances. Property dualism speculates that there is only one substance, which exhibits both physical and mental properties. This is similar to another intriguing school of philosophy/consciousness known as *neutral monism*. Here, the world is also only one substance, which is labeled neutral, since it is neither physical nor mental; these both arise from that neutral *something*. (Much of this stuff, the reader may be realizing, can be pretty difficult to follow!) Leibniz, who was a contemporary of Newton (and who lived immediately after Descartes), thought that perhaps, in some synchronistic fashion, consciousness was separate from and yet ran in identical parallel tracks to the physical, so that the two seemed as one. Ultimately, perhaps neither dualism or monism is correct. Perhaps the answer will lie in new thinking on the subject, new discoveries, a new paradigm.

***

Most of the modern theories about consciousness are designed to show that consciousness is a natural consequence of biology, and are rooted in more classical scientific models and mechanisms. But what about the things that we learned of modern physics in the last chapter? The vast majority of consciousness researchers are running on a separate philosophical track from the physicists, which in a way seems an odd lack of communication, since they are basing their theories of consciousness *on* the physical. One *physicist* who is venturing into the realm of consciousness is Roger Penrose, who has advanced an intricate theory involving physical quantum processes occurring in "microtubules" in the brain itself, which have a connection to gravity. If true, it would somehow unite gravity, quantum, and consciousness together. The Holy Grail, Theory of Everything would be here. Unfortunately, he has had quite a bit of difficulty getting others to join with him on this idea. There are other physicists, including Henry Stapp, who are also producing theories trying to connect quantum and consciousness. On the consciousness side, David Chalmers has written about the various interpretations of quantum mechanics, and has thrown his hat into the ring in favor of the "many minds" interpretation of quantum, which he considers a more correct reading of the popular "many worlds" version. (But then again, he is a consciousness theorist, so this is not surprising.)

Rene Descartes was an Aries, as is David Chalmers, and it seems entirely fitting that Descartes's philosophy began with "I think, therefore I am." (If one reads beginning astrology texts, the first thing that we learn is that the keyword for Aries is "I am.") Another Aries who has been very concerned with consciousness is physicist Henry Stapp (mentioned above), who, like Penrose, is interested in possible quantum processes *in the brain*, or in consciousness, which could collapse the wave function: in other words, a *mechanism*. This is in contrast with physicists John von Neumann and Eugene Wigner, who simply were interested in the idea that consciousness *does* cause the collapse of the wave function (thereby creating reality, as Berkeley had suggested), not so much in how it does so. Although this occupies one of several cutting edges in the philosophy of physics *for certain physicists*, many consciousness researchers seem hesitant to wade into this area; it is possibly an intimidating and difficult realm for them to join in the discussion on.

Let's dive in ourselves. If it is true (and again, this is an area of much disagreement) that consciousness or its handmaiden, measurement, can collapse the wave function and influence physical matter (as seems to be the case in the dominant Copenhagen interpretation of quantum mechanics, and the double slit experiment), then what does *that* say about consciousness? Few in the mainstream community are brave enough, or foolhardy enough, to wade into this and risk being ostracized. A word of curiosity, and one is automatically marginalized and put in the corner with a dunce cap on. However, the acceptance of "measurement" collapsing the wave function in the Copenhagen interpretation would seem to beg the question: who or what is doing the measuring? It seems likely that consciousness is the undeclared elephant in the room here, although von Neumann and Wigner make it explicit. And while consciousness may not be *required* to collapse the wave function—another topic of debate—it seems that it certainly *can* do so. So even if one posits that the measurement may be mechanical, there is indeed a ghost in the machine lurking nearby: the humans with their consciousness, who have put this together. (Some religious folk would punt this up to the next level.) And even if the measurement is mechanical, there is always the possibility that I, and my consciousness, can *choose* to intervene and measure things, thereby changing the way reality manifests.

The question lingers: what is quantum theory trying to tell us about consciousness? It certainly seems as if it's trying to tell us *something*. This seems like a particularly pertinent question, especially in view of the current consciousness researchers trying their best to put together a physical model. Why not then start with physics? Is consciousness again dualistic? Is there a mysterious and larger "Consciousness" that is somehow able to collapse the wave function and determine reality, and if so, what is it and how is it that humans (at least) have a "piece" of it, or are connected to it? Or is reality again *non-materially* monistic after all, all of a One as the sages have said, including such disparate elements as rocks and consciousness? Perhaps neutral monism *is* the way to go.

Another interesting take on things that would actually attempt to *quantify* an object, animal, or system's amount of consciousness is Guilio Tononi and Christof Koch's "Integrated Information Theory." This would assign a value ("Phi") to rocks, amoebas, thermostats, dogs, and humans. This seems to be the first formal attempt at *quantifying* consciousness, or at placing it in a framework that might someday make it compatible with other parts of modern science.

Regardless of all these speculations, it seems unlikely that everything will turn out to be nothing but currently identified matter and physical energy; consciousness as something immaterial, or as yet unknown and undiscovered, seems likely to be implicated and involved at some level. Perhaps, as Descartes said, consciousness is primary; perhaps, as Berkeley mused, consciousness is everything.

> "We are what we think. All that we are arises with our thoughts. With our thoughts we make the world."—Gautama Buddha

What *is* it like to be a bat?

I know You Are, But What Am I?

To get a taste of where the current state of discourse on consciousness theories stands in some cases, one need only peruse John Searle's book *The Mystery of Consciousness*. Searle is the originator of the "Chinese Room" rebuttal to Strong A.I. (artificial intelligence), which states that computers may have their own "consciousness." Searle doesn't agree. The title of the book, however, is somewhat of a misnomer: the point of the book seems more to demonstrate that consciousness is a mystery to everybody *but* him; Searle is quite sure that he has a pretty good handle on it. Searle, a philosopher and professor at the aforementioned U.C. Berkeley, believes that consciousness is "above all a biological function, like digestion or photosynthesis." He is not quite sure of exactly how consciousness arises from biological processes, but he is quite sure that it does.

This puts him squarely in the monist camp, although he apparently chafes at that designation. His personal label is "subjective ontology," although he falls back on materialistic arguments. No one in the consciousness field, in fact, seems to particularly want to be pinned down or pigeonholed; probably because the field is so unsettled that they want to stay flexible towards future developments. Also, moving targets are more difficult to hit. And God help you if you're not in Searle's corner: he comes across in the book as the Hulk Hogan of philosophers, ready at a moment's notice for a WWE Smackdown. In this book, he goes after fellow philosopher David Chalmers with a vengeance reminiscent of Hogan going after Rowdy Roddy Piper. (With both of these pairs, we have Leo vs. Aries.) It annoys him that Chalmers won't fall into line with the monist camp; and that he in fact has a convoluted system involving biology for the lower brain functions, along with a dualistic "something" keeping the higher consciousness functions separate from, and greater than, the merely physical. In fact, both philosophers have some good points (and some not so good ones), but Searle is having none of that easy-going, live and let live thinking. He is very attached to his point of view, and does not suffer disagreement lightly. He is willing to argue anyone down to the mat.

Searle states that Chalmers' book, *The Conscious Mind,* "is a symptom of a certain desperation in cognitive studies today." Chalmers' arguments are "invalid." "It gets worse," and "even worse is yet to come." He accuses Chalmers of the "absurd view" of panpsychism (which Chalmers apparently hedges, and is unclear on himself. To his credit, Chalmers retains a bit more humility in his writings and speculations). He points out that Chalmers actually has a section of his book titled "What's it like to be a thermostat?" (Thermostats possibly being an example of a low-level consciousness, since they "carry information.") Searle self-confidently states that "It is just a plain fact about nature that brains cause consciousness. It does not seem implausible to me because I know, independently of any philosophical argument, that it happens. If it still seems implausible to the biologically uninformed, so much the worse for them."

Earlier, Searle bemoans, "It seems that to accept dualism is to give up the entire scientific worldview that we have spent nearly four centuries to attain." OK. So perhaps *that's* the issue: a simple and natural resistance to change, as well as an attachment to all of the work that went into current ideas, his own and others, in addition to a straightforward difference of opinion. That's all pretty understandable; that's human nature. Unprovoked attacks often smell like fear, however, and there seems to be a slight whiff here. But while it's fine and appropriate to revere the past much of the time, progress throughout history has only been accomplished by challenging the status quo. And if it were the case that consciousness studies were a pretty well-agreed-upon discipline, with everyone on the same page, that would be one thing. But four centuries later, they're not. And quantum seems to keep throwing further questions into the mix. As a simple point of fact to be mentioned here, the Copernican, Newtonian, Einsteinian, and quantum revolutions have forced the giving up of quite a few more than four centuries of entrenched thinking. So it can be done.

It's not as if Chalmers is completely accepted, and has all of the answers, either. He is a major new player in consciousness studies, but not everyone is on board. The two are mentioned here because they represent contemporary versions of the dualist/monist polarity. Chambers himself is the focus of another book, *Explaining Consciousness—The Hard Problem*, edited by Jonathan Shear, which consists solely of a series of essays that are in response to Chalmers' ideas. People seem to love to rebut Chalmers; maybe some of it is simply because he is a younger "upstart," and is getting a lot of attention aside from his actual theses. There is absolutely no widespread agreement that Chalmers is either correct or not.

***

So what are we to make of all this? Several points occur. The first is that consciousness researchers might benefit from some serious hunker-down time with quantum physicists, Buddhists, and Hindus, in addition to biologists and the more traditional Western philosophers. These three groups also deal with the subject of consciousness as a part of their disciplines (or at least some quantum physicists do), have some ancient as well as modern wisdom, and could likely contribute much to the discussion. Secondly, the entire state of consciousness study is seemingly in disarray: arguments and opposing formulations abound. The field has been left largely to philosophers, because few other disciplines wish to wade into the swamp. Thirdly, although we are dealing with an ultimately unexplained phenomenon here, the materialists and functionalists mistrust and deride anyone with a more alternative view of consciousness. And finally, the question of "what is consciousness" remains in pretty much the same state as it was in Descartes's time: no one knows. It is in this darkness, confusion, and vacuum that the various players are arguing their theories. And like many arguments, the more vague and unproven the surrounding information, the harder some people will argue that their views are the definitive ones. It may remind one, uncomfortably, of a picture of medieval philosophers arguing about how many angels might be able to dance on the head of a pin. They were arguing about oranges, when the subject turned out to be apples.

It may ultimately prove to be the case (if panpsychism is not the answer) that the brain is necessary but not sufficient for consciousness. It could indeed be (Chalmers takes this position), that the materialist brain is responsible for all of the basic functions that we perform in our everyday lives, while consciousness itself is a separate thing, somehow anchored to the brain, and yet not solely of the brain. That's the dualist perspective, although Chalmers goes through various undulations to try and make this more palatable to some of his peers. But really, when all is said and done, what *is* one to make of ESP? Synchronicity? The fact that I can change the material world by how I choose to perform the double slit experiment?

Consciousness as Dimension

In the understandable disarray of current thinking on consciousness, in the revelation that consciousness may play a role in physics, in the primacy accorded it by certain spiritual traditions, and in the desire (given its ubiquitousness) to find a larger role for consciousness in the investigation of the world around us, where might we turn? What *is* consciousness? What role *does* it play in our day to day universe? Let us, just for fun, entertain three serial contemplations here; two are to be explored in the next sections, but let us first turn our open minds now to a possibility that, while obviously far-reaching and speculative, may not be quite as strange as it seems at first glance. We are keeping in mind, of course, that the universe is likely to ultimately prove, as J.B.S Haldane noted, stranger than we even have the ability to imagine in advance, and will continue to surprise us at every turn.

In 1884, two decades before Einstein published his special theory of relativity that placed time in the unique position of being a 4th dimension, there was an obscure novella published titled *Flatland: A Romance of Many Dimensions* by Edwin A. Abbott, an otherwise poorly remembered headmaster of an English school. The book, a slim volume, was meant to be a satire of Victorian class sensibility, in addition to its scientific and mathematical speculations. It has succeeded over the years in being better at the latter than at the former; Victorian eras fade, reality doesn't. Like Poe's book (*Eureka: A Prose Poem*—mentioned later in this volume), timing would allow that the great Einstein may conceivably have been exposed to this, prior to his own theories: but that may be unlikely. Great ideas often emerge together, however, and it was presumably simply the right time for these thoughts of other dimensions to take form. (It was actually Hermann Minkowski, not Einstein, who was more responsible for the eventual popularization of time as a 4th dimension.)

The book *Flatland* introduces a (then) novel concept: that there may be other dimensions existing that we are unaware of. The narration is provided by A. Square, who is a... square. He is living in the mythical country of Flatland, which is a two-dimensional (i.e. flat) world. The world is populated with a social strata of flat geometric forms such as triangles, squares, circles, hexagons, etc. The triangles are the lowest class, who aspire to more and more angles, eventually moving up socially to becoming circles, the ruling class. They are trapped in their flat dimension, which does not seem odd to them, since they have no knowledge of any other. Abbott spends quite a bit of time (and uses diagrams) to think through how someone in Flatland might live their day to day lives. To the reader, it is mentally visualized as if looking at a flat map, with the houses being like "schematics" or house plans laid open, with the various two dimensional polygon shapes moving around, going about their business.

The day before New Year's eve, prior to the year 2000 (or 116 years into the future for Abbott; he was thinking ahead!), A. Square falls asleep and dreams of a visit to Lineland. The Flatlanders are aware of the dimensions below them, just not of any dimensions above. A. Square (the narrator) dreams that he is transported to one-dimensional Lineland, where there is no spread-out x-y axis, but where everything exists on a single line. Again, Abbott goes to great lengths to try and explain the practicalities of how that might work. A. Square meets the ruler there, and attempts to help him to broaden his vision by explaining his own world, the one of two dimensions. The king will have none of it, not believing that there is any dimension higher than the one he himself perceives: his own. Short-sightedness of perspective seems not to be confined to our own world; that is one of Abbott's points in the book. The king gets angry at the attempts to open up his view of reality, and threatens A. Square, who returns to his own 2D world. (Later in the story, A. Square also gets to visit Pointland, a place of *no* dimension, a single point ruled by a single king who is lost in solipsism and can't conceive of anything outside himself: he, too, is stuck.)

Returning to Flatland from Lineland (the dream is over), A. Square the very next day sits contemplating what the new year of 2000 might bring. He has just finished expressing skepticism to his nephew (a hexagon), who has been wondering if there might be some other dimension beyond their own two, when he feels a strange presence in the room. At first, there is only the intuition or feeling of something unseen; shortly thereafter he observes a circle appear nearby on the flat plane. As he watches, the circle grows and shrinks. Eventually, an invisible voice announces himself as A. Sphere, and says that he is speaking to our protagonist from the 3rd dimension, which is invisible to A. Square. He tries to explain to A. Square that the reason for the circle expanding and shrinking in size, is that it is actually the form of a three dimensional sphere, which is interacting with the second dimension: A. Square's plane world. Because A. Square can't see the 3rd dimension, he is only able to view the circular 2D plane intersection (manifested as an expanding and contracting circle), which results from A. Sphere's movement across the plane. (Look for *Flatland* on Youtube.)

A. Sphere explains that every thousand years, someone from the 3rd dimension attempts to contact someone from the 2nd dimension, to form a sort of mentor relationship; hoping that the chosen 2D initiate might spread the word, and thereby bring enlightenment to the 2D world. A. Sphere attempts to convey this new dimensional knowledge to A. Square, but A. Square is confused and not getting it, because he is unable to fully visualize or understand what is going on, even though he has just had a similar interaction with the dimension below him. Ultimately, A. Sphere drags A. Square up out of his plane world and into 3D Spaceland, to let him see the next dimension in all of its glory. Here, A. Square can see that the houses are like open boxes, and he can see the pancake polygons as they move from room to room. Now, he understands. While living in Flatland, if a person went from one room to another, they disappeared from sight. Looking down from his new perspective above, however, he can now see (as if a god) the people moving from room to room. His entire perspective and view of reality has changed.

Excited, he can also see where this is going. If he has had knowledge of Pointland and Lineland, has been living in Flatland, and is now privy to the glories of Spaceland, then what else could lie out there? Might there not be a 4th dimension? A 5th? He approaches A. Sphere with this idea, but is not prepared for the reaction: A. Sphere shuts down and denies any dimension beyond his own three; and while he was earlier attempting to show the 3rd to the 2nd (as A. Square had tried, in his dream, to show the 2nd to the 1st), he is now blind and uninterested in the possibility of a 4th dimension, and seems threatened by the idea. He sends A. Square back to Flatland, where, in trying to convince the others there of a three dimensional Spaceland, he is thrown in jail for his heresy; the ruling powers— although they, too, have heard rumors of a 3rd dimension—are protective of their kingdom and willing to use force to squelch any dissidence involving the teaching of higher dimensions. It is from his jail cell, after seven years, that A. Square narrates the memoir that is the book *Flatland*. A mere twenty-one years later, Albert Einstein took all of us from our 3D Spaceland world into the 4th dimension, which could easily be called Timeland.

The book is actually more popular today than when it was written, and there have been several (animated) movies made of it. *Flatland: the Movie*, a 34 minute short from 2007, in fact ends with the animation of a tesseract, a 4-dimensional cube spinning in time that gives visual hints of future possibilities. (The tesseract also appears as a plot point and special effects delight in the 2015 movie *Interstellar*.)

***

So what are we to make of Flatland? What meaning might it hold for us? What lessons can we learn from it? One is certainly that dimensions may be mathematical and geometrical: A. Square learns that each dimension builds geometrically on the last. The tesseract would seem to fall into this category. These sorts of dimensions are "spatial"; there are quite a few visualizations of tesseracts on the internet, some with animations. A question that arises here, however, is this: what exactly qualifies as a dimension? Do dimensions *have* to be spatial or geometric? Of note is that currently there is more than one competing "4th dimension." and there are ongoing discussions and disagreements about this. Is the 4th dimension spatial or temporal? There is the spatial 4th dimension, represented by the tesseract, with physical attributes that we can't see; just as the folks in Flatland couldn't "see" the 3rd dimension, but only theorize about it. But then there is also the 4th dimension of *time*, that we learned about as kids: time is a 4th dimension according to Einstein's spacetime ideas, adding an extra dimension onto the existing three spatial ones that we live in; in fact, it can be thought of as defining them. And time itself, while somewhat more amorphous, is also mathematical and geometric: the block universe depends on it. Perhaps there are two "branches" of dimensions, with the spatial, represented by the tesseract, heading off towards the theorized eleven mathematical dimensions of string theory, and that of time defining our own day to day existences. For our purposes here, we will certainly acknowledge that there may be more than one "extra" or further dimension, but we will concentrate on time, as that is the more culturally visible and intellectually accessible one at this point.

***

Let's talk about other implications of the book also. For the 1983 Harper Perennial edition of *Flatland*, Isaac Asimov wrote an introduction that concludes: "In short, *Flatland* is not just an amusing and witty exercise in geometry, but is a dissertation that could lead to very profound thought about our Universe and ourselves." Indeed. For starters, we note A. Square's perplexity in trying to visualize the 3rd dimension from his own flat plane, which is all that he can see. The directions that he is familiar with are north, south, east, and west: all points on a two dimensional plot. His bewilderment in trying to come to grips with the new thinking is best expressed by his trying to digest the idea of "upwards, not northwards," which initially makes no sense at all to him. Physicists of a hundred years ago trying to digest Einstein and the fledgling quantum field would likely be able to relate.

One important concept to talk about here is that *it takes the currently perceived dimension to perceive the lower dimensions. The knowledge of these lower dimensions is evidence that the currently perceivable dimension must exist: It is this dimension that is being used to visualize the previous or lower dimensions.* A point has no dimension: it takes the perspective of a line to be able to visualize a point *on* the line, to be able to see the difference, to use the necessary perspective. Similarly, if one is living on a line (1st dimension), it is impossible to see the line itself. It takes a plane (2nd dimension) to be able to see the line moving across the plane, somewhere on the x-y axis. If one were stuck on a plane, such as in Flatland, one would not know any higher dimensions, and would not even be able to see their own plane clearly, although they would be living "in that dimension." It takes the next dimension (the 3rd) to be able to see the plane. Only by being in space above Flatland can we see it clearly, see its parameters and properties. This was the secret knowledge given to A. Square by A. Sphere. We can *speculate* regarding the 3rd dimension from a lower one, but if we can *see* Flatland, we can know that we are actually *living* in the 3rd dimension. That is very important.

Thus it is with the 4th dimension. By being able to *see* three dimensions spread out before us, we are assured that we are living in the next one, the 4th. (Although we can't see the 4th clearly because we *are* living in it, just as A. Square couldn't see the second clearly because he was living in it; he could only see it clearly when he got to the next dimension, the 3rd.) According to Einstein (and brought to fruition by Minkowski), we are now dealing with spacetime, with time being the 4th dimensional component. The perception of 3-dimensional space is, in fact, intimately connected to time. Einstein's equations show this, as does common sense. We internally process, without thinking about it, the fact that when we look out the window at our car, our car is a certain distance which correlates to a certain amount of time that it might take for us to get out to the car, or for light bouncing off of the car to reach us. Time and distance are thus joined together as a whole and define each other, just as in previous dimensions width and length were joined into a whole—that of the plane. If there were no movement in time, there would be no way to move from this mark to the next mark, and therefore no meaning to a sense of space regarding these two points. Although invisible, it is actually *time* that gives us the perception of 3D space.

The addition of time as a dimension, however, is a very interesting thing. What exactly *is* time? That (in addition to consciousness) is a question that philosophers and researchers have argued about since, well, time immemorial. The previous dimensions were all spatial, geometric ones. Some future ones (tesseracts, the 11 dimensions of String Theory, etc.) are also built around geometries of one sort or another. Time, however, while being amenable to calculations involving geometry, and while being banded together with space, seems to be something else, something harder to pin down: what *is* it? The first Google hit states: "Time is a measure which allows events to be ordered." But what does *that* mean? In keeping with the idea of higher dimensions being mysterious, time seems to be one of the ultimate mysteries. You can't see it, you can't hold on to it, you can't saw it into lengths like a 2x4. It feels *different* from the purely spatial dimensions.

But here's the point, to continue on: by being able to experience time, know about time, and in being able to see how time interacts with space to form a 4D universe, *we must be knowing this from the perspective of the next dimension. That* is the message of Flatland. We can only know about each dimension from the perspective of the next. What could the next (i.e. current) dimension be, after time, such that we are already living in it, are dimly aware of it on some level, and are surrounded by it? One clue is that all of the previous dimensions were not hidden, occult, or complicated: they were right there in front of us. Time has always been right there with us, although it took the genius of Einstein to point it out as a dimension, connected mathematically to space. Obviously, length, width, and depth have always been a large part of our lives. So, in regards to the invisible current dimension following the 4th: the 5th, or current, is likely something that is all around us, but that we don't "see" or recognize as a dimension, in the same way that we didn't see that time was the 4th dimension, until it was pointed out to us. And time lets us know also that dimensions don't have to be spatial to interact with and help define our world; they need only have the characteristics of expanding our overall view of reality, and allowing us to see the dimensions below them, in addition to interacting with those dimensions.

If we are indeed living in a 5th dimension that lets us appreciate the four below it, then what could that dimension be? Let's return for a moment to Abbott's *Flatland*, and keep in mind that it was written 21 years before time showed the first hints of becoming the 4th dimension. 3D character, A. Sphere, is talking about speculation that others have had regarding higher dimensions: "But men are divided in opinion as to the facts. And even granting the facts, they explain them in different ways. And in any case, however great may be the number of different explanations, no one has adopted or suggested the theory of a Fourth Dimension. Therefore, pray have done with this trifling, and let us return to business." A few more words are exchanged, and A. Sphere continues: "But most people say that these visions arose from the thought—you will not understand me—from the brain; from the perturbed angularity of the Seer." Following which, the narrator A. Square, now being the one pushing for more dimensions, and more knowledge, jumps in: "Say they so? Oh, believe them not. Or if it indeed be so, that this other space is really Thoughtland, then take me to that blessed Region where I in Thought shall see..."

Wow: Thoughtland. The 4th dimension as time turned out to be quite likely different than what Abbott may have imagined—or that anyone else could have imagined, for that matter. New things always are. But it's solidly in place now: we know about it, we're aware of it, we work with it, it's a part of our cultural touchstones. But what about the 5th? What is it that allows us to know about, visualize, work with, and appreciate the first four dimensions? What's hiding in plain sight? What about Consciousness? What about Thoughtland? Consciousness is lurking in front of us like the proverbial 500-pound gorilla. Think about it. It's what allows us to see the three spatial dimensions that surround us. It's what allows us to use the 4th dimension of time to measure those dimensions and to order events, as stated above. It's what allows us to grasp the entire spacetime continuum, splayed out so elegantly before us. It is, in fact, what has allowed us to *formulate* that spacetime continuum: to know it, to acknowledge it, and to appreciate it. The current dimension always views, frames, and gives meaning and perspective to the previous ones. From modern physics to ancient poetry, consciousness is what has allowed us to "see" our world, and *to interact with it.*

Can consciousness be used in equations, as other dimensions can? An intriguing, and not ridiculous, question. There are differing interpretations of quantum collapse. Some specifically include consciousness. Perhaps if these versions were pursued, instead of trying to force things to stay within a known materialist perspective, there *might* be a way to factor consciousness into equations. Interestingly, (*are* there any coincidences?), the symbol for the wave function in quantum mechanics is the Greek letter psi (ψ), which is also the term being used at this time for alternative consciousness studies. It is also visually connected both with the planet Neptune, as well as the Hindu god Shiva (who appears on the cover of this book, and is further explained in the essay "Lord of the Dance."

Breakthroughs (Uranus) frequently come from the fringes, rather than from the mainstream, which is often bound (Saturn) by structure, protocol, and inflexible paradigms. There is always a flavor of the unexpected: the expected is anathema to discovery. Golda Meir aptly noted that "The dog that trots about finds a bone." Staying on the porch gives us the same food that we had yesterday, and the day before. Who would have thought, prior to Einstein, that *time* would have turned out to be the next dimension? Think about it. Time seemed an entirely unlikely candidate: besides the fact that no one even knew what it was (sound familiar?), it would have been difficult to visualize time as being capable of assuming the place of moving forward the progression of dimensions that began with the visible, tangible, and spatial ones. We took time for granted; we are taking consciousness for granted. Consciousness, too, may seem at first glance to be a very odd choice for the next dimension, but it is the nagging itch running through many different threads and questions regarding our modern view of the world. It therefore may be deserving of more respect and research; not only as to what it *is*, but as to how it may *interact with*, help modify, or even create the world around us.

> “I regard consciousness as fundamental. I regard matter as derivative from consciousness. We cannot get behind consciousness. Everything that we talk about, everything that we regard as existing, postulates consciousness.”
>
> and
>
> “A new scientific truth does not triumph by convincing its opponents and making them see the light, but rather because its opponents eventually die, and a new generation grows up that is familiar with it.”
>
> —Max Planck, seminal originator of the quantum revolution.

We certainly have a long way to go before consciousness might become a “new scientific truth”; but as the saying goes, the longest journey begins with a single step. That single first step which most benefits any journey is an air of broadmindedness in being open to new experiences, dimensions, and ideas. One never knows as they trot around where the bone may be found.

Consciousness as Energy

Physics, Consciousness, Synchronicity, Astrology, Metaphysics. Five interlinking circles. Five shifting views of reality. Five components of the world around us. How might they be connected? Where is the link? Perhaps it might seem that the most difficult association would be that between physics and consciousness, the concrete and the ephemeral. So let's continue with another alternative speculation regarding consciousness that may also tie it into physics. Remember that this book is intended more to ask questions than to provide answers. We have started with the idea that All is One (from metaphysics and supported by modern physics), and we are endeavoring to look at ideas that foster the connections that may show this to be true. We continue with the possibility of consciousness as energy.

What is energy? Energy can be a slang term: "I'm feeling a lack of energy today." It can be a metaphysical or mystical term, as in the energy often associated with whatever concept of God that we might have, or with other spiritual manifestations or abstractions. It can be an astrological term, as when talking about the various "energies" that are displayed and interacting within a horoscope as it interfaces synchronistically with the larger cosmos. It is most commonly a physics based term: nuclear, electromagnetic, chemical, gravitational, mechanical, thermal, potential, kinetic, zero-point quantum, etc. Let's talk about physics.

Electrical energy powers our modern world: lights, computers, television, phones, rock and roll, and Facebook. Interestingly, prior to Benjamin Franklin and a few other pioneers in the 1700s, electricity didn't even exist. Are you surprised? To clarify: it didn't exist as a force in the world that we knew about, or could use. For all practical purposes, it was invisible and nonexistent. Earlier people had certainly made note of lightning and novelties involving static electricity, but other than that, electricity wasn't around. It was "discovered" in the same way that Columbus "discovered" America: America was obviously there, but to the people writing the history books, it didn't exist. For people writing the science books, electricity was nowhere to be found. The same is true with atomic energy, which, although it has powered life on earth since its inception (by being the mechanism through which the sun operates, allowing life to take root here), didn't "exist" either until the last century's amazing discoveries.

We as humans, of course, had possessed various thorough and internally consistent cosmologies and proto-sciences prior to the discoveries of electrical and atomic energies. They were, however, obviously incomplete, as we now realize looking back. (Hindsight, as they say, is always 20/20.) Of course they didn't seem so at the time, and were only revealed as incomplete after the fact, after these new discoveries had been made. So R=K+1, always. In the same manner, there will undoubtedly be things coming in the future which will make us bang our heads that we hadn't realized sooner, they were so obvious. Which may (or may not, depending on our temperament) lead us to ask: what else is out there that we may either not know about, or hubristically discount? *Might* there be other forms of energy about which we are completely unaware? Energies that are hinted at, all around us, and yet lie "undiscovered?" Why not? Is everything known?

Physics defines energy as "the capacity of a body or system to do work," which is as good a definition as any. Physics also states that "work is done when a force that is applied to an object moves that object." So we have a situation wherein any movement is an end product, or result, of the occurrence or use of energy. And in fact, in a colloquial sense, energy intuitively implies movement: energy is dynamic, not static; this is true even of "bottled up," or potential, energy. An example might be that of heat energy applied to a teakettle, which then changes water from a liquid state to a steam state, and moves the molecules faster and faster. Or perhaps a chemical reaction produces heat as a byproduct, and then has the same result. Force, mentioned above, is a second cousin, carrier, and handmaiden to energy.

Consider the scenario where a person may have a certain potential energy, which is then used actively to throw a ball. Energy (through force) is now transferred to the formerly stationary ball, which now has kinetic (moving) energy. This may in turn exert force on something else, perhaps a neighbor's window. The key here is that energy is making something move. In both of these scenarios, it may be seen that energy is not isolated, but is instead part of an endlessly changing and connected chain of energy events: someone had to put the teakettle above on the stove, for example, so we must then consider *their* energy, and so on backward and forwards. So energy is always part of an endless succession. But a question that one may ask is this: is every link in the chain purely physical? Where did the ball hitting the window event begin? What energy was it that was associated with the *decision* to throw the ball, or to boil water for tea?

Let's consider another situation. Let's suppose that an author (not this one; someone more inspirational, perhaps *your* favorite author) eats a candy bar during a particularly lethargic stretch with the quill one morning. The added sugar gives him or her an energy lift, providing chemical energy in their body, which boosts them to a point where they have a sudden burst of inspiration, and finish their masterpiece at long last with an ecstatic flourish. The chemical energy has performed work, allowing their tired arms to lift and furiously scribble in a burst of activity. But the energy has also had a more indirect effect: by providing glucose to their brain, it has supported what may be thought of as mental or "psychic" work, moving their minds and ideas forward to finish their opus, which, as everyone seeing it comments, was "a lot of work." This is not normally taken to mean that there was a lot of arm lifting involved in writing the book; this is usually meant in a more abstract sense, in terms of the effort needed to come up with ideas and words.

Let's look at that hint of more ephemeral forms of energy and work. We are venturing here outside of the strict physics definitions of these two, and yet hopefully keeping some of their sense and intention. Where do ideas come from? Is it just a matter of feeding more glucose to the brain? It seems a bit more difficult to pin down than that. And we cannot deny it, looking at your author's tome: a lot of work was needed. So let's continue the scenario. Through various forms of energy transferences, your favorite book is printed and distributed to various bookstores (if those still exist at the time of this printing). And now let's suppose that you see a review of this book online somewhere, and in the review some of your author's *ideas* from their new book are laid out and explained. No quotes, just ideas. However, you are so excited by these ideas, so intrigued by them, that you want to buy the book and find out what your author has to say. So you find your wallet or purse, get in your car, drive to the bookstore, purchase the book, come home, make a cup of tea, and settle in by the window with your cat. Alternatively, you look online, push a few buttons, and wait for the book to be delivered with the same feline/glass portal ending.

So what has happened here? In a nutshell, your author's *ideas*, i.e. their *consciousness*, has caused *you*, through interacting with your own consciousness, to perform physical actions. *Work has been done.* There is a direct and traceable path here. *Their* consciousness, or mental energy, has moved *your* body. Many, many authors have moved both my own body and my mind, and I've been the grateful recipient of those efforts and energy. Work can only be done if energy is available. Work can only be done through the use of energy. What energy? How can we look at this? *Could* consciousness be a form or type of energy? It seems, in a way, to be performing work.

And what of another sort of movement: that which may occur if you read your author's book (Einstein, Schrödinger, Krishnamurti, Watts, Plato, Arroyo, Greene, Jung, Buddha, Bible, Wilson, Upanishads), and have a personal revelation, leading to a whole different outlook on life? Your *ideas*, so to speak, have been moved. Maybe a prejudice or preconceived notion has been pushed to the side, under the sofa. Movement has taken place, energy has been used to do work. Consciousness has moved consciousness. Perhaps, then, energy or work as being only physical is too limited a concept.

If looked at with an open mind, this can lead to some very serious questions. It's easy enough to leave things in their own particular isolated baskets, where ideas can interact only with ideas, and physical objects can interact only with physical objects. But can ideas interact with physical objects? Perhaps they can do so through a mediatory consciousness. What are the chains of connection here? This is getting to the core of our possible speculative bridge between these two circles. These are also obviously questions coming from a place that has been subject to much discounting, ridicule, and scorn. But many ultimately productive questions and ideas throughout history (and not just in science, but in politics, history, theology, and philosophy, to name a few other disciplines) have been met with these same sorts of reactions from critics. That alone is not enough reason to back off. Some questions need to be asked, and asked more than once; and this question is not nearly as settled as many would have us believe. Let's take a brief detour before we continue on to the next speculation:

Max Planck, in trying to solve the black body radiation problem mentioned in the earlier physics section, came up with a constant (mathematical value) in 1900 that not only solved the dilemma, but that has become one of the most-used numerical values in all of physics. Planck's constant (h) shows up in many varied facets of the discipline, and in fact plugged perfectly into calculations astronomers made in 1990 using COBE satellite measurements to give a picture of the background radiation of the universe: the radiation that was left over from the Big Bang, 13.8 billion years ago. The number itself ties together energy and wavelength in the electromagnetic spectrum.

As important as it is, what's *really* amazing is how *small* a number it is. Planck's constant is rounded to 6.6×10^{-34} Joule-seconds (a measurement of energy). What does that mean? Probably many people's math is rusty, so let's just say, as a refresher example and reminder, that 10^3 (10 to the 3rd power) is 1000 (10 times itself 3 times). 10^{-3} (10 to the minus third power) is then 10 divided by itself 3 times, or .01 (a hundredth of one). 10^{-34} then would be 10 divided by itself 34 times. Needless to say, this would be such a small number as to be nearly infinitesimal. Specifically, crunched and divided by a calculator, factoring in the 6.6, it would be .0000000000000000000000000000000006.6 That's pretty tiny. *And yet it powers the universe.* Planck units take part in many measurements at the sub-nano scale, including length, mass, time, and energy.

(A recent article in online *Symmetry* magazine by Rashmi Shivni puts it into more visual perspective. Recall first that protons are *very tiny* themselves. They are only part of the atomic nucleus, and atoms are pretty darn miniscule. But the Planck scale? Shivni lays it out: "if we scaled the proton up to the size of the observable universe, the Planck length would be a mere trip from Tokyo to Chicago.") Wow: that's *small.*

So what's the point here? Suppose, for the sake of argument, that consciousness *was* a form of energy. Now suppose that it wasn't a 50 pound, 10 gallon, big old hunk of energy that was immediately visible to everyone around, but a more shy and subtle energy; one that perhaps revealed itself somewhere around the Planck scale, the scale of photons (not protons). This actually may be an appropriate scale to consider, since in the double slit experiment, it is possibly consciousness (through measurement) interacting with photons which produces the odd results. Indeed, the Planck scale might be a good place in general to look for interactions between matter and consciousness, since matter at that level doesn't really even exist as we know it. There are only energy patterns and probabilities. What if one of those energies *were* consciousness? *Something* is causing those potential, buzzing energies to form into people, houses, and planets. I can easily change the results of the double slit experiment according to my whims of the moment. Might consciousness then play a role?

Perhaps it may be the case (as mentioned in the previous section), that there will one day be a way to quantify consciousness, or to plug it into an equation. We are moving along on a never-ending journey towards solving the mysteries of the cosmos; there is no shortage of ground yet to cover. Erwin Schrödinger's great contribution to quantum physics was his equation for the wave function (using Planck's constant!), which describes the behavior of vibrating, potential, and probabilistic energy at the quantum scale. Here, energy makes its transformation, collapses its possibilities, and finally coalesces into matter, into our world. Paul Dirac came behind Schrödinger and added to the equations, making them compatible with Einstein's relativity. So the precedent is that nothing is ever finalized: knowledge in physics, and in life, can change, and can be added to. All is a work in progress. If one is an imaginative sort, it may be conceivable that one day Consciousness will be added to these equations, to round out our picture of the world.

Consciousness as Field

According to physics, a field is a force that is spread out over a particular area, which is often quite large: theoretically up to, and including, the universe, although its actual effectiveness drops off pretty quickly with distance. Examples may include temperature, gravitational, magnetic, and electrical fields. Fields themselves are invisible, and may be thought of simply as carrying the qualities, characteristics, or forces of that particular field. They are described mathematically, and they are continuous and omnipresent within their domains. In a way, they are almost like the ancient idea of an aether that pervades all of space. For example, regarding the gravitational field surrounding the earth: it is invisible, and yet anywhere within the field, one is subject to the effects of gravity. These effects diminish the further one gets away from earth according to Newton's inverse square law, which is what allowed him to predict planetary motion. That's also why one "weighs" less in space, or on the moon, than on the earth's surface. Fields contain energy and occupy space, and are thus considered "real" entities; quantum field theory, in fact, is currently understood to describe the most basic constituents of physical reality. Fields may also be thought of as carriers of information, or as being informational: the gravitational field, for example, gives us information about how gravity may affect us at a particular point in space and time. Thus, information and the physical world are connected.

Fields surround us at every moment. If we could color and visualize all of the fields around us at any particular point in time, we would seem to be awash in endless flashing and changing rainbow hues. (Probably anchored by the electromagnetic glow of our cell phones!) "Psychedelic" would likely be an understatement. So it is probably not surprising that assorted individuals over the years have proposed various field theories of consciousness. These fall into two basic categories; the same two categories that we have already met several times. There are those who still hope for physical or biologically based fields, usually electromagnetic; and there are those who simply postulate fields of some unknown composition: of just "consciousness," whatever that may turn out to be. These tend to lean towards a more spiritual basis or connotation.

The electromagnetic versions of consciousness field theory still fascinate some, but have never really caught on. One reason is simply that they are more amenable to testing, and thus may actually be examined and discarded if not applicable. Consciousness has shown itself to be not only more slippery, but just plain *stranger* than such a simple explanation might provide. Radio talk show host Eva Herr has a book out titled simply *Consciousness*, in which she interviews ten alternative consciousness thinkers. To a person, they state that whatever consciousness is, it is most likely not electromagnetic (although of course there *are* electromagnetic *processes* in the brain). So what then *is* it?

Benjamin Libet (who was a pioneer in discovering that much of what we consider volitional free-will decisions have, in fact, been put in place prior to our conscious "deciding") proposed in 1994 that consciousness is a field which is "not... in any category of known physical fields, such as electromagnetic, gravitational etc." In Libet's words, his proposed Conscious Mental Field "may be viewed as somewhat analogous to known physical fields... however... the CMF cannot be observed directly by known physical means." (taken from an article on Scholarpedia by Dr. Susan Pockett in 2013). Of note here, however, is that this particular speculation is envisioned as a field that operates strictly *within* the individual's brain; Libet was not venturing beyond the cranium.

Others have been more experimental. David Chalmers and Andy Clark have written a paper titled "The Extended Mind" (1998), in which they wonder whether objects in the environment can become part of the functioning of the mind. The words here give a clue that this is a more functionalist approach. And although Chalmers has elsewhere been "accused" of panpsychism, this is actually a rather timid venture outside of the orthodox walls. Others have ventured much further. Physicist John Hagelin, who once graced the cover of *Discover* magazine for what was considered to be one of the most brilliant Unified Field Theory (or "Theory of Everything") attempts to date, has lately been persona non grata in the conventional physics world. Besides his cutting edge work at CERN, Hagelin—unfortunately for his mainstream career—at some point latched onto a larger vision of things, and is currently the director of the Transcendental Meditation movement in the United States. Physicist Amit Goswami has pointed out that "as for physicists, philosophy is said to be like the gutter—once you fall in, you just go deeper and deeper and never come out." Probably in connection to this, Hagelin has proposed a very far-reaching and extended Theory of Everything that involves consciousness, not only as a factor in quantum mechanics, but as an active and extended field that we are able to tap into through meditation. He trained under the originator of TM, Maharishi Mahesh Yogi.

Hagelin's not alone. Herr's book mentioned above includes interviews with such fellow trained physicists as Henry Stapp, the just-mentioned Amit Goswami, Elizabeth Rauscher, and Thomas W. Campbell, in addition to rocket scientist Robert Jahn, psi researcher Dean Radin, and several others. All seem on board with the general idea of a field of consciousness which is not specific or isolated to a particular person, but which is indicative of a larger and more distributed field. Of course individual consciousness exists also, but it draws upon the larger version for its energy and ideas, and is always connected at some level. (Fields may always coexist and interact.) The interviewees in the book draw upon history, and seem agreed that whatever consciousness is, it is likely something outside of known physics: *known* being the keyword for several of them. They thus reject any electromagnetic theory, frequently pointing out that the field of greater or universal Consciousness is probably something which is beyond our conventional notions of time and space and the traditional fields associated with these concepts. Thus, consciousness as they envision it may at some point come to terms with physics, but not with physics as we currently understand it.

Ideas of consciousness as a field, although not specifically named as such, have in fact been around for quite some time. They are some of the earliest ideas that man has produced. Hindu versions going back 6,000 years or so, and eventually laid out in the Vedas, the Upanishads, and the Bhagavad Gita, treat the universe as a single great Consciousness, manifesting constantly and creatively in a multiplicity of ways. One difference between this scheme and the Western Abrahamic religions is that, for the Indians, one may call this Consciousness "God," but it is in fact beyond anything that we could actually conceive of: it is the unknown, the manifested *and* the unmanifested, That Which Is. The various Hindu "gods" are simply poor (though beloved) representations of the unknowable energies associated with this Consciousness that we all take part in. We are (for the Easterners) *part of* the One, of Consciousness, the Unknowable; part of God, if you will. There is no separation. We, as well as everything else in the universe, take part in this sacred Consciousness, and our task in life is to awaken to this fact, and to see ourselves correctly as amnesic nodes of the One, as connected and *part of*. It is important to note that this One includes not just interconnections in a physical or physics sense, but (just as *information* may be a key component of the universe) assumes a certain level of intelligence and meaning; after all, that is what consciousness is all about, even within our own skulls. And our own puny consciousnesses here are simply maya-drenched outposts of this greater Consciousness, whiling away time in the swampy backwaters of a much larger field.

In the more dualistic West, by contrast, where God is "up there," and we are subservient to Him and separate from Him, there is more fragmentation, and therefore more discord. We all remain separate from each other, and from God: we are trapped in our fragile and contentious little egos, looking for "salvation": to be taken out of this world of woe. In the East, there is nothing to be taken out of: we are the world, we are Consciousness, and they are us. In the West, we can salute our higher natures and pull together towards peace at times, but it is more difficult than in the Eastern system, where it is taken for granted and understood that we are all each other, and all part of the One, part of the Godhead. In the

Western traditions, there *is* a greater Consciousness, that of God, but we are not a part of that; we spend our lives struggling to align our personal and isolated consciousnesses to that larger one of God. One may find an interesting take on this by returning to George Berkeley, who was introduced earlier as the originator of idealism. He thought that consciousness was primary: it created reality. However, when faced with the conundrum of how reality could exist when our consciousness wasn't around, he posited that it did so because *God's* Consciousness was always around. With these examples, we see clearly the idea of consciousness as a field, and the connection, for many, to religious or spiritual ideas.

These traditions, and most others that may be called spiritual or religious, presuppose a more universal Consciousness field of some sort, and most presuppose the primacy of Consciousness over the material world. But does one need to be religious to support a field theory of consciousness? Not really. Let's remember, first of all, that no one really knows what consciousness is, or how it may interact with our personal selves, or how it may interact with the physical world. So the opportunity for interpretations and ideas is fairly wide open. Let's also drop back for a moment to revisit quantum physics. Here, again, consciousness may not be *required* to collapse the wave function, but it is true that if my consciousness decides to measure the photons in a double slit experiment, I can make them act like particles rather than waves. So again we don't know if consciousness is *mandatory* in bringing physical reality into being, but we do know that consciousness is *able* to do this.

So it is entirely possible for the completely non-religious to speculate that there is this secular "force," consciousness, continually acting in accordance with quantum principles, and in concert with unformed potential, to produce reality at the level with which we are familiar. (We are trying to avoid the word "cause," which may turn out to be completely archaic in this context.) The *field* of consciousness would carry this force, just as the gravitational field carries the force of gravity. (See the earlier discussion, however, on gravity vs. general relativity.) It would be a real field, but one which perhaps may exist at a level of physics that we haven't become acquainted with yet. Of note here is that fields themselves may be quite different in their properties: the fields being investigated at the quantum level are already vastly different than previous macro-level fields; and who knows what a new and undiscovered field of consciousness might be like? At the level of physics with which we *are* working, we do know that fields can overlap, that they can influence each other, and that disparate fields can induce (bring about) other fields that are of a different type than their own, although there may be an underlying connection. So, for example, electric fields can generate magnetic fields, and vice versa. Scientists are still looking for the connection between gravitational fields and electromagnetic fields. Perhaps the speculative field or force of consciousness is something that we (perhaps unconsciously) take part in, and which could then interact or induce some of the more familiar fields, including quantum ones. These would then create "reality," and the physical world.

Another mention of note here, in keeping with our general themes of open-mindedness, is that it wasn't too long ago that we actually knew nothing of fields. Gravitational and electromagnetic fields, for the greatest minds on earth, simply didn't "exist." They were unknown and invisible. The progressive discovery of fields since then may, for the intellectually adventuresome, bring about a question launched earlier: might there be other fields out there that we haven't detected yet, or are we pretty much done, everything having been discovered? And if we restrict ourselves only to those discoveries in the future that we perceive will be "non-weird." then we are denying the very, very, strange history of science so far.

So we are left back at the question: is it possible that consciousness may be a field of some sort? If so, what does that then suggest regarding our concept of the way the world works? And even more importantly, *is* it possible that consciousness may actually be primary, as some have suggested? In an August 2013 article in *Scientific American* titled "What is Real?", author Meinard Kuhlmann (who has dual degrees in physics and philosophy) writes about the complicated Unruh effect, wherein two different observers will find a patch of empty space to be either a vacuum or teeming with particles, depending on their relativistic relationship to that space. He then notes, importantly, "if the number of particles is observer dependent, then it seems incoherent to assume that particles are basic." Indeed. Take your pick: dimension, energy, or field. Whatever it may ultimately prove itself to be, consciousness is likely to turn out to be *something* more than simple, materialist/reductionist biochemical processes in the brain.

> "The doctrine that the world is made up of objects whose existence is independent of human consciousness turns out to be in conflict with quantum mechanics and with facts established by experiment."—physicist Bernard d'Espagnat

> "Consciousness cannot be accounted for in physical terms. For consciousness is absolutely fundamental. It cannot be accounted for in terms of anything else."—physicist Erwin Schrödinger

> "Thou Art That"—the central theme of the Upanishads, equating and tying together personal consciousness with Universal Consciousness. We are manifested points on the field of potential.

> "The stream of knowledge is heading towards a non-mechanical reality; the universe begins to look more like a great thought than like a great machine."—physicist Sir James Jeans

OK, I Get That

It is normal to feel that we are pretty sharp, pretty aware of what's going on around us, and pretty good at analyzing things. Not many things can get by *our* astute perception and scrutiny! So here's a fun demonstration of just how much we move through life on autopilot, not examining things in our surroundings or consciousness, and taking things for granted without thinking much about them. How much are things around us every day, and core parts of our daily lives, really in our awareness? Let's briefly consider the word "OK."

It's an impressively useful and widespread word. Most of us use it easily hundreds of times per day, and sometimes per hour. It is likely the most universally understood word across the face of the earth. You can go to the jungles of Borneo, or the rural villages of Kazakhstan and say "OK" about something, and the person that you are talking to will nod their head knowingly, repeating "OK" in return. It is the universal word for agreement, in addition to its many other uses. But have you ever considered the word itself? What does OK mean? Where did it come from? Is it an abbreviation for something? If so, then what? What are its origins?

It's a pretty versatile word: it can act as a noun, verb, adjective, or adverb, depending on one's needs at the time. It can be a complete sentence in and of itself: "OK." It can be a question, a statement, a description, an agreement, or an acknowledgement. But where did it come from?

Amazingly, for something used so frequently and universally, no one actually knows. The best guess by scholars so far is that it came about through the newspapermen of Boston making fun of poorly educated rubes in the 1830s by using the phrase "Oll Korrekt" (as they imagined an uneducated person might spell it) in their proofreading notes. This was abbreviated in their jottings in the margins, as "O.K."

So there you have it. OK?

The Relativity of Consciousness

Everything is relative. Space and time are relative, but so are consciousness and perspective. Everything is relative, however, within defined parameters. This was the great society-wide structural change and understanding that grew out of Einstein's epiphanies. Certainty was on its way out, thanks to our boy Albert, and quantum closed the door on it. Relativity appears everywhere we look. In the astrological world, different practitioners often follow different versions of astrology, using differing techniques with differing horoscope emphasis, but still produce equally valid results. Similarly, studies done in the psychological counseling field regarding competing therapies most typically show an equal rate of success no matter what school is followed. Both depend on many factors, including the skill and the consciousness of both the practitioner and the client. Perspectives that are different relative to each other can produce identical results.

Comparably, whatever version of quantum mechanics *interpretation* that you prefer, the *results* are the same. My ideas may be different from your ideas. They may come perhaps from different sources, they may be processed in different ways, and they may come at the world from different angles: there are many perspectives and ways of viewing reality. And yet, for quantum, the *results* of the calculations are the same: it is the understanding and interpretation that are different. And so it is, finally, with our lives: the "results"—how our minds interact with the external world to produce our personal histories—may all arise from independent, and often quirky, paths that demonstrate quite dissimilar perspectives; but ultimately the results are always consistent with the overall "laws" of human nature and karma.

Consciousness, as seen peeking through above, is also relative, but relative to what? It is relative to other consciousnesses, and to the material world itself. It is relative to our internal processing of external (or internal) stimuli, and to how our thoughts, dreams, hopes, fears, and beliefs interact with the world and the people around us. As has been demonstrated, it is even in a relational and relativistic aspect to the physical world surrounding us. Where we "sit," cognitively and emotionally, as well as physically, determines everything. Will we observe a particle or a wave? Our consciousness will determine that one particular person looking away from the double slit experiment will find a wave at the end, while another monitoring the slits will find a particle at the end. Our consciousness will also determine what meaning the character of an *event* in our life will have *to us*. Will the event be a particle, or a wave? Will an event in our life lead to new possibilities for growth, or to a downward spiral? The event may be either: we choose one or the other.

How do we even know that we are seeing things clearly? If someone is color blind, but does not know it (does not know that color exists), he will naturally assume that he is seeing things appropriately and clearly, as they are. He has a flinty eye for reality; not much gets by his keen perceptions. Why wouldn't he assume this? Most of us have a fairly egocentric view of the world: what *we* see is the way that things are. Only when this person is around other people that have full color vision will he be able to understand that he is lacking in this perceptual ability. (Although, of course, he may still continue to insist that he is actually seeing things more clearly than they are, simply because that's the way that *he* is seeing them!) So who has the better grasp of the full spectrum of reality? Who should we listen to? And what about the "full color" people? What else are *they* missing? Are they seeing reality clearly? Can they see ultraviolet or infrared? What additional information about the world around them might these frequencies impart? What about those people who may be more, or less, sensitive to *emotional* clues regarding others around them? The deaf, vs. the acute of hearing? What does *their* world feel like? What's it like to be a bat?

Consciousness is relative to our own frame of reference. Just as Einstein showed that there is no ultimate or fixed spacetime frame of reference, perhaps there is no universally knowable consciousness frame of reference. That would mean that there is no ultimate Truth, at least that we can know, since human truths come out of consciousness. Plato would not like this idea very much. On the other hand, the true strangeness and obvious relativity of Einstein's ideas only come out at the far fringes: in everyday life, things mostly hew, on a grosser level, to good old-fashioned classical rules. So, for ordinary (especially community) existence, we may not have to get rid of, or mistrust, all of the hard-won, transmitted, and agreed upon bits of human wisdom that we've accumulated. We can keep them, albeit with caveats.

Nonetheless, in our own lives—apart from these sometimes dubious mass agreements—everything that we see, think, or know is colored by our own biases, perceptions, and awareness. All *is* relative. Like time and space, consciousness is fluid, malleable, and subject to perspective. We know, but we don't know. More frighteningly, we don't know what it is that we don't know. As pointed out in the introduction, this simple idea has likely been at the core of many of the world's problems. There is no universal agreement on the way things are, or on the way that things "should be." They should be the way that *we* think they should be. (Our ideas, of course, are always the correct ones!) But others think that also. We are normally able to interact on a day to day basis simply because we share enough consensus between consciousnesses that we can function together at some level; and yet most people have had the experience of being very surprised at how different someone else's consciousness may actually be. "Really? They think *that*!?" Yes, they do.

The Relativity of Consciousness, Part 2

On the other hand:

Individual relativity aside, there *does* seem to be much consensus regarding certain universal human "truths," and so let's look at that. The most likely explanation for these common bits of wisdom to have arisen is that, due to genetics, most humans share the vast majority of traits in common, such that "people are people" around the world. Jung's ideas figure in heavily here. Stories, myths, fables, and morals resonate from one culture to another. Indeed, they may be imprinted into our genes, such that an isolated tribe, raised without cultural touchstones, would automatically develop such archetypes as the Journey, the Hero, the Lover, the Mother, etc. Similar to Plato, it is astrology's view that these archetypes exist independently from any particular person, life, or culture. They may indeed exist eternally in some form that both the universe and humans tap into and understand.

So perhaps, the relativity of consciousness notwithstanding, Plato would not be so unhappy after all to see the commonalities between all people, and their ideas, ideals, shared myths, stories, and wisdoms. If there were a universality, connectedness, or pan-conscious nature to things, then this would not be surprising. One question then to ask would be how individual consciousnesses might interact with and influence each other, and how they might interface with a possibly even larger and more distributed Consciousness. One model here might be that of wave interactions producing a blended picture of merging energies. It is certainly possible that there may be a "global consciousness" (or larger) that is a composite of individual consciousnesses. There may also be intermediary levels of aggregate consciousnesses existing on a smaller scale, such as local groups, friends, partners, etc.; these may then combine into something larger. They may be like ripples in a greater consciousness field, somewhere between the individual and the Whole. Whether individual or in composite, consciousnesses may interact with other consciousnesses in a wave-like fashion, negating or adding to the waves nearby, and forming interference patterns. What would the relationship then be between an individual or aggregate wave, and a more Universal Consciousness? Might it be possible that there could be some sort synergistic, skewing effect from the combining of individual waves with this more Universal Consciousness? And further, could it be that this larger Consciousness may then be responsive to, and at least partially composed of a conglomeration of individual consciousnesses, bending and twisting the Whole with the combined energy of their various permutations? If all is connected, then a pull on B will deform A. If A is much larger than B, however, the pull will be very small. The gravitational waves recently detected by LIGO produced a disturbance only the width of a thumb in relation to the size of the Milky Way galaxy. We are likely talking of very subtle effects here.

A radical and creative way of attempting to discern if this is true in a literal sense is what is known as The Global Consciousness Project. It has been in process since 1998, and uses constantly running random number generators to see if combined human consciousness can influence or skew the random numbers in some way. The idea relies heavily on the *emotional* component of consciousness (see the next chapter), and claims, for example, that the random numbers globally showed a marked deviation at the time of the 9/11 attacks in New York on the World Trade Center, as a shocked world reacted. Interestingly, the researchers claim that the random numbers started to deviate slightly *before* the actual event, and so that is material for additional speculation. As usual with any sorts of alternative consciousness explorations, however, it is difficult to know what the actual facts are, because while there are claims and data from the researchers on the experimental side (with statistical evidence), there is the traditional *guarantee* that orthodox science (which has more manpower and resources) will automatically, and in every case, find some reason that the methodology, design, sample, results, or verification is flawed. It will never be found to be of any value. The stone wall will not be breached by upstarts. So it is usually difficult to get the real story, or to sort through claims.

Combined consciousness may also shed light on another issue. The idea of consciousness “creating” the physical world has been mentioned as one solution to the measurement problem in quantum mechanics. It is also compatible with many spiritual traditions. However, questions arise. If we exaggerate to the macro level, then who gets to create the table that you and your friend are sitting at? Is it arising from her consciousness, or yours? Does it exist only in her consciousness or also in yours? How do we move away from solipsism? If the two of you share the table in front of you, then how could that work? How can the world be so seemingly full of shared experiences, points of commonality, and yet be created by *us*? How might we share a common reality? Might there be parallels to the current movement towards computers sharing in “the cloud?”

One solution might take place if consciousness was *not* in fact limited to the weak little bulb between our ears, but was better visualized as a shared, amorphous, and changing field of energy that we communally contribute to and take part in, and which then interacts with a shared, amorphous, and changing energy or field that is the physical and energetic universe. We would all then co-create reality, we would be participatory nodes, but not alone. Reality would then be an ever-changing, ever-flowing creative mix of consciousness and matter laid out before us as conventional spacetime, and produced by a host of contributors. We would share the world because we *were* the world.

There are a myriad of alternative but popular science books built around the idea that consciousness creates matter. There are dozens on Amazon. And just because it is speculative, doesn’t mean that it is wrong or ridiculous. In the relativity of consciousness, it simply occupies a particular frame of reference. It derives directly from the mainstream physics literature, which allows consciousness as a possible solution to the wave function collapse. These cutting edge questions in physics do *not* have universally accepted answers at this time. There is room for debate and alternative ideas, but in all fairness, these farther out speculations of consciousness also beg other questions.

When we walk out at night and look up at the stars above, perhaps we might see Alpha Centauri, the nearest star system to us. Although it appears as one point, it is actually three stars very close to each other. It's effortless to speculate that perhaps your consciousness (maybe in conjunction with your friend's) had some part in creating the table in front of you, but what of Alpha Centauri? Whose consciousness created *that* (if we are still on the consciousness-creates-matter conjecture)? If matter is created by consciousness, then who created Alpha Centauri? Was it the proto-human whose consciousness first noticed it? Aliens with *their* consciousness, perhaps? Was it a conglomeration of scientists, ancient or modern? Was it God in His infinite field of Consciousness? And finally: does this quandary make the possibility of mind/matter interaction any less likely? Why would it? It's just a very large question, and there are a lot of very large questions. We mustn't let the magnitude of the questions make us less open-minded; it should actually make us more so. What it would seem to make *more* likely is the idea that, for a lot of this stuff, we really just don't have a good idea about what's going on.

Owsley's Ghost

Einstein showed that everything is relative. There is no permanent, fixed, and unchanging frame of reference that we can ultimately point to. Life "works" so well simply because most of us share fairly similar physical and cultural frames of reference that we can all agree on—at least on a grosser level. The idea of an immutable shared frame of reference breaks down pretty quickly, however, once the finer and more personal forms of consciousness-relativity enter the picture.

Our perceptions of the physical world itself are more subject to consciousness-driven relativity than they may initially appear to be. We like to think that we (unlike other people) see the world pretty clearly. However, regardless of what may be out there in some philosophical "objective" reality, our personal world is always determined purely by our perceptions, and the way that we process them. Our perceptions are ultimately conceptual, and working in tandem with our biases; but they at root depend upon our physical sensory apparatus, which is often not nearly as reliable as we would like to think. Thus, things aren't always what they seem. In 1905, Albert Einstein showed that physical reality and time were not fixed, but were simply relative to a particular observer. In 1943, Albert Hofmann discovered dramatically and conclusively that consciousness and perception were not fixed either, but could be relative and changeable. The relativity in this case was within our own mind and its aforementioned sensory apparatus.

For those who have done psychedelics, in addition to experiencing distortions of space and time, there is often also an overwhelming *feeling* and sense of Oneness and Meaning. The question is: are these effects (whether perceptual, or of understanding) simply a matter of altered brain chemistry, or are the drugs themselves providing us a concrete experience of relativity, and possibly even allowing us to encounter a level or form of consciousness hitherto unexperienced in our ordinary lives? There has been more than one well-known and published psychedelic "researcher" who has intimated that the function of these drugs is to actually let us see reality in its larger or truer form, putting into perspective the illusory and limited nature of our day to day visions and perceptions. Generally this has to do with precisely the "relativistic" effects of the experience: it (the experience) reveals in graphic detail just how dependent what we know as reality is on our personal perceptions and assumptions. By shattering these in a very palpable way, it has the potential to lead us towards a higher level of understanding. Those who have done psychedelics often experience a lasting effect that may integrate into their permanent awareness and sensibility, and may thus inform the way that they see things for the rest of their lives. So it is certainly possible that the effects may help to give us a clearer picture regarding the ephemerality of what we call reality; if nothing else they allow us to know, in a very clear and graphic fashion, that the way we see things is a construct of our mind, and not necessarily the way that they really are. (As a side note here, it would seem that certain physicists have done a variety of psychedelics at times over the years. Psychedelics are all about consciousness, and therefore there is a chance that some originally more materially-bound physicists may eventually be more sympathetic to this component of existence. The ones who have done psychedelics certainly seem to be.)

***

For those readers who have not done psychedelics, come with me as I imagine a hike on a trail in the mountains of my youth, while in just such an altered state of consciousness. Hopefully, one may get a taste for the odd and relativistic effects mentioned above. Ready? Here we go:

The drug is just starting to kick in; the sun is up for the day, but low in the sky. Leaving early on my hike, I soon pass by a dad with three little kids all stopping and stooping down to look at a grasshopper, frozen and motionless, temporarily, glistening in the sun, latticework wings shining. Not to intrude, I pass them by, but am fascinated by the quartet's interaction with nature; why have we lost touch with nature in the modern world? What *is* more amazing than a grasshopper? Later, a bicyclist rolls by. His wheels stir up little plumes of dust. He seems at first very, very far away, as if he were at the end of a long tunnel. Space has been stretched. Then suddenly, in a flash, he is by me and past. His helmet and sunglasses make him look like a giant insect fighting its way through the world. He is kin to the grasshopper: they are somehow the same, and the connection becomes obvious. Something about him looks so pleasant, so real, and so funny that I smile and laugh to myself. The trail behind him seems to be lengthening further as I watch, stretching away towards infinity, undulating with living and breathing hills caused by the shadows on it. I can feel the respirations of the earth. I see a tiny troll with a green hat way down at the end, and then he is gone. The bicyclist's nod seemed as if it were from another dimension; I have a brief moment of paranoia, and then it is gone. The clouds, fluffy and white, drift across the impossibly blue sky and arrange themselves to form personal messages to me; and then I join them, looking down, floating and flying with them. And the breeze carries good news, caressing my skin as if I were taking a bath in it: warm and soft, like a delicate cashmere blanket. The pines bend over towards me in a gesture of friendship, and I am awash in the smell of pine sap: I can see the molecules drifting towards my nose, leaving trails behind them. I think of the lyrics to the Beatles' song "Lucy in the Sky with Diamonds." We have definitely left the dock.

The sound of my feet crunching in the gravel of the trail begins to sound like a miniature locomotive: it achieves a rhythm of its own and I am only a carrier of it, a part of it, going along with it. The trail, the sound, is walking *me*. It's becoming increasingly difficult to keep moving forward, however; walking is starting to seem as if I were moving through molasses, and yet it's OK. I have to stop every few minutes to inspect the bark of the trees around me from about an inch away. Amazing stuff! I try to make sure that no one is looking. It's kind of fun in a way, and extremely funny. I can't stop smiling. The total absurdity of how seriously we take life is becoming apparent. I sit down on a large rock. Suddenly a real miniature locomotive appears in the brush nearby, although it doesn't seem to be moving, just kind of vibrating in place. I glance away and look back, and it is gone. The brush holds geometric patterns as far as the eye can see: intricate henna-work with stunning depth and dimension. There is a humming and buzzing in the air: the sound of the universe.

Bees and birds. The bees are the source of the buzzing, moving from plant to plant. They seem to be messengers of some sort, but I can't decipher this further. The faint impressions of another bicycle track heading off through the mehndi also seems to portend meaning; my mind goes off into the distance, trying to follow. I close my eyes for a minute. Cartoon characters in my imagination tell a lightning-speed story that my mind makes up on the spot, second by second. The fecundity of the images pouring forth when I close my eyes is astonishing. "So *this* is what the human mind is capable of!" I think in amazement, grateful to be the possessor of such a wonderful tool. It's true! We *do* use only a fraction of our minds—I am burning up with mental creativity. I can't stop it, or slow it down. I can also feel the earth rotating below me, and can feel myself flying through space; all of this energy is massive, moving, changing, tumbling forward. Always in flux, always in motion. No thought lingers for more than a second, the miniature trains appear and disappear. The world is a Blooming Lotus Flower, dazzling in its manifestations. All is Becoming.

The sun breaks through the clouds and the trees, too blinding to look at; we humans must bow our heads in deference. So this is the source of all life here on earth! The plants that I walk by now seem to reach up towards it in supplication, their tiny tendrils waving and beckoning. Little purple and yellow flowers teach me lessons about the electromagnetic spectrum, and about kindness. It all becomes clear: the sky is alive with radiation filling every square inch, and yet it's all benign. The very atoms around me are all droning and vibrating; I can hear them. All are working together in concert to produce the beautiful vista that I now see. But wait: this seems in a sense to be all coming from my own mind; I can recognize that, and can see the connection, as if disembodied from both my own mind and my surroundings. How *does* my mind interact with the vista around me? What is the separation? Is there any?

My watch, upon noticing it, now seems to be the most amazing technological accomplishment that I have ever seen. I gaze at it, turn it over, try to imagine its workings. I marvel: how did we as humans get from the dirt below us, all the way up to this watch? My watch seems like the most exquisite jewel in the universe; the Faberge eggs pale in comparison. And what *is* time, anyway: how does it flow? What does it mean? What does my watch measure? I now feel suddenly that I can't trust my watch: I am now suspicious that it may be in collaboration with time, able to manipulate time, with me left out of the loop. How reliable *is* it? Since I started my hike, time has either been standing still, or disappearing in big chunks. It suddenly seems as if it were almost mocking me. Then I laugh: *of course* time is ridiculous! *Everything* is ridiculous: that's the meaning of things. Silliness rules the cosmos. Rocks themselves nearby jutting up out of the grass seem to speak of time and silliness. They seem to know more about time than my watch. What processes have turned them into the gravel in front of me, inch by inch, millimeter by millimeter, nanoparticle by nanoparticle? Isn't it silly that a rock should turn into gravel anyway? I can't stop smiling; the wonder of the surrounding world has again overtaken me.

I take a deep breath and all is beautiful. All is connected. The breeze that embraces my skin also touches the flowers and the bicyclists. We are one, we are coupled and undivided. There is no them or me. The world is a series of infinitely projecting mirrors facing each other, and we are all in the middle. The warmth of the sun that shines down goes through me, goes through the earth as it takes its own part in the distant patterns of solar systems and galaxies. The sun and I have that in common. I get up and start walking again.

***

Of interest here is an idea from Aldous Huxley, author of *The Doors of Perception*, written after his experiences with Mescaline. Huxley theorized that all of our consciousnesses may tap into, and be part of, what he called the "Mind At Large," and that the actual function of our brain was to act as a "reducing valve" to allow us to live our day to day lives without being overwhelmed. Philosopher C.D. Broad adds to this, "The suggestion is that the function of the brain and nervous system and sense organs is in the main *eliminative* and not productive." (Per Michael Grosso in the compilation book *Beyond Physicalism*.) Quite a concept, and this is certainly true at least in relation to these sorts of experiences; once the doors have been opened, the flood of sensory and perceptual input is poorly tamed. One hangs on and goes where the car goes. Keep your hands inside the ride at all times!

Please note that this is not to advocate for psychedelics; they are powerful chemicals with less common but significant risks attached to them. I personally haven't done them since my early 20's. They are especially *not* for anyone with mental health issues. This is simply to demonstrate how different our perceptions of the world can be, depending on our mental state; and while drugs provide an overwhelming example, such subtle things as everyday emotional states can cause us to misinterpret our physical, sensory information as well. If this is so, then how, really, do we know what is certain or solid? Relativity is not just physical, but is a key component woven throughout our consciousness and perceptions, and indeed our entire lives, as well as the universe.

And a special side note to those in recovery: like all other mind-altering chemicals, psychedelics are to be avoided. There are other more lasting and deeper passageways for getting to where they lead. That is a thrilling discovery in itself. Naomi Judd (of all people) has said "There are many paths, but only one journey." That's true.

Spukhafte Fernwirkung

Is Consciousness local or distributed? Is it emergent from physiologic processes, or primary as a force in the universe?

Modern scientism is a pretty tightly sealed vessel, and it would be tempting to think that consciousness *does* strictly arise from, and is confined to, personal fleshy matter, if it weren't for the darn outliers that keep popping up. What are we to make of the role of the observer in quantum physics? Of the many documented psi experiences? Of synchronicities? Of the placebo effect?

In physics, there are two versions of reality. One is termed "local realism." This is the version favored by Newton and Einstein, in which particles and events can be "connected to everything," or part of a whole, by *interactions*; but in which they remain essentially discrete. Interactions are limited by the speed of light, determinism rules, and causation is the connecting factor. The clockwork universe, in other words. However, there is another, and more modern, version of reality emerging from quantum theory, in which things may be "non-local," which is quite a bit stranger. This a component of the weirdness that is supplanting Newton and Einstein, but about which there is no general consensus as to what it fully means yet.

Non-locality, produced by entanglement, is the property demonstrated by the EPR and Bell experiments; the idea that Einstein called "spooky action at a distance." It is the idea that at some unknown level, the universe may be both deeply connected, and beyond our conventional ideas of time, space, and causality. It's well to recall here again that we don't get to choose how the universe works; the universe gets to choose. The universe is not what we would wish it to be, but what it is. Wikipedia points out, matter-of-factly, that "quantum nonlocality is a property of the universe that is independent of our description of nature." An old Zen Buddhist analogy talks of an adept pointing towards the moon with his finger, and giving a caution to the neophyte. The moon exists, the moon is what it is. The finger is simply a pointing device towards this reality. We must not confuse the two.

So how does this relate to consciousness? Most mainstream consciousness theorists have training in philosophy or biology rather than in physics, and most physicists do not have training in philosophy, although modern physics has incredible philosophical implications. So that is good to keep in mind. The world is a whole, and philosophy (including metaphysics and spirituality), biology, and physics *must* tie together in some fashion, at some point. One physicist trying to tie them together is Freeman Dyson, who has been savaged in the past by evangelical atheist Richard Dawkins for daring to suggest that one may be scientific and spiritual at the same time. Dyson has collected quite a lot of scientific honors in his field, but has also speculated regarding the subject of consciousness, especially as to how it might interface with his physics background. Again, from Wikipedia, Dyson has stated that, "The universe shows evidence of the operations of mind on three levels. The first level is the level of elementary physical processes in quantum mechanics. Matter in quantum mechanics is [...] constantly making choices between alternative possibilities according to probabilistic laws. [...] The second level at which we detect the operations of mind is the level of direct human experience. [...] [I]t is reasonable to believe in the existence of a third level of mind, a mental component of the universe. If we believe in this mental component and call it God, then we can say that we are small pieces of God's mental apparatus." This interestingly parallels the microcosm, the mesocosm, and the macrocosm, as well as Hindu Vedic teachings.

Of course, in talking about his particular version of God, Dyson immediately moves from possibilities for inclusiveness to fragmentation, as everyone now can begin arguing about which version of God is better or more correct, or whether God even exists, etc. Nonetheless, the issue is a good one to bring up: if physics has implicated consciousness in the workings of the physical world, and if the physical world is now demonstrated to be synchronistic and connected—non-local—then what might one say about consciousness? There is indeed a *lot* of food for thought here. Although this speculation in our traditional-science culture has been mainly confined to those on the fringe (where of course much of the truly paradigm-changing innovation frequently takes place), there are a few mainstreamers who have hiked into this territory. Besides Dyson, other trained physicists including Eugene Wigner, Henry Stapp, Fritjof Capra, and Amit Goswami specifically state the primacy of consciousness; other followers of the Copenhagen interpretation use consciousness in a less acknowledged fashion. ("Measurement": By whom? By what? What even constitutes measurement?) Outside of the physics world, we have already talked about David Chalmers' flirtation with both panpsychism and information as the underlying strata of consciousness; some in the physics world also see information as the key component of non-locality. Others engaged in consciousness speculation, such as C.J.S. Lewis and Ted Honderich, have also espoused a philosophical externalism. Perhaps we will move towards a distributed and external monism that includes both physical and consciousness components. That is what neutral monism attempts to get at. It is entirely possible that non-locality and "spooky action at a distance" may ultimately apply not only to the physical world, but to consciousness as well.

It may be that consciousness, as separate from the physical, and especially if non-local, is the very basis of what separates spirituality from science, and yet what may finally bring them together. This may or may not include "God," of whatever sort or interpretation; in the following sections there will continue to be speculation as to how consciousness may tie into physics. It may also be true, as the Hindus espouse, that there is a Universal Consciousness permeating the universe that we "tap into," or are pieces of, manifesting our own little portions. In this vision, we are nodes of the One, of God, of Consciousness, of What Is. We are connected with, and take part in, a Universal Mind. It may also be, that as *part of* this larger schema, we ourselves have input into the more distributed system; and in fact, although there may be a universal and more powerful Consciousness, our particular nodes act in concert to form what we know as the local reality around us. The overall arc of local manifested existence may be partially an aggregate of dimly perceived shared minds. E Pluribus Unum. Whether that may be the "ultimate" reality, however, we may or may not ever know. R=K+1.

It's a Miracle!

"Whether you think you can, or you think you can't—you're right."—Henry Ford.

My dad, as he got older, had some problems with gastroesophageal reflux and especially with esophageal spasms; he would often have to stop eating a meal because of the spasms. Somewhere along the line he discovered Zantac™, and for him, this became his "miracle drug." Whenever he felt like he was going to have a spasm, he would take a Zantac. The amazing thing was, not only is Zantac not prescribed nor known to be effective for esophageal spasms, but my dad would also claim "instant" relief: within seconds, before the pill even hardly had a chance to reach his stomach, let alone get into his system, he would have relief. "It's like a miracle," he would say, "this stuff works instantly!" The rest of the family just smiled. Welcome to the placebo effect.

The placebo effect, surprisingly, is actually a good example of "holistic" medicine, meaning that which recognizes that the mind and body are working together. We often think of the placebo effect in a negative way, as if it were "cheating" or something. The fact is, my dad never once had an esophageal spasm after taking his miracle Zantac. Research with antidepressants has often shown that the placebo effect actually trumps real medicine in many cases. Skeptical folks often like to make fun of the placebo effect, but how then to account for demonstrable results? A very recent study, in fact, showed that placebos not only work, *but work even when people are told and know that they are taking a placebo*. Wow. What's not to like? Who cares what they're about if they work? But *how* do they work?

The placebo effect (and its opposite, the nocebo effect) are woven through our lives, and there is no doubt that even the most cynical researchers can be found taking part in these experiments, whether they realize it or not; it's a human nature thing, and it's hard to avoid human nature (unless you're a bat). It's baked into our genes. In more primitive times, it was likely the reason that witch doctors or shamans were able to cure people of various illnesses. Many people, in fact, still love the idea of shamans—it's the ongoing fascination with that mind/body thing, which has often been ignored by Western medicine. The placebo effect is related closely to superstitions and lucky talismans also: the special necklace that keeps one from harm in stressful situations, the personal mantra that helps us calm down. It's OK. They work.

The placebo effect and superstitions have the same mechanisms. They are rooted in *belief*. It doesn't matter how smart one is: if one is human, then believing is seeing, to whatever greater or lesser extent. Believing can be both the cause of dysfunction or illness, as well as its cure. Believing against frequently contradictory evidence (my child would never do *that*!) is also human nature. Welcome to our species. And since our personal worlds are constructed as much or more from beliefs as they are from facts, we can all share in this. What's interesting is how this effect points up the connections between consciousness (and the associated unconscious) and the body. Real physical effects are happening here, arising from mental processes. Placebo blood pressure medicines can actually lower the blood pressure. Placebo "spasm meds" can prevent esophageal spasms. Placebo antidepressants can increase one's sense of well-being. Studies have shown that prayer (which some would consider a placebo or superstition) has a documented positive effect on the survival rates and courses of serious illnesses. For myself, minor illnesses such as colds or flu occur rarely, but when they do it often seems as if my body is telling me that I need to slow down, to take a break, to get away from the hustle and bustle of the exterior world and concentrate on getting back to a more important introspective place, to things that really matter (to me, anyway). Can my body, possibly prompted by my mind, somehow "choose" when to get sick? Or is that just a belief in itself?

Anyone, again, who states that *they* are seeing things clearly, that they are not prey to projecting their beliefs into their lives, or would never fall for the placebo effect, is simply not in touch with themselves or the way that human consciousness works. Most importantly, with placebos, we see tangible evidence again that consciousness can influence the physical world—in this case, our own bodies, hormones, neurotransmitters, etc. It goes without saying that the physical world can influence us; but we are seeing, more and more, a reciprocal effect. But what exactly is the connection? Is it a philosophically dualistic situation, where some sort of ephemeral consciousness is somehow affecting the material world? Or is it physical monism, demonstrating that indeed our minds are nothing but extensions of our gray matter, tied to the rest of the body, mere biochemical processes? Does it have to be one or the other? What (to flog a dead pony) about neutral monism? And what about the extended mind idea? What about whole groups of people all falling in lockstep to the same idea, belief, or placebo? Is that just an issue related to the material consciousness within each person's own mind, or is there some sort of shared consciousness that we take part in to produce these communal effects?

Enquiring minds want to know!

Wegener's Folly

Believing is seeing. Anyone who believes that their consciousness and its observations are solely dispassionate and objective, may need to examine that in itself as a belief system. Our reality is not *reality*, but only our particular version, our own projections on the world around us of our beliefs, thoughts, prejudices, pet peeves, enthusiasms, hopes, and fears. This is actually quite a subversive take on the way that we are normally used to looking at things. It stands in contrast to the supposed objectiveness of scientism, and as the stories below demonstrate, it can have global consequences when everyone buys into a particular version of reality that may not be true, but seems likely, and seems to make sense.

Armand Diaz, writing in the online *Astrology News Service*, notes that "Scientists consider themselves objective and impartial, but it is not scientists but the scientific method that has objectivity. Participating in the scientific method doesn't wipe out the partialities and prejudices that are endemic to human experience." Entrenched belief dulls our ability to be truly open-minded. If we want to more effectively see the world as it is, and to grow in understanding, we have to be on guard against our own prejudices and projections. Here to demonstrate this are some stories from the scientific literature; politics, religion, astrology, and psychology all have plenty of examples in their own spheres.

***

Dr. Barry Marshall is an Australian physician and researcher. In 2005, he received the Nobel Prize in Physiology or Medicine—a prestigious award, as one might imagine, associated with acclaim and honors. But his reputation wasn't always quite so elevated. Barry was born in Kalgoorlie, Australia, and received his Bachelor of Medicine and Surgery from the University of Western Australia in 1974. Shortly after this, along with Robin Warren, he came up with the idea that stomach ulcers were caused by a bacterium known as H. pylori. This went counter to the current thinking of the time: that ulcers were caused by stress and spicy food. Marshall presented his ideas to various physicians, researchers, and medical conferences, only to be met with scorn and skepticism. Time and again he was shut down and told to go home by the medical establishment. Medical experts at the time "*knew*" that bacteria couldn't live in the stomach: it was simply too acidic. Hydrochloric acid, after all, was strong enough to dissolve nails. Anything alive would be killed instantly in this environment. Besides, they also already knew the cause of ulcers. What more was there to look at?

Frustrated with being discounted by the existing experts, Marshall persisted in a uniquely spectacular way. In 1984, he willfully drank a solution containing H. pylori bacteria, expecting that later on it might cause him some problems. Much to his surprise, within three days he was vomiting, and within a week an endoscopy showed massive gastric inflammation. Two weeks from his ingestion, he then took antibiotics, and miraculously cured the documented ulcer that he had given himself. The medical world of stomach ulcers was at that moment instantly and completely turned on its axis. Now, for next to nothing, with a dose of inexpensive antibiotics, anyone can be cured of an ulcer in a very short time. In an interview with *Discover* Magazine in 2010, Marshall stated "To gastroenterologists, the concept of a germ causing ulcers was like saying that the Earth is flat. After that I realized my paper was going to have difficulty being accepted. You think, 'It's science; it's got to be accepted.' But it's not an absolute given. The idea was too weird." Marshall, in the interview, credits himself with maintaining an open mind during his investigations, and *Discover* states that "Marshall's story serves as both an inspiration and an antidote to hubris in the face of the unknown." Indeed. For the previous ulcer researchers, believing was seeing. They already "knew" what caused ulcers. They didn't need to be bothered with new ideas. They were unable initially to see the new way of looking at the problem.

***

"Like saying the Earth is flat." Not much of a controversy there today, nor is there any controversy regarding the earth orbiting the sun. But in 1473, when Nicolaus Copernicus was born, that wasn't the case. As early as the 3rd century BC a Greek, Aristarchus of Samos, had speculated that the earth revolved around the sun, rather than the other way around. But this line of thinking had largely been lost to history, and it simply made the utmost sense that the earth was the center of the cosmos, being orbited by the sun, moon, planets, stars, and the odd comet. The Catholic Church made sure that heretics to this view were quickly shut down. The whole philosophical basis of theology at that time rested on man's special importance, and his central place in the universe, directly under God.

So Copernicus's idea that the earth orbited the sun was quite revolutionary, and he was not only thinking outside the box, but was willing to go against the entire establishment's view of the universe—at least in private. It is difficult to imagine at this point in history just how radical the change from a geocentric to a heliocentric perspective must have been. Einstein's later revolutions were likely no more anarchic than this novel line of thinking, which also helped push forward the Renaissance in Europe. In addition to being a cosmologist, Copernicus was also a "physician, classics scholar, translator, governor, diplomat and economist" (Wikipedia). Obviously he was a very bright man. So bright, in fact, that he kept his new conception mostly to himself throughout his lifetime, publishing his conclusions only in the year of his death, and then dedicating them to Pope Paul III, likely a pre-emptive strike that didn't fool the Catholic Church for very long.

Giordano Bruno and Galileo were not so skillful in dealing with the Church. Bruno, born in 1548, five years after Copernicus' death, was quite advanced in his thinking. He not only embraced Copernicus' heliocentrism, he went on to propose that the stars themselves were in fact distant suns, each surrounded by their own planets as in our own solar system, and in fact possibly harboring life of their own.

He also proposed that the universe itself was in fact infinite, having no center at all. For his avant-garde thinking, he unsurprisingly underwent a seven-year trial for heresy, during which he paid minor lip service to being contrite, but remained largely defiant and proud of his vision. He was burned at the stake in 1600, and his ashes dumped in the Tiber river.

The Church's Cardinal Bellarmino, who was instrumental in Bruno's demise, also had a bone to pick with Galileo. Galileo Galilei, the last in our cosmological triumvirate, was born in 1564, 16 years after Bruno. Like Copernicus, he was a Pisces with Sun/Uranus aspects. (See Richard Tarnas' excellent meditation on this configuration in his 1995 book *Prometheus the Awakener*. Tarnas himself is also a Pisces with Sun aspecting Uranus.)

Galileo is often considered to be the "father of modern science," and his accomplishments were many and varied. Among them, he improved the telescope, and discovered the moons of Jupiter—which was ultimately to be the last nail in the coffin for an earth-centered cosmos. But at the time, a heliocentric universe was still very controversial, and the Church, perhaps noting with alarm the additional people joining up with Copernicus's and Bruno's ideas of a few years earlier, again put their foot down with Galileo. In 1616, under orders from Pope Paul V, Cardinal Bellarmino went after Galileo, the first of the great scientist's many ongoing run-ins with the Church. These ultimately culminated in Galileo's spending the last nine years of his life under house arrest, dying at age 77 in 1642.

It is easy to think, in light of all this, that it was simply a case of the Church holding back scientific progress. But in an excellent article in the January 2014 issue of *Scientific American* titled "The Case Against Copernicus," by Dennis Danielson and Christopher M. Graney, they point out that in fact "Copernicus's revolutionary theory that the earth travels around the sun upended more than a millennium's worth of scientific and religious wisdom.... Most scientists refused to accept this theory for many decades—even after Galileo made his epochal observations with his telescope... Their objections were not only theological. Observational evidence supported a competing cosmology—the 'geoheliocentrism' of Tycho Brahe." It simply *made sense* that the sun revolved around the earth—why, anyone could look out of their window and see that! Why would anyone want to tax their brain to entertain ridiculous ideas to the contrary? Again, all people—even highly intelligent and educated people—find it extremely difficult to change their thinking, to let go of things that they "know" are true, that seem self-evident. Is it any wonder that astrology has been written off by much of the modern world? Of *course* the planets can't influence us! Just look out the window. See how far away they are? Ridiculous!

In 1992, celebrated as the 400th anniversary of Galileo's telescopic observations, the Catholic Church finally apologized for the way he was treated. New ideas can sometimes take a while for us to get used to.

(As an interesting aside regarding the oft-repeated idea that people used to think that the earth was flat, Douglas Main wrote an article in the January 28, 2016 edition of Newsweek titled "Even in the Middle Ages, People Didn't Think the Earth Was Flat." He notes that "With extraordinary few exceptions, no educated person in the history of Western Civilization from the third century B.C. onward believed that the Earth was flat," per historian Jeffrey Burton Russell, writing in 1997. Main points out that this seems to have been an after-the-fact idea and fiction concocted in the 19th century. But why? Why bother perpetuating falsehoods? "Russell and Gould suggest that the flat-earth myth was used to demonize Christians and religion in general, and to lionize scientists...the falsehood about the spherical earth became a colorful and unforgettable part of a larger falsehood: the falsehood of the eternal war between science (good) and religion (bad) throughout Western history." Hmmm.)

***

Even the great Einstein was subject to the occasional error of thinking, and stuck in his beliefs in at least two significant ways. First, his calculations about the cosmos showed that the universe was not stable, but likely either contracting or expanding. This did not sit well with Einstein's beliefs about the universe as a durable and unchanging cosmos, and he found that by fudging things a bit and adding in a "cosmological constant," he could make the universe stand still. (He later called this "the biggest blunder of my life.") As mentioned earlier, Einstein also came to an impasse in his ability to accept many tenets of the new quantum theory, although he had previously helped set this revolution in motion. He balked at Bohr's quantum discoveries and ideas (particularly during the EPR paradox episode), and could never fully accept the implications of Heisenberg's uncertainty principle. He approached entanglement, the basis of the upcoming quantum computer revolution, with derision and disbelief. It would seem that believing is seeing, even for great men.

***

Finally, although there are many other examples throughout history and throughout science that are readily researched, we will tip our hats to Alfred Wegener. Although several people through the years had remarked on how the various continents were shaped in such a way that if rearranged they might "fit together," It was Wegener who formally proposed in 1912 that all of the continents on earth had at one time formed a single landmass called Pangaea, and that they had somehow become separated. He coined the term "continental drift." but was unable to explain how this might have occurred.

He was immediately and thoroughly attacked from every side: German, British, and American. How *dare* he propose geological theories; he was merely a lecturer at Marburg University, and his specialties were meteorology and astronomy, not geology. Richard Conniff, in an excellent telling of this story in the June 2012 *Smithsonian* magazine titled "When the Earth Moved," talks of German geologists referring to his theory as "delirious ravings" and

American geologists calling it "Germanic pseudoscience." He also points out that one geologist who set out to crush Wegener—Thomas, C. Chamberlain at the University of Chicago—had an unstated rationale that apparently went "If we are to believe Wegener's hypothesis, we must forget everything which has been learned in the last 70 years and start all over again." The naysayers prevailed, and Wegener was marginalized for decades. Finally, according to Conniff, "The turnabout on his theory came relatively quickly, in the mid-60's, as older geologists died off and younger ones began to accumulate proof of seafloor spreading and vast tectonic plates grinding across each other deep within the earth." Wegener, unfortunately, did not live to see this. On a humanitarian mission to bring food 250 miles to some arctic researchers in Greenland during the winter of 1930, he had died in the cold along the way; he was 50 years old. His body was later found, and a cross now marks the spot.

***

So what are we to learn from these, and countless other similar stories that exist—many on the personal and smaller scale of our own lives and experiences? We learn that beliefs are deep, lasting, and entrenched. They are not easily changed. We learn that people mistrust the new, the odd. We learn how difficult it is to change the status quo, the dominant paradigm. We learn that many people, not just scientists, have vested interests: they have spent their whole careers "betting on red" so to speak: staking their reputations on a particular idea or belief set, and are understandably threatened and disconcerted when storms arrive that might swamp their boat, or prove them wrong. We learn that people have an ego attachment to their supposed expertise, and God help those questioning their ideas that don't have the "proper credentials." We learn that professional cliques form and are difficult to break into. People circle the wagons: "you can't come into our club—you're different." We learn that "the devil you know is often better than the devil you don't." We learn that changes do happen, but they often happen only after a sizeable, decades-long, hard-fought and messy battle; and then frequently only after the original stake-holders pass away, and a new generation takes their place. We learn that many people can believe (and control the established party line on) certain things, even with very sketchy evidence, but if you want to change the paradigm, you'd better have immaculate and irrefutable proof.

But things do eventually change. Science, cosmology, racism, women's rights, environmental consciousness; on and on, they all change. Change, in fact, is the nature of the universe. Nothing is permanent. Astrology was run out of town by the solidification of the then-new scientific paradigm during the Enlightenment, and religion is currently waning in the age of posthumanism. Things change. But science continues to have (and always will have) unsolved mysteries, and perhaps some more open-minded scientists or physicists at some point will once again deem astrology or alternative consciousness to be worthy of investigation. Perhaps there will appear some brave soul such as those listed above, unafraid of ridicule, who will test the waters, pay attention to the various canaries in the coal mines out on the fringes, and tie things all together.

Zuni and the Doorknob

We have at this writing a white and tan cat named Zuni. He's half Tabby and half Siamese, and is a great little guy, very inquisitive, very social and involved, and very intelligent. (He's an Aquarius.) He always wants to be in the middle of whatever's going on, and his kitty IQ is probably a good cut above average. We got him from a nearby no-kill animal shelter at only a couple of months old, and he is a joy to be around. We were told that he was from Gallup, New Mexico, and was brought here with a bunch of other kittens that would otherwise have been killed there. Driving home with him from the shelter, my wife and I were putting some effort into coming up with a name that sounded "Western," in deference to his origin, and settled on "Zuni" because we were aware that there was a Zuni Indian tribe somewhere out West; they are the ones who, along with the Hopis, are known for their colorful Kachina dolls.

Good name, we decided, and after getting home we looked up the Zuni Indians, and discovered that their reservation sits right on the outskirts of Gallup, New Mexico. Synchronicities are described as meaningful coincidences. Hmmm.

Zuni is smart, but how smart can a cat be? Zuni is smart enough that he has figured out that opening a door has something to do with the doorknob. (Animals always seem to be wanting to go in or out through doors—that frustrating quest for freedom.) He watches us open doors, and whatever brain processes that are involved in doing analysis in the cat brain go to work. What are his conclusions? He definitely knows that the doorknob is the key. After watching, he stretches up and touches the doorknob, plays with it, tries both paws. He knows it opens the door, but there is something missing. Nothing happens. Eventually, he gives up and goes back to simply waiting for someone to open the door. He may go through this for several times before he gives up for good.

He doesn't seem to try and turn the knob; he just bats at it or touches it. He knows that the knob opens the door, but perhaps hasn't noticed that it is the turning motion that opens it. Or perhaps he has and realizes that he simply is unable to do so. But what does he really know of the doorknob? Does he really know that it is the turning that is the key? Does he understand the mechanism that this turning effects? Does he understand all of the engineering and pieces that go into a lock? Does he understand how a key works, how a lock works, that the concept of "lock" even exists? Does he understand that a doorknob is made from metal, and how that differs from wood? Does he know of or understand the smelting process, or the mining process? Does he understand that metals are composed of atoms and molecules, and that they are of certain types that conduct electricity, as opposed to others that don't? Does he understand electricity? Does he understand that molecules are composed of atoms, and that these atoms are composed of smaller units still? Does he understand that this doorknob exists in a house, and what a house is all about? Does he understand that this house is resting on a planet that is flying through space in a universe full of stars? Is he able to convey his knowledge of the doorknob to fellow creatures?

He of course knows none of this, and most importantly, *he doesn't know that he doesn't know*. These are the questions not asked, questions that would never occur to him to ask, that he is in fact unable to ask. This knowledge, this level of reality exists side by side with whatever reality he lives in. He is infused in it. He looks at it every day, and yet it is invisible to him, forever beyond his access. He lives in this reality, and yet knows nothing of it. It is not a parallel universe: it is *his* universe, and yet it is hidden to him. His world is a smaller subset, and more limited. What portion of "actual reality" (our own hubristic version) does he then perceive, one might ask? For him, his vision of the reality around him is complete, or nearly so. There's just that nagging doorknob thing...

It's easy for us (as "superior beings") to hover above, and see and talk about all of this, and about Zuni's limitations. We know that cats do not have the brainpower that we have, and that's OK. We understand that simpler creatures on down the phylogenetic scale have even more limited realities. But what of ours? We *assume* that we see, and have access to, a fairly complete vision of reality. But do we? What portion of reality are *we* actually privy to? What are *our* questions not asked, our questions that we don't even *know* to ask, the portions of reality that may be forever closed off to us? Man as the centerpiece of the universe died 400 years ago when Galileo trained his telescope on Jupiter. Are we alone in the universe? Are there superior beings out there who have a vaster knowledge, a larger grasp of overall reality than we do? Even bringing that up is actually somewhat of a red herring, as if there were, then they themselves may also have limitations in their own knowledge and perceptions. R=K+1 leaves room for a lot of really large numbers.

So the question is: *do* we ourselves have the brainpower to ultimately understand everything? Where *is* all of that dark matter that we can't find—dark matter that wasn't even known about a few decades ago, dark matter that was the question we didn't know to ask? (Dark matter here simply being the latest example in a string of ongoing and completely unforeseen things popping up out of nowhere, while we're busy searching for something else.) I saw some graffiti in a bar in San Francisco called The Plough and the Stars many years ago that read "There's been an alarming increase in the things I know nothing about." Indeed. What don't we know that we don't even have a clue that we don't know?

We're pretty clever, and our self-congratulating ability to figure things out has given us the sense that we'll one day be able to understand everything: it's only a matter of time. But is it? *Do* we have the capabilities to finally perceive everything there is to know about everything? That seems somewhat presumptuous. Why should our brains be the ultimate clumps of cells that could never be topped by other brains (natural or artificial) that have increased capacity to perceive things not even on our radar? Perhaps in all of our braininess, we are actually not so much further along than Zuni standing on his hind paws batting at the doorknob. Perhaps reality is that big, that amazing, and that unknown. We know something is out there that might allow us physically or mentally to open the door, but we can't quite figure out what it is. Wouldn't that be something?

Great Idea!

The Greek philosopher and author Plato died in 348 BCE, and the Swiss psychiatrist Carl Jung died in 1961. The gulf between these two men, both in space and in time, was large. The world that existed for each of them was quite different, and yet in certain ways, they travelled parallel intellectual tracks. Both of them were in search of an unseen substrate that they felt somehow stitched together reality as we live it daily. Additionally, it was between these two dates that the current version of Western astrology was laid down, added to, amended many times, and has achieved its current organic and adaptable form. Each of these men, consciously or not, added to that development.

What *is* our world? What does it consist of? What is its substance, what is its structure, and how might we understand it? These questions have puzzled man throughout his history, and will no doubt continue to do so for quite some time to come. The quest for how the world works may somewhat arbitrarily and artificially be broken down into two camps for convenience. They might be labeled physics and philosophy. There are those who feel that the world is largely physical and mechanical at its base, although allowing for the bounds of probability, or multiple worlds, or whatever current exotic speculations might exist. This camp bases their understanding on energy, but uses only physics-based energy; generally this is energy that might at some point be able to be converted into matter, or understood on a material basis. The other camp consists of those who feel that there exists something beyond our current conceptions of the material: some energies, forces, or structures that may not fit into our current models of the manifest, concrete world. There are many that fall into this camp; Plato and Jung were two of these.

Plato's idea was that the world was a manifestation of invisible "Forms": archetypal, non-physical, informational energies that organized reality into certain categories. Plato was a student of Socrates, and was very enamored of his mentor and his philosophies. There are no writings existing from Socrates himself; all philosophy related to Socrates comes down to us through Plato's *Dialogs*, which feature Socrates and his thoughts. Thus, it is difficult to ascertain what portion of the concept of Forms came from Plato vs. Socrates, but it is likely that this idea is much more from Plato himself than from Socrates. At any rate, it is an idea that attained a lot of respect in its time, and is still taught in philosophy classes. It is such a part of Plato's writings that it would be difficult to separate it from him.

Plato approached the world using primarily deductive reasoning, and sought to derive specific truths from general principles. He observed that a tree seemed more real than its shadow (as the shadow was more ephemeral and changing), and thus came to the conclusion that the actual tree had a higher level of reality than that of its shadow. Similarly, he looked around at the various varieties of trees, noted that trees appeared and disappeared (were born and died), and asked what it was about trees that could possibly be more real than the trees themselves; what could be beyond the temporal and changing physical trees that we perceive with our senses? He came to the idea of what he called the Forms.

His writings are ultimately not firm and final when it comes to the Forms; they were apparently a work in progress, even in his own mind, and throughout his life. Nonetheless, the basic idea is fairly simple. The Forms are more or less abstract ideas, or organizing principles of various sorts, that actually exist nowhere and everywhere, but that may be perceived by the mind, and are unchanging and eternal. Thus, the idealized Form, or idea, of a tree may exist and be tapped into by our consciousness as an image (although the Form itself is beyond image). This Form may then be found manifested in the world as the lesser sense objects of actual trees, or, to move one step further away from the Form, as their shadows. Both of these may be understood as lower level examples of "Treeness." There is a direct analogy here from shadow to tree, as from tree to Form. Forms are the highest reality, and math was one of the Forms that held particular interest for Plato and the Greeks, as math seemed plainly immutable, eternal, and never-changing. Although not as straightforward as math, these same universal qualities were assigned to other Forms such as Beauty, Reason, etc. Another well-known Form was that of "The Good," which Plato felt should guide human life and society. Ultimately, the Forms themselves were reality, and any perceptions by us were simply sensate subsets or sub-examples of this higher plane. There are strong parallels to astrology here.

The idea that reality is of a higher level than we ordinarily perceive is portrayed beautifully by Plato in a very famous scenario known as The Allegory of the Cave, from Plato's *Republic.* (There are quite a few visualizations of this online.) In it, he describes (through Socrates) a situation in which a group of prisoners have been chained together since childhood, seated, facing a wall inside a dark cave. Their heads are fixed so that they cannot see anything but the wall in front of them. Unseen by them, there is a fire burning behind them, and a low wall in front of the fire (but still behind them), on which are paraded various people and objects in a puppet-like fashion. The shadows of this play are projected onto the wall in front of them. All of their lives, they have been able to see only the two dimensional shadows of these objects, and thus for them, the shadows, and their limited two dimensions, are the only world that they know. They get to know the various shadows and give names to them, as they have become their only reality. They know no other, and suspect no other. The outside three dimensional world is the question that they don't know to ask, that doesn't occur to them. They are metaphorically and literally in the dark.

At one point, however, a prisoner is freed, and though afraid, is dragged up out of the cave and into the sunlight. At first, he is confused and dazed, blinded by the light, and disoriented. After a while, however, he is able to slowly see what is going on around him, and begins to understand—dimly at first, and then possibly in an "aha!" moment—that what he has previously seen and experienced all of his life is but a poor imitation of reality; a pale shadow of the way things really are. The full three dimensions now wash over him, and he is amazed and transformed. Excited, he descends back into the cave to share with his former fellow dwellers what he has seen, his newfound knowledge and insight. However, upon returning to the cave, his eyes, now used to full light, are clouded and he is nearly blind. He is not comfortable in his former world. He attempts to share with the prisoners his new insights; but they, seeing that he is blind and stumbling, make fun of him, and discount what he is saying. In fact, comfortable and entrenched in their known reality, they agree that if anyone else should try and drag them up to this blinding, obviously inferior world, he should be summarily killed!

This allegory is beautiful, useful, and instructive to anyone wanting to improve their understanding of the world. It can be applied to every facet of life, from science to metaphysics. It is today the 4th dimension; it may be the 5th. It is similar to the allegory of *Flatland*. Whether it is physics or consciousness. other insights, or spirituality: some self-examination will reveal that *we* are the ones in the cave, and the fact is that we don't know what is up that passage to the light. We can get reports, or hear stories; we can form opinions and speculations; but we must each find out for ourselves what lies up there. For Plato, it is the Forms that lie above us, up the dimly lit shaft to the bright sun of reality. The Forms are above and give rise to what is below. The Forms, although invisible and sometimes difficult to discern, determine and structure reality. In the same way that time provides dimension to space, they provide dimension, depth, and meaning to the shadowy manifestations of the world below them.

It may be noted that Plato's student, Aristotle, did not side with him in this more philosophical and deductive method of investigation. Aristotle, a towering figure in his own right, had a more concrete turn of mind, and did not hold with such abstract thinking. He developed, in many ways, the forerunner of today's scientific method, by using empiricism and inductive reasoning to discover things about the world. Instead of Plato's top down method of using the Forms to explain reality, Aristotle preferred to examine things carefully and scientifically from the bottom up, and to then draw inferences from these experiments and examinations, leading to higher level conclusions.

The two opposing views from two millennia ago still today beg the question as to whether there is any place for questioning existence apart from materialism and the scientific method, which has come to dominate Western thought. Many people certainly feel that there is, even in light of the wonders that science has brought us in the 21st century. The question of *meaning* still hangs out there, often unanswered, and this is more Plato's realm than Aristotle's.

***

Jung started out as somewhat of a protégé to Freud. He was younger, in the same field, and his Taurus Moon was conjunct Freud's Sun. (There was later on for Jung another very interesting relationship with physicist Wolfgang Pauli, another Taurus.) Freud was initially somewhat of a father figure, but Jung soon began to chaff. Jung, from his early days was interested in a larger realm, and no doubt felt confined by Freud's intense emphasis on the personal unconscious, as well as Freud's preoccupation with sexuality. Jung began to develop his own theories about the personality, and about human consciousness and behavior. He was very interested in how various cultures across time, and across the globe, appeared to have many of the same motifs in their stories, art, and traditions. Mother goddesses on one side of the earth seemed to reflect and mimic Mother goddesses on the other side of the earth. They both seemed to have echoes in contemporary Western art and literature as well, and to show up in film and other media. Wherever humans were, the same ideas were to be found.

Jung was a well-educated man, and it is certain that he had been exposed to Plato's Forms. He questioned reality in the same way that Plato had: all of what we see is changing, manifesting and disappearing. What might be permanent? What might be constant, what might give rise to the ephemeral world as we know it? What might be constant in our psyche, that is also always changing? He also saw that many of the same themes that appeared in personal psychoanalysis and dreams were displayed in world myths. What was the connection? What was the unifying force? He proposed the idea of archetypes, which are very similar to Plato's Forms. They would function as the unifying force that he was looking for, and would function, as the Forms had for Plato, as an unchanging matrix independent of time and space that would give birth to the sensate items of the world, as well as to the structure of our consciousness. Indeed, human culture and societies could be laid at their feet. Where *were* the archetypes? They were here and nowhere. Jung compared them to the structure of a crystal: the structure itself was invisible, and did not exist in any material sense; and yet the crystal depended on it, and only revealed itself in a way that displayed the crystalline structure giving it form. Similarly, for Jung, it was their amazingly consistent *appearances* which indeed announced the invisible archetypes. They were similar to math in Plato's Forms: the archetypes could not be seen, felt, or touched, and yet manifestations of various phenomena depended on them, and expressed them.

Jung saw that the archetypes were not only often unconscious and always invisible, but that they appeared both within the individual psyche, and in the world at large. Thus, he posited the collective unconscious as a counterpart to the personal unconscious, a concept which Freud had pioneered. Now there could be a connection, an invisible thread that wove through cultures, and through humans, and connected the two. A thread that allowed human consciousness to be, if not the expression of the Divine, at least the expression of larger forces that connected the varied and diverse cultures of the world. And it made sense: from a small beginning, it has increasingly become part of our way of looking at and talking about the world.

Archetype as a word and concept was once rare; now anyone with the slightest bit of education is familiar with it, and uses it in everyday life. Joseph Campbell did much to popularize this concept with his books and media appearances, especially in talking about *The Hero with a Thousand Faces*, his examination of the Hero archetype throughout various cultures, and in people's personal lives. We all live the Hero's journey: our lives *are* the same journey, driven by the Sun, the Self, played out each in our own way. Campbell's work (in addition to Jung's) also reinforced the idea that archetypes are not only people (the Mother, the Wise Old Man, etc.), but can also be events, myths, situations, concepts, and similar things. Jung was a Leo, and Campbell had his Moon in that sign: who better that these two to understand the Hero's journey? For a modern example of this principle in action, one may investigate the wonderful movies made by fellow Leo James Cameron, and watch the movie *Deepsea Challenge*, which documents his quest to be the first human to descend to the lowest known point on earth, in the Pacific Ocean. Challenger Deep lies 35,787 feet below the surface of the waves, and Cameron succeeds in his Hero's journey here, in a craft he himself helped design. His Moon is in Pisces, and he has stated that he always felt drawn to the water; his most famous movie is *Titanic*.

Nearly every movie features a Hero, and the archetype goes back through Shakespeare to the Greeks. It is universal—that's what archetypes are. Plato's journey of the prisoner leaving the cave can be easily thought of as a "journey towards enlightenment" (or knowledge) archetype that many people can identify with. In fact, it is just another variation of the Hero's journey.

The archetypes then, like the Forms, are ideas in a sense. But they are not ideas that only occur to us individually, or that are only in our minds. They seem to exist independently in the universe (or at least in human culture), and then give rise to, or manifest as, our personal ideas. We are the visible crystals expressing these structures. They are universal ideas, or ideals, or organizing principles. The question then is, are they "real?" What does real even mean, if we can easily speak of love, beauty, justice, math, and understanding as being things that have a real existence? This is the same problem that Plato faced. Aristotle took many people with him when he brought reality down to what could be seen and measured by empirical evidence. But many of those pragmatic people still glanced backwards with fascination and curiosity at Plato and Jung. There are even those who, attempting to straddle the gap, have tried to "find the archetypes" in a more physical sense, by looking at DNA, etc. But this has proved elusive: the archetypes seemingly belong to a realm that we can easily see in action around us every day *if we are looking*, and yet one which is not amenable to statistical analysis or calculators. There are parallels here in the quest to "prove" astrology, which is talked about in a later section. Both lie closer to the realm of magic than machine. Nightly, our dreams attest to this realm; but by day many often scoff and deny, or simply ignore.

Later in his life, Jung expanded even further his understanding of the archetypes. He had started with *psychological* principles which tied the individual unconscious to the collective unconscious of the world, of humans. He began to consider, however, that the archetypes could also be used as a bridge between the world of matter and the world of consciousness; could act as an invisible connecting principle. This again was territory that would have been familiar to Plato, and this was also part of Jung's discussions with the physicist Wolfgang Pauli at one point in his career. Jung came up with the idea of a Unus Mundus, a single underlying reality that gives birth to all else in the world, and of which everything is an expression, a subsidiary shadow, so to speak. This Oneness would be similar to that spoken of by the many sages of history. Its expression in the known world would be through the mechanisms of archetypes and synchronicity, a concept also pioneered by Jung, and covered in the following chapter. The relation of all of this to consciousness should be obvious. The ideas of the Forms and the archetypes have more apparent connections to the mind, than to matter.

***

Between the time of Plato and that of Jung, Western astrology developed, flourished, waned, waxed, waned, and yet, although on the ropes, it remains a daily presence for many in the modern world. So we might ask: how is astrology any worse, or even different, than Plato's Forms or Jung's archetypes, both of which (or at least Jung's version) are taken seriously in the modern world? Archetypes, as popularly considered, are mainly confined to psychology, literature, anthropology, or cultural studies—fields that have found tolerance for their difficult-to-pin-down, benign quirkiness. These are assumed to be minimally predictive, non-"hard" sciences, mainly because they deal with those unpredictable and frustrating humans. Guess what? So does astrology. Just a point of note. The larger philosophical implications of Jung are rarely considered. *Are* there non-physical structuring elements to reality that may work through interactions with consciousness, or do these elements simply arise *from* consciousness? An interesting chicken and egg question. Add in Jung's synchronicity to the archetypes, and things start to get philosophically uncomfortable very quickly.

***

Arthur Koestler, in his book *The Sleepwalkers*, writes: "Some six thousand years ago, when the human mind was still half asleep, Chaldean priests were standing on watch towers, scanning the stars..."

John Anthony West and Jan Gerhard Toonder, in their 1970 book *The Case for Astrology*, quote this, and update the idea: "Vilified by science for three centuries, derided by philosophy, psychology, medicine, the law, and every other orthodox branch of modern learning, astrology refuses to die." Their book, of course, attempts to convey exactly why that is.

Astrology is nothing more than a specific group of Archetypes expressed in conjunction with the dynamic movements of various celestial bodies. So where *do* archetypes or astrology fit into human explorations? Searching the stars (mainly the planets, sun, and moon, actually) for signs or guidance goes way back with us humans, and it would be foolish to think, as some scientists apparently do, that the entire enterprise has been one of haphazardly making things up and convincing others to buy into random delusions. Even gullible people would likely tire of this after a while. People have stuck around because there *is* something to it that they can perceive.

These early searchers were using what would later become enshrined as scientific techniques, ones that would be recognized by Aristotle and others after him: empiric investigations and careful observation, coupled with attempts to correlate positions of the celestial bodies with known events or occurrences on earth. One must not underestimate the pragmatic intentions and keen observations of these early proto-astronomer/astrologers. In actuality, they were, whether consciously or not, trying to bridge the ephemeral idealism expressed by Plato with the boots on the ground approach of Aristotle.

Modern astrologers *also* come to their interest in the subject in the exact same way that those nascent astrologers did 6,000 years ago: they investigate for themselves, and find correlations. That scientists don't see that they are doing so says more about the scientists than the astrologers. These correlations hint at, or lay bare, predicted themes and commonalities that astrologers can see operating in the people and the world around them.

Greek (Hellenistic) astrology developed from mainly Babylonian influences, but also included some Egyptian ideas, as well as other scattered contributions. It eventually reached its flowering, and was codified in Ptolemy's *Tetrabiblos*, around 160 AD. The Greek Stoics contributed philosophically to its development, as they were keenly interested in fate, and how this could best be determined and worked with. At the same time, the flowering of Greek gods (especially the "Twelve Olympians," although there is only a partial correlation to astrology) assisted in putting into place not only the fated nature of astrology, but also the archetypal one. Astrology became solidified as being archetypal, and the archetypes became disseminated and accepted. And astrology has indeed developed a very intricate and sophisticated archetypal system.

So if we talk about the Jungian archetype of the "Lover," what are we talking about? Certainly at minimum we are talking about a common theme for humans that reverberates across time and cultures; one that everyone can relate to, and one that appears constantly in dreams and art. But astrology goes further than this: it takes the archetype of the Lover and shows that there are different types of lovers: there are star-struck lovers, jealous lovers, generous lovers, parsimonious lovers, friendly lovers, controlling lovers, disappointed lovers, happy lovers, quirky lovers, constant lovers, and many more. The level and amount of archetypal detail with astrology blossoms and explodes. But astrology goes even further: it states that these various archetypes not only exist, but that they can be correlated with the position of the planets in our solar system.

Wow.

It's not difficult to understand why astrology is so difficult to accept for those who haven't investigated it. What an odd and radical idea that is. It was radical 6,000 years ago, and it is radical today. Scientists don't like it, because there is no "physical" explanation or mechanism. But that just gets us back to the question of whether there may be things in the universe that cannot yet be explained by known physical processes. The more one studies these various alternative disciplines, the more likely it seems that there may be. That is up and out of Plato's cave, however: most people are still staring at the shadows on the dim walls below. So whether astrology has any (yet unknown) physical mechanism remains an open question at this point, although most scientists would have us believe that it is closed.

***

Evolutionary biology attempts to explain some human behaviors that may be confused with archetypes, such as altruism or attachment, and it is certainly true that hormones play a role in all lovers' behaviors. But that is not what we're talking about here. The archetype of the Lover exists independently from any actual human relationships or biological processes, just as trees exist independently from their shadows, and the archetype of "Tree" exists independently from any actual trees. Venus moves into certain positions in our charts, and the archetype of the Lover raises its head in our lives, either positively or negatively. The archetype is constant and ever-present; our experience of the archetype is varying.

The bottom line in all of this, as in many things that we are considering, is simply a series of open-ended questions: are there archetypal, organizing principles in human life, or in the cosmos, that our behaviors (biologic or not) are subsets of, or influenced by? Are archetypes or Forms "all in our heads?" Are they simply a way that human consciousness organizes itself, or do they somehow have an existence outside of human consciousness? Are they possibly part of, or evidence for, a more collective, distributed, or universal Consciousness, or unconscious? Do they, as Jung began to speculate after his conversations with Pauli, somehow tie consciousness to matter? Might they have some sort of a biological basis, somehow be "hardwired" into our brains? How and why do they seemingly affect us differently as the various planets move in their orbits? As long as Plato and Jung are taught, these questions are still valid ones.

Final Comments

So what *is* consciousness? We have looked here at some hints that consciousness may be more difficult to pin down than we might have thought, and we are looking throughout this book at some examples that hopefully demonstrate how difficult it is to keep an open mind. Because the thing is this: if we want the good stuff, if we want the magic, if we want the whole picture, then we need to get out of our boxes. If we are to do an honest and open examination of any of the issues in this book—modern physics, consciousness, synchronicity, metaphysics, or astrology—then the freedom of new ways of looking at things would seem to be an absolute prerequisite. The status quo, the accepted paradigms will not suit us well here. We are leaving the charted paths, the well-worn trails, and must pay attention not only to what is right in front of us, but to the seemingly insignificant rustle in the bushes off to the side, for that may turn out to be where the important thing is to be found.

Does consciousness then create the world, and is consciousness primary over materialism? We don't know, but consciousness is likely, at the very least, to play a *role* in its creation. We *do* know that consciousness creates our own particular worlds at the personal level: believing is seeing.

Synchronicity

A Curious Thing

At some point during my later college days, I had come home to visit and stay with my parents in New Orleans. I was out one evening with some friends, driving around the city, killing time, listening to music, talking, and smoking pot. I came home, not late, and lay down to sleep. Full sleep did not come, however; I tossed and turned, and entered a half-conscious no man's land of nod. That is, I was in a state sometimes known as "lucid dreaming": I was not awake, and yet I was in a twilight place where I was seemingly dreaming, and yet aware that I was dreaming. I dreamed this:

In New Orleans, there is a large building at the foot of Canal St. on the Mississippi river, which was then known as the World Trade Center (not to be confused with the better-known one that was in New York). It is still there, but as of this writing is empty, and future plans are up in the air. It was built in 1967, and stands 33 stories tall. Near the top, there is an observation deck with a metal railing surrounding the whole building, on which one could walk out and around the building, high up, for views of the city. I have never been to the observation deck, but one may see it even by looking up from the ground.

In my "dream" (which was more like a vision, or an observation of myself from the outside), I imagined myself up on the observation deck with some friends. These friends were taunting me and daring me to hang over the side, suspended 33 stories up, only holding onto the railing by my hands. As young men often do, I took the dare, and found myself dangling, my hands gripping the railing, looking out over the city below, my feet waving free. Oddly, no fear seemed to be part of this. In fact, as I hung there, looking down and around, the strangest feeling washed over me. It was one best described as peace or serenity, and the thought came to me: "why not just let go?", which I then did.

(It should be pointed out that I had absolutely no interest in, or any thoughts of suicide in my life.)

What made this so vivid, however, was not just the dream or vision itself. It was that this same scenario played itself out over and over again in my mind for what seemed like about a half an hour. I simply could not move on, simply could not get my mind to progress towards something else. The vision was very intrusive. It was like a tape loop, and I had no option of stopping it. I would again be on the observation deck, my friends would again be daring me, and I would again hang by my hands from the railing. I would again have an overwhelming feeling of peace: that very distinct emotional feeling being coupled with the thought of "why not just let go?" Again, I would loosen my grip and start falling. The falling itself was untroubled, but never consummated; and this was where the loop ended each time, only to start over again. It was the *feeling* that struck me the most, and stayed with me about the whole thing. Each time, I would again let go, and the tape would return yet again to the beginning. This must have played out six or seven times. It was quite disturbing to me that I couldn't stop the loop (even though the last emotion of the scenario was one of peace). I couldn't seem to "turn it off." Finally I drifted off to real sleep.

The next morning, a woman jumped off of that same observation deck of the World Trade Center and killed herself. It was not someone that I knew. It was the first time that had ever taken place, and, as far as I know, has never happened since.

***

The late poet Maya Angelou said, "I've learned that people will forget what you said, people will forget what you did, but people will never forget how you made them feel." Emotions are more important, and carry more power, than we give credit to in the modern world. With all of these synchronistic vignettes, what's missing from the dry descriptions are the *feelings* involved. Every one of the incidents laid out in this book had certain (and often very strong) *feelings* attached to them, which are impossible to convey in the dry black and white of print. As we examine these sorts of episodes in our own lives, or in others', we see over and over that emotions often, or always, seem to play a key role in synchronistic events.

The only other time that I've matched the same odd feeling and compulsion of repetition presented above was less than a year later, when I was living with my sister in New York, on the Upper East Side. We were by no means in an upscale area, however: we were on the top floor of a 6th floor walk-up between 1st and York, not far from the river. Again one night, I lay down to sleep, and again I was distressed and locked in, as I had been during the above incident. I had the same eerie emotion of not being able to control the replay of a certain vision: this time it was not a sequence of events, but only an image. Try as I might, I could not get out of my mind the picture of a dead baby. That's all there was. Just the visage of a cold, somewhat blue-gray dead baby, lying on a blanket or fabric of some sort. There was no interacting with it, or anything else to the dream/vision. Just the baby lying there. It wouldn't go away for quite a long time, and I had the same not awake/not asleep frame of consciousness that I had had in the earlier episode. The same feeling of being deeply disturbed, but without the peaceful component this time.

It was so upsetting, and it felt so much like the other incident, that the next day I talked to my sister, and started calling people in New Orleans to see if anything had happened. I scoured the local newspapers. When I reached my parents a bit later, they told me that at nearly the exact moment that I had experienced this vision, the son of one of their neighbors two homes away had committed suicide.

This might be chalked up to simple coincidence by the reader. The reader, however, isn't privy to the odd *feeling* of significance that was involved. It was the emotional component that stuck in my mind, not the dry facts of the event. Curious, indeed.

***

Fast-forward to many years later. After meeting my present wife, we decided that it was best to look for a larger place than the small apartment that I had been living in, and we began to look together at houses for sale. One of the ones that we looked at seemed charming and near perfect: nice yard, and just the right atmosphere. My realtor was also impressed, but my wife had some nagging doubts. “There is a weird, musty smell in the living room,” she said, as we toured the house. Neither the realtor nor I could detect anything of this nature, but we looked around to appease her. We discovered, under the large rug in the living room, an actual trap door. Pulling up on this, however, revealed only a view of the ground 3 feet below; it showed that there was a crawl space under the house, which apparently gave access to the plumbing and so forth. My wife peered down into the hole below the house, but said that this didn’t seem to her to be where the musty smell was coming from. It was just coming somehow from the living room itself, although the living room was freshly painted and sunny. We looked around at the rest of the house and left; it was a nice house, definitely in the running for what we were looking for. For my wife, however, there was this lingering and difficult to pinpoint olfactory apprehension.

A few days later, my realtor called me. He had been at a meeting the night before, and just by coincidence a neighbor that lived near the house had also been there. It wasn’t somebody that he knew, and it’s unclear how the conversation drifted onto this particular property, or why he even started talking to the woman in the first place; the meeting itself had nothing to do with real estate, and was not near either of their homes, nor the house in question. Perhaps he had asked her where she lived, and mentioned that he was looking at a property nearby. Synchronicities work in mysterious ways. At any rate, she gave him some information about the person who had lived there, prior to the current owners (who may or may not have been privy to this knowledge). She stated that it had belonged to a middle-aged woman who had become despondent, and ended up committing suicide in the living room by sitting on a sofa there with a plastic bag tied around her head.

Onward and Inward

> "...thou canst not stir a flower, without the troubling of a star."—Francis Thompson (and a thank you to Victor Mansfield)

It hardly needs to be pointed out that synchronicity is currently the favorite amongst the competing theories of how astrology may work, but why *is* that? What is it about synchronicity that appeals? And what exactly *is* synchronicity? We will delve further into various astrological speculations in the next section, but because the idea of synchronicity has moved into such a core place in modern astrology, it bears a few words of its own at this point. Synchronicity itself raises the same questions of fate and connectedness as many of the other essays found in this book. Ghosts and intimations of both the block universe and the butterfly effect lurk here, as does consciousness.

(As an aside, Denver astrologer Chris Brennan has done a nice job in some of his material online in laying out four possible philosophical positions that one may take in approaching fate. He does this through examining Hellenistic astrology, but the orientations may be derived from other systems as well. These positions also need not necessarily be limited to astrologers; to varying degrees they may be considered by the curious in general. The four possibilities regarding fate are that the astrological universe is: a) completely deterministic involving causes (i.e., a physical mechanism); b) partially deterministic involving causes; c) completely deterministic involving signs (i.e. correlations, rather than causes—synchronicity, in other words); or d) partially deterministic involving signs: synchronicity again). In the modern, "humanistic" era of astrology, the last seems to be the most appealing at this time, although there is certainly wide latitude for discussion and position on this issue amongst astrologers. Note that all four involve some degree of fate or determinism; that is a prerequisite for any sort of astrology at all. If life were 100% free will, there would be no room for astrology to exist. Astrology *is* a to-whatever-extent fated connection between human life and the powerful archetypes associated with the planets and their movements.

The idea of planets "causing" their effects in terms of rays, or some other physical mechanism, has really fallen by the wayside in our modern world, simply because no one has come up with a plausible scheme for them to do so; and this seems even less likely as time goes on. So we are left almost by default with synchronicity. The two versions of synchronistic interpretation mentioned above (Chris Brennan's "signs"), in fact, mirror certain philosophical issues in modern physics. Does the synchronicity demonstrated by astrology indicate a completely deterministic situation (the "block universe," as brought to fruition by Einstein's ideas), or does it reveal an only partially deterministic one (addressed further in the next section, but more compatible with the current quantum view)? Physics itself is of course at odds with these questions, stemming in part from the difficulty of reconciling Einstein's general relativity with quantum. Even *within* quantum, Schrödinger's wave equation is deterministic, while the collapse of the wave function that it leads to is probabilistic. Might it be that astrology may actually help to shed light on this quandary? First, however, let's talk about synchronicity.

***

Jung first began mentioning synchronicity around 1930, but it was not until 1952 that he wrote his seminal paper "Synchronicity, An Acausal Connecting Principle," which pretty much "invented" synchronicity as a subject, and brought the idea out into the world. It didn't take long for this idea to take root in popular as well as more academic culture. It has fascinated more than a few people since then, not least of whom is astrologer and author Maggie Hyde, who has written cogently and extensively on Jung and his relation to this topic, and to astrology. Her 1992 book *Jung and Astrology* would seem to be the most important work here, and is highly recommended. It may be purchased from her website. (Thanks again to Chris Brennan for the tip.)

Synchronicity stemmed from Jung's fascination with, and investigations of, divination. He saw divination and synchronicity as ways for us to connect with what he called the "Unus Mundus": the underlying and unified Ground of Being from which all of reality arises. He was aided in some of these speculations by his friendship with the physicist Wolfgang Pauli, and he was also influenced by many of the world's varied cultures, which frequently spoke of this Oneness in myth, legend, and canon. The interconnectedness of all things is a given in Eastern thought, and has many adherents in the West as well; physicists and astrologers among them.

A note here is that there is more than one view of what synchronicity actually is, however. Prior to continuing, we need to step to the side for a brief clarification. The subject of synchronicity has often produced confusion in discussions at times, by actually having two separate components or variations that are frequently not spelled out; Jung himself didn't address the difference. Interestingly, however, astrology would seem to neatly bridge the two. More on that later.

One version of synchronicity may be thought of as being more "secular," physics-based, mundane, or mechanical. Maggie Hyde terms it "synchronism," and that is the term that we will use here; it seems descriptive in an appropriate way. ("Synchrony" is the root.) This alludes to only the most base level of synchronization. This version speaks simply to the connectedness of all things in a fashion that is compatible with the physical/energy world of spacetime as we currently know it, i.e. materialism. If one takes away movement, dynamism, and change, it is also compatible with the block universe.

Some physicists may be comfortable with this particular version; others with a larger vision may find it lacking. It admits no "meaning" to coincidence: coincidence here at all times remains simply mathematical chance. It is the expression of a mechanical coupling of matter and energy in spacetime. It is dry and lacks fecundity. It is intriguing in and of itself, however: again, like the block universe, anything in this particular space and time may be discovered to be connected in some fashion (which may be demonstrated through equations, if one ignores quantum) to whatever else one may care to examine in another space and time. The "butterfly effect" is found here.

All that's missing is the component of personal and emotional connection: how we actually *experience* the network, or may be able to use it. Connections are there, but like the block universe, are static and frozen (which again is somewhat of a contradiction, since physics models presuppose an energy field as primary). The positive element here is that this model very likely *does* contribute in some fashion to astrology's workings. The negative is that we are once again back to the clockwork universe, which is inadequate in explaining both our current physics as well as our current astrology.

Regardless, this really isn't what Jung himself was talking about; it is not his conception of synchronicity. For Jung, synchronicity and synchronistic events were *always* tied together with *meaning*, that is, with *consciousness* and *emotion*. Synchronicity's most common definition, in fact, simply identifies it as "meaningful coincidence." The "Curious Things" appearing throughout this book fall into that category. *Are* they simply random or incidental occurrences falling in line with the mathematical laws of chance? They certainly don't *feel* that way. And what really *are* the odds? It is not difficult to suspect that there is more going on here than mere statistics: there are very few people who haven't had at least an episode or two of these types of events on their own, although some people certainly seem more "prone" to them than others; and it may even be a talent that can be developed.

It is our mindsets that determine our interpretation of these events: believing is seeing. If, for you, the world is nothing but math and science, then there will be no meaning to these events beyond the odd coincidence, which, with a small amount of rationalization, will not even seem so odd. (And you may also likely be less predisposed to experiencing these sorts of coincidences yourself. *If* it is true that we help create our own worlds, then the "doubting Thomases" may be shutting themselves off from wherever these experiences come from. Commitment to yang can trample yin.) But if you suspect that the world may be more than what we currently call physical, then the possibilities open up. For our purposes, synchronicity may be thought of as a synchronized underlayment (with nods to entanglement) of the universe in general that is linking consciousness and emotion with the physical world, and which seems to be operating outside of normal spacetime constraints. Meaning may drive this, or may emerge *from* it; it's likely a two-way street, which then circles back around to the idea of acausal connection.

It's interesting that many people seem more ready and open to talking about synchronicity than about astrology; that there seems to be less of a taboo, even though astrology is perhaps the most obvious and consistent example of synchronicity that there is. Astrology perhaps has too much baggage, has been the object of too many pogroms; synchronicity is newer and fresher, and likely also has a larger base of people who can dredge up events in their own life to identify with. But astrology *is* synchronicity, as are meaningful coincidences, psi experiences, divination, and the general spiritual experience of the Oneness of all things. In regards to the latter, one may ask again: if all is One, then what *is* that One? Material? Immaterial? A combination of both? Regardless of which way you lean, it is still of value to know about the material (our world in which we live) and the immaterial (our world in which we live). Beneath both, connection trumps causation.

***

Synchronicity has also become somewhat of a glib catchword that is easily batted around without much thought: "That is, like, *so* totally synchronistic!" may be heard more often on a California beach than in serious academic discussions. Don't be fooled, however: synchronicity *has* been the topic of discussions by some very bright minds. Like the basic forms of relativity or quantum, the term itself is only the tip of the iceberg. Vast philosophical, as well as physical and cosmological, implications may arise from that one simple word. These are, in fact, many of the same implications that we have run into in our discussions so far pertaining to physics and consciousness. In fact, and most significantly, synchronicity may seem to be evidence of a natural bridge or connection between these two odd bedfellows.

Many orthodox physicists love quantum, and are fascinated by entanglement, but ("shut up and compute!") hate the questions that for some emerge naturally from these ideas. What *is* one to make of the idea that two electrons, or atoms, or even macroscopic objects may be connected in such a way that they are effectively one thing together, that they are effectively two parts of a single entity *even if they are separated in space*? That's exactly what entanglement *is*: they share a common wave function, and what happens to one is *instantaneously* revealed as simultaneously affecting the other, though it be on the other side of the universe.

Entanglement may or may not have a direct connection to synchronicity. But consider the hints that it throws at us: each separate thing must have its own wave function: therefore if the number of wave functions decreases, then the number of separate things decreases; some have taken this all the way to the idea that the universe itself may ultimately have a single wave function, and may thus be a single *something*, an undivided Whole. This idea, for some, would be physical proof that the universe's natural state is that of Oneness, and that our dualistic and fragmented view is false and distorted, missing out entirely on the most key ingredient of reality. If all is indeed One, then that also throws causality out the window (which has also been verified by modern physics at the subatomic level), as for example my self can't cause my self: they/it are/is the same thing. My arm can't cause my arm, my leg can't cause my leg. Everything arises, is connected, and exists together. Causation is a temporary and illusory subset of correlation. I am: that stands without causation. The universe is: that also stands without causation. However, there is no difference between myself and the universe: that also stands without causation. We are One, we are entangled, we co-exist without causing each other, we emerge and manifest together, we are part of the stream of Whatever Is.

***

We have looked at the idea that it's entirely possible that the physical world may be connected to, may be changed by, or may even be dependent upon, consciousness (through measurement, in the Copenhagen interpretation. Although "changed by" may be seen here to be a convenient shorthand for something more complicated, just as gravity and general relativity were shown to be in the Physics section: correlation again trumps causation). We have looked at the relativity and plasticity of space and time. We have touched on Jung's conversations with Pauli, and the fomenting spark that perhaps archetypes might be a mechanism through which consciousness may join the physical, and provide meaning to the connections. We have noted the frequent emotional component to all of this.

Putting all of these factors together, we yet again, in a self-referential ouroboros, arrive at a possible world where all is connected, where all is One and where consciousness swims with physics in a world of correlation rather than of causation. In short, we arrive at... synchronicity, an "acausal connecting principle," manifesting as meaningful coincidences that seemingly use consciousness to transcend matter, time, and space.

Why Is That?

Prior to Jung, a quirky Austrian biologist named Paul Kammerer became very interested in what he called seriality, the coincidental repeating of certain patterns or *components* of events in a seemingly meaningful way. He might, for example, sit on a park bench and observe passers-by to see if perhaps the day might lend itself more to women wearing green rather than red hats at some significant level. Upon closer examination, this can be seen to be an early attempt to examine the same phenomena that Jung spoke of as synchronicity. The observations from the park bench could easily be chalked up to typical human pattern-seeking, or standard fluctuations through chance; but occasionally certain patterns break through that seem to defy the laws of coincidence... Einstein himself called the idea of seriality "interesting, and by no means absurd." Whatever might be behind synchronicity, then, would be behind its predecessor, seriality.

Kammerer himself loved to tell the story, oft repeated since then, of M. Deschamps and M. Fortgibu. It seems that when a certain M. Deschamps was just a boy in Orleans, France, he was presented with a piece of plum pudding by a guest of the family, a M. Fortgibu. Fast forward to young adulthood, and Mr. Deschamps was later sitting in a restaurant in Paris, and decided to order plum pudding. Unfortunately, he was informed that the last piece had just been ordered and taken—by a diner across the restaurant who turned out to be none other than M. Fortgibu. Curious, but not that amazing so far, perhaps. Many years after this, however, M. Deschamps was at a party where plum pudding was again being served as a special treat. Jogging his memory about the earlier coincidence, M. Deschamps was engaged in telling the other guests about this odd occurrence when the door suddenly opened, and who should stumble in, uninvited, but none other than M. Fortgibu himself:

now a confused and elderly man who had simply gotten hold of the wrong address and had walked into the party completely by mistake.

Possibly you will find this denouement a bit more interesting; likely you will find your own stories of synchronistic experiences much more so—*to you*. Why is it that these sorts of synchronicities seem so amazing and fraught with meaning when they are happening to *us*, but much less so when we read or hear about others' tales? There are likely a couple of reasons for this. First, in keeping with the emotional component of synchronicity, our own experiences call forth emotion (amazement itself has an emotional feel to it) in us, while hearing of others' tends to be a much more cerebral experience. We *experience* ours, we *analyze* others. Ours are filled with significance and wonder; others' are just words on paper. Skillful novelists or writers are adept at eliciting emotional responses in others; perhaps synchronistic experiences retold by accomplished wordsmiths may carry more weight in this regard. There are examples in literature.

The other reason is likely this: attached to the idea of cosmic Oneness though many of us may be, most of us live within our little self-created worlds dominated by ego, belief, and partial (at best) awareness. We care most about our own ideas, feelings, thoughts, and goals. Others' are often simply less interesting to us. We can't directly feel the emotions that others are encountering. That doesn't mean that we don't care about others—it simply recognizes that we create our own realities and that we are the center of those realities.

The more mystical may well see how synchronicity in general ties all of us together, ties us together with a larger Consciousness and with matter and energy themselves, and sees clearly the falseness of the personal ego. And yet, it is that ego, *our* ego, our selves, that actually *experience* the synchronicities. It is paradoxical: in recognizing these meaningful coincidences, we are brought towards a direct experience of the connectedness of all, and yet it is our personal selves that experience that dissolution of ego. This should, in fact, give hints as to the nature of the self. There are many contradictions and ambiguities to be encountered in our journeys. Perhaps this is another example of complementarity.

Regardless, the unpredictability and quirky personal nature of synchronicities makes them impossible to study from an experimental or predictive perspective, and therefore leaves them permanently outside of science as we know it today. Indeed, meaning of any sort, synchronistic or not, lies outside the bounds of science, although it of course may be informed by those disciplines. The intimate nature of these experiences means that they must forever remain our own personal canaries in the coal mine, alerting us to the possibilities of a larger vision or reality. We are nodes of the great Wholeness, yes, but these coincidences seem tailored to our own particular nodes.

***

Like all things non-analytical, synchronicities thrive when the hamster-on-a-treadmill, nonstop "monkey-mind" (as the Buddhists say) is put to rest. A Tarot or I Ching reading, for example, requires a clear and receptive intellect and psyche in order for a meaningful reading to occur. This receptivity opens up the potential awareness of the world that synchronicities thrive on, and are actually trying to point us towards. Distracted or skeptical frames of mind will not find the coincidences and meaning that they know aren't there. Synchronicity in its larger sense, in fact, is not just the odd coincidences that we have mentioned so far, but may indeed manifest itself as any feeling (and there *must* be a feeling involved) of deep connectedness. Any noting of disparate occurrences coming together in a meaningful sense which points towards a deeper field of connections below the superficial level that we normally exist in may be considered synchronicity. This includes numinous or "peak" experiences.

Going to back to physics, David Bohm hinted at a hidden "implicate order," which gives rise to the explicate order: our world. He did not specify consciousness, but he left the nature of the order open to further musings, and in fact speculated that it may contain the seeds and connections of both mind *and* matter. This again has echoes in the philosophical position of consciousness known as neutral monism, mentioned earlier. This synchronistic peak feeling may be the physicist contemplating the laws of the universe; it is the astrologer lost in amazement and delight at the intertwined dance of a natal chart interacting with an actual life. This is Jung's Unus Mundus. This is the mystic's religious experience. For the mystic, every moment is one of meaning.

***

Those studying the more distributed models of consciousness or spirituality will feel right at home here as well. Synchronicity has to do with the connection between matter, mind, spirit, and emotion. For many, this is demonstrated only by occasional, haphazard, and wayward clues. For the mystic, however, matter has already disappeared into active relationship. For the mystic, there is nothing *but* connection: God, Consciousness, meaning, matter, thought, and energy. The visionary lives where most of us only have the privilege to visit.

Synchronicities point, moreover, towards the unknown. What *is* out there, or in here? *Is* there a difference? What *is* going on? Synchronicities point us towards the awe and wonder of the undiscovered. How *could* that coincidence have happened? Contrary to an oft-repeated stereotype, it is not true that we use only 10% of our brains, but it certainly may be true that we only experience 10% of our reality.

We are more likely to experience synchronicities when we are open and receptive; when we let go of our yang, masculine, problem-solving minds and let ourselves sink into our yin, feminine, experiential minds. We often need to let our intellectual guard down for the truth to sneak past the gates. We are more likely to experience synchronicities at peak emotional or crisis points in our lives, or when we are in love, or lost in creative pursuits, or dreaming. When we are able or forced, that is, to move away from our driven and dualistic monkey-minds. These synchronicities are more likely when we step back from the day-to-day minutiae in our lives and meditate on the larger pictures. We are normally staring at the equivalent of pointillist paintings from an inch away; we need to step back to view what's really going on.

We can train ourselves in the direction of synchronicities by being attentive, and attuning ourselves to look for them. Believing is seeing, so we must hold a model that includes their possibility. Quite often, when we look for them, they actually appear. They are never far away, lurking out of the corner of our eyes. They are naturally foreign to our Western minds, but they are there. They do not have to be dramatic; they can be quietly talking to us as well, pointing us in the direction of understanding and wholeness, over analysis and fragmentation. They may be surprising, sudden, and shocking; or alternatively, relaxing and meditative. They *always* point towards, if nothing else, the import and significance of their own manifestation and its implications. They are a self-sustaining loop of demonstration and essence. Math and meaning. Duality and completeness. In synchronicity, the divisions disappear.

> "I am open to the guidance of synchronicity, and do not let expectations hinder my path."—the Dalai Lama

> "With synchronicity, all the resources we need are made available for us at the precise moment that is appropriate. The people who come into our lives are the ones we need at that moment in time. Everything is perfect. We only need to recognize this to tune into the flow. Everything happens for a reason and every experience is a learning experience."—Alex Chua

Getting Emotional

Earth, Air, Fire, and Water. When looking at the universe, it is easy to visualize how the first three of these may relate to the "Big Picture." Earth is physics. Earth is materialism. It is the current scientific way of viewing reality, which is reductionist: it attempts to "reduce" everything to physical causes and conditions. It has seemingly been very successful in many ways in achieving this, but for many people, nagging questions remain. There are suspicions, there are pieces of the puzzle that don't fit. Enter Air: perhaps our world *isn't* just physical, but in addition has consciousness as a key component. Along with Descartes, we can then wonder if consciousness, in some way, is separate from and yet connected to the physical world. We can wonder if consciousness merely resides within our own craniums, produced by gooey biological reactions, or whether there may be a larger version of it. And it is also easy to visualize how Fire may play its part in the larger scheme: the cosmos, even by the standards of mainstream science, is a humming Oneness of energy, a vast vitality of interlocking motion and potential. Without energy, without Fire, there is nothing. Fire also governs the spirituality that seems to have infused human culture through the ages.

But, for an astrologer, what of poor Water? Where does Water fit in? In our modern yang world, water as the feeling component of life often seems to be a weak afterthought: things are moving along and working so well, and then there's this feminine emotional stuff that gums things up. There is an internet joke which reads "Newton's Third Law of Emotion: For Every Male Action, There is a Female Overreaction." So emotion gets no respect. This is not the place to launch a lengthy discussion of the place for the feminine in our picture of the cosmos, but suffice it to say that the feminine is, by definition, half of our world. Perhaps we should act like it. It's just that we have chosen to de-emphasize it, in favor of logic and linear reasoning. Meaning has become subservient to math. We have relegated emotion to an aberration over on the sidelines. We have created a lopsided view of things. So much the poorer for us.

But as astrologers, we must take it as a given that the four elements need be of equal importance, at least for our personal worlds, which is all that we can finally know. Everything is filtered through our human, our psychological and sensory, and our astrological glasses. So emotion must be on an equal footing with the other elements. As well, we must make astrology, and thus again all four of the elemental aspects of life, ultimately compatible with other disciplines such as physics and consciousness. *All* must be harmonious and intertwining parts of the Whole. There is no "which contains which." They are all part of the Klein bottle. So what role *does* emotion play? How might we bring emotion to parity with the other three? Although currently (at least in terms of Western scientific paradigms) the poor stepchild of the other astrological elements, there are clues.

For starters, we may note that studies have shown that pure consciousness, or reason, without emotion is not only sterile, but is not as effective, at least for humans. "Emotional intelligence" is the buzzword here. Pure thought and reason gets bogged down with endless possibilities. It is difficult to do weighting, and to make effective decisions without an intuitive component. Part of the greatness of Einstein was his ability to bring in the feminine, emotional, and intuitive functions to his examinations of reality. On Star Trek, one may admire Spock's logic, but it is ultimately Captain Kirk's more human, emotional, and balanced approach that effectively steers the ship from episode to episode. One may examine the yin-yang symbol itself: there are equal parts male and female, reason and intuition. *The Whole is not half.* Apart from science, much of what is experienced as worthwhile in our culture arises from the Feminine, including much of the art, music, and literature which pulls at our sentimental nature and reflects back to us insights on what it means to be part of the fallible but striving human race.

And what of "enlightenment" itself, if one should take that ambiguous term to be a high point in our relations to the various explorations of reality? One normally jumps first to consciousness here, but an equal component is emotion. For those who have had an experience of Oneness, there is always a *very* strong emotional component. It is not just "knowing," it is *knowing*. This deeper knowing is accompanied by emotion. There is a delicate, and yet intoxicating and overwhelming, *feeling* of the unity of all things. It is a dispassionate excitement. Emotion, for us humans, is a key component or adjunct to consciousness. The two are technically separate, but it is in their synergy that we experience our world. They also act as a whole, as complementary partners. That alone is a strong argument for emotion, but there is more.

Emotions, although their own entity, seem to exist in a place that lies somewhere between consciousness and the physical. Emotions are a part of consciousness; they are a key part. And yet, they are part of the physical world also. They arise from the churning stew of hormones, neurotransmitters, and chemicals that our body and our brains are awash in. They are part of feedback loops between mind and body. As such, they provide a primordial, paradigmatic template of consciousness/matter interactions, or of the mind/body problem. They provide function and intuition, and yet it is certainly true that they may also at times turn *dys*functional: we have all been held hostage at times by the very chemicals that can make life wonderful. The Buddhists (and their Western counterparts, practitioners of "mindfulness") attempt to minimize the destructive components of emotions, in favor of their intuitive and productive expressions. But, rarified and difficult though the fumigation process may be, this purification of the emotional mind does not in fact get rid of emotion: passivity itself is emotion. Only pure analysis is not. Mindfulness in fact speaks of the pursuit of the "Wise Mind," which is produced at the proper intersection of logic and emotion. It is the pairing of the feminine with the masculine, it is the perfection and appreciation of complementarity.

***

Our minds and our bodies, consciousness and the physical world, are in constant interplay. A strenuous bout of exercise uses mediating endorphins to produce an emotional sense of well-being that washes through our conscious minds. Conversely, our minds may hear bad or fearful news, and we then mysteriously find our bodies to be exhibiting headaches, or other pains, or digestive problems, or other illnesses. We are one and whole within ourselves as well, mental and physical, mediated by emotions. We are a reflective part of universal patterns. The entire field of holistic medicine is built on this simple idea. But might this be extrapolated even further?

Gratefully, we have the freedom within this book to simply ask questions. This is not a scholarly endeavor. We can note that emotions seem to bridge consciousness and the physical world, at least within our own bodies. But our bodies *are* the world: whatever rules of consciousness and the physical world there are that may be operating within ourselves must also echo and parallel the larger principles of the universe. We can remember that, in the line of quantum physics that we have been pursuing, generalized and impersonal consciousness and the physical world seem to have some connection. Yet emotions have a role in mediating the two within our bodies; might this mediatory force affect larger systems?

We can note that, curiously, the unifying component of psi or synchronistic experiences, both of which seem to contain clues to a reality beyond day-to-day spacetime, is that of emotion. It is an emotional experience in which Jung notices his famous scarab: a story not told here, but repeated endlessly in articles and books about synchronicity. It is in an emotional context that most of our own synchronistic experiences take place. Switching over to psi experiences, which are perhaps best seen as second cousins, or special cases of synchronicity, we find precognition, telepathy, near death, and remote viewing. All have a strongly *emotional* feel to them. Why is that?

Emotion has power, no doubt: those who have had any dealings with Scorpios can attest to that (!), and the power of water (the astrological symbol for emotion), has long been accepted and revered, especially in the East. The I Ching talks about the strength of water, and about its ability to overcome all obstacles through wearing down, through erosion, through the filling up of all the spaces in earth and air, through spreading, connecting, dissolving, and influencing. Cancer springs to mind here, with its quiet and almost unobserved ability to get ahead when it wants to, using its softness at times to mask ambition, using its empathy at times to further its causes. Even Pisces, the "weakest" water sign, can subtly make itself indispensable to those around it, who are seemingly much stronger, in order to bring to fruition its aims. And the sympathy, emotional empathy, and flowing all-connectedness of Water brings us back full circle to the Oneness experiences mentioned above. It is no wonder that Pisces, Neptune, and the 12th House have the function of "dissolving" boundaries. The ego of course goes first, for in the 12th House it is more hindrance than helpmate, if understanding in that realm is to be achieved. Here, we are all simply mirrors of each other, and of What Is. "I am That," as the 20th century guru Nisargadatta Maharaj put it: being born "at the break of dawn" gave him Sun in the 12th, opposing Moon in Libra; a double dose of non-duality and complementarity. Emotion was not absent, but was placed into its proper percentage in the cosmic scheme. It is one quarter of the whole: no more, no less.

Consciousness and emotion are similar and connected in another respect: they are both powerfully in existence, and yet they are both invisible, ephemeral, just beyond grasp, and unaffected by attempts to squeeze them into a box. Possibly this is due to their arising from a deeper level of reality than we are currently able to fully know. They are like Plato's Forms, and they are also like a Taoist yin-yang pair: our thoughts are always (although we like to fancy ourselves personally immune from this) being skewed by our emotions, and our emotions in turn are being constantly influenced by our thoughts: they are a system. That's the basis of Cognitive Behavioral Therapy (CBT), a popular and effective form of psychological therapy. Given all of this, might it then be that emotion, in its quest to take its place as equal partner in our world with Earth, Fire, and Air, may actually turn out to be the missing bridge or connecting piece between consciousness and matter? (In our world, at least—it is likely that our particular astrology is local to our solar system and may exist beside different versions throughout the universe, interacting in some fashion.)

Might it be that emotion may assist consciousness in collapsing the wave function and producing physical reality? Or could emotion at some times and in some ways be a kind of "trigger," acting at other points of confluence between consciousness and matter to produce some of the strange circumstances talked about in this section? That would certainly give it equal standing with the other elements in the Larger Scheme. It seems far-fetched, but then again almost everything that is known about the way that our surprising and changing world works seemed far-fetched at one time. Wegener's continents may not be so far from the curious emotional states that often accompany synchronistic events.

As stated, these are simply fun speculations: who knows if they will go anywhere? More alarmingly for those who have difficulty coming to terms with the idea that *consciousness* may interact with matter, what then could be made of the idea that *emotions* may interact with matter, or help create reality? Curiouser and curiouser, as Alice would say. There are always things hidden and unknown, and even entirely new worlds down the rabbit hole. It *is* of note, finally, that the Water signs have a reputation for being able to sense and manifest things on a more subtle plane than that of the grossly materialistic, or even of the cognitive. The intuitive function is deep and unseen, and adds the emotional to the mental. It may turn out to be coming from the same place wherein synchronicity resides.

Bridge of Psis

One may ask: what is the relationship between synchronicity and what is currently known as "psi" phenomena? Psi has come to be the label for all things involving consciousness that are odd or unexplained by traditional science. It is, of course, derided as a "pseudoscience" by the mainstream. It includes ESP, clairvoyance, precognition, psychokinesis, and more. Psi comes from the first letter of the Greek word meaning soul or mind, and is also known as parapsychology. Parapsychology was popularized in the 1930s by investigator J.B. Rhine, who coined the term extrasensory perception, or ESP. It has had a bumpy history, to say the least, and its study has been handicapped by both wishful thinking and accusations of fudged results on the psi side; and on the skeptics' side, by a determined stonewall of mainstream scientists who are so predisposed to discount it that one suspects that there can ultimately be *no* study that they would be willing to accept as legitimate. Believing is seeing, and this goes for both sides.

But how is one to explain the "life-sized statue," or the other odd and curious anecdotes presented in this book? Simple coincidence? Perhaps. And yet again, they don't *seem* like coincidence; they seem connected to many other people's stories of similar events: this is the motivation for the explorations, formal or informal, that people have taken over the years in investigating psi events and experiences. Like synchronicity, psi events are fairly common, and most people have one story or another involving something odd. More "holistic" societies that have shown aptitudes for Oneness and the feminine over our more analytical and masculine orientation have been more comfortable with these possibilities. Ours has felt a bugle call to arms to hunt down and eliminate any talk heading in this direction. Here reason, separateness, duality, and mathematical causality must rule, or the demons of inarticulate and anarchic boogeymen will be peering in the windows. But perhaps there is a middle way. Perhaps the two sides (yang, intellectual; and yin, intuitive) might actually hint at a wholeness that could include them both.

The problem with "proving" psi is the same problem that is encountered with proving synchronicity or astrology: they are all so damn slippery. They appear when they want. They appear most when we seem to be looking away. When we ask them to appear on demand, they get coy and shy, and retreat. Perhaps they want to be teaching *us*, instead of us teaching *them*. These particular interactions, in fact, somewhat recall in flavor those modern physics experiments, including the double slit, in which human conscious interaction appears to skew the results of experiments. The physics experiments, of course, ultimately have a more predictable outcome, but some of the *feel* is much the same: the odd slipperiness and uncertainty as to what's going on. That in itself should be a clue towards something. But things are what they are, and we are where we are in our current investigations of the universe. Ignoring our own lessons from the quantum realm, we revert back to the idea that if things aren't presently quantifiable or predictable to us with a known physical mechanism, then they simply can't exist.

William James, the "Father of American Psychology," was also the founder of The American Society For Psychical Research. Being a Capricorn, he was methodical and cautious of reputation, surrounding himself in this new Society with those of status in many fields: a mini "Who's Who" of American thinkers at the time. Although enthusiastic regarding all possibilities of psychic phenomena, he also maintained a healthy skepticism, and was instrumental in the debunking of many so-called mediums and other charlatans who seemed to flourish in the decades after the discovery of Neptune in 1846.

(One runs a fine line here in acknowledging that the field is ripe for poseurs to work their "magic," while striving to demonstrate the view that not everyone interested in these issues is gullible or fraudulent. It's just the state of things in the psi field, tied into the fickle manifestations of psi itself. Things at some point may sort themselves out a bit more, one hopes. It's also, as astrologers will know, the nature of Neptune itself, planetary ruler of all things psi: Neptune includes the dishonest and the gullible, along with the inspired and the visionary. It rules the intentional maya of the movies, as well as the clear eyes of the enlightened. Neptune can be associated with the highest that humans can aspire to, but with this planet it is always caveat emptor. Interestingly, at around the same time that Neptune was discovered, Scottish surgeon James Braid coined the term hypnotism, and wrote his first book on the subject. The second half of the 19th century also saw significant inroads for Eastern religions and disciplines making their first forays into the West. The Theosophical Society, which introduced Krishnamurti to the world, was founded in 1875.)

But back to James: whatever else one may think of James's dabbling in this area, he had a nobility of intentions regarding research here, and had the foresight to call for a scientific program "first to investigate psychic phenomena according to the methods and criteria of science; and second, to enlarge the scope of science to include the study of phenomena that are random, non-repeatable, and dependent on universal personal capacities and dispositions." The problem, unsurprisingly, turned out to be too much concentration on the first half of his suggestion, and not enough on the second half. (This story is part of an examination of science's dismissal of psi told by Elizabeth Lloyd Mayer, in her book *Extraordinary Knowing*.)

***

What then *is* the relationship between psi and synchronicity, other than both being very strange experiences? This book is too short to delve into psi experiences in depth, but the two are at minimum first cousins, and are likely closer relations than that. As an aside, when I was just out of college, a friend and I tried some card-guessing experiments on our own, and achieved a level that seemed significantly higher than chance, although there were no scientific controls or monitoring involved. I have a suspicion that were we in a laboratory performing these same guesses, the results may not have been as notable. Why? It may be that consciousness is simply more delicate and unpredictable than other forms of energy, or may be more sensitive to setting, emotional state, and other variables that are difficult to reproduce in the lab. It may be similar to the quantum Zeno effect, wherein too closely observing quantum processes can cause them to "freeze" and stop performing their tricks. Electricity and atomic energy, though right in front of us, eluded us for thousands of years; and yet they are large, dramatic energies. Even though it is also "right in front of us," and part of our daily lives, it is likely that consciousness is subtler and more difficult to understand, notice, and pin down. Perhaps we are simply not in the portion of our knowledge evolution yet in which we are ready to, or meant to, discover certain things.

So both synchronicity and psi have in common that they point us towards the confluence of consciousness and matter; they may ultimately turn out to be the same phenomena, manifesting in different forms. This would be similar to how electricity and magnetism were once thought to be separate things, but were eventually shown to be two facets of one force (and they have since additionally been joined by the nuclear weak force.) As mentioned previously, it seems eerily synchronistic in itself that the Greek letter and symbol psi (ψ) not only currently stands in for the oddities of the mind, but that it was chosen by Schrödinger to represent the wave function, the energy field that the mind may have a hand in collapsing into the material world. (Schrödinger came first here.) Most curiously, it also coincides nearly exactly with the glyph for the planet Neptune. The ouroboros appears repeatedly in human culture: This is That, and the Whole is round and self-referential. Both psi and synchronicity point to the subtle ephemerality of normal, everyday consciousness, and also to its amazing ability to magnify and become prominent during periods of crisis, or other emotional turmoil. One day we will know the formula. Both seem to throw causation and time to the side; both give us direct hints as to a more universal substrate lurking below our focus on the tangible, visible, and verifiable material world.

Is Water Wet?

Kevin Loria, appearing in 2015 in the *Business Insider*, has written of an interesting phenomena that came to his attention after listening to a Radiolab podcast called "Colors." In 1858, William Gladstone of England did some research and noted that the color blue was apparently and surprisingly a recent human invention. To clarify: no one knows what primitive people saw when they looked up at the sky. But he pointed out that in the Odyssey, Homer describes the sea as "wine-dark" in color rather than blue. After doing research into the literature of other ancient cultures, including Chinese, Islamic, Hindu, and even the Icelandic sagas (from around 800 years ago—and those Norse seamen should have known a bit about sea color), he could find no mention of blue except in Egypt, which coincidentally was the only country to have developed a blue dye. Guy Deutscher, author of *Through the Language Glass: Why the World Looks Different in Other Languages* even performed an experiment with his daughter Alma in which he raised her as long as possible without describing the color of the sky. When he finally asked her, she initially called it white before finally settling on blue. To her, it really had no color at all until it was labeled. Loria summarizes: "If you see something yet can't see it, does it exist? Did colors come into existence over time? Not technically, but our ability to notice them may have..."

Good point, and an example of what is known as "linguistic relativity": the idea that our language itself constrains what we may know about the world. A common example of this that is often given (but that has scholarly issues), is the idea that Eskimos (Inuits) have many more words in their language to describe snow than English does. Regardless of word count, it is certainly true that someone in a country not used to snow will show a poverty of description about the subject. For example, a Jamaican may well call anything that is white and comes from the sky snow, while an

Inuit may make a distinction for slushy snow, new snow, crusty snow, powdery snow, and many more variations. So what are each of these people seeing? Obviously, they are both seeing different things, or more to the point, they are seeing things differently.

This is somewhat analogous to the famous optical illusion of the vase and faces that everyone has seen at some point: what are you seeing? How might you see this illusion if you've never seen a vase or don't even have a word in your vocabulary for vase? Would vases exist? And yet the vase is there for those trained to look for it. One can in fact take this idea of how our language is intimately connected to our thought patterns to a much higher level than colors. In Western religions, the word "God" connotes a single, personalized, omnipotent Being who is separate from us, watches over our every move, and can be influenced by prayer. Mention the word God to someone from India or the East, however, and the word is more likely to evoke the image of a spiritual force which pervades everything, manifests in and as everything, and that everyone is a part *of*, rather than separate *from*. Entire cultural gestalts are based on different languages' interpretations of one single word. So who is correct? *Is* there a "correct"?

We see the world as our culture teaches us to, as our language structures it, and we take the world as we find it. I see a small, older lady at the grocery store frequently. She has blue hair (although she wouldn't have in Homer's time), and frankly her makeup is what is best described as "garish": she has a bit of a clownish look to her, although sweet and friendly. What does she see when she looks in the mirror? Obviously something quite different from what I see. So who is seeing things accurately? Who is to say? I have lived in my house now for ten years. My doors throughout are brown stained wood, but my door frames are painted white. It is highly likely, because it was the style at the time that the house was built, that at one time the door frames were also stained brown wood to match the doors. I never really thought about this until today; it never occurred to me. Now I see that this was probably the case. It allows me to see my doors in a new light, one that I had never considered before. I took the world as I found it. It's difficult to see things in a new way, to break out of our paradigms, our cognitive laziness. The world for us isn't *what* we see. It's the *way* that we see it.

Isaac Newton is best known for his laws of motion. But Newton also laid the foundation for our modern understanding of light. Specifically, in 1672, Newton published the results of a series of experiments that he had performed using prisms. He demonstrated conclusively that white light was in fact a *mixture* of the various colors of light, and could be "taken apart" and put back together again by the use of prisms. This was a revelation, in that the thought at the time was that light was simply a mix of light and dark (although objects themselves had colors), and that prisms somehow "colored" the light passing through them. Interestingly, Newton chose seven colors (red, orange, yellow, green, blue, indigo, and violet) largely because of his occultist beliefs in the power of seven (7 visible objects in the skies, 7 musical notes, 7 days of the week, etc.). It appears, looking back, that indigo was not really a distinct color, but was "shoehorned in" for the sake of symmetry. Many current charts show only six colors, leaving indigo out.

It was not known in Newton's day, but we know now that the visible light spectrum is only a small part of a much larger entity known as the electromagnetic spectrum. In fact, the first hint of this was laid out by William Herschel (who also found Uranus) in 1800, when he discovered the infrared portion of the spectrum, followed a year later by the discovery of the ultraviolet portion by Johann Ritter. The race for extension was on, and by the 1860's, Faraday, and then Maxwell, had discovered that electricity and magnetism were entwined forces, that electromagnetic waves traveled at the speed of light, and that visible light was but one part of this spectrum. Other parts of the spectrum, including many types of radio and microwaves (on the low frequency end), and x-rays and gamma rays (on the high frequency end), were soon put in place.

As humans, our primary input as to what the world is like is through our eyes, although we of course have at least four other senses. Our eyes are filled with receptors that, out of the entire electromagnetic spectrum (EM), are sensitive only to the very tiny portion that we call (for obvious reasons) visible light. We are dumb to all other frequencies. This should be a humbling experience for us, but we homo sapiens are hard to humble. There are other animals that can sense different frequencies: for example some snakes and bats have longer-range infrared (heat) detectors, and many insects and birds can "see" ultraviolet rays.

In addition, our other senses are also limited in many ways compared to other species; one common example is dogs' ability to hear higher frequencies than we can; bloodhounds also have forty times the number of olfactory receptors that we have: our noses are particularly limited and "dumb." Again, the world opens up to these animals in new and novel ways from our own views. One wonders what the world "looks like" to them. It no doubt looks different than it does to us. So which is the "true" world?

The point is that the world is in fact not the way that we see it at all: we perceive only what our particular sensory receptors and cognitive processing apparatus allow us to perceive, further modified by our filtering and belief systems. Of course, it is true that our cognitive abilities, coupled with instruments to extend our receptors, can form a larger picture of things, and we have done an excellent job of this, amazingly so. However, again it may be asked: what is it that we *don't* see *because we don't know what to look for*? You cannot see the thing you're not looking for, or not aware of. If you've never seen a vase, you will not suddenly see one in the Rubin's vase illusion. Or if you are looking for faces, you will not see the vase. There are lessons here regarding those who don't like astrology failing to see it in action. Electricity was there before our "discovery" of it, but it was not there for us. Atomic energy was there before our discovery of it, but it was not there for us. If you're Jamaican, you cannot see the various forms of snow, because you don't know how to look for them. The world is ever hiding from us in plain sight.

***

There is a phenomenon called the "signal to noise ratio," which those in the electronic or broadcasting industries are very familiar with. Many signals, for example, are specifically broadcast at certain frequencies that a receiver is looking for, and thus are strong and easily identifiable. This is true for a radio or TV signal, and our eyes take part in a selective receptivity as well. Our eyes are trained to pick out certain frequencies as red, blue, yellow, or whatever, which our brain then turns into an identifiable picture. As outlined above, this also depends somewhat on our cultural and linguistic heritage, as well as our belief systems, since we are often restricted in our cognitive perception only to those signals which correspond to our personal "belief receptors."

But what happens if the signal is weak, unclear, or obscure? In dim light, we may have trouble distinguishing between black and blue or green, but yellow may stand out. An analog radio receiver in between stations may produce sound that seems only to be white noise static, but (if you are old enough to remember traditional radios) one may occasionally catch snippets of a distant station fading in and out of the noise. These fragments are often too faint to be able to do much more than identify them as some sort of far off signal, obviously produced by humans. It is often very difficult to ascertain, in fact, whether one is hearing only noise, or whether there may actually be a faint signal mixed in. A better antenna may often bring the signal in more clearly. The level and coherency of the distant signal above the level of the background noise is called the signal to noise ratio. It can be described numerically, and it can vary up and down. Again, it can be amplified. This is actually the technique that allows cosmologists to search for "alien" signals amongst the background noise of the universe. (Perhaps in return, aliens will at some point be receiving from us faint flickers of the "Big Bang Theory" in some far-off locale.)

***

Well into the 20th century, miners brought canaries with them while working in coal mines. The canaries were more sensitive to carbon monoxide than the miners were, and thus there was a way for the miners to tell when that danger was increasing. The miners couldn't smell, taste, feel, see, or otherwise perceive the gas, but they knew that it was there because of their animal intermediary: the canaries died. They could thus get hints of something that was invisible to them.

Primitive man saw lightning all around him. Had he known what to look for, he could have identified it as a "canary in a coal mine," providing hints to an unseen force that he would later harness to run a civilization. Throughout history, there have been signals and events which have (or could have, were they recognized) provided clues to unseen events, forces, and paradigms. The continents on a map fit together like a jigsaw puzzle, but most people dismissed the idea of continental drift out of hand, and so simply didn't "see" it. Often in history, the death of a metaphorical canary left questions, but no answers.

***

So how are we to look at astrology, synchronicity, and psi phenomena today? Isn't it possible that all of the anecdotal events of this nature, while not "scientifically" understandable or reproducible, are simply canaries in an unknown coal mine? Isn't it possible that those odd synchronistic experiences that almost everyone has at some point *aren't* just dry coincidences, as the mathematicians would have us believe? Why do they usually seem to correspond with strong emotions or in settings that evoke emotional responses? What *does* it mean when an astrologer can guess someone's zodiacal sign just by looking at them, or talking with them? Why can't they then do that consistently, so that it could be pinned down and analyzed as a chi-squared event?

Perhaps psi glimmers are to us what random lightning was to primitive man: get back with me in a few thousand years—maybe we'll have a new civilization powered by consciousness. Perhaps the hit and miss of astrology is like cartographers 200 years ago staring at a map of the world, and wondering why the continents could, if moved, fit together like a puzzle laid out on the table. What was missing in their knowledge that could have made that possible? What could have tied that together? How *could* they have made sense of that with the limited knowledge that they possessed at that time? Why *do* we only get glimmers of some of these psi things, but no real consistency? Is there some principle that we haven't discovered that would answer that question? In the science realm: what *will* end up being the missing link that will tie together Einstein's ideas with those of quantum mechanics? What about all of the other questions? *What are we missing?* What are the questions we don't know to ask? How will we find out?

Relativity only becomes glaringly apparent at extremes, specifically when we get close to the speed of light. In our everyday world, it is "invisible." That's why it wasn't noticed earlier. Quantum effects only become apparent at extremes, specifically at the atomic and subatomic level of reality. In our everyday world, they are invisible. And yet relativity and quantum are everywhere, and describe the reality that we see in a way that we *can't* see.

Gravity also only manifests itself at extremes: at the atomic level, gravity is negligible, being far overshadowed by the other three fundamental forces. Gravity only manifests itself at what seems to be the "extreme" level: ours! At the atomic level of size, what might seem normal to us might be seen as extreme and gigantic, although of course there are much larger levels above us when looking out at the cosmos. So again, everything is relative, everything is perspective, and there are always things about reality that we will never be able to see in our "normal" mesocosmic level of perceiving reality.

So might it be possible that the signal to noise ratios in astrology, synchronicity, or psi only become apparent at certain levels, and then only to those who are looking for them, who are attuned to them, and who open-mindedly have their receivers turned on? Might the fleeting nature of competing and overlapping astrological cycles confuse and obscure the signals to those not trained to receive them? To pick the signals out of the fuzz and ever-changing clatter often takes some training, effort, and willingness; to others, only what seems to be white noise is apparent.

But the white noise contains the colors, the signals. What percentage of reality *do* we perceive at any given moment? Our attention, after being woken up by our reticular activating system (RAS), chugs along through the day governed mainly by two processes: "sensitivity enhancement," and "efficient selection." Efficient selection weeds out those things that we don't consider necessary or interesting to our attention at the moment (astrology for scientists), and sensitivity enhancement allows us to magnify the signals that we *do* find interesting, valuable, or necessary (astrology for astrologers). This goes a long way towards explaining how two people can see the world so differently, and it also goes a long way towards explaining how one person might be very in tune with and skilled at physics, while another person might have the same skill with intuition or horoscopes.

We're always missing something. It's the nature of reality. R=K+1. The best that we can do is to remain open-minded, and to check our beliefs and preconceptions at the door. We will always be proved, if not wrong, then at least having a continually incomplete picture of the world. Humility of perspective is always in order. Perhaps astrology and psi are not only like the canaries in the coal mine for some brave new vision of reality; perhaps they are also showing themselves in ways that only those with (or willing to develop) more advanced or specialized "antennas" can discern. Perhaps the signals are fleeting, ephemeral, and difficult to detect. Perhaps the signals are there with the noise, but few have taken the trouble to listen carefully. Perhaps with most people the signal-to-noise ratios are present, but are low—low enough that those with grosser antennas or strongly held preconceived beliefs are deaf or blind to them. Perhaps it's a matter of intention and willingness. The subject of intention, in fact, figures heavily into alternative consciousness speculations. Perhaps believing is seeing might be true on *both* sides (science and consciousness). More will be revealed.

So our vision of the world is dependent on our biologic senses, on our language, on our culture, and on our beliefs. The world is what it is, and we are only limited and ego-opinionated antennas and processors. Why are we so sure that we know what we know? *Is* red, red? Or is it just electricity and magnetism vibrating at a certain frequency? What really *does* exist, how will we know, and how shall we understand it?

Is water wet?

Curiosity du Jour

Synchronicities are all around us, if we look for them. They seem to pop up more if we are receptive to them. Major synchronicities we remember, but we often write off or discard the more minor ones as mere coincidences. And perhaps they are. Those with a hard-core paradigm of materialism and skepticism, of course, write off *all* synchronicities as mere coincidence.

Which begs a question. In life in general, is it possible that those who are more open and receptive to the yin as well as the yang reap the benefit of a richer depth of experience than those who stay on a flat, literal, and doubting plane? Our society encourages us to strip away the intuitive and feminine, in lieu of the analytical and masculine. But is something lost in the process?

A female friend of mine recently told me of watching a total lunar eclipse (a media-hyped "blood moon") with a group of NASA scientists. As the eclipse became near total, she made the mistake of casually remarking that the vague penumbral/annular effects made the moon look almost like an eye with an iris and pupil. The intent was simply to convey something artistic or interesting. Note that she didn't say that it *was* an eye, or that it was God looking down at us, or something equally extravagant. She simply said that it kind of resembled an eye. They looked at her as if she were a simpleton or an idiot, which gives a clue, perhaps, as to why there is such a gulf between scientists and astrologers, or artists of any medium. From the scientists' perspective, the moon in eclipse *doesn't* look like an eye; it looks like a moon in eclipse.

Astrology and synchronicity are built on symbolism and meaning; the idea that things can be "like" other things, and that we may draw significance and understanding from that fact. The idea that there may be unseen layers of meaning beneath the apparent, superficial, and obvious world around us. They are allegorical and not literal. The symbolic is an ever-present and powerful force in human life, and if one strips it away, our existence somehow becomes smaller.

It must be stressed, however, that there is room for both the literal and the symbolic in the world, and that they form yet another complementary pair. Art, empathy, and allegory have contributed as much to our daily quality of life as have math and reason, and we need not diminish either one. So this is not to lessen the importance of science; it is simply to bring in additional realms of seeing and knowing. Scientists operate on a very concrete and literal plane, while astrologers exist in a realm of simile, metaphor, analogy, symbol, archetype, and image. Things can be "like" other things: in fact, *most* things are like other things in some way. It is the cognitive stretching that these links produce that drives not only astrology, but art, literature, philosophy, fables, and most other wisdom traditions.

We learn about our own lives, in fact, because they are like other lives, like stories that we have read, or sayings that we have heard. We ourselves are analogies. At our best, we may maintain a sense of humor about the whole thing. Metaphoric connections get us back from the linear and logical to the holistic, adding the feminine, the intuitive, back in to the masculine. The Whole is fecund, self-referential, intuitive *and* creative. Linearity and logic are part of the Whole, but are not themselves the Whole.

It is possible, in a nod to complementarity, that simple coincidences *do* exist alongside synchronicities, which leave math (at least as we know it) behind. Who is to say at what level coincidence becomes synchronicity? The emotional component again is a clue: true synchronicities most often have an emotional component, *meaning*, associated with them. The emotional component may be only noticed after the fact, in our reaction to the events; or it may seem to be a complicit partner, in some way helping to actually produce the occurrence. Regardless, it is typically there at some level. Mere coincidences *do* exist, but they do not normally engender an emotional response. (There are those indeed, it must be pointed out, who feel that there are in fact *no* coincidences whatsoever: that all is connected at the synchronistic level, and that everything therefore has meaning and is meant to be. That is certainly possible also.)

It is not every day that meaningful coincidences happen, but that is probably due more to our lack of receptivity, distractions of everyday life, and attachment to the materialistic model, than to any actual frequency issues. If you'll bear with a few more quick anecdotes, following are some coincidences that happened during the writing of this book, or just previously.

***

Not long ago, I arrived upstairs from the basement to visit with my wife Margaret on her break from work (she works out of the house). I said to her, "Guess what I just did." She said, "you wrote me a check for $5,000 to buy clothes." Of course she was kidding. As if. However, think of what she could have guessed that I had been doing. Surfing the internet, writing the book, emailing friends, or sorting through ever-accumulating stacks of various things would have been likely suspects. Joining the Peace Corps would have been possible, but farther out in the probability cloud. What I had actually just done was this: move $5,000 from my checking account online to a Home Equity Line of Credit that we have, that is primarily used by my wife. I really never use it, and had used it only to purchase my current car, which, due to some accumulated savings, I decided to finish paying off completely and early. Other than this, my wife had been the "administrator" and 99% user of the HELOC. (She had not looked at it that day.)

So she got several things right: 1) that I had just done something financial involving my checking account, 2) that it involved her (the HELOC), and 3) that the amount was $5,000, far from a typical amount that we normally deal with. The only thing she actually got wrong was the clothes angle, and that's probably just wishful thinking for a woman. Being downstairs is not something she has ever associated with financial things; typically I pay all of my bills upstairs with my paper checkbook. This, by the way, wasn't intended at all to be any sort of "guessing game"— it was just a brief, casual conversation on both of our parts.

Like the woman who guessed the "life-sized statue," My wife is also a Sagittarian, although with Moon in Pisces: both signs are known for having good intuition. Also during the synchronicities mentioned in this particular section, transiting Neptune was in conjunction with her moon.

***

The reason that I was paying off a new car was that my old one had met an untimely death. It was an older car, but was not ready to go yet. To give some backstory for astrologers, in late November of a couple of years ago, transiting Pluto was coming up to an exact conjunction with my natal Moon, less than a degree away. To my mind, this would likely involve my 89 year old mother, and to be honest, I feared the worst. But we learn over and over again in astrology that the *character* or archetypal energies of events may be dimly perceived, but that we are more often than not surprised by the exact event itself. Perhaps as humans, certitude is not meant for us.

Margaret and I had decided to take a trip to Mount Rushmore over the Thanksgiving holiday, and had rented a cabin in advance and planned our itinerary. Thanksgiving night, around 6-7pm, we were driving through remote Wyoming, and it was already pitch black; the nearly new moon meant that the sky was dark. My wife was driving, and rapidly so, since it was open highway. I was sitting in the passenger seat "bobbing for apples," repeatedly dozing and waking. Suddenly I heard her cry out, and raised my head just in time to see a large buck deer with a huge rack of antlers appear in the road thirty feet in front of our car. There was no time to plan, think, or react: we slammed into the deer, which in a split second hit us like an explosion, careened over the top of the car, and was gone. There was no way that he could have lived.

He hit on my side of the hood, and I got the briefest view of his eyeball looking at me as his antlers broke the windshield 6 inches in front of my face, prior to flying over us and disappearing. The airbags deployed for both of us, and our lives were saved likely, and only, by my wife's ability to pilot the vehicle to the side of the road with a fully inflated airbag in her face at 80 mph in the dark Wyoming night. Prayers of gratitude were said. As for myself, a curious experience took place within the overall event. One sometimes hears about time slowing down at certain significant events in people's lives, for example, the idea of one's life "flashing before their eyes." Here, my life didn't flash, but time definitely took on an Einsteinian relativity. As the deer hit us and flew up and over, time seemed to stretch and slow. I saw every detail of the deer: his eye, his antlers, and his coarse fur; saw the cracking of the windshield in front of my face. I saw the airbag explode, which could only have taken a split second, and yet for me it took on a closely observed sequence. Airbags apparently have an inch or so in diameter hole in them so that they can quickly deflate after their momentary expansion. I watched as the airbag grew slowly outwards like a large white puffy blossom; I saw the round hole with its stitching curiously heading towards me. The hole and the stitching stuck in my mind as much as the deer, although I know that the explosion of the bag must have been unbelievably fast. Perception and relativity were displayed in action.

So *that* was my Moon/Pluto experience: how could one have predicted that, predicted the event that would synchronize with the transit? The event itself was synchronistic, as all powerful astrological events are, and laden with emotion. We were cold and stuck in the middle of nowhere in the inky blackness on a Wyoming highway. The hood of the car was crumpled up, the engine was useless and smoking, pushed back nearly a foot into the frame by the collision. There was deer blood and hair stuck all over the wreck. My wife was crying, the radiator was hissing. But we were alive. Later, several friends told us stories of people who had been killed when a deer's antlers punctured the windshield, or when the deer itself crashed into the driver or passenger seat of a car. We were lucky, we were blessed, or we were simply players in a synchronistic event. We were possibly all three.

My mom was the most likely scenario in my mind for this transit, but I've slowly learned to never try and second guess the universe; I'm usually wrong, or missing something. Surprise and discovery are the fruits for the open-minded, not finding confirmation for "what we know." The wreck involved: a (near) death experience (Pluto), involving a woman close to me (Moon); I'm fortunate that my wife didn't try to swerve, which may have rolled the car, but in a cool presence of mind hit the deer head on. It wasn't my time, or hers. Or my mom's.

***

During the writing of this, I saw an ad for chest CTs (cat scans) connected with a research project for former smokers. Even though I had quit smoking many years ago, I had been having an intractable cough recently, and started to worry about just what might be going on inside my ribcage. So I signed up for one. This sounds pretty cut and dried if you weren't involved, but emotionally for me it was a fearful time. I worried quite a bit in the couple of weeks leading up to the CT. I practiced drawing upon my more zen-like resources, and even planned out how I would live the rest of my shortened life if the news were bad. The *morning of* the CT, I sat eating breakfast, and in between bites of cereal, opened up for the first time the new edition of *Nutrition Action*, a monthly newsletter that we receive. The magazine had come with an outside cover containing ads that obscured the real cover. Thus, I couldn't see what the issue was about until I finally opened it up. When I opened it up, I couldn't believe my eyes. In giant letters, taking up the better part of the front of the magazine, was just one word, staring me in the face: "CANCER." Wow. Not the most encouraging synchronicity. The whole issue was about nutrition and cancer. Skimming this, I left for the hospital to have the test. Along the way,

I called my previously mentioned elderly mom just to say hello. She was sobbing so hard I could barely make out what she was saying. "What's wrong?" I asked. It turned out that for some reason (she didn't know anything about my own scheduled radiography) she had suddenly that morning decided to focus on my sister's own smoking, and was very fearful that she might get cancer and die early. She was so upset by this that she could hardly get a word out. I went into the test very unnerved. The test turned out to be negative, but the synchronicities weren't. This particular morning demonstrated very clearly the amazing coming together of consciousness, emotion, the physical world, and meaning that synchronicities seem to generate.

So two separate camps could look at these incidents and come up with quite different conclusions based on their worldviews. One (skeptical scientists for example) might say "well that's mildly interesting, but coincidences happen all the time—you're reading way too much into these." Or alternatively, those who are more interested in the hidden connections of life might say (regarding the payoff of the car), "Wow, she almost nailed it perfectly," or "Wow, what a surprising playing out of the Pluto/Moon transit," in addition to similar comments on the last one above. Which group would be right? Do we really know for sure? R=K+1. We've probably only scratched the surface of reality. It's way too soon, anyway, to think that we actually know how it all works.

Believing is seeing: that in itself shows us that our consciousness determines our reality. It's true for the physicist, and it's true for the mystic. Belief comes from consciousness mediated by emotion, consciousness is tied to matter, and the connection is called synchronicity. The rest is not known to us yet. Reality is always a work in progress: if one feels that they have all of the answers, then they probably haven't gotten all of the questions yet.

What's the Matter?

Synchronicity often seems bizarre or far-off. It sneaks up on us, it pops up in the oddest of circumstances, it reveals itself as it wishes—and yet this isn't even true. We are always a partner in its manifestations: *synchronicity itself is an indication of how we are co-creating our realities in every moment*. For most of us, this is unconscious and unnoticed, so that we are normally taken by surprise when the seams reveal themselves, or when the hidden mechanism below breaks through to the surface. Our consciousness is determining our reality, and yet it is doing so only within certain pathways or boundaries that we are complicit with, as will be more fully discussed in the next section.

We often get sidetracked in considering with amazement the less important implications of synchronicity. We focus on the coincidences and their improbability. But that is only part of the story, and actually the lesser part. The greater part of the story is this: synchronistic experiences demonstrate in a very tangible way that consciousness, emotion, and matter are in fact inseparably connected and dynamic. Modern physics has, amazingly, hinted at this; but physicists themselves, with a few exceptions, have been reluctant to consider the import of their own findings. Those with no scientific reputations to uphold have often proved more daring. In fact, this notion is so bizarre for *most* people that it is much easier to revert to the comfort of pure random coincidence than it is to fully examine the connotations of what appears to be going on. Somehow, in some way, the material world (including ourselves and other people) is seemingly being influenced by our thoughts and emotions, just as we are being influenced by *it*. The relationship is reciprocal, and in fact, influence is the incorrect word for this elegant movement in concert. The level at which this occurs is beyond separateness or duality, and is ultimately acausal. There is no better example for this reciprocity than astrology itself, and our consciousness-driven actualizations of the planetary ballet. If astrology exists, then synchronicity exists; and if synchronicity exists, then astrology exists.

But how is one to reconcile the vastness of the universe with our own personal interactions between consciousness and matter? It is one thing to look in the ephemeris and tie an accident experience (for example) of ours to the conjoining of the planets Mars and Uranus, even using a symbolic perspective. That seems so local, so self-contained: it is within our own little solar system. But what of the fact that there are more stars in the sky glowing from untold galaxies than there are grains of sand on all of the beaches on earth, with many of those galaxies being separated by billions of light years of rapidly expanding space? How big is *that*? How can our puny consciousnesses possibly interact with *that* fact? What are the limits of our personal consciousness?

As mentioned previously, perhaps we are but nodes of manifestation for a more universal Consciousness energy; this would explain the fact that the "power" of our personal consciousness seems barely strong enough to create our own lives, let alone the universe as a whole. It does *not* leave the universe, however, barren of the possibility that some sort of consciousness energy *might* take part in its creation. More will be revealed here, always.

***

This book opened with a curious incident involving natal Mars and transiting Uranus in the author's own chart. A similar Mars/Uranus synchronistic incident of an even more spectacular nature may be found on pages 108-110 in physics and astronomy professor Victor Mansfield's excellent book *Synchronicity, Science, and Soul-Making* (1995, Open Court Publishing—the book itself is one of the best ever written on the subject, and is highly recommended). For him, the event associated with this same astrological configuration involved a plane crash. Here we have two independent and yet similar stories of Mars/Uranus synchronistic accident experiences. Astrologers will not be surprised. The incidents are in fact, in their qualities, just the sort of events that astrology would predict as possibilities for this confluence of energies.

The bigger message here isn't in the dramatic, life-changing events themselves, but that they mirrored each other, and coincided in time with the angular relationships between gigantic balls of rock and gas flying through space millions and billions of miles away from us, and billions of miles away from each other. No wonder astrology is so difficult for many people to get on board with! And yet, we look at the two synchronicities with the same two planets involved, and note that they are associated with just the type of events that would be predicted by astrology. It's pretty stunning when one really sits down to meditate on this; and yet, except for the scope, it is no different, or more or less amazing, than the throw of three I Ching coins that deliver a meaningful reading. Both speak to the underlying connectedness of all things, and are our own little windows into this process. In fact, as astrologers, we sometimes have to remain strong ourselves and stay on track to avoid the incredulity that can make us sink back in doubt, and ask, "How *is* this even possible?" But it is.

So we have here synchronicities, the vastness of the universe, astrology, and matter/consciousness/emotional interactions. What could it all mean? How could it work? It's difficult enough for many people to accept that there may be some connection between matter and consciousness without throwing in emotions and astrology. But there it is. A little investigation from friends, family, literature, and the internet will turn up story after story that is difficult to explain through pure coincidence. Marie Louise von Franz has stated that these experiences are "an empirical indication of an ultimate unity of all existence," which her mentor Jung termed the Unus Mundus. David Bohm termed it the Implicate Order. It is assumed and taken for granted in the Eastern traditions.

Astrology explains that occurrences of this nature are the external manifestations of internal energies: of us, *and* of the universe. The alchemists called it the Law of Correspondences: As Above, so Below. All of these ideas point to synchronicity as being, not a random aberration or curious coincidence, but in fact the way that the universe actually *works.* The external and the internal are a Whole, a single unifying principle that does indeed manifest continually on both the interior and exterior levels of both matter and consciousness/emotions. It's not that the external, physical world doesn't exist; it's rather that we are its co-creators, just as it is the co-creator of us. This takes place through what astrology calls Fire, which is associated with the spiritual realm, however one chooses to interpret that: physics energy, God, Tao, creative manifestation. It doesn't matter what terminology is used. If all is One, then those, too, are One. We are synchronized together. We are evolving together and discovering insights together. Krishnamurti stated that "the observer is the observed." The observed and the one observing it are One. This is getting at what we are talking about here.

So we don't need to worry about the vast array of galaxies billions of light years away, or whether we "created" them somehow through consciousness. Oneness presumes participation, but in realms of this magnitude, our personal participation is likely small. All of this is too mysterious for us to know the final answers to. Our personal experience is more provincial and closer to home. Consciousness *is* connected to matter, *is* connected to other consciousnesses, and perhaps to some Ultimate Consciousness or Energy; and the rest is then details. Consciousness, like matter and energy, likely pervades the universe, likely exists as a field, or dimension, or unknown force. We are active nodes, taking part in a correlated and complementary exchange with other consciousnesses, with energy, and with its ephemeral counterpart matter. It is all part of one system, whether Unus Mundus or Implicate Order or Ground of Being. Although connected, we are nodes only, we are not all. We do not have to create all of reality, but only our own little portions. The exact percentages, or qualities, of our interactions with Consciousness, energy, and matter, we can never know.

***

As a corollary to this, if everything is indeed connected, then there is also no possibility for causation (although this doesn't get rid of probability, which has been well verified through experiment. The challenge is to discover how quantum possibility and probability may interact with a completely connected universe.) Alan Watts used to ask: how can a cat cause its tail? As a cat moves along on the other side of a hole in a fence, we at first see the head, the body, and then we see the tail. Each follows the other in time. But does the body cause the tail? Synchronicity is the real-world experience of this.

Alan Watts additionally used the visual analogy of the world being a rubber sheet: our seeming separateness is as if we poke our fingers up from underneath, producing a bump in the rubber sheet, which we may then move around. It seems separate, but it's not. At birth, we poke up from the sheet, appear independent for a moment, and then before we know it, at death, we simply relax back into the sheet. We were never apart from it. According to Watts, we don't "come into this world" so much as we "come out of it." For some, this concept is as difficult to grasp or accept as astrology is. The two go together. They stem from the same vision or concept of the universe: one which is connected and holistic. It is difficult for us to grasp, because our temporary and illusion-ridden egos cry out for separateness and uniqueness. But our egos, too, are simply part of the Whole. The challenge is for us to see that. That is the riddle that has been assigned to us this lifetime.

***

The difficulty in accepting that, whether in physics or in synchronicity, matter may be tied to consciousness, comes from a misunderstanding of matter itself. We are taught from an early age that matter is solid and separate, and interacts with other matter only in a time-ordered linear and causative sense. Billiard ball A rolls across the table in a time period of x seconds, and strikes billiard ball B, causing it to fall down into pocket C. Except that this isn't at all what it seems to be when one drills down to the deeper levels of what is really happening—or rather that it is only the most surface manifestation: what some traditions call the world of maya, or transient illusion. The two billiard events are connected, that much is true. There is an audible "crack" as they knock into each other that is difficult to ignore.

But let's dig deeper. Quantum physics has shown that, in the first place, besides being 99.999% empty space, the billiard ball is in fact nothing more than the temporary manifestation of a series of wave function collapses of the atoms and subatomic particles that it contains. There existed simply an energy *potential* for a billiard ball, which has been actualized through a solidifying of possibilities into the form that we see. The greater realities are the wave functions themselves, which are nothing but mathematical descriptions of energy fields. All is energy, and the billiard ball is only one of a multitude of physical forms that the anonymous atoms and molecules could have taken. The collapse of these energies into a billiard ball may or may not have had to do with interactions involving consciousness. *The potential is always there that it could have.* Were the billiard ball part of a synchronistic experience, then consciousness likely *would* have interacted with it. In addition, the time ordering of the interaction is also illusory. Stepping back perhaps into another dimension, we can see the causative misconception of the billiard interactions fade into a matrix of swirling energy events that are connected only acausally, because they ultimately express a level of reality that is beyond matter, time, and space. So consciousness is not really interacting with what we know as physical matter, but on subtle and invisible energies that may be more compatible with its own ephemerality.

Synchronicity is then a concept that combines all of this, and more. The "meaningful coincidences" are merely the localized expressions of a larger principle which hides in the shadows. The meaning derives from the interactions of consciousness and emotion with matter and its unknown energy substrate. Again, we have: Earth, Air, Fire, and Water. Again, the world is complete, a whole.

Whether experienced as a localized curious occurrence, an astrological transit, an "a-ha!" moment, or an overwhelming sense of meaning and connectedness, the largest import of synchronicity is, again, that it is evidence in front of us that consciousness, and what we are calling the material universe, are partners, are indeed two sides of an unknown coin. We have only to open up our eyes and minds to see.

***

ADDENDUM: BYE, BYE, AMIT

Let's follow up here on how problematic it is to make headway towards having orthodox science look at consciousness, or synchronicity. How stacked is the deck? How difficult is it to get past the dominant paradigm checkpoint? A short while back, on a trip to New Orleans, I observed in the newspaper a notice that there would be an exhibition of drawings from the Prohibition era in Louisiana, by a woman named Olive Leonhardt. Mildly curious, I googled her. She of course came up on Wikipedia. She was an obscure Louisiana illustrator and artist, who died in 1963. But she was there.

While doing research for this book, I also had occasion to google another personality, Amit Goswami. I couldn't find him on Wikipedia. Curious. He is a fairly well-known physicist, teacher, and consciousness/synchronicity theorist. He has at least ten books listed on Amazon, including a 500-page mainstream quantum physics textbook that is used in schools, and has been translated into 9 languages. He has hundreds of videos on YouTube. (Olive Leonhardt has one, announcing her posthumous show.) He is a teacher and lecturer. He has his own DVD out, and has appeared in other movies. He was a professor of physics at the University of Oregon for 30 years.

Apparently, Olive is good enough for Wikipedia, but not Amit. Further googling offsite from Wikipedia unearthed a link to a page titled "Wikipedia: Articles for Deletion/Amit Goswami." Does this mean that Goswami once had a profile on Wikipedia, but that someone has taken it upon themselves to put it into a process of actual *deletion*? Rubbed out like a mafia hit? Taken off the shelf of available information like the burned books of the Nazis or Mao? The author of the Wikipedia deletion page writes, "I'm just not convinced that this article really demonstrates notability... I'm just not buying it... Perhaps something can be salvaged, but I'm not convinced the case has been made." There follows several threads of discussion, pro and con, including one person's suggestion to "Keep regardless of if he is right or wrong, at least his theories are new and fresh and deserve that we reflect on them. I say that we should at least have an article on him in Wikipedia to at least see what books and articles he has written." That's followed by a reply: "That's not a policy-based argument, the issue is whether he's notable."

Hmmm. Not to be paranoid about the scientific community's lack of embrace, but there couldn't be *any* possibility that some folks at Wikipedia simply don't like "new-age" people with alternative views, could there? Here's a way to kill a few minutes: forget about Olive Leonhardt; try some experiments for yourself. Google on down to some of the most obscure things that you can think of. I'll bet they're on Wikipedia. Now look for Amit: professor, lecturer, movie personality, author of ten plus books, hundreds of YouTube videos. Blank. Draw your own conclusions. I love Wikipedia, I use it daily, and I contribute to every fund drive that they have. But there is possibly some room at the ranch for more open-minded writers to step in, if these writers would not somehow be "written out" themselves, or overridden by the dominant paradigmers at Wikipedia. Who's up for it?

In the physics world, he is not the only one who has been voted out of the club for his heresy. (Fortunately, unlike the days of the medieval Catholic Church, folks nowadays can't be literally burned at the stake just for entertaining contrary views.) When one sees the discounting of consciousness as a possible factor in the physical world, much more prevalent than Amit is the favorite beanbag target: Deepak Chopra. Chopra, because he is so outspoken, visible, and "new-agey," stands there with a bulls-eye painted on him. Obviously very smart (he is a medical doctor, and was Chief of Staff at New England Memorial Hospital after moving to the US from India), he seems to arouse particular ire.

But Chopra is not a physicist, and so an argument could be made that, unlike Goswami, Chopra does not in fact have the training to be voicing opinions regarding this branch of science. (Never mind that many scientists are happy to put their two cents worth in on a variety of subjects for which they themselves have no training, astrology being exhibit A.) It's apparently easy to pick on new-age types. But what you *don't* often hear about in the attacks on "irrationality" are the names of actual physicists themselves (other than Goswami) with more far-reaching ideas on how consciousness may interact with physicality. One might mention here David Bohm, Fritjof Capra, Roger Penrose, Fred Alan Wolf, F. David Peat, Wolfgang Pauli, John Hagelin, Henry Stapp, Brian Josephson, Eugene Wigner, Bernard d'Espagnat, and Freeman Dyson. The list goes on, and in fact dates all the way back to many of the original quantum pioneers, including Schrödinger himself, who was fascinated with Hindu Vedic thought, and said, "The material world has only been constructed at the price of taking the self, that is, mind, out of it, removing it; mind is not part of it...," and "The world is given to me only once, not one existing and one perceived. Subject and object are only one."

Those bent on defending the fortifications of the materialistic party line love to pick on Deepak, but don't often mention the above names, all of whom who are well-educated physicists who have had distinguished careers (there are at least four Nobel Prize winners among them), but who have also had the temerity to consider possibilities beyond rank physicalism. And as far as synchronicity and astrology go? Forget about it. Go away. The doors are closed.

Astrology

A Curious Thing

In high school, I was starting to be curious about astrology, but was only at the level of sun signs. I made a note in my mind that two of my best friends, David and Charlie, were both Cancers, as was my Dad. It wasn't until my college days that I became interested and dedicated enough to spend the time learning to set up and interpret full natal charts. This was in the days of tables of houses and logarithms, prior to computers, and so it required a fair amount of interest to want to spend an hour or so doing the calculations involved. But it was always rewarding. I learned that my dad was a Cancer with Moon in Aries and Leo rising.

Doing the charts of my two friends, I discovered that *both* of them were not only Cancers, but also had Moon in Aries and Leo rising, although they were born a year apart. Coincidence? Only one in 1,728 people will have this exact combination of the three factors. I am not an overly social person. What are the odds that I would not only find the two within my small circle that matched my dad's horoscope, but that I would bond with them as best friends? I am still in touch with one of them to this day. I had a very difficult relationship with my father at that time (which became much better later in life), and this was obviously energy that I needed to come to terms with and work through. After college, I also dated a woman for two years who, although she had a different sun sign, also had Moon in Aries and Leo rising. (one in 144) I think that this may have finally helped me to resolve and digest that particular combination of energy in my life. I began to make inroads at this time towards developing a better relationship with my dad, and we eventually became very close. I've also learned quite a bit more about astrology since then.

Is Astrology Divination?

Question: Is astrology divination?

The short answer: Yes, sort of, in a way, partially.

The long answer:

We are going to shortly present the idea that astrology is not predictable; or rather that it is only partially so. At the opposite end of the spectrum from astrology as a predictable clockwork science, then, lies astrology as divination. If astrology isn't a block universe, if it isn't a giant set of gears simply awaiting the correct key or formula, then might it be pure divination, divorced from any such mechanical calculability? This idea has gained some popularity in recent years.

The popularity of the idea is generally attributable to Geoffrey Cornelius' 2003 book *The Moment of Astrology,* which has been the subject of more than one conversation in the astrological world. It does a great service to astrology by keeping alive and providing fresh thoughts and insights into the age-old question of how astrology works. The book postulates that astrology is most properly thought of as divination; as being not much different from other divinatory practices, such as the I Ching, or Tarot cards. Cornelius is not alone here: in a podcast with astrologer Chris Brennan, he describes how a whole group of British astrologers involved with both the Astrological Lodge of London and The Company of Astrologers had been moving towards this orientation since the 1970's. They were encouraged in this direction not only by a revival of William Lilly's teachings involving horary, but also by the relative failure of scientific studies involving astrology.

The book traces the roots of astrology back in history to more primitive cultures looking for divinatory signs from the heavens, and states that there is a "hollowness" to the way that most people practice it today: using the natal chart in a mechanical and mathematical way, with an assumption of some degree of determinism, to map out the possible courses that a life (or other event) might take, while giving short shrift to the immediacy of the moment. For those interested in astrology as divination, the "live" time point of the interaction, whether in a horary situation or in a life reading, is really what counts. In fact, every reading here is essentially a horary reading. Of note is that Cornelius comes from a self-professed divinatory background, and as we may note with everyone from physicists to philosophers, if one's tool is a hammer (as the saying goes), then every problem turns out to be a nail. Believing is seeing. Our worlds are a projection of ourselves; this is true for everyone. Where we come into astrology is more often than not where we stay. If we learn Placidus cusps, we tend to stay with Placidus. If they tell us in Physics 101 that astrology is ridiculous and impossible, then we tend to stay with that also. You do this, and I do this. It's human nature.

Cornelius' book is well worth reading. He has a lot of great things to say, and he has opened up some good dialog in the astrological community. His book is well written, erudite, and brings out many questions that astrology has often shied away from examining. And yet, after one has digested the book, the core question remains: *is* astrology divination? That's a valid question. The idea that there is a "secret mutual connivance" (Jung's term involving synchronicity) between the astrologer and his client, or the client's chart, is undoubtedly true. So is astrology then simply a divinatory expression of the moment, or is astrology a mechanical block universe of fixed fate forever frozen in spacetime, but discoverable by thumbing through the ephemeris? Those two are very different ideas. Is the "moment" of astrology the reading itself, or is it the previous birth moment with its attendant dynamics and predictably moving chart? Might it be both? Is it augury, or quantum, or humanistic, or scientific, or spiritual, or *what*? Is astrology causation or synchronicity based, or something else? It's always of value to ask what *are* we studying or attempting to know, what *are* our prejudices (importantly), and what are the implications of any of this in a larger sense?

The main issue that some astrologers seem to have with this thesis is not that astrology may have some divination involved in its workings, so much as the emphasis on a "pure" and solely divinatory model for much of astrology outside of horary (which is already divinatory). It seems undoubtedly true that there is a strong element of synchronicity-associated divination in astrology, and in the book's historical examination he is entirely correct. But our views of many things (physics, biology, astrology) have changed through the centuries, and usually in parallel with other events and discoveries in the world at large. We must always continue to examine existing truths and paradigms, and that includes astrology as well. It is likely no coincidence, for example, that humanistic astrology came about just at the time that quantum mechanics was starting to describe the world in more probabilistic and observer-influenced terms, rather than in the previously more deterministic ones. In light of the modern gestalt and various scientific findings, it then is natural to inquire to what extent divination *may* be a viable way of looking at the mechanism of astrology in today's world. One might actually make a case that it is perhaps *more* appropriate today to take a divinatory approach, in view of quantum's triumph of probability and observer interaction over clockwork. So Cornelius is conceivably on to something here.

Cornelius does throw the non-divinators a bone by dividing the discipline into two camps: his pet Divinatory division, and what he calls "Natural" astrology, which is what most people think of when they consider astrology at all: a knowable and foreseeable world (at least as to the cycles), featuring predictable orbits of the planets and other bodies that can somehow, and to some imperfect extent, be correlated with life on earth, or our own histories. However, this is then discounted as somehow inferior. The rules of Ptolemy are rejected in lieu of the more primitive omenistic origins of astrology. It's actually a shame, as this "moment" could have provided the perfect opportunity for bringing together in a meaningful way the two versions of synchronicity mentioned earlier (synchrony, and consciousness with emotionally mediated coincidence).

Part of the rejection of many of the techniques of astrology as currently practiced, by those who gravitate towards divination, is related to the failure of astrology to be able to "prove" itself scientifically, and the repeated frustrations encountered by astrology banging its head against that particular wall. For those who have fought that battle, it indeed must have been tremendously frustrating. At one point, Cornelius acknowledges some valid scientific studies, including the Gauquelins and Vernon Clark, and even acknowledges that they were unfairly neglected and picked on by mainstream science; but then seems to ignore this, minimize them, and declare that there is no scientific validity, or way to find any. Like many other astrologers today who have been disillusioned by the scientific quest, he reverts towards the somewhat sour-grapes, burned-hand position that astrology simply doesn't need science, and in fact would be better off without it. Somehow, a further leap is made here wherein the discouraging interactions with science have left divination as the only logical option. Is that even true? And yet, like everyone else, he seems to long for more mainstream acceptance, and correctly names science as the gatekeeper for approved knowledge; a role that used to be filled by religion. It's unclear, however, how reverting to talking about astrology again as occult, magic, divinatory, a product of the daemon, or similar terms, will further the cause.

The divinatory camp, it must continually be stressed, isn't wrong, but simply seems incomplete. Divination *is* part of the astrological process. Again, this could have been an opening to place astrology more firmly in its traditional formulary of art + science, while recognizing the mainstream scientific bias against the objective studies that *did* pan out as being an important factor in the astrology vs. science standoff today. This whole subject would seem to cry out for a more nuanced middle ground beyond the either/or of divination *versus* ephemeris based, or even (to extend the continuum) completely deterministic astrology.

Regardless, if there actually *is* a particular "moment" of astrology, then what *is* that magic moment? Is it truly that particular instant associated with a reading? It is correct to say that if things are a Whole, if time and space are connected, then *every moment* of our lives is a divinatory moment, not just a particular one. My life is a continuance, unbroken, and of a single piece of cloth. That includes this moment, but it also includes the moment that I took my first breath. They are connected and inform each other. They exist and take part, not only in my own life, but within the unfolding cosmos around me. That is the basis of synchronicity. In every moment of our lives, we take part in the evolving fabric of existence; we are connected and we have the potential to be aware. Divinatory aids such as I Ching coins or horoscopic charts may help us to focus, but the potential is there to divine things even without them, and at any particular moment. Our own insights, as well as that of talented psychics, readers, or divinators testify to this. And, dropping back to our previous consciousness speculations, it is also likely that in our interactions with others, in our explorations of either synchronicity or the moment of astrology, there is an additional synergistic *mixing* of interpersonal consciousnesses that factors into achieving the results of any divinatory effort involving more than one person. Then: looking at all of this, looking at synchronicity's apparent role in the universe, and looking at modern physics' movement towards the involvement of consciousness and observers, it is *entirely* proper and instructive to take up the subject of divination.

But that's not what astrology is (except for horary). That's what the I Ching or the Tarot is. Astrology takes *part* in a divinatory *aspect* of reality, of the moment, but it is far more. Astrology *does* have a basis in the natural world: that is its most salient and important feature. Otherwise, why have an astrology chart at all? Why not just use a piece of scrap newspaper for divination? The very premise of astrology is that there are predictable movements of the sun, moon, and planets, and that these are somehow synchronized to the fates of those on earth, who can then in turn find meaning in these knowable cycles. Astrology as divination may sidestep and negate the problem of making it compatible with science, but as a sole explanation, it doesn't feel true to astrology. It feels more authentic to continue with the art + science model, and to continue to hope that science, in its own explorations, will one day make itself compatible with astrology. Admittedly, that is not exactly darkening the doorstep of the discipline at this time; but we are always surprised at the turns that science and its investigations may take. Who'd have thought that the earth wasn't the center of the universe? All problems will not be solved in our own lifetimes.

The very idea of divination is that we tap into the flow of things at a particular moment. We will continue to remain suspicious of the notions of space and time themselves, as we have discovered that they are not always what they seem to be, and are possibly not always even operational—though that is difficult to comprehend. We will let them stand for now. So it would seem that there are at least two factors in a divinatory experience that are operating here. One is the idea that things simply move along at their particular pace and in their particular way; that path being beyond what we can ever fully comprehend. That is the Tao, that is God's will. At the same time, things are connected in time and space, and beyond or across time and space. That is synchronicity; that is the basis for common divination, the coming together of various archetypal elements. That is why a divinatory reading seems to be relevant to the moment. Those are the wormholes of reality that produce the a-ha! moments found in a Tarot or an I Ching reading. All of these factors assume, and indeed cannot exist without, the component of active and involved consciousness, and likely Consciousness. And as there is more than one consciousness involved in the typical reading, this begs a question of weighting, revisited later in this book: which, or whose, consciousness is creating more of reality at the moment? Emotion plays a part, as does concentration, personal will, and most importantly, the needs of the universe. So we have here, so far, making up the divinatory moment: the flow of the cosmos, intelligent or not, personal consciousness, transpersonal consciousness, and synchronicity. These are the factors that exist with us as we sit down at the table and attempt to make our minds receptive.

All of these also exist in astrology, but now there is an additional component: the flow of the Tao runs in meaningful parallel to the movements of the planets. (Actually, of course, *everything in the universe* runs in meaningful parallel.) The movements of the planets are mechanical, are predictable, and are laid out clearly in black and white on the pages of the ephemeris. There *must* be a connection here, or there is no astrology. The connection is acausal. Our personal development, experiences, and awareness also parallel the cycles of the planets. Like the rest of reality, there must be an acausal and yet predictable-to-whatever-extent connection here as well. If everything is a Whole, then everything is by definition connected. Various interacting consciousnesses, in fact, act in concert with the positions of the planets, and pull or incline their effects slightly in one direction or another; a sort of psychic gravity bending time, space, and consciousness in the same way that Einstein's general theory of relativity did for the purely material. Our personal consciousness is the most important for us in our own little corner of the flow, but it is not the only influence: we are part of the Collective, and our own influence must interact with others. Randomness and unpredictability also contribute. But for the astrologer, interacting and predictable cosmic cycles, focused on the birth chart (or other chart of interest), are a key factor in any reading, along *with* divination. Synchronicity ties them together. Ultimately, for astrology (and unlike the I Ching or Tarot), the ephemeris rules.

So divination as a metaphor for using the intuitive to get in touch with consciousness and synchronicity *is* part of an astrological reading, but is not the whole story, or possibly even the most important component. The beauty of astrology is in the harmony and synergy between intuition/divination and the established and predictable mechanical cycles; between the known and forecast archetypes and the interactive consciousnesses of the people involved. Synchronicity itself, as it relates to astrology, contains both the divinatory and the cycles; that, in fact, is what synchronicity *is*: "an acausal connecting principle." It connects *meaning* expressed through archetypes with predictable mechanics, and in astrology, personal meaning is *always* attached in some way to the cycles of the cosmos. One cannot have astrology without synchronicity, although one can have synchronicity without astrology. But then, of course, it's no longer astrology. A reading is of a whole, as indeed are our lives as we move through the cosmic patterns, attempting to find direction and significance. But, regardless of the exact percentage of divination involved in readings, there are larger questions that exist in astrology...

A Modern Model for Astrology

Which is stranger: the ideas that the universe appeared initially perhaps from pure mathematical quantum possibility, arising from an infinitesimally small point, and is dilating outwards due to the creation and expansion of space itself; that nothing is fixed in the universe, but is subject to relativity of reference frame, laws of chance, and observer participation; that not only light but also matter are simultaneously two completely incompatible concepts, waves and particles, and that our measurement may determine which; that we can't find 95% of the universe that's right in front of us and we're comfortable with that; that an electron on the other side of the universe can instantaneously "know" the results of our lab experiments; or that we are somehow in synch with or influenced by the solar system around us, the system that includes our own sun, powering all life on earth, aka astrology? Just a question.

***

Astrology, like physics, can't seem to decide whether our lives are ruled by free will, or by fate. Astrology has traditionally had a very fated quality to it; but then again, so has physics: the clockwork universe lasted a long time. But physics has moved on to quantum uncertainty, and astrology has moved on towards the mainly "humanistic" position that it occupies currently, which presupposes some level of choice and input from us towards the stars as well as the time-honored reverse path. So which is correct? Is it all one or all the other, or might there be some sort of hybrid?

Physics is currently stuck at a massive impasse involving this exact same problem. The logjam is keeping scientists from moving forward with a "Theory of Everything"; one that would stitch

Einstein's ideas together with quantum mechanics, the macrocosm with the microcosm. Both ideas are stalwarts of physics, both have been proven to be true, and yet they are incompatible. As it stands now, Einstein's theories of spacetime and general relativity point towards a predestined and predictable universe as much as Newton's ideas did. It is one that would be ideal for astrology: a block universe in which it would be easy to comprehend, if not fully divine, the connections between events in both time and space. Everything would be relatively straightforward math, everything would be fixed and predictable. Versions of astrology such as Hindu Jyotish, which is heavily fated, may find this interesting. Unfortunately, the universe itself hasn't seemed so willing to cooperate in this regard. Quantum mechanics, the only slightly younger upstart which has also been thoroughly investigated and successfully tested many times, specifically states that there is *no* predictability or predestination for anything; that *everything* is subject solely to the laws of chance and probability, with the final direction possibly skewed by consciousness. As may be easily seen, there is a big problem here.

It's the same ongoing problem that affects astrology, and, just as astrology in some ways has mirrored the course of physics, the answer to one may provide the answer to the other. What could the solution be? Let's take a look at a couple of things. The current fate/free will choices for *anyone* are a) everything is fated, b) everything is a product of free will and/or randomness, or c) there is some sort of combination of the two. For astrologers, really only a) and c) are viable options, as astrology pretty much (except possibly for the divinatory positions) presupposes some level of determinism, either complete or partial.

Now, here's an interesting thing: the world is what it is. Things turn out the way they turn out. That means whether you *believe* in fate or free will, the end product is always the same: things are the way they are. That is all that we can ever know completely and unequivocally. We can never know the answer as to whether they turned out that way because of fate, or because of free will.

However, there are some intriguing speculations that may be drawn from this. We will assume up front that not everything about reality has been detected or made known to us yet. R=K+1. We will note (moving back and forth again to physics) that light is currently both a wave *and* a particle simultaneously (while in superposition); the particular version that it exhibits being determined by measurement, interaction, and consciousness. We will note again that *matter itself* conforms to this wave/particle duality: our entire material universe is, at its root, as indeterminate, unformed, and pliable as the results of the double slit experiment. We will wonder if perhaps this dualistic incompatibility may one day be resolved through the discovery of a deeper level of reality that will show how this seeming discordance was illusory all along. We will wonder, perhaps, if apprehending these two qualities of the material world could be seen as the Indian parable of the Blind Men and the Elephant. One blind scientist says "I know what matter is like - it's like a particle," and another says "No, matter is like a wave." They get together, and puzzlingly, decide that it is odd, but matter is like both a particle AND a wave. But why should it end there? They are at this point apprehending perhaps only the elephant's trunk and right leg. What else is missing from their assessment? What else haven't they noticed or touched?

The *seeming* dichotomy of fate and free will may be a similar situation. We need to work backwards here. A clue is that again, whichever of these you prefer, *the end results are the same*. That speaks to an equivalence. Fate = Free Will. *There is no difference whatsoever in outcomes* related to your preference. Perhaps this is because we are seeing only part of the elephant; perhaps there *are* "hidden variables" that would explain this seeming difference, coming from a deeper level of reality. The type of hidden variables proposed by Bohm (for example) were designed to obliterate chance or free will and return the universe to certainty and predictability. But what if there were another, or deeper, level hidden to us that allowed both fate and free will to exist at once, as well as their cousins predictability and indeterminacy? Or perhaps the nature of systems in general is to include disparate components, and we are noticing a system here that is simply too large for us to comprehend in its entirety. Perhaps it is another example of Bohr's "complementarity," which was also expressed millennia ago by Taoist spiritual masters in the yin-yang symbol. Perhaps you *can't* have fate without free will and vice versa, just as you can't have black without white, or good without evil. For one to exist, the other must also be known: we perceive or recognize one only by knowing the other in contrast. Reality itself, of course, is beyond these dualities, and is beyond waves and particles. It incorporates them but is above them as well as below them, outside of them, and inside of them. Black and white are both separated *parts* of a greater whole that contains them: as with everything else in our world, misleading duality continually arises from the One, generated by our trying to parse and understand its components.

So fate and free will perhaps *must* be part of a greater whole that contains them both. You can't have one without the other: they define each other, and are thus inseparably linked. Though seemingly incompatible, they both must exist, and they both must govern the behavior of our universe. They are of the same thing, they produce the same results. Black and white are not the same, and yet in a way they are: they are parts of a whole without which either partner is meaningless. It is in their working in tandem that the visual contrast of the world as we see it is produced. Fate and free will are not the same and yet they are: they are parts of a whole without which each partner is meaningless. Is light a particle or a wave? It is both, depending on how we choose to measure it. Are our lives governed by fate or free will? They are directed by both. Analogous to the measurement of light, perhaps they show us one more than the other in the way that we choose to see them. The deeper level of reality that allows this to be true is hidden from us by clouds and smoke; we catch brief glimpses of it, but only fleetingly. One day it may be possible to know it in greater depth. It may very well be Consciousness, or at least something connected to that force. It is consciousness that produces our personal reality; it is consciousness that apprehends our fate; and it is consciousness that guides whatever free will we may have in our interactions with our destiny, chance, or karma. It is indeed consciousness through which we interact with, experience, and know our natal charts and transits.

Life is but a dream, the old saying goes, and this may be more true than we might imagine. Quantum mechanics says that the world around us is produced by the collapsing of possibilities into actualities. Inchoate and formless possibility produces manifestation and structure. Uranus produces Cronus (Saturn). We can see this in our own lives, in fact: the observation of nature has been the instructor of man throughout his history, and why should the modern world be any different? In the modern world, quantum is now a part of nature. We can see that at our birth, we are 100% possibility and 0% actuality. At our deaths, we are 0% possibility and 100% actuality. Our lives then are nothing but a continual manifestation of possibilities into actualities, driven by our consciousness interacting with circumstances, and bound by whatever portion fate may play. Our charts, starting from nothing but quizzically marked circles on paper, turn into the richest of experiences throughout our lives, including a-ha moments, understandings, disappointments, and reorganizations. We dream our lives into existence, and we give flesh to our charts.

So: Do we manifest these actualities ourselves, or are we passive travelers, viewing the scenery from the window, enjoying the ride as our train rumbles along its fixed and fated track? This would seem to get at the very crux of the matter, especially for astrologers. We don't *feel* like completely passive travelers. We feel like active participants. And yet, we look in the ephemeris, and we see that, unnoticed to us previously, there was a Saturn square that marked our divorce a few years ago. Wow. (Hindsight is always 20/20, as the saying goes, and synchronistic meaning, interestingly, often appears only after the fact.) Einstein has been telling us that space and time are both connected and predictable. Quantum has been telling us that nothing is certain until possibilities are collapsed into actualities. And spirituality tells us that this is accomplished by consciousness. What can we make of all this?

If fate exists in any fashion at all, then astrology must exist. The existence of fate, or predictability, or certainty, presupposes some sort of connection in time and space between events and physical objects. The pool balls must be knocking into each other; we will know where and when the event will occur. The position of the planets must have a raw association in time and space with events in our lives: these events at minimum occur *alongside* whatever positions the planets are currently exhibiting. This is not *causation*, but simple *correlation*. That's synchrony. The only question is one of meaning; whether these parallel connections produce meaning. That's synchronicity. Both of these are acausal. But if things are fated or block-like, this would have to include the events in our lives, as well as the parallel locus of the planets. One need then only to discover and delineate the association or connection. The question is, whether this correlation is fixed in predictability, or may include some opportunity for free will or randomness. The principle of indeterminacy states that it must.

Einstein. Quantum. Fate. Free Will. No one knows yet how these ideas, tied to physics, will all play out. Great minds are working on these issues as we speak. The problem with our latest version of physics, quantum mechanics, is not that we can't use it; the problem is that we really don't have any idea of what it actually describes. It seems, especially in its in conflicting relationship to geometric spacetime, to be pointing towards a level of reality that is deeper, and would be more explanatory: but *what*? Consciousness, either personal or transpersonal, is certainly, for the adventurous, a possible candidate; but no one knows for sure. Regardless, let's move forward and use these three items (spacetime, quantum, and consciousness) to construct a model of how astrology may work in the context of fate and free will *both* being equally extant and operational, and in the context of synchronicity.

***

Let's go back to the block universe, and specifically to the idea previously mentioned of using a loaf of raisin bread for a model or metaphor, last seen in the Physics section under "It's All Relative."

(This popular loaf of raisin bread is also frequently drafted into service to explain the expanding universe.) Here, then, is the partial skeleton for our model of reality: the loaf represents time, the universe, and the spacetime continuum; and the raisins contained in it represent events. In this visualization, a "slice" of bread would be like a moment in time: we would not see the parts of the loaf in front of us (although, due to the mysterious arrow-of-time that flows only one way, we could see the slices behind us). We would be confined in our vision to the slice that we were currently in, the present, with whatever raisins (events) that existed in this particular slice, at this particular moment. Other slices have already been baked and fixed as they are, but exist either in the past or in the future, behind or in front of our own slice. But there are oddities: if it is true that synchronicity involves some sort of consciousness which is beyond currently known space and time, then there are those who, on certain occasions, may get glimpses of the raisins in other parts of the four dimensional loaf, including the "future," although that term is a somewhat inaccurate description. The loaf, after all, is all of a whole, with everything (bread and raisins) existing at once and connected to every other part. Thus, past and future are arbitrary labels pasted onto different parts of the bread. This was Einstein's vision. The promise of Flatland is that, due to our consciousness, we may magically hover outside or above the loaf to see all of this.

So here comes astrology. Astrology is very compatible with this model so far. One could simply say that *synchrony* (as opposed to true synchronicity) shows that everything in the loaf is synchronized just as in geometric spacetime, and that therefore events (raisins) are fixed and synchronized with our "map" of the bread, if we could (similar to Flatland) visualize the whole loaf from outside, from a higher dimension. One could further hypothesize that since everything is geared together, the known and projected wanderings of the planets shown in the ephemeris may be laid out and act as just such a map, at least for our local corner of the universe, the solar system. The mysterious archetypal energies through which astrology operates may then form nodes in the loaf in the places that they either intersect with each other, or intersect with our personal charts. The visualization would be that of invisible, crisscrossing, and yet predictable lines of energy running through the fixed loaf, with the raisins forming nodes correlating with events. These raisins may thus be predicted and placed in the loaf through using the ephemeris. Planetary paths, it might be noted, would actually look like spirals corkscrewing through the bread rather than flat orbits as they moved forward in time. Visually, this would be very similar to A. T. Mann's wonderful diagrams in his book *The Round Art*. The ongoing energies of our own charts would also trace imperceptible helixes into the future. Connections would be invisible as they would deal with unseen energies; only events themselves (raisins) would be visible. Our charts, as mentioned, would take part in this illusory movement through the loaf: we are our own little raisins or nodes, in a sense fixed in a certain time or place in the loaf, but whose energies stretch throughout the raisin bread and interact with all other points in the loaf. It is the energy of consciousness that allows this meta-view, this seeming perception of movement.

OK. So far, we have a fixed (and actually infinite; don't get too hung up on the picture of a loaf) quantity of bread with raisin events in it. The events may be known and foreseen throughout the loaf by interpreting invisible yet predictable lines of energy, and maps of the synchronized planets acting through the archetypes (love, war, intellect, etc.). Whew. That seems like a lot, and seems like it might be enough. But it isn't. Quantum won't let us settle on anything this predictable, and neither will our real-life experience with astrology. Try as we might, drill down to the most microscopic minutiae of our charts, learn every possible secret, mathematical, and occult technique of astrology, and we find that we still can't predict the future.

Or rather we can, but the success rate is quirky, to say the least. We *can* predict the future *sometimes*, and we can predict it in *certain ways*: if this were not true, astrology would have died on the vine a long time ago. One can only live for so long on raw hope or delusion without some sort of concrete results. (Although the Flat Earth Society is still in existence, it must be noted!) People stick with astrology because they *do* find something there. Many are frustrated that things aren't *more* predictable, but that is exactly where we are moving now in the discussion. In many ways, the predictions of astrology show a situation very similar to Heisenberg, who showed that in paired quantum variables, the more we know about one, the less we will know about the other. Similarly, we can predict some astrological events exactly, but only once in a great while, or we can predict "weather-report"-wise ("70 percent chance that you might change careers") constantly and consistently, but with less accuracy. We can predict the general *character* of events a lot of the time, or the *exact event* very rarely. This smells like quantum, and gives us a clue as to the next ingredient needed.

This next step gets us into all sorts of complicated things in physics, many of which are incompatible with the fixed and predictable raisin bread model. The arrow of time was mentioned previously, and those who enjoy cognitive challenges may also look up light cones and thermodynamics for some really speculative discussions of time. We are going to keep the arrow of time for our own purposes here; that is the apparent flow of time (using quantum) moving away from the actualized past and towards the unrealized future. We move in that general direction through the bread loaf, but the raisins are now, while still present off in the distance, getting hazier. Einstein would love the loaf of raisin bread as described previously, but quantum theory states that events are not finalized or manifested until the unformed potential of their wave functions are collapsed in the present. Everything may have a wave function, it will be recalled, but most collapses take place at the atomic or subatomic level; that is why our mesocosm looks so normal, why we don't see bizarre materializations or de-materializations in our everyday world. But, in adding this underlying uncertainty and randomness to the loaf of raisin bread, we find that the future now is there, but it is not fully known. It is predictable, but indeterminate. It is fixed, but fuzzy. The past is concrete: the future, while still perceivable in certain ways, is unmanifested and gel-like; the concrete hasn't hardened yet. Possibilities walk hand in hand with probabilities. We now have fate and free will working in tandem, with a dash of quantum randomness thrown in for good measure. That's exactly why astrology has the tantalizing feel that it does. This in turn is our whispered clue towards a deeper level of reality. It is this deeper level that produces astrology as we know it, and indeed, existence as we know it.

***

As to the raisin bread model: let us now adapt it, to make it more compatible with the modern world. Let's add some quantum uncertainty, as well as some consciousness, into the mix, and see what we come up with. In service to this, we will again start with the original loaf containing the raisins: fixed and expected spacetime. But in deference to this idea of deterministic predictability collaborating *with* quantum uncertainty collapsed by consciousness, let's create a new schema. Let's keep the raisins that are "behind" us in the loaf of spacetime as they are: they are known, they can be seen, and they are collapsed and solidified. They are the past. Energy and potential have become matter, space, and associated events. Hindsight is 20/20. But let's look more closely at the raisins that are in the loaf "in front of us" according the arrow of time, which is how we actually experience things. The raisins (events) must exist, because spacetime is an accepted part of reality, and because they are right there in the ephemeris. But why do they look so fuzzy? Why don't they look clear like the raisins behind us? Why can't we "remember" the future? Why can't we fully and exactly *predict* the future?

The upcoming raisins/ indeterminate events lie in wait like psychic and archetype-loaded landmines standing in place to be stepped on, to be triggered. They are there, they exist, but they are fuzzy. They are fuzzy because their quantum potential has not yet been activated; because our consciousness has not yet interacted with them. The fuzziness that we see is their *potential*, their possibilities, their event cloud; their actualities have not been finalized yet. They have not been collapsed.

It may be that our currently known spacetime is laid out all of a piece like a dimension in Flatland, but that most of us as humans are not privy to the larger vision, and are only able to move through the loaf of bread as if linear time existed; and perhaps it does. In accordance with the arrow of time, we move through in one direction only, slice by slice. As we go, we encounter new fuzzy raisin events which can be predicted, but which have not yet been brought to full manifestation. As we encounter them, our conscious interaction with the archetypes and their associated energy lines collapse the fuzzy event-possibility-clouds of the raisins, and turn them into actual events. We *are* creating our own reality as we go, just as the sages have said. At the same time, we *are* living out our charts and our transits, just as the astrologers have said. If consciousness *is* the next dimension that allows us to visualize and "look down" on spacetime, then what do we see? We see the residents of Spacetimeland going about their business. We see the raisins behind them, fully formed and concretized. We see them as they encounter the fuzzy raisin-events ahead of them on the timeline, and watch as their consciousness interacts with these events, producing new finalized versions in their lives that will also soon move behind them. We see the crisscrossing lines of transits and progressions dancing together in their spiral helixes. We see the archetypes light up and fade as they play their parts. We see the "future" (if that is even the right word) ahead of them with its fuzzy pockets of possibilities for their lives, and we see how their *interactions* with these possibilities have forced the potentials to reveal themselves and become part of their ongoing history. We watch as their lives change, through sequentially processing the slices and the raisins, from 100% possibility to 100% actuality.

Just as ours do. Nature is a great teacher. Intuition is a great teacher and innovator. Astrologers have intuitively moved, since Rudhyar in the 20th century, towards a view of results that is compatible with just this sort of model; our analysis above merely explains what their intuition has drawn them towards. (Quantum is the new wrinkle here, acting as an explanatory mechanism for this; the idea of indeterminacy in astrology is certainly not new: the pseudonym "Marvel Brilliant," acting as a writer and researcher for

Kepler College, points out online that the popular phrase "the stars impel, they do not compel" can be traced as far back as a 1632 quote by Sir Francis Bacon, which reads: "Wiser astrologers [believe] that there is no fatal necessity in the stars, but that they rather incline than compel.") Real-world experience bears this out. That is why astrologers today are more likely to produce the above-mentioned "weather report" type of predictions than something more exact and fatalistic. The future is determined, and yet it is not. Fate and free will are working together, and this is a solution to the quandary.

We move through life as if in a dream: our consciousness and course determining, and being determined by, other consciousnesses and pre-ordained possibilities arising from some unknown realm. Life is "conditioned and unfree" as the I Ching puts it, and yet we have the privilege of contributing to our fate in some small way, and working in tandem with the universe itself. The word for this is synchronicity.

An electron orbiting the outermost regions of an atom may, according to quantum theory, potentially be found at any location in the universe. It is, however, most likely to be found sticking fairly close to its nucleus, close to home, close to the place that is "right" for it. Similarly, we are most commonly found close to our own "homes," our astrological dharma, the paths that are laid out for us, fuzzy though they may be. Those who wander far are often less happy. Life becomes out of balance. We *have* choice, we have some limited ability to steer, but our best choice is usually to simply actualize who we are *meant* to be. That is shown by our charts. The level of reality that is producing these paths, this dharma, is not fully known to us. We can only look up, or look out, or look in, and simply wonder at it all.

A Modern Model, Continued

What then are the upcoming events in this model, which is trying to simultaneously be second cousin to both physics and philosophy, as well as astrology? What is the character of the "raisins" which lurk ahead, waiting for our own lives to be ready for them? We see them dimly, but they are unformed, like impending ghosts. They are part of the fabric of spacetime, but the fabric is not entirely woven yet; it is loose and gauzy on the far side of our slice of the loaf.

These future events, to refer back to quantum again, take on the appearance in physics of an electron cloud, which is simply the probability distribution of where an electron might be found surrounding its atomic nucleus. These are also known as orbitals, and good visual representations may be found online; there is a beauty in their mathematical symmetry. They speak to the fact that, in keeping with Heisenberg's well-verified uncertainty principle, the exact position of an electron may not be known until we measure it, and conversely upon measuring its location we then will not be able to know its momentum, or trajectory. The modern universe has a frustrating ambiguity *built into it*. The fabric of the future is there in some form, but at the same time we are weaving it as we go. The loom is never still. We can't know what the *exact* nature of an event will be until we get there, and once the exact nature of an event *is* known, we cannot know exact nature of the *next* event that it will then lead to. Like dogs going in circles, we are forever chasing the tail of the future, always just beyond our reach. If we are stagnant, we are tracing circles. If we are moving and growing, we are tracing spirals.

So the picture of the atomic orbital, or electron cloud, is really a picture of the probabilities of finding an electron at a particular point in space. Prior to measurement, the electron may theoretically be found at any point in the universe. Its location does not become definite until we measure or observe it. Quantum does not disallow any possibilities. However, *probabilities* dictate that the electron is much, much, much, more likely to be found in a particular location close to the nucleus, just as one would expect. That's the genesis of the cloud picture itself. Higher probabilities lead to greater densities in the cloud surrounding the nucleus.

It is the same with astrological events. From a distance, they are perceived, but a blur. They appear in a fuzzy, cloud-like fashion with varying densities, just as the electrons did. Saturn square Sun by transit: what could this mean? What would the event cloud look like? It could conceivably lead to an event which would mean a new love affair, but this would be unlikely; that's not really the nature of these energies. But again, according to quantum, no possibilities may be disallowed. So that would be within the realm of possibility. But this would be the equivalent of an electron circling an atom on the screen in front of me being found perhaps somewhere a few feet away from its atom: possible, but highly unlikely.

The position of the event in its probability cloud would be more likely to hover near more appropriate locales: circumstances (in this example) which would relate to delays or obstructions in expressing our essential energies or self, problems with authority figures, careers, etc. But what would the *exact* event be? Why can we not predict that? With collaborative astrological factors, common sense, or intuition, we can perhaps get closer; but the exact denouement will remain indeterminate until the event itself, unless we have a lucky guess. It may be losing our job. It may be a project that drags on due to problems. It may our dad dies. It may be a bout of depression or disappointment. It may be an authority figure blocking our progress in some area. It might be a heart attack. It may even be positive things, if we are attuned to Saturn: it may be new insights or the *overcoming* of struggles; it may be the planting of unknown seeds which will come to fruition in more auspicious times. It might be that a failure of a pet project opens a door to a whole new mode of expression. It may be million things, but the density of the event cloud centers around those circumstances which are most appropriate to the involved archetypal energies. The final collapse into actuality takes place when our consciousness interacts with the potential event cloud to produce a physical circumstance. (Pure quantum randomness may additionally play a part.) And even though our own consciousness is implicated, the circumstances may often take us by surprise: there is far more to our consciousness's involvement with archetypes, time, our own dharma, and the world around us than our worrying frontal lobes are aware of, or privy to. We and our ego's wishes and desires are always and ever revealed as small and meager in the larger scheme of things.

The beauty and the usefulness of astrology is that it allows us a peek into the workings of the non-physical cosmos. What an awe-inspiring array is there, and what an endless source of wonder! A lifetime is not enough to appreciate its delicacy and elegance. We are able to see into the very fabric of spacetime. We can see the raisins, the event-clouds hovering ahead, and can experience the archetypal energies as we engage with them. We can feel our oneness with time in the form of patterned events. The Whole becomes, if not clear, then clearer; as clear as it can ever be for our limited minds to ponder.

Eureka!

Edgar Allan Poe, the famous author, was born on January 19, 1809, at possibly around one o'clock in the morning. ("Mother gave birth about 3 hours after leaving the theater.") He had a stellium in Pisces which included the Moon, Venus, Jupiter, and Pluto clustered on his 5th house cusp and Leo on the Midheaven. A certain level of drama was guaranteed to be part of his life, and with the Sun conjunct Mercury in the 3rd, writing and stories were a natural outlet. In addition to the heavily aspected Pluto, Scorpio rising on top of his native Saturnian nature gave a clue as to the direction that these scribblings might take: "Murders in the Rue Morgue," "The Fall of the House of Usher," "The Premature Burial," "The Masque of the Red Death," and many more. He was the first of the great gothic horror writers, and has inspired everyone in the genre since then. His personal life was also one of tragedy and darkness: losing both parents before he was four years old, he himself suffered from crushing poverty, episodes of madness, and end-stage alcoholism.

But in addition to the secrets of his lurid stories, Poe himself had a secret interest that not many know about: cosmology. In 1848, one year before his premature death at age 40 (likely from alcoholism), he penned a slim volume titled *Eureka: A Prose Poem*, and actually considered it to be his most important work, his crowning "masterpiece." It was subtitled "An Essay on the Material and Spiritual Universe." In it, he presents a vision of the universe based on his own intuition, rather than on prevailing science or math, but one which is still being examined and discussed to this day for its prescience. Included in it, for starters, is the idea of a "Big Bang," and an expanding universe, presaging orthodox researchers by 80 years. (The universe, he speculates, came from a single "primordial particle" in "one instantaneous flash.") He further posits the Big

Crunch by speculating that the universe is actually endlessly expanding and collapsing, analogous to a heartbeat. He also gives a plausible solution to Olbers' Paradox, which was a mystery at the time, as well as exploring the idea of black holes.

He opens the third paragraph of his narrative with a modest goal: "I design to speak of the Physical, Metaphysical and Mathematical – of the Material and Spiritual Universe: of its Essence, its Origin, its Creation, its Present Condition and its Destiny." Amazingly, during the course of the essay he not only lays out the schema for the Big Bang, but declares that "space and duration are one," and that "matter and spirit are made of the same essence." One may recall that, in the earlier physics section, two of Einstein's biggest breakthroughs were the discovery that space and time were part of a single system, spacetime, and that matter and energy were simply different versions of the same phenomenon. Pretty impressive for a morbidly inclined poet with no scientific training writing in the mid 1800's!

The word "eureka" means "I have found it." (The image here is of Archimedes sitting in his bathtub.) It was an optimistic title for the summation of Poe's amateur philosophical and cosmological thought. Leaving his astronomical conjectures, he turns near the end towards more spiritual matters, which have a distinctly pantheistic tone, and then addresses the spirituality of Consciousness. He believed that ultimately, individual consciousnesses will collapse back into a single One (similar to the Big Crunch), a "final ingathering" where the "myriads of individual Intelligences become blended." He sums up his view of God as a "Divine Being, who thus passes his Eternity in perpetual variation of Concentrated Self and almost infinite Self-Diffusion," and talks about "those inconceivably numerous things which you designate as his creatures, but which are really but infinite individualizations of Himself. The Universe is but his present expansive existence." He touches on Karma (though he doesn't name it that), and lays out his overall theme, which is that of Oneness, as opposed to the illusion of duality.

It's not known whether Poe, who was obviously very intelligent and presumably well-read, was exposed to any Hindu literature or teachings. It *is* known that his contemporary Ralph Waldo Emerson (though there seemed to be a mutual distance between Emerson and the Transcendentalists, and Poe) had, in the 1830's, obtained copies of the Rig Veda, the Upanishads and other Indian texts. (Emerson's personal favorite was the Bhagavad Gita.) Much of Poe's thesis sounds very close to classic Indian ideas of spirituality.

Moving forward in time, it's also not known whether Einstein may have been exposed to *Eureka*! prior to developing his own theories; there were known to be European translations in circulation at that time. It is more likely a case involving the synchronicity of ideas, which occurs over and over again in culture and science. Einstein did acknowledge reading it in 1933, and wrote regarding Poe that it was "a very beautiful achievement of an extraordinary, independent mind." But after re-reading it in 1940, he inexplicably not only denied having read it earlier (despite his documented comments), but backpedaled, wrote a scathing condemnation, and called Poe a "pathological personality": pretty harsh words. It was at this time that Einstein was battling against the idea of an expanding universe, so that may have had something to do with his newfound dislike, in addition to the possibly uncomfortable prefiguring of his own contributions.

But Poe had his limits. In addition to his uncannily accurate cosmological pontifications, he also spent time theorizing on what Darwin later called the origin of species: how the various animals and humans on earth came to be in their present configuration. Here, he was wildly off base, recognizing a sort of evolutionary process, but attributing it to solar activity and other geocosmic effects. (It sounds like astrology, but it isn't; at least not in any meaningful way that we might commonly regard that subject.) But how was he to know? He wasn't privy to Darwin's insights, which were published ten years after Poe's death. Here, his intuitive abilities failed him. Absent these discoveries, he did his best with what knowledge he had. If nothing else, it's an interesting historical footnote to follow how someone from that era might hypothesize the origins of the various animals on earth.

But let's talk again about Poe's Pisces planets. In regards to those who, like Poe, seem prone to enlightenment, religious visions, or a feeling of Oneness and non-duality, some have theorized a biological or genetic process of some sort. There would then be a "God gene," which would be more prominent in certain people than in others. It is certainly possible that there may be some mild effects to be found there, but this line of thinking doesn't really explain the fact that most people who gravitate in this direction are singletons in their family: most of the time, other family members with similar genetics show no aptitude for this cosmic perspective.

But what if it were once again simply a case of researchers not being privy to information that is right in front of them, and yet which is effectively invisible to them? Those who write off astrology a priori leave a lot of information unexamined, and on the table. Astrology delineates that those with a positive Neptune in their horoscope, or a positive Pisces influence, or with positive planets in the 12th house (these can all be equivalent) may be able to see beyond the veil of materialism and duality, may be able to see the connectedness of all things, and will tend to be spiritual and visionary in their approach to life. Neptune is the Pisces planet and the 12th is its house. Its principle, or mode of action, is to dissolve boundaries and duality, revealing the underlying unity beneath. Perhaps, then, it may not be so much a coincidence that Einstein was "The Spiritual Physicist," George Harrison was "The Spiritual Beatle," and Edgar Allan Poe was apparently "The Spiritual Mystery Writer."

Eureka!

Here's Some Astrology

The purpose of this book is not to explain astrology or to delineate charts; there are a plethora of books out there that do exactly that, and very well. The current book assumes that the reader has some familiarity with the subject, and some knowledge of the basics. If you are somehow reading this and don't (which seems unlikely), by all means stop right now, and read some of the other excellent and instructive books on the subject. The purpose of this book is simply to provide food for thought on the philosophical underpinnings of astrology, and on how astrology might interact and be connected with physics, consciousness, and synchronicity. The book is a question rather than a statement, and yet some may be baffled by a book using astrology in the title with so little actual astrology in it. So here are a couple of thoughts that arose after a recent conversation with a friend, regarding those who are skillful with words.

In his book *Prometheus the Awaker*, Richard Tarnas mentions several authors who have Uranus/Mercury aspects in their charts (which may lend themselves towards a certain genius for cleverness and communication.) One that was left out was Vladimir Nabokov. Nabokov was a fascinating personality in general, and one well worth studying from an astrological perspective: born to an aristocratic and wealthy family in Russia, he was, in addition to being a writer, a lepidopterist, artist, teacher, translator, composer of chess problems—and at one point taught tennis and boxing. His native tongue was Russian, and his first *nine* novels were in Russian. After the Bolshevik revolution, he moved briefly to England and then spent many years in Berlin, although he was never fond of it. He and his family fled Berlin in 1940 ahead of the Nazis, and settled in the U.S. He immediately turned to writing in English (as if that were as easy as flipping a switch), and in fact, achieved his greatest success in that language. He is known for his intricate and incredible wordplay, which is best seen on display in his most famous work, *Lolita*, which currently stands as #4 on the Modern Library's list of the 100 best novels of the 20th Century. One cannot read that novel without the force of his Mercury trine Uranus leaping out from every page. In keeping also with Uranus's reputation for the revolutionary flaunting of convention, many places in the U.S. ended up banning the book for its fearless, intentionally shocking, and yet humorous head-on plunge into a very taboo subject. (A middle-age man falls in love with—and becomes obsessed with—a 12 year old girl.) One can almost see Mercury the Trickster winking at his co-conspirator Uranus here. But it is really not so much the subject of the book that is ultimately so shocking, but rather Nabokov's uncanny command of language. It's just incredible to realize in reading Lolita that English was Nabokov's second (or perhaps third, after German) language. He composed it during lengthy trips to the Western U.S., where, interestingly, the same Jupiter/Sun lines that ran through his native St. Petersburg appeared again after their trip around the world. (In an article on Nabokov in the New York Times, author Landon Y. Jones writes that something about the Rocky Mountain West reminded Nabokov of his youth in Russia. "Some part of me must have been born in Colorado," he wrote to the critic Edmund Wilson, "for I am constantly recognizing things with a delicious pang.") During the writing of Lolita, his wife Vera (a Capricorn who completed a trinity with his Sun in Taurus and Virgo Moon) acted as his cheerleader, manager, and typist. You can find Nabokov's chart on Astrodienst (www.astro.com), and his bio on Wikipedia.

One curiosity that most people will have after reading Lolita is "how could a middle age man know so much about a middle age man's lust for a 12 year old girl?" A great question, and one that has been danced around and explored by various pursuers of Nabokov, including the Pulitzer-Prize winning author of his wife Vera's biography, Stacy Schiff. Much is revealed by her in an internet article that may be found by searching for "Stacy Schiff on Nabokovian frottage." Of interest from an astrological perspective, is that in addition to his literary Mercury trine Uranus, Nabokov in the romantic department had Venus in Pisces in the 12th, squared by both Saturn and Neptune. Uranus was in the 8th house, trine Mars in the 5th. The Taurean sun gave a love of beauty, and of physical pleasure; the Pisces Venus produced a confused idealism. Could there be any chart more appropriate for unusual and unrequited love, and lust for the perfect and yet unobtainable? For frustrated longing? The key, though, was that the tension formed by Venus-Neptune-Saturn found completion in a Mutable Cross with his Moon in Virgo completing the picture, and keeping the tension under wraps and on a (mostly) mental and literary plane. During the year or two preceding the publication of Lolita (meaning during its writing), transiting Uranus was back and forth with exact trines to his Venus, no doubt further inflaming the theme in his mind. Also at the time of his greatest literary achievement, Nabokov had a stellium of five progressed planets in Gemini trined by a progressed Moon in Libra.

***

Speaking of Gemini (and of course they like to speak!): in examining their literary, musical, and poetic output, Walt Whitman and Bob Dylan may appear in many ways to be chronologically separated twins. In their style, they are similar: both have a beautiful, prolific, and nearly uncontrollable ability to produce fantastic tossed salads of words that excite and amaze. They throw forth phrase after phrase, rapid-fire, often seemingly with no thought other than the sounds of the words themselves, and how they might rhyme or fall together. It is as if they are drunk on language, and the love of sharing it with others. They are additionally, in persona, both rootsy, ramblin' kind of guys: trains, roads, paths, explorations, wonder, hobos, and life without cares or ties appear throughout their work. (One of Dylan's songs is called "The Drifter's Escape"). They both give body to the term "Americana." American curiosity, adventure, optimism, and experimentation come to life in their lines. In early pictures, Dylan even resembles tintype photos of the young Whitman in stance and dress.

There is a distinctly mercurial quality to their writing (Dylan has in fact been described using that word in the press over and over), and it's probably no surprise that both share a Gemini sun. Neither can stay in one place very long, either physically or intellectually. Their writing is always on the move, in rapid-pace fashion, and their endless fascination with language burns through at every turn. To keep them from drifting away in pure intellect however, both are firmly grounded by the hand of Taurus in their charts. Dylan has a stellium of Taurus planets in his 5th house, and Whitman has Mercury and Venus (the two planets probably most important to a poet) in a wide conjunction in that sign in his 1st house. Whitman was controversial in his day for the sensuality that he wove into his verse, and his poetry is indeed at once earthy and yet philosophical, as is Dylan's; though Dylan is a bit more ambiguous. In addition (again, no surprise here), both have a very strong Uranus presence in their charts.

Mercurial Whitman, as one might expect, had a variety of jobs and experiences before determining to be a poet, shortly after his first Saturn return. He wrote in his spare time, and ultimately not only published his first volume of poetry himself, but actually wrote and published his own enthusiastic review of it as well! (He had Aries rising and Moon in Leo; his best known poem is titled "Song of Myself".) This was in his 36th year, 1855. Over the previous several years, as he was writing, transiting Uranus had tagged his Venus and was now conjunct his Mercury. Pluto in that year had also taken its place exactly conjunct his Venus. The earthiness of his Taurus Mercury and Venus informing his restless Gemini Sun had produced one of the most important and best-loved collections of American poetry: *Leaves of Grass*.

Dylan, for his part, had honed his own restlessness at home in his bedroom in Hibbing, Minnesota. A skinny, suburban Jewish kid, he had teased himself into a fever listening to clear-channel radio stations from Shreveport, La., blowing hick country and poor black blues tunes like a blanket over the Midwest. In 1960, he could take it no longer. He dropped out of college, and the next year, 1961, he headed for New York to visit his sick idol, Woody Guthrie, and to throw his hat into the ring of the American music that had seeped into his bones. Progressed Jupiter had landed on his Sun, and with transiting Uranus squaring his entire Taurus stellium, life in a cold-weather Minnesota mining town had become unbearable. The world was waiting for him, and he was off to see it:

> "Long enough have you dream'd contemptible dreams,
> Now I wash the gum from your eyes,
> You must habit yourself to the dazzle of the light
> and of every moment of your life"

Had Dylan been born an itinerant printer/poet in the 1800's, those words of Whitman's might just have well have been his.

***

On a less cerebral note, astrologers reading this may find humor in a news article that appeared in January of 2015. It was in the Wall Street Journal, and was titled "Fans Commemorate 'Toystory', a Dairy Legend With a Ravenous Libido." It celebrated the passing of apparently the most prolific breeding bull in history; "an ornery, 2,700-pound bull named Toystory—a titan of artificial insemination who sired an estimated 500,000 offspring in more than 50 countries." He apparently had only one interest, and other than that was "meaner than a snake," according to one vet. One of his managers (he had his own t-shirts, hats, and birthday parties) clarified that "as long as he was interested in sex, he wasn't interested in you. But if he lost that other interest, you had to be careful." Toystory was born May 7, 2001, which made him a Taurus with Moon in Scorpio, and Mars sextile Uranus.

The Age of Aquarius

There are various schools of thought as to how much "bleed" or blend one might give the signs or houses as they move across the cusps from one to the next. In terms of the natal horoscope, this can engender debate: if one is 29 degrees and 59 minutes of Aquarius, how much Pisces influence is there? The answer is, no one knows. Some astrologers have very strong opinions based on what they've seen in their personal research, but another might contradict the first, and state that they have found the opposite to be true. So, like many things in astrology, this falls into a rather subjectively interpreted category.

Unlike natal astrology, however, most in the astrology world would agree that the Great Ages have a significant amount of bleed-over from one Age to the next. We are not one year in the Age of Pisces and the next year in the Age of Aquarius. This is congruent with the constellations themselves up in the sky, which have no fixed lines drawn that we can see, but have very indistinct edges, and actually overlap at times. Like most things in astrology, the determination of the *influences* of the Ages boils down to a simple "it works." So the question is: where does one Age end and another begin? Should we attempt to pick a sort of "midpoint" of waning and waxing influences, or just accept that there are transition zones and leave it at that?

It's a subject that has been exhaustively written about by many, many astrologers, including Ray Grasse, and was even talked about by Carl Jung in his book *Aion*. In fact, one could argue that Jung's examination of the symbolism of the Age of Pisces in this book is actually what brought the subject to the attention of many astrologers of his generation. The Great Ages, of course, are brought about by the precession of the Spring Equinoxes, caused by the earth's "wobble" on its axis. Most agree that the general character of each Age corresponds with the attending sidereal zodiac constellation: for example, over the last several thousand years, the Cancerian age was associated with the development of agriculture, mother goddesses, and the settling down of people into fixed homes; the Age of Gemini was associated with the advancement of language, communication, and the birth of writing; the Taurean Age had massive building projects such as the Egyptian pyramids, in addition to extensive bull worship and imagery in various cultures; and the Age of Aries coincided with the Iron Age: no fitter image occurs for the Age of Aries than that of the Roman Legions, although they took power just as the age was waning. Aries is not just a warrior, however, but also a trailblazer and thinker, and the Age of Aries also contained what Karl Jaspers has called the "Axial Period" from about 800 to 200 BC, during which there was an explosion of religion, philosophy, and science throughout the world, including (most notably for Westerners) the Greeks, and their strivings for intellectual advancement. Unknown in the modern world, examination of the natural world (later known as science) coexisted fully and peacefully with philosophy. It was, in addition to the Greek philosophers, the age of Buddha, Lao-Tse, Confucius, and the Old Testament prophets; in India, the Upanishads, the cornerstone of Eastern philosophy, were finally being written down. The ancient Hindus, as well as the Hebrews, blew a ram's horn to call the faithful. It was a time of travel, exploration, and trade; and in examining the ideas of the Greeks side by side with those of the Indians, one becomes suspicious that ideas travelled the world a bit more freely than we are normally taught to think.

So almost everyone in astrology seems to agree that the Ages make sense, and it's fairly easy to out pick the point at which the Roman Legions of Aries gave way to Piscean Christianity (in the West) with its fish imagery, and the emotion-over-logic, religion-over-knowledge paradigm that ushered in the "Dark Ages" of Europe. But since we are enmeshed in the transition, who is to determine where the point should be placed as to where the vaunted Age of Aquarius will finally subsume and supplant the Age of Pisces? Quite a few astrologers search the horizon for the Age of Aquarius as if it were difficult to find. Some, using various calculation methods, have put the ingress as far ahead as 2150 or later. However, a case may be made here to do a simple weather check. That is, if the weather forecaster on TV is telling you that it is sunny, but you look outside and it is pouring down rain, it's probably more appropriate to go with the rain. Regarding the Age of Aquarius: perhaps we are already in it.

***

The planet Uranus was discovered by William Herschel on March 13, 1781; the date perhaps serving as symbolism that the Age of Pisces had just received notice. Sun in Pisces was in square to Uranus in Gemini, which opposed a conjunction of Mars and Saturn in Sagittarius, pointed at the galactic center. The discovery, and its surrounding period, was bookended by two conjunctions of Uranus and Jupiter in 1775 and 1789. Uranus immediately staked its claim for being new and unusual, exhibiting itself as the only planet with a lateral rather than a vertical axis (spinning on its side, so to speak), and also rotating "backwards" compared to all other planets except Venus. The discovery itself threw the astronomical world, as well as the astrological community, into a frenzy: the Cosmos had been considered perfect and complete, and during the entire history of humanity, the planets through Saturn were thought to have constituted the entire solar system. Quite an unexpected and sudden shock!

But in addition to this surprising discovery, it was an exciting and revolutionary time in general. It was the Age of Enlightenment, as well as the beginnings of what is now called the Scientific Revolution, which had been partially kicked off by Sir Isaac Newton's amazing understanding of motion, including orbital mechanics. Rene Descartes famously stated "I think, therefore I am," and the focus slipped away from dark superstition and blind belief towards the rapidly-blooming accomplishments of Man, his mind, and his societies. What is known today as "secular humanism" was being born. Religion was losing some of its grip and authority on at least the more educated classes.

Also being born at this time was what has been called, with apologies to other countries, the "world's greatest democracy"—The United States of America. The American Revolution started in 1775, followed by a formal Declaration of Independence in 1776. The French Revolution followed a few years later, and the template was set for many other countries to follow, around the world. Humanity was moving towards an awareness of, and more power and respect for, the masses, the people.

One of those people was Benjamin Franklin, often nicknamed "The First American" for his contributions to these efforts, as well as for his amazing accomplishments in almost any field one could choose to name: politics, diplomacy, writing, creating a Post Office, inventions, university founding, abolitionism; oh, and science. Let's talk about science.

Although interested in many areas of science, it was Franklin's well-publicized experiments with, and ideas about, electricity which eventually brought him fame in the scientific realm. Franklin's dramatic experiments with lightning boosted growing interest in the subject, and finally put electricity into the public mind as an object of endless fascination, as well as spurring more scientific research and knowledge about this "new" phenomenon. Many have heard of his kite experiments, and that he invented the lightning rod, but don't know that it was actually Franklin who came up with the idea for positive and negative charges in electricity, a significant move forward in the accumulating insights. He was quite a guy. He didn't "discover" electricity, but he popularized it and moved it along in the period of time leading up to the discovery of Uranus.

***

So, to recap: amongst other things that are easily researched, we very visibly have, within a short window: the discovery of Uranus, the Aquarian planet; the founding of the best known democracy in world history; the age of Enlightenment, science and humanism; and the popularization of a previously (nearly) unknown new force, electricity. These certainly would seem to give hints as to when the Age of Aquarius first began making itself felt.

According to basic astrology textbooks, Aquarius/Uranus is associated with independence, science, electricity, astrology, sudden insights, humanism, eccentricities, and freedom of both thought and movement. Hmm. As I write this, I am syncing my new smart phone to my computer. Using this small device, an astrology program will instantly generate a horoscope chart for any moment that I desire. I can read the latest research on quantum mechanics, and even watch videos explaining those difficult ideas.

However, at the same time, in the news on my phone are stories of various backward-looking religious fundamentalist groups around the world attempting to drag humanity back to a medieval age and sensibility, replete with beheadings, but without the positive aspects of the Age of Pisces. One may easily see this as the last desperate gasps (and the most dysfunctional ones at that) of a 2,000 year old paradigm that is dying. Transitions are always difficult, and many fear the future, but we will not go back. We have put men on the moon. We have decoded the human genome. My new phone has 2 *billion* transistors packed into a few ounce package the size of my palm that connects me instantly with any other human on the planet who holds a similar device. We connect through geosynchronous orbiting satellites which are continually and automatically adjusted for variations predicted by Einstein's theory of relativity. No, we will not go backwards: the Age of Aquarius is here.

Welcome.

What's Up, Doc?

In 2014, there was a small documentary produced called *Into Eternity*. It was made by Danish director Michael Madsen, and concerned a nuclear waste repository, Onkalo, on the west coast of Finland. The documentary itself was somewhat redundant, but it highlighted the Scandinavian tendency towards Saturnian glumness and a strong sense of reality and responsibility. The Finns, recognizing that nuclear waste is the inevitable result of using nuclear reactors for fuel (karma is obviously in Saturn's domain), and recognizing that this will be a burden on future generations for many thousands of years to come, open up their thought processes in trying to reconcile these two notions in a responsible way. Contrast this with the U.S., whose Sagittarian rising chart gives it a ruler of Jupiter, with that planet conjunct both Venus and the Sun. A Saturn square notwithstanding, the U.S., in contrast with the Scandinavian countries, is known for its breezy optimism, excess, and focus on possibilities rather than limitations. It's the Swedish Bergman movies vs. the United States' *Field of Dreams*.

And yet, in the United Nations' annual "World Happiness Report," of the globe's varied countries, the Scandinavians occupied six of the upper ten slots in 2015. The U.S. was nowhere near the top (contrary to its "we're the best" jingoism). Why is that? How can "Saturnine" people be some of the happiest people on earth? (And this additionally in spite of what is normally thought of as not being the most ideal of climates.) One clue is that a strongly reality-based orientation to life has been shown through psychological studies to frequently be associated with the above-mentioned "Saturnine" personality, and metaphysical studies in turn tell us that the secret to happiness must begin with the acceptance of reality as it is. If we attempt to "be happy" without accepting reality, we are building our quest on a foundation of sand which will ultimately crumble. The point of the above is not to imply that one attitude is intrinsically better than the other, but simply to bring out that happiness is a slippery thing, and is not nearly as simple as some stereotypes would lead us to believe. Many have pointed out that happiness is best thought of as being a by-product of correct living and correct attitude; and as something that cannot be chased, but that lights upon one as a butterfly might if one's energies are in harmony. What are those energies?

Jupiter and Saturn in astrology, and in archetype, represent two great poles of a single principle, two sides of a cosmic coin. They represent most importantly grace and work, but they also represent luck and karma, and they therefore represent the two forces that shape *results* in our lives, and thus the quality of our lives themselves. One pole requires our effort, and dishes back to us our just rewards, while other is seemingly good fortune of a random nature: if it were not random, but justified, then it would not be Jupiter, it would be Saturn. And yet, one notes, the randomness interestingly accrues more to those with a strong Jupiter in their charts than otherwise, or to those who are pursuing a Jupiterian outlook. There is something of a quantum flavor here, as well as the taste of yet another of the mysteries of life. A strong Jupiter gives more opportunities for random and unpredictable grace to appear: that in itself seems fated, or Saturnine. And so the two are a pair, complementary, in the same fashion that light is both a wave and a particle, and in the same sort of paradoxical, contradictory, and yet both-are-true fashion that fate and free will seem to exhibit. The quantum world allows for this: everything is intertwined, part of a whole, and influences every other part.

These two as a pair seem to produce the results of our strivings in life. Either one of these principles may produce positive or negative results, and each result may lead to its converse through conscious interaction with them: disappointment and resulting hard work can produce wonderful fruits from one's efforts just as easily as seemingly lucky gifts can produce heartache and misery. Just ask the big lottery winners: there are as many unhappy ones, years later, as there are happy ones. Jupiter is not always good, and

Saturn is not always bad: that is one of the first lessons that we learn in beginning astrology. All planetary principles are part of the Whole, and all are necessary. Jupiter without Saturn is profligate, and Saturn without Jupiter is miserly. Saturn, for example, often operates from a "zero sum game," fear-based model, where an increase in your money or happiness comes at the expense of mine, and vice versa. Jupiter, in contrast, operates from a faith and generosity model, where all can have increasing wealth and happiness at no other's expense: there is more than enough to go around for everybody. It is the fishes and loaves. It's all perspective, and it's all in what we *do* with these principles. Are we wasting, taking for granted, or misusing our Jupiterian good fortune? Are we giving in to Saturnian setbacks, or are we working hard to learn the lessons that we are being taught, so that we can constructively change things for the better in the future? All of life consists of lessons, work, grace, chance, faith, love, karma, and learning: these are the factors that make up the results of our lives, whether in love, in business, or in other matters. If we are learning our Saturnian lessons, then perhaps we are more likely to notice and wisely use the Jupiterian grace elements. The Scandinavians seem to have an intuitive feel for this dynamic. We are meant to take care of the few things that we *can* effect, and to be grateful for the small presents thrown in our lap, using them wisely and not squandering them.

***

Perhaps you have noticed the two different figures of the Buddha that are most popular: there is the serene Buddha, usually shown in a seated and meditative pose, and there is the "Happy Buddha," often engaged in walking with a bag over his shoulder, an expression of joy on his face. Why *are* there these two? What do they mean? Which one is a more accurate expression of Buddhism? Which *version* of Buddhism? Historically, Happy Buddha is actually a folkloric figure known as Hotei or Budai in the East, and while not the same as Siddhartha Gautama, is revered as an additional Buddha or Bodhisattva. He also figures comfortably into Chinese Taoism. Likely, the cosmic principle of complementarity needed Hotei to balance the more serene Siddhartha. The universe produces what it needs.

Serene Buddha appears to be contemplating, although the purpose of that contemplation may be to become free of contemplation, to empty the mind. Effort and accomplishment are in evidence, even if the goal of the work is to go beyond such concepts as "effort," and to simply be, to be part of the One, to lose the ego. A particular posture is carefully chosen and worked on; the eyes must be just right, perhaps the proper mantra is performed. One hopes that results will follow from effort. The aura of seriousness and Saturn permeates the visage, although the image also portrays the progression into passionless acceptance, compassion, and understanding.

In contrast, Happy Buddha seems little interested in such efforts or with work at all for that matter, although he may well work: "chop wood, carry water" seems to apply here. He seems very Jupiterian: breezy, unconcerned, trusting to fate, living his life. Happy, joyous, and free. Going about his business without worries or cares, and with the appearance of having a generosity of spirit towards all. He perhaps doesn't *have* to think, or to contemplate, or strive to be somewhere - he is already there. Grace over work permeates the air. Even their physical forms are telling: one is slim, spare, and austere; the other is fat and jolly. It is perhaps not difficult to see in these two figures the great dyad, Jupiter and Saturn in their stereotypical incarnations. (Santa Claus is also Jupiter; Ebeneezer Scrooge is Saturn.) In fact, the more that we look, the more ubiquitous these partners seem to become. They are the two Great Principles upon which the world is supported: work and grace, analysis and understanding. As trans-personal planets in astrology, they are the link between the more personal inner planets, and the more generational and spiritual outer ones.

When one looks for them, Jupiter and Saturn appear everywhere. Aristotle thought that matter either tended to sink down (gravity) or rise up (levity). The very words gravity and levity speak of the heavy, serious, and pulling-down-to-reality of Saturn, and the humorous, light, bubbling up and gaseous nature of Jupiter. In Greek theater, the famous masks of Comedy and Tragedy gave a face to these antipodes. In the Bible, they are the stern Old Testament God of demands and punishments, testing and grudgingly rewarding his faithful, versus the New Testament Jesus, sowing love and grace to mankind, and delivering messages of hope, kindness, and generosity. Jesus says, "You shall be redeemed, simply through love for me and from me." Work vs. Grace. In Hinduism, one may contrast the sterner forms of Shiva or Kali against the vision of little blue baby Krishna playing in the fields: gentle, laughing, and stealing butter from the milkmaids. The two planets shine on all of human culture. Both are necessary. The duality is also epitomized in a mother's love vs. a father's love: unconditional vs. conditional. Like the yin-yang symbol, they are part of a whole. One without the other is meaningless; life would be out of balance.

It's Bugs vs. Daffy. In 1937, Warner Brothers studios introduced the hand-drawn animated character of Daffy Duck. He was an instant hit, but perhaps the universe was silently squirming at the imbalance: we'll never know. At any rate, a year later, in 1938, Bugs Bunny made his debut. He quickly took the spotlight, becoming even more popular than Daffy; next to Mickey Mouse, he was probably the most beloved cartoon character of the 20th century. He completed the duo, and again Saturn and Jupiter took their rightful places as co-rulers of human fate. (Currently we have a similar duo in Jupiterian Spongebob Squarepants and Saturnian Mr. Krab.) The episodes in which both Bugs and Daffy appear in the older series are particularly telling. Bugs is Jupiter personified: self-confident, amiable, relaxed, never needing to over-think, and just plain *lucky*. Everything simply goes his way, regardless of any effort on his part. He always comes out of every scrape "smelling like a rose," chomping on his carrot. Never is he in a bad mood, and his sense of humor is on frequent display in many episodes. He wears his ego lightly, as evidenced by his forays into drag and other characters that some, including Daffy, would likely find demeaning. Regardless of what's going on in the rest of the universe, things will work out for him.

Not so much so for Daffy. Daffy's lot in life is that of the eternal striver (and eternal optimist, so there is just a little bit of Jupiter in his temperament also, if not in the results). He is forever trying to make things work, to *force* things to work out for him, which of course they rarely do. He then spends much of the time disappointed, disgruntled, irritable, and angry. His ego is much more on the line, and "flop sweat" is a constant companion. He has a frustrated scowl on his face as often as a hopeful smile. Bugs is all grace and no effort; Daffy is all effort and no grace. Both are exaggerations, of course; in real life, there is no pure Saturn or pure Jupiter—everything is a blend. That's probably why we enjoy these amplified versions of ourselves: we sense these forces within us, and the stories may help us to understand, and put things into perspective. Plus they're just plain funny. Tex Avery, who really kicked these cartoons into shape, had Moon in Sagittarius; Chuck Jones, who presided over arguably the Golden Age of Warner Brothers animation, had Jupiter in Sagittarius. (Walt Disney, of course, had a Sagittarian Sun.) Mel Blanc, who did most of the voices for Warner Brothers, was (what else!) a double Gemini with Jupiter in sextile to both Sun and Moon. A fun bunch: no wonder Daffy had to have just a little bit of optimism tucked in there. These wonderful folks, in true Jupiterian form, gave us an irresistible invitation to set aside our Saturnian gravity and earnestness for a moment or two. Perhaps there is a reason that the center of our galaxy lies in the direction of Sagittarius!

***

Faith and Fear are two of the most potent manifestations of these opposite principles, and ones that would benefit us from the understanding of their roles in our lives. Ignorance (in its more willful meaning of ignoring) here can have large effects on both our histories and our happiness. Bugs shows no fear simply because he has faith that things are going to work out for him; and they always do, at least in the cartoons that he stars in. Daffy on the other hand, is frequently a vibrating, sweaty mass of fear and nerves, hoping for the best but secretly expecting the worst, as that is how things usually work out for him in *his* cartoons. Like attracts like. But we see that his sin is often hubris, or pride, or attachment, or the negative over-optimism of Jupiter; and thus there is a connection to a violation of universal principles in his failed results. The Jupiterian cartoonists and humorists (Sagittarians Mark Twain, Rodney Dangerfield, and early Woody Allen are other good examples) love to puncture our over-inflated egos, for it reveals the truth, which is that of our commonality: the antithesis of the personal ego. Most of us take ourselves way too seriously.

Faith and Fear. Far-reaching thoughts can be attached to how these play out in our lives. They steer not only the outcomes of our personal stories, but our *perception* of these outcomes, which is actually what finally determines our happiness. Faith will lead us to acceptance, and connect us to greater levels of understanding; fear will build upon itself, and we will forever be waiting for the next shoe to fall, and the next. Faith and Fear are a pair, and are indeed the same pair as Jupiter and Saturn. Faith comes from Jupiter, and Fear comes from Saturn. (But fear is of course far from being the only manifestation of Saturn. The list of constructive positives is long, and seems to be even longer in Scandinavia.) Fear is an incomplete understanding of the fullness and workings of life, based on Saturn alone. (Delusional over-optimism is Jupiter alone.) Faith and fear are, unlike most things in life (see above), a *true* zero-sum game. That is, if we have 100% faith, we will have zero fear; conversely, if we are 100% fearful, then that is an indication that we are not showing any faith at all in the way that the world works. It works through free will and karma; it works through grace and work. They are two sides of a single coin. Most of us, of course, lie somewhere in between these two extremes.

Faith as used here may require a bit of explanation. It does not necessarily connote a religious faith, although it certainly may be tied to that. It is essentially a faith in *what is*, in the way that the world is unfolding: that things are unfolding perhaps exactly as they are meant to be, and that it's OK. Fear is ego-based worry that things might not unfold to our liking; quite often they don't, of course. But we don't get to control outcomes— we only get to control our portion of the inputs. Life is free will *and* fate: only one of these is within our dominion. Buddha and many of the ancient Hindu gods are often seen holding a hand up, palm out in reassurance, exhibiting a pose that is known as the *Abhaya Mudra*. The Abhaya Mudra simply means "let go of control and worry, have faith, it's going to be OK; things will turn out as they're meant to be." The OK-ness is dependent upon our attitudes and acceptance. Jesus frequently shows the same gesture, although this time it is conveying more of a blessing; perhaps it is the blessing of faith, the blessing that we will come to understand all of this.

In addition to fate and free will, since a certain element of chance or randomness seems built into the fabric of the cosmos, this might require a stretch in their understanding of the way things turn out for many people. For some who search for certainty, its elusiveness is frustrating. Perhaps God is not only playing dice, but is, in addition, chuckling at the foibles of fate, and at the search for certitude in humans. The overly serious will not want to hear that. And yet, the stretch can be made: perhaps the universe, *even with chance*, is moving along in just the way that it is supposed to. It certainly is moving along in just the way that it is, Jupiter and Saturn combined, and that's really all that we can know, or need to make a start here. Again, we run across one of the many paradoxes of life. Acceptance leads to more happiness and peace of mind than white-knuckled attempts at control. Chance and fate coexist as part of a larger whole that we are not privy to. Our minds, egos, and desires seem large and important, but perhaps they are not. Perhaps there are things that we will *never* understand or find a logical reason for, things that we just have to accept as being the way that they are. Perhaps that includes everything.

There is a good argument to be made, in fact, that the way things *are* is equal, in some spiritual equation, to things being the way that they are *meant to be*. There is no provable difference: again, we run into the fate/free will paradoxes. Whether things are happening by chance, effort, or fate in the end produces the same results, which often (some Jupiter ego-puncturing humor here) have a marked disinterest in our petty petitions and strivings. In Eastern traditions, the concept of the Tao seems to sum this up nicely, and bears study, especially for those who may not consider themselves to be otherwise "religious." The Tao is a spiritual concept that lends itself well to the secular.

***

Ultimately, things do move along in their own way, and at their own pace. Whether we choose to see this as the Will of God, or as physics, or as Taoism, or as astrology, doesn't matter. Things are *still* going to move along in their own way regardless of our interpretations. Things are the way they are. The universe *is*. The planets move, molecules and atoms move, consciousness moves. We really only have two choices in life: to move with them, or to attempt to resist them. If we resist them, we will always lose: we are fighting fate, chance, and the flow of the world. The forces are larger than we are. Our only real choice is to accept things as they are and work with them. If things are flowing in our lives, we are probably working in harmony with the Tao, God, the Jupiter/Saturn combination, or What Is. If we find ourselves continually stymied, blocked, frustrated, or unhappy, there's a good chance that we are fighting the flow.

There was an African-American disc jockey where I grew up who used to sign off every show with, "And remember —the only difference between a good day and a bad day is: your attitude." What could be wiser than that? Perhaps we need to watch more Bugs and Daffy cartoons. Astrology is our greatest ally here. It can lay out for us the direction of travel so that we may join in meaningful movement, rather than attempting to work at cross-purposes to the universe, or to continually be making attempts to place square pegs in round holes. In life, it is often difficult for us to see our own paths, just as it is difficult to see our own backs or the direction we are heading. It is thus often advisable to seek assistance, to have an outside observer watch our meanderings, to see if we are moving straight and strong, and in harmony with our surroundings.

In fear, we are not trusting the process. We are blocking grace by micro-managing, and attempting to maintain certain ego-structures. Fear is Saturnian: fear is always the fear of losing something that we have, or of not getting something that we want. It is clinging to something: a physical object, a desire, a person, an idea, anger and resentment, or even another fear. Attachment connotes structure, even for a desire, and is thus ruled by Saturn. It blocks the Tao, the river, the personal chi, God. Fear is often attached (through "bargaining," which an is attachment in itself) to feverishly working at controlling things, exhibiting another aspect of Saturn: we *hope* that the results of our work will manifest in a certain way, although we *fear* that they may not; nowhere in this is faith in the process, or in the outcome, which is out of our hands. On the other hand, fear can also be allayed by work: the correct understanding of the Saturn/Jupiter combination may allow us to perceive the proper path: *that of working, but not being attached to the results of the work*, or to a particular outcome. Doing the right thing, and then letting it go out to the universe for results. (Of course the trick is in knowing what the "right thing" is.) That is a productive understanding of, and way out of, fear. We can hope and work, but we must not be attached to the results, or to the desire for a particular result. We must be ready to accept whatever the outcome is. Hope is not bad; refusal to accept outcomes is bad. The path of Jupiter is that of faith, of trusting that the results which materialize will be (even if not what our desire attachment wanted) what is appropriate for us, and what we need to grow. Life is teaching *us* lessons, we are not teaching life lessons - a hard truth that some people never learn. Hopefully we are learning our lessons, and not ignoring them.

So faith is a trust in the process, in God, in Jupiter and Saturn, and in whatever you conceive the flow of the universe to be. Ultimately it doesn't matter what your preference is: life is a Oneness, and so all roads lead to the same results. The important thing is that we don't try to micro-manage those results, but accept them graciously, after we apply whatever "right effort" we feel is appropriate. Jupiter is faith and grace. Grace can only enter if we have some modicum of faith, of any sort. Grace cannot enter in the terror-sweat of Saturn.

Saturn himself knows this: he works in cahoots with his partner Jupiter. They are a team. Our main efforts should be in trying to divine the direction of the flow, and accepting it. That's the way of happiness.

Gratitude, acceptance, autonomy, and getting out of our self-centered egos and helping others have been identified by several meta-studies on well-being as the core components of a happy and meaningful life. ("Only a life lived for others is a life worthwhile." — that's Albert Einstein, not Mother Teresa.) Again, we are sniffing around the Scandinavian effect. All of the above are associated with the *combination* of Jupiter and Saturn: generosity and practicality working together for some greater good. All speak to the necessity of seeing our personal paths as aggregates of free will and fate, of grace and work; as expressions of a greater commonality, which necessarily sparks an altruistic streak—related to the awareness that we are all in this together. Gratitude needs to produce concrete expression, as well as the reverse; Jupiter needs to lead us to Saturn, and vice versa. Those who want concrete expression or results without gratitude, faith, and acceptance are missing half of the equation.

A fable from Aesop:

The wind was challenging the sun one day about which of them was stronger. Suddenly, they noticed a traveler coming down the road towards them, and they agreed on a challenge: whoever could remove the traveler's coat first would be regarded as the more influential. The wind jumped in and began to blow as hard as he could towards the traveler, who could barely make headway against the strong gusts. But the harder the wind blew, the tighter the traveler wrapped his coat around him, until the wind was exhausted and gave up in despair. Then it was the sun's turn. The sun came out from behind a cloud and did little more than gently let his rays shine down, but in a short while the traveler began to feel pleasantly warm, and removed his coat, slinging it over his shoulder as he continued on his way.

The above may sound a bit over-Jupiterian. The complementary, and equally valid, perspective on this may be the view that life is a blend of both principles, but that reality (Saturn) must come first. Ultimately, we come to see that the two are entangled and inseparable. Pure Jupiter may not plan adequately for the future, may over-estimate and misjudge, and may see life through rose-colored glasses. Saturn at its best may lay a firm foundation and show the practical results of carefully building something; at its worst, it may simply be ego-driven and harsh. Tempering Saturn with Jupiter in a positive way, we can find an optimism-based acceptance of reality, plan for dips in the cycles of life, and develop a sense of responsibility and connection with others, in addition to finding a humble gratitude—whatever our circumstances. Happiness lies in performing voluntarily that path that has been allotted to us in life, in joyfully (Jupiter) performing our dharma (Saturn). It is in the full understanding of this that we find peace. Hello, Scandinavia.

Life requires effort, but the effort should be effortless.

Jupiter and Saturn.

Little Things Mean a Lot

Dr. Benjamin Spock was well known to the "Baby Boom" generation: as a general rule, our moms had one hand on the cradle and the other on his book *Baby and Child Care*, first published in 1946. He was the hero of a generation of mothers, and taught new and terrified moms the ins and outs of dealing with their squalling infants (even though moms had been dealing with these for quite some time!). He was the very model of the kindly old pediatrician. In addition to helping a generation of moms raise babies, he also became well known for his opposition to the Vietnam War, and in 1968 was named "Humanist of the Year" in response to his work in this area. He was a Taurus with Moon in Cancer.

Adolf Hitler was a Taurus with Moon in Capricorn.

Donald Trump is pretty well known (at least on the U.S. stage) for his flamboyant personality, his amazing and narcissistic run for president, his nouveau-riche schemes, and his eccentric comb-over. It's not surprising that he has Sun conjunct Uranus in the 10th house, and Jupiter in the Second House of money. Less considered is that he also has Neptune in the Second House, and many of his investments have not turned out as planned—as well as there being nagging questions regarding him allowing others to "take the fall" for poor personal and investment decisions. His Mercury square Jupiter allows him to fire off grandiose comments without spending much too time in the analysis portion of the process. His colorful and ostentatious persona, however, is certainly consistent with his chart: a Gemini with Leo rising - and he is certainly getting his money's worth out of that last degree of Leo!

The Marquis de Sade is a much darker figure; he stands as the exemplar of aristocratic decadence played out on the field of sexual debauchery. The word "sadist" comes directly from his name, and he spent much of his life in prison and mental institutions for his sexual misadventures. His Sun was joined by the planet of excess, Jupiter, as well as Neptune in the 8th House, and he, too, is perhaps consistent with at least the lower possibilities of his chart: a Gemini with Scorpio rising. It's really quite amazing the ramifications that a few hours—or even a few minutes—of difference in the time of birth can produce. We are all very finely-tuned persons. Who needs multiple universes to awe us with the philosophical possibilities of how our lives may have turned out differently? The simple tick of a bent black iron hand on an ancient grandfather clock standing in the hall can generate a wholly divergent life for any one of us. Sir Richard Burton, the famed British explorer from the 1800's, also had Scorpio rising, and produced the first English translation of the Indian *Kama Sutra*.

***

> "Two roads diverged in a wood and I - I took the one less traveled by, and that has made all the difference."—Robert Frost

We have all of us taken the road less traveled, and with some knowledge of astrology, it is astonishing just how fine a line there is between the way we are and the way that we might have been, the path we may have taken. Minutes can easily translate into a completely different lifetime and person. There's a lot to meditate on here. We have all taken our *own* road, and there is no one traveling with us. We have not *taken* the road less traveled, though, so much as we have been *assigned* to it; for those into certain variants of spirituality or karma, the choice may be seen as a mutual and forgotten decision between us and the universe. It is *our* road. We have some choice as to how we actualize it or pick the various side-paths as we go along, but there are no passageways connecting us to the roads of others. We are forever on our own paths. And while it can easily be an object of fantasizing, meditation, and idle speculation as to what our lives may have been like had we been born a few minutes or a few days earlier, or later, here we are. We can look over and see others moving in parallel to us, living their own particular lives, seemingly separate from us on an alternate route across the field, but their paths are not ours. We are here to play the cards that *we* have been dealt. Our choice is to work within the parameters that have been given to us, to reap the seeds that have been sown, to grow into ourselves, and to express as best we can the higher version of our particular natures. We are forever unique, just like everyone else, and we are our birth moments.

A Great Dane

Tremendously influential modern astrologer Dane Rudhyar was born (in France) midway between Niels Bohr and Werner Heisenberg, in 1895, and his formative years roughly coincided with the physics upheavals taking place in the early decades of the last century in Europe. Like the later 1960's, the "Roaring 20's" were a time of general excitement, new thought, and a feeling that "anything goes": a phrase later immortalized in a song by Cole Porter. Also like the 1960's, there was a strong Uranus/Pluto aspect in effect, instilling its energy into the period. (Interestingly, this combination also appears again in the mid 2010's with the US's first black president, the legalization of gay marriage, and the legalization of marijuana in many states. Anything goes again. Well—a little bit, anyway: Uranus and Pluto are talking again, but in the present case with a bit more disagreement; this time it's a square.)

Rudhyar, while originally a musician, emigrated from Paris to New York, and began to study theosophy, Jungian psychology, and astrology under Marc Edmund Jones. As physics began to see reality as less deterministic, and more correlative and probabilistic, Rudhyar in parallel helped to further the concept (using many of Jung's ideas) that astrology was probably not due to some sort of physical mechanism, but was more likely due to some process similar to Jung's synchronicity, although Rudhyar typically didn't use that term. But his talk of a holistic view of reality and astrology, manifested partly through what Jung would call individuation, is eminently compatible with this concept. As physics moved from a model of absolute predictability to one of only possibilities (thanks to Heisenberg), Rudhyar began to champion what he called "humanistic astrology" which gave much more latitude for free will and self-development, as well as a greater connection to consciousness. His breakthrough book, *The Astrology of Personality*, was published in 1936, and pushed astrology in a whole new direction that continues to this day: astrologers since Rudhyar are much more likely to talk of each person's capacity for growth and development, and to take a "weather report" approach to predictions or personalities. These use the idea that infinite possibilities may exist in unmanifested form, but that certain ones are more likely. These in turn may be influenced by free will, spiritual development, and other factors during the individuation process. This contrasts with the somewhat more prevalent astrological fatalism of centuries gone by, and is likely a result of the quantum discoveries of the early 20th century exerting an osmotic effect on the both the general understanding of the world at that time, and on Rudyhar. The synchronicity of larger societal movements with scientific as well as astrological understandings is fascinating. The world is a whole, and in its larger manifestations, it moves as a whole. Indeed, depending on the planetary alignments, anything *does* go.

Secondary Progressions—This Is Where We Take Our Leave

Who knows how astrology operates? That is a work in progress. The model that astrology is being judged by in the scientific community, interestingly, does not even use the current scientific paradigm or information, but uses a paradigm from several cycles ago. Physics itself is swirling in quantum mysteries and surprises, but astrology is still being judged by Newtonian mechanics. How could it work? Rays of some sort? Gravity? Electromagnetic flux? Nothing is revealing itself in this regards, and in fact these sorts of speculations seem almost quaint in their retro feel and lack of imagination. We are stuck with ideas from Buck Rogers when the CERN lab is discovering the Higgs boson. The problem is twofold: astrologers have little scientific training to defend themselves, and scientists have dropped astrology into the dustbin many decades ago.

And while modern physics is starting to feel closer to the Godhead from Hinduism than a giant machine, astrology itself at times has strained to stay in touch with this fast moving thinking. One sign that it has is the move towards probability, rather than the idea that one may make definitive predictions. Quantum ideas have infused the whole of modern culture, and taken astrology along with them. But besides the "weather reports," the fact that specific predictions are still made at times with success again accents the need for a new understanding of the universe that would encompass not only astrology, but psi phenomena and synchronicity (in addition to science). Synchronicity is rapidly becoming the explanation of choice for how astrology works. But how does synchronicity work?

The solution to the problem of astrology is likely a few cycles of discovery away yet. We've had to wait hundreds, or even thousands of years for many of the scientific truths that we take for granted today; things are revealed on a timetable that is often frustrating to the impatience of our own lifetimes. And if things ever get to the point where astrology seems too tantalizingly close to being explained by current physics possibilities, one need only move to a study of secondary progressions (or solar arc directions, AstroCartoGraphy ™ , or other more symbolic techniques) to move the goalposts further ahead, and to be grounded in just how strange this discipline really IS. This is really where we take our leave from any possible explanation that might be tied into modern science (but possibly not future science). Secondary progressions have no connection whatsoever to the physical world: they are solely and purely symbolic, mathematical, and conceptual. But then again, so is the Pythagorean theorem, and it certainly has an "existence" of some sort. An interesting parallel there.

For those not familiar with them, the two methods most commonly used by astrologers to forecast upcoming events or trends are transits and secondary progressions (followed by solar arcs). Transits are tied to the physical solar system, and reflect the actual movements of the planets, sun, and moon as they "transit" around the natal chart, or amongst themselves. Conclusions are drawn by examining their aspects, or angles, to the natal, or birth, planets. Thus, current meets past to predict future; a nicely holistic scheme indeed, and the main technique for prediction. Transits are mainly used to predict *external* events or *conditions* that the native might meet as the cycles move, although of course external events may well change a person's internal consciousness considerably.

Secondary progressions, on the other hand, have more to do with a person's inner self and development, and how they approach the world—in an analogous way as to how one may read the natal chart. They are frequently used side by side with transits, although typically secondary in importance as well as in name. Many would say that transits have the ability to set off or "trigger" possibilities shown in the more slowly developing secondary progressed chart. Secondary progressions are based on the purely theoretical, mathematical, and archetypal idea that a person's inner nature progresses through life in the fashion that, for each year of life, there is a bit of the additional flavor of where the planets were a day (for each year) after they were born. The idea is "a day for a year." For example, using an ephemeris, if a person born on Jan 1st were to turn 10 years old, one would look up where the planets were on Jan 11th of their birth year (10 days after they were born) to see what changes in outlook and consciousness may have occurred. In practice, it is primarily the Sun and Moon that are looked at the most, largely because their faster apparent speed shows more movement; in this scheme, the slower planets may often move barely at all through a lifetime, and therefore most would say that when they do so, it shows a time of extra significance.

To those who haven't investigated this, the idea at first seems ridiculous. It seems made up, arbitrary, silly—just a fun idea that someone had, that sounded good at the time: "Let's say that a day equals a year and see what happens." However, for those who take the time to investigate, and who are open-minded, it can be quite revelatory. Since the sun moves at about a degree a day, everyone will "progress" through at least another Sun sign or two during their lifetime, depending on what degree of their birth sign they are "starting from." The subtle changes in character and interests are often dramatically evident if one examines their life carefully. For example, if one is a Gemini, and their progressed Sun moves into Cancer, they may often have children, or become more emotional and caring. They may possibly change careers to one more compatible with feminine values, one considered a "helping" profession, etc. The natal Gemini Sun sign is never lost; one simply becomes a more emotional, or caring, or family-oriented, or motherly Gemini: there is a sort of mild "Cancer overlay" to the native Gemini. Again, if one examines the long narrative of their lives with an ephemeris handy, they can often pick these intervals out. Later, the Sun may progress to Leo, and this time there will be a "Leo overlay" onto the Gemini, with all of the characteristics which *that* may connote.

The progressed Moon is similar in that it, too, provides its own distinctive overlay to the life and interests, but is unique in that this happens roughly every two years or so, instead of every thirty years, as with the Sun. So here we have an overlay on an overlay! It's easy to see how astrology can get complicated very quickly, and why it is so difficult to isolate a particular factor to "test," if we are so inclined. All factors work together to produce a whole. And yet, if we learn, and if we look, we can clearly see each individual element in play. We can pick the signal out of the noise, pick the color out of the rainbow. It's really quite beautiful.

But this is where we finally must take our leave: there is no way whatsoever in our current understanding of science that any of this can be reconciled. Whatever is going on with astrology, it is beyond any current comprehension as to mechanism. And that's Ok. It doesn't mean that it doesn't work: it just means that we don't know *how* it works; its "mechanism" (if that even turns out to be the correct word) is beyond our current knowledge and vision. There is something there, but we don't know what it is (to paraphrase an excellent movie of a similar name, as well as a Bob Dylan song). Likely, there *is* no unique mechanism; most likely, a better understanding of the synchronicity of the universe itself is the answer.

Trying to evaluate astrology, or to understand it according to current physics or science, perhaps would be like someone from the Middle Ages hoping to get a handle on magnetism, or to measure it, by putting it into a bucket and trying to see how many gallons there were. It's using joules to measure apples, or kilograms to measure light. It's evident that magnetism exists, and yet it would be an imperfect understanding of it to try and measure it with a bucket: it would not further the apprehension of it, because the units of measurement are wrong, *reflecting missing knowledge*. Similarly, it's obvious to many people that astrology exists, but one cannot capture it by trying to stuff it into current physics models; there is something else there, something incompatible, something missing and yet to be discovered. And yet, for those willing to be open-minded and investigate, the beauty and power of astrology are there for anyone who makes the effort.

One Shift, Two Shift, Red Shift, Blue Shift

Most people are familiar with the phenomenon, if not the physics, of what is known as the Doppler effect. It used to be explained by the sound of a train horn whizzing by, but not many people today are privy to train noises. And since it requires a sustained sound, car horns don't work very well (except perhaps in India). I had the recent opportunity, however, to have a large motorcycle pass by me with a loud radio going, blasting a rock tune out to the world. Mick Jagger and the Rolling Stones were being featured, and just before the motorcycle overtook me, I heard Mick's voice sounding a bit odd and higher pitched than usual. Then, as the bike flew past, Mick's voice suddenly dropped in pitch. Very odd.

The doppler effect works like this: sounds emit waves. Tighter waves (more cycles per second) are associated with higher pitched sounds, while lower pitched sounds have "longer" waves. But when something is coming towards one, the frequency will seem to be "compressed": the waves are sort of pushing together, which leads to the perception of a higher frequency. Thus, Mick's voice seemed higher as the motorcycle came towards me. But if that something is then flying away, the waves seem to relax and spread apart more, and thus the frequency to the observer drops, and Mick's voice lowers noticeably. (Although of course the frequency from the moving object's point of view never varies; Mick sounds just fine to the motorcyclist.) Thus, objects speeding by us have the typical MRRRRRowwww..... as the sound drops in pitch during the pass-by.

It turns out that this phenomenon occurs with any wave, and not just with sound. Astronomers long ago discovered that this allows them to determine which objects in space are either moving towards us, or moving away from us. Using visible light instead of sound waves, galaxies or other objects that are moving towards us will have a "blue shift," as the wavelengths of their light will seem compressed, and thus generate a higher apparent frequency *to us*. (Blue light has a higher frequency than red light.) However, if the galaxy is moving away from us, then the frequencies will relax and stretch out a bit from our point of view, and generate a "red shift" (a color shift towards the red, or longer wave, end of the spectrum). As it so happens, due to the expansion of the universe, almost every object outside of our galaxy appears to be moving away from us, and thus one hears mostly of a "red shift."

But let's talk a bit about how astrology may take part in the Doppler phenomenon. Years ago, I worked for a summer in Denver at a company called Mile-Hi Psychics. This was just before the internet broke, and "900" pay telephone numbers were all the rage, and big money makers for many companies. Mile-Hi advertised in various magazines and newspapers, and did quite a good business. People would call up to talk with a "psychic," and be billed by the minute. Consequently, we were paid by the minute. Most of the people who worked there (it was a sort of boiler-room type of setting) seemed to have a sincere interest in things psychic or alternative, but most also seemed blessed with the gift of gab. (No, they weren't all Geminis or Sagittarians!). Most— well, everyone except me—were Tarot readers. This seemed to work well for them, as there was always another card to turn over and talk about, and this kept the chat going. Some could talk for hours. They were probably driving Mercedes.

I've never been a huge talker to begin with, and I have that stereotypical guy thing going on: "get the problem solved, and move on." Plus, and especially in the realm of how an astrological reading might affect someone else's life, I've always done my best to be honest, and tried to respect and elevate the art, rather than cheapen it. Consequently, even though there were many calls per day, I didn't make nearly as much money as some of the other readers, because I couldn't see extending the conversation on the phone for too long, just to run the tab up. I saw myself as mainly a problem solver, not so much as a therapist at that point. I later realized that one could be both.

Astrology is just so amazing. Here's what would happen in about 90% of the calls that I took: I had both my ephemeris handy as well as one of the first portable laptop type of IBM computers, with Matrix astrology software installed. Someone would call up. They would be, I could tell, pretty distraught about one of the usual subjects: relationships, money, other losses, change, etc. My heart usually went out to them, because I could tell that they were hurting, and really just wanted someone to tell them something good. Normally, they would have been dealing with the problem for quite some time; they were now at the end of their rope, so to speak, and were desperate for some positive news.

The great thing was, in almost every case, I could provide it to them. It was uncanny. Looking solely at their natal charts and current transits, it was not difficult to see where the trouble was. Invariably, it was a difficult outer planet transit that had been going on for some time. In fact, it was spooky: most of these callers would have something like Saturn square Venus, Uranus square Sun, Neptune conjunct Mars, or something similar. I could see that this transit had been bothering them for "x" period of time, and they would agree that this was the case. But the amazing thing was, *they always called just before the transit was about to end*. No one ever called at the beginning of a transit. The saying "it's always darkest just before the dawn" is certainly true. It was as if they had initially suffered stoically for a while, became more alarmed or discouraged, and then were at their wit's end as to what was going on through the whole difficult time. Now they were ready to throw in the towel. They were desperate. There seemed no way out, or nowhere to turn; it seemed to them, at that point, that nothing would change, or get better. I could tell that some of them were people who wouldn't ordinarily turn to a psychic or astrologer, but were now so beat down that they were willing to listen for any message of hope, wherever they could find it. It felt good to be able to explain to them just what had been going on, for how long, and most importantly, that it was usually just about to end. These conversations almost always ended with positive feelings and optimism on both sides.

Why is this? Why did they always call towards the end of a difficult transit? It's likely that transits, like every other wave (waves are cycles), take part in the Doppler effect. As a transit approaches and moves into its manifestation, the "frequency," the archetype, begins to compress and become heightened, the tension mounts, things become thrust into our awareness, and we become a bit disoriented, as the status quo is rocked and subjected to this new energy coming towards us. Our normal sleepy, auto-pilot awareness and routines are assaulted, and forced to wake up. The energy is blue-shifted; coming at us in a pushed, compressed, and amplified form, even as the cycle progresses. It is often not until the middle of the cycle or so that we even realize (although some pretty major effects may have been felt by then) that this particular moment in time really is *different*, that the character of our passage through time has been part of a collision with something unknown, and something often very scary. Midway through, we suddenly realize that the past is gone, and that we have been thrust into new territory. We can't go back. The planets want us to wake up, and to grow. They are asking us to leave the warm and cozy pub by the dock and to head out to sea: the horizon looks far away, dark, and blank to us: what is out there? The blue shift compresses the archetype and compresses the fear and disorientation. Like it or not, however, sail we must: that is the message. Midway through, we realize that we actually *are* at sea, not remembering our disembarkation. (Positive cycles, of course, we typically take in stride, and take for granted: it's simply our native *right* to have good things happen to us. So these often blow by us with minimal gratitude or appreciation for them.) And unless we have some astrological knowledge, we will often not be focusing on the "lessons" that we are supposed to be learning from a particular time, but simply on the pain and alarm.

And then it's over. Mick's voice rushes by, drops in tone, and then is gone. The same thing happens with our transit: we have had it rush upon us, or sometimes explode upon us, if we have not noticed the subtle blue shift coming. We have endured it as it passed by, maybe learning something, or maybe having our world turned upside down. And then one day we simply notice that it is, without having announced the exact point of its final passing, in the rearview mirror. Now it's all behind us, a relaxing red shift marking with relief its final moments as the lengthening wavelength stretches off in the distance, corresponding to a drop in tension and effect. It is done. We've survived. We can relax. The acute power of the archetype is diminishing, and sinking back into the larger matrix. Hopefully, we've gotten some insights along the way. Hopefully, we will hold on to the remembrance of the experience, if for no other reason than to remind ourselves that life *is* cycles, and that our only choice is to work with them, and not to fight them; to get whatever meaning we can from them, and to be more prepared for the next one. To learn and know that we mustn't take the good times for granted, because they don't last forever; and to know that neither do the bad times. The only way that we can screw up or prolong the period of a particular cycle is to fight it, to try and hold on to the status quo, to resist the lessons being presented to us (or forced upon us as the case may be). The wheels always keep turning, each cycle makes way for the next.

MMMMMRRRooowwwww....

What's the Story?

Humans are storytelling animals. We'll always tell stories. Stories are how we learn about ourselves, about others, and about the world around us. Stories are magical, informative, and mundane. They are in a galaxy far away, and sitting on the sofa next to us. Stories exist from out of the earliest fog of man's history, to the sitcom that we watched last night. Gilgamesh is forever meeting Clark Kent. Stories can be placed into several categories. There are many stories that are obviously fictional, but that provide (besides entertainment value) psychological and other insights into our fellows. Such a sprawling masterwork as Gabriel García Márquez' *One Hundred Years of Solitude* falls into this category. (It is interesting that the term "magical realism" was coined to describe his writing style, and that he is a Pisces with Taurus rising.) Even simple children's fairy tales are laden with meaning and peeks into the darkest recesses of the human mind (as noted by Jung and such others as Marie-Louise von Franz). The world indeed would be a poorer place if not for a dollop of magic and wonder at the unknown.

Star Trek was stories, and there is a reason that there was only one Spock on board. If the whole ship had been Spocks, there would have been no stories. That's the difference between humans and Vulcans. Earth, Air, Fire, and Water. Spock was pure Air: dispassionate, logical, and intellectual. But pure anything is, by nature, limited and false in some way. The world is *not* pure; it "contains multitudes." Humans are contradictory and messy, and it is this messiness that drives their stories, whether of triumph or tragedy.

Other stories are designed to explain things, often things that we're not too sure about. Creation myths associated with various religions fall into this category. As explanations of physical reality, religions of course have had their day; the world has moved on. But they carry on because they meet other needs. Some folks who are not religious will insist that those who *are* religious have a greater need for certainty than other folks, or a greater fear of the unknown; but maybe this isn't the entire story. Religious stories are primarily designed to bring people together with spiritual truths. This is why they have lasted in our societies beyond their ability to explain lightning, or the origin of species. Science, on the other hand, now writes our current version of the "explanation" stories. This is not to say that they aren't "true"; simply that science itself qualifies as a story. It is the way that we are currently interpreting the world. But science as an explainer, unlike solidified religious dogma, has going for it that it has a built in expectation of transformation and updates, which will always keep it fresh. It is always a story in progress. There are quite a few cliffhangers involved! As to whether science will ever finally provide a *definitive* picture of reality is a topic that is open to question. And open questions are, in fact, much in the very spirit of the scientific story. 'Round we go.

In addition to the above, there are anecdotes, fables, folklore, jokes, legends, myths, news stories, parables, paradigms, and urban legends. We love sharing things: look at Facebook. It's important to note that stories may be factual or not; the Associated Press disseminates stories as surely as the Brothers Grimm did. The story about your neighbor may be a dry recitation of the facts, or a fanciful and embellished masterpiece of gossip. Many stories have elements of facts and speculations mixed together; that is why science may be thought of as a series of modern stories, as much as scientists may protest being associated with that term. How much of science is true? Were the stories that we tell today true 300 or 500 years ago, or were there other "truths" or "facts" that people believed at that time? Will the current truths of our scientific stories be the same 300 or 500 years hence? We see that maybe some of the stories told in the past were different. So we must come to the conclusion that, for all its credibility and self-importance, science, too, contributes to humanity's stories.

> "The world isn't just the way it is. It is how we understand it, no? And in understanding something, we bring something to it, no?"—Yann Martel, Life of Pi

It is through our own personal storytelling that we may most clearly see how our consciousness creates our reality, at least in a psychological sense. Believing is seeing: we may enjoy a multitudinous variety of external stories and have no difficulty telling the true from the fanciful (although of course we might), but when it comes to our own stories, we are often curiously blind, often aggravatingly or humorously so to our fellows. Others can often tell our story better than we can; they are privy to a level of perspective that we usually cannot muster. In our own stories we are perhaps one particular thing, and the world is a particular way; in our friends' versions, we may play a different or slightly less elevated (or less diminished) role, and the world may not be as we see it.

All of us wear rose (or other) colored glasses. Astrology is incalculably valuable in this regard, as it allows us (as much as anything in life can) to take our glasses off, and to see the whole spectrum, *because we can discover what color glasses we are actually wearing*, and we can see what color glasses others are wearing. It is this self-awareness and vision of our own reality being only one of many possible choices that allows us to perform this miracle. We will never see through another's glasses, but without wisdom traditions or self-awareness techniques such as astrology, we often do not even understand that we are seeing the world through a filter, or that others are using different colored filters than ours; and that no particular pair or color of glasses are necessarily "better" than another. They are all required to make up the Whole, of which we are only a small part. White light contains all colors; the various colors are subservient to a greater whole. If we have a model in our minds that only our particular color is "correct" then we are at risk for a frustrating uncomfortable, and incomplete life.

Astrology does this, of course, through stories. Through stories of Jupiter, or Mercury, or Venus, or other mythological archetypes that informed the birth of Western astrology; through the story of energy: cardinal, fixed, mutable (beginning, middle, end); through the fabric of human existence: physical, emotional, mental, and spiritual. Earth, Water, Air, and Fire. Astrology is a rich loam of mythology, observation, and correlation. It has walked side by side with humans since the swamp. It matters little if the stories aren't literally "true"; that isn't the purpose or point of myth and archetype. They are true for us as humans, as they describe our quirky, maddening, and chaotic journeys through life.

Astrology is a symbolic language, and humans are symbol-using animals. Our knowledge of the physical world has improved and accumulated over the millennia, but we are the same people who prayed on the Ghats at Benares, or walked the streets in Babylonia, or debated in the Greek agoras in years gone to the mist. Our technology is different, but our personal journeys are as well described in the books written by the sages of those eras, as in the ones of today. Mars still lives with us, as does Neptune. We may find as much insight in these primal archetypes and stories as our ancestors did (the warrior and the dreamer are going nowhere soon), and yet we continue in our own journeys and stories as well, adding to and verifying the symbols, myths, and tales of humankind. More to the point, our own lives and beliefs are ultimately nothing *but* our personal stories about the way we are, or the way others are, or the way the world is. We are all writers of our own tales.

Study, Study, Study

Why has astrology been so difficult to study scientifically? Why have those of us who had some hopes in this direction repeatedly had them dashed or delayed? There are a multitude of reasons for this; let's look at some of them. Primary, of course, are simple biases against this sort of research on the part of the established scientific community, combined with a lack of funding and training on the part of the astrologers. That is, most mainstream scientific studies are performed by those with the resources to do so, and for a particular topic that can generate funding. The resources are typically provided by established channels, those working within current paradigms. One can be innovative, but only so much as is tolerated by the group controlling the money to be dispersed. Science today has little interest in investigating astrology; it's a subject long considered dead and put away. Astrologers themselves, meanwhile, are not a rich lot, and the ones who make the most money frequently have little interest in research of this nature. *Most* astrologers, in fact, have minimal interest in research, often coming from a place of perceived defeat prior to investigation (resulting from past experiences), knowing that the deck is stacked against them, or simply not caring whether things are "proved" scientifically or not. Some feel (not unjustifiably, as this book has shown) that astrology is incompatible with science as we know it today, and therefore not worth the effort. It simply works for them, and that's good enough. In addition, astrologers tend to be a quirky lot, quite the antithesis to the methodical and concrete scientific mindset.

So science itself has no interest in investigating astrology, and the few scientific researchers who do find astrology on their radar screens tend to see it simply as an annoying gnat that must be swatted away. Thus, any studies that might be examined by these investigators usually involve charging forward with armored biases minimally camouflaged, gunning for the poor fuzzy headed folks in their sights. At their noblest, they simply assume that astrology is bogus and meaningless and one must grudgingly take time out of their day to demonstrate this; and at their worst, they exhibit a vindictive, questionably ethical, and mean streak about the whole thing.

Wikipedia, for all of its strengths, has been generally unkind to astrology. For example, their entry on "Astrology and Science" touts negative results regarding Shawn Carlson's 1985 research, "A Double Blind Study of Astrology," even though the biases and limitations of this typical study have been carefully analyzed and examined by Edward Snow of the Astrology News Service. They also mention anti-astrology crusader Geoffrey Dean, and in another article The Committee for Skeptical Inquiry (CSI), formerly known as CSICOP (Committee for the Scientific Investigation of Claims of the Paranormal). Of note is that Carl Sagan, although no fan of astrology, refused to sign CSICOP's 1983 "Objections to Astrology" statement on the subject; he apparently felt that it sounded like an unscientific diatribe in and of itself, somewhat of a "witch hunt," and not compatible with the ideal of objectivity that he would have liked to have seen among supposedly otherwise objective scientists. Regarding Geoffrey Dean's integrity as a credible researcher, meanwhile, according to Astrodienst, "for years he lied about his own data (his birthday), ...apparently amused that astrologers would then tell him bits of delineation about his (made up) chart." Ha-ha. What a jokester. No bias *there*!

Astrologers are *not* scientists, by and large, and thus normally have no training in research and statistics, although there are rare exceptions. Consequently, they are poorly trained to defend themselves, or to investigate the subject "properly." Most, but not all, astrological "studies" boil down to a particular person looking through the charts in their files, and arriving at certain conclusions, or speculations, or insights. This is in fact the way science itself approaches things, but the astrologers do not normally have the resources (or often the energy, time, or desire) to statistically study or verify these observations. The verification is haphazard and anecdotal. Nonetheless, it has moved the discipline forward. A good example is Doris Chase Doane's book *Astrology: 30 Years Research.* Although, again, this is exactly the way that astrology actually *did* develop through the millennia in an empirical and observational fashion (as did science), it certainly leaves giant holes in terms of being verifiable, reproducible, or "respectable" by the scientific community. Specifically, it provides huge opportunities for selection bias and confirmation bias.

And yet, we can *see* these things working in our lives, and with those around us, on very obvious display. For us, it is the ability to pick hidden colors out of the rainbow, and to see an invisible spectrum in all its glory—with all of the amazement that may engender. For others, it is simply white light, noise. It is so frustrating!

***

Suppose that I have an idea for a study that might show that, on the average, Sagittarians weigh more than Capricorns (Jupiter vs Saturn). An intriguing idea, and one that might be easily verified using large samples in one way or another. In fact, it could even be done anonymously, using the large databanks that hospitals have, for example. But who would fund this? Who would organize it? Who would publish it? Would the scientific community even care, or simply ignore or bury it? And most importantly, would it show validity? Would the p-value be significant? Would there be a signal pushing out of the noise? (See the "signal to noise ratio" discussion elsewhere in this book.) And if it did not show significance, then what would that mean? Would it mean that astrology is silly and stupid? Who that interpreted the results would have enough of an understanding of astrology to correctly see the problems that there might be with the study? Perhaps it could be that a more predictive variable might turn out to be Jupiter or Saturn aspects to the ascendant, the rising sign, or one of a hundred other possibilities.

This points out another extremely problematic issue in investigating astrology: how *does* one isolate a variable to test? Scientific studies thrive on isolating a single variable to avoid contamination by other factors, and to demonstrate things more purely, clearly, or simply. The typical horoscope chart is, unfortunately, replete with hundreds of potential astrological factors, many of them contradicting each other. One is not simply an Aquarian, that we can then test or experiment with. One is an Aquarian with Moon in Cancer, squaring Neptune, in the 8th house, progressed to Aries, conjunct Mars... one can go down the rabbit hole pretty quickly here. As another example, suppose that I am a Leo, which an investigator may read to be sunny, open, dramatic, generous, and optimistic.

But now suppose that I also have Moon in Scorpio, which is obviously a quite different kettle of fish, a very different personality. I now enjoy reading Dostoyevsky's dark (but often humorous) *Notes From Underground*, and I am fascinated with murder mysteries and revenge. Who am I? How does a researcher, who is trying to "prove" what Leos are like, deal with this? In this particular case, I am Alfred Hitchcock: a Leo with Moon in Scorpio, who managed to merge introverted dark mystery with dramatic storytelling, and a fair amount of ego. As *astrologers*, we can easily "see" these two disparate energies at work, but how could a scientist ever tease them out in a study? And if you don't even believe that these energies exist, then how in the world could you *ever* see them, or even talk about them? Would this individual show up as a Leo, a Scorpio, or something else in tests? What about the rising sign, the aspects, the houses? We are like the various and distinct colors in the rainbow vs. white light. Signal vs. noise. We are all white light until someone looks through a prism.

There are perhaps ways to get around this, but again it would require statistical and research expertise, along with time and money: and those who have these qualifications are generally not astrologers. When I was pursuing my degree in psychology, I did an independent study course in which I used a small sample (less than 10 each) of Sagittarians and Taureans (perhaps Scorpio or Capricorn might work as well here) to show that there was a significant difference in "authoritarianism" in those two personalities. I specifically chose a test known as the Pensacola Z-Scale due to its reputation for being difficult to "fake" (face value): it was difficult to discern what the test was looking for by reading the questions.

Who knows if this would be reproducible or not? It was a small sample, but it was statistically significant at the time. But who would have the money, time, resources, or interest to reproduce it? And would it even be reproducible? It was done quite a while back, and perhaps the gestalt of society has changed since then, and the way that authoritarianism plays out may be different. (Although recent history doesn't show much change in human nature.)

Which brings up another problem with studying astrology from a scientifically reproducible standpoint. With astrology, in addition to the frustratingly unpredictable nature of those quirky humans, you have the additional variable of an ever-changing cosmos that may affect experiments in ways that we don't even know. A person filling out a questionnaire this week with Jupiter conjunct their Sun may fill it out differently a month from now with Saturn squaring their Moon. Transits multiply the problems of investigation; such symbolic forces as secondary progressions or solar arc directions add to the difficulties.

So, using the hypothetical Aquarian above, how could we check whether "Aquarians" have certain traits, if every Aquarian has a different chart in other respects, and all charts are dynamic and responding in real time to current cosmological conditions? And if we use twins, what percentage of their lives and personalities are astrological, vs. genetic, environmental, or just subject to a willful choosing to go in different directions in order to establish their own identities? "Time twins" improve this, but are still problematic. There is *human* nature in addition to astrological nature, and, like universal spiritual principles, this inconsistently-manifested variable may actually trump astrology. Genetics and nurture may be predicted by, or tied to, astrology, but they may not be. We don't know for sure, and this would be one of the most difficult studies imaginable.

And regarding the "human" factor: those damn, wiggly, changeable humans are not only possibly responding to monthly, daily or even hourly transits in their charts from various astrological factors, but from who knows what other influences. They argued with their wife this morning. They just got fired from their job. They won the lottery. It's like trying to nail jelly to a wall. It's like trying to study psychology, or love, or generosity, using math, or physics, or chemistry. There is a potential mismatch here; there are certainly myriad difficulties in the design of these studies.

***

There are two people looking at a light beam. One of them has a prism and the other doesn't. The one with the prism states that they can see a variety of colors: red, blue, yellow, etc. The one without the prism says, "you're nuts. The light is white, and that's the end of the story. You're hallucinating, or delusional, or gullible, or making things up. And it's not even worth wasting time proving you wrong." Borrowing the prism would be the equivalent of learning astrology; an offer that is normally declined: "no, I'm good. I don't need to investigate your viewpoint." On top of this, the person with the prism has the difficult task of not only convincing the first person that the colors exist, but that one particular light beam may have a slight preponderance of green over another, although they appear approximately the same: subtle, but noticeable. How does one tease *that* out? How does one explain that? How does one explain that although the two light beams contain all colors, one appears to have a bit more emphasis on green?

That said, it is still entirely possible that experiments may be designed to tease out some signals from the noise in an effective, significant, and reproducible fashion. But again, that would require more resources and expertise than the field of astrology generally has. I don't want to cut short or minimize the sincere and productive efforts of those in the astrology field who *have* put a lot of effort through the years into attempting to validate our understanding (In fact, *thank you.*); but the reality is, in the larger quest for man to know his world through research, astrology remains a marginalized backwater. What would it take to turn things around, to break through the stasis and prejudices in order to invite another look? Perhaps research in astrology could somehow be linked to a new weight-loss program, miracle mop, or something else that marketers could smell might make money. Just a thought.

***

An interesting example of what might seem to be a rigorous scientific study that ended up being sympathetic to astrology is, of course, that of the Gauquelins' research, which began with the "Mars effect" for sports champions. This is a long, involved, and rewarding subject for further reading; most serious astrologers are already familiar with it, and so it won't be gone into detail here. Suffice it to say that Michel Gauquelin and his wife Francoise, through the analysis of thousands of French birth charts with accurately documented birth times, found that the planets Mars, Jupiter, Saturn, and the moon corresponded roughly, in certain segments of the horoscopic wheel, to various professions that were appropriate for each planet by ancient tradition. Pretty astounding, and even an analysis by CSICOP's Marvin Zellen seemed initially to confirm this. The only astronomer at CSICOP, Dennis Rawlins, also agreed that the methodology and results looked valid. However, this was not to stand, as CSICOP, no doubt alarmed by the implications, soon began to backpedal furiously, and began to produce many obscure reasons as to why the Gauquelin study was not to be trusted. The scientific moat had been rocked, but the invaders were ultimately repelled. Of note here (one may refer to several online articles), is that CSICOP itself is not an actual scientific group (although it solicits scientists to add their names to its roster), but is more of a public relations and lobbying group, hoping to convince the public that anything alternative (astrology, psi, etc.) is worthless and delusional.

The controversy has never had a firm resolution: believing is seeing, and both sides here will find what they are looking for. Interestingly, although the Gauquelin research identified planet/profession combinations that would be familiar to any astrologer, the *segments* that he found them in were shifted a bit from those traditionally seen as prominent by astrologers. Thus, many astrologers have basically ignored Gauquelin's research, continuing to use houses 1, 4, 7, and 10 (the "angular" houses) as the prominent houses, rather than larger segments of the "cadent" houses (especially 12 and 9), as Gauquelin's research showed. So what does this mean? Was Gauquelin right with his sectors, and should astrologers be using his "cross-house" sectors preferentially in delineation? Most astrologers will tell you that (while agreeing with the planet/profession correlation of his study), intuitively for them, and in the results that they see in their own anecdotal studies, the 12th house still seems to deal with obscurity and the 1st or 10th houses with prominence. So what are we to make of this? Were astrologers right? Were skeptical scientists right? Was Gauquelin right? It seems impossible for all of these to be correct. Perhaps what it really shows is the excitement and possibilities that could come with further large-scale research into the subject.

***

And then there's consciousness and synchronicity. The whole of this book is infused with speculations about how consciousness may tie into astrology, or physics, or synchronicity, or our lives otherwise. This is somewhat of a wild card, but it may also be a key limiting factor in how to investigate astrology, just as consciousness and measurement interact with certain predictive parameters of quantum physics experiments. Carl Jung did an informal experiment (retold by Maggie Hyde in *Jung and Astrology*), in which he had three people whose mental/emotional makeups were familiar to him try and match up couples among 20 horoscopes of married people that were jumbled together. What he found was not that they were able to accurately match the couples (they were not astrologers, anyway); rather, he found that they matched horoscopes which ended up corresponding to *astrological traits within themselves*, within their *own* charts, tying inner energy in a synchronistic fashion to outward, "objective" events or choices. (For example, an "angry" person might unconsciously match two charts that had strong Mars links, etc.) Maggie's husband Geoffrey Cornelius also has a lot to say about this. So this would seem to be yet another wild card that may skew any astrological studies.

We must also ask ourselves another simple and parallel question, one that is understandably confusing, but one whose omission doesn't aid astrology in any quest towards rejoining mainstream thought: *what exactly are we studying, and how exactly are we studying it?* As pointed out above, we must be sure that we are not studying psychology with physics, or physics with psychology, or botany with geology. The fact that we're not even sure exactly what astrology is, or how it works, is a limiting factor here. One thing that we *can* be sure of: astrology is not simple, its possible mechanisms are not simple, and therefore it will not be surprising if simplistic efforts to tease them out are ambiguous or inconclusive.

Dennis Elwell, in *The Cosmic Loom*, brings up something that has been pointed out several times here; that "the new physics, which has been immensely fruitful in practical terms, contrasts starkly with the old Newtonian model, with its simplistic reliance on cause and effect. The new orthodoxy is agreed that Newtonian physics no longer adequately explains what is happening. Yet when it comes to the business of discrediting astrology, scientists happily scamper back to Sir Isaac's arms, demanding to be told how the planets can exert significant gravitational or electromagnetic effects at a distance. Then they have the temerity to accuse astrology of clinging to an outmoded model of reality!"

Stephen Hawking, for example, has said that "The reason most scientists don't believe in astrology is because it is not consistent with our theories that have been tested by experiment." Forget the fact that he himself has moved way beyond Newtonian simplicity. Forget the fact that he himself has done radical reversals on his own ideas, including coming to the conclusions that black holes aren't even black, and that, contrary to his early theories, they probably eventually "evaporate" and disappear. He apparently doesn't recall that most things known in science were at one point radically in contrast to existing theories. Scientific knowledge is a dynamic and moving thing. So when he says, "our theories that have been tested by experiment," one may ask: *which* theories? *What* experiments?

Finally, all of this also points up an unfortunate feedback loop: no interest in astrology = no money for research = no research = no results = no interest in astrology (in the dominant scientific community).

Let us end all of this, however, on a more open-minded note, by quoting astrology skeptic Carl Sagan once again:

> "That we can now think of no mechanism for astrology is relevant but unconvincing. No mechanism was known, for example, for continental drift when it was proposed by Wegener. Nevertheless, we see that Wegener was right, and those who objected on the grounds of unavailable mechanism were wrong."

Thank you, Carl. Speculated mechanisms at this time are limited, and may in fact turn out to have nothing to do with how astrology actually works. So where does that leave us in terms of scientifically "proving" astrology? Pretty much back where we started: limited hard evidence, but an ocean of anecdotal evidence, and hope. It leaves us with that odd prism that others are either unable or unwilling to look through. It demonstrates not that astrology will never be compatible with science, but simply how difficult it may be to find the common ground. We can see astrology in action as clearly as the nose on our face: bringing that deep and prismatic vision to uninterested skeptics remains a challenge. There is a tremendous opportunity here for someone young, intelligent, and energetic to perhaps make a difference that would literally affect mankind and our vision of reality for all ages to come. The opportunity is open.

That Sounds Just Like Me!

Astrology is real. Astrology works. For this simple reason, astrology will never "go away." Astrology can be one of the most rewarding and amazing studies that any human being can undertake. But astrology quite often can also be the Wild West of human development/consciousness/social/psychological/ personal growth disciplines: anything goes (to reference Cole Porter again). One can almost say anything they want, come up with any sort of theory or idea, put it out there, and usually have at least some group of people enthusiastically sign on. (The irony of this book's "Modern Model" is not lost here.) Unlike science, there are no constraints, minimal peer reviews, and very few evidence-based studies or experiments to reign in some often very unusual ideas. Formal attempts at standardized training are out there, but are spotty at best in their levels of acceptance and use.

So how do we decide what's good, solid, lasting astrology and what's more "fringe?" Where do we draw the line? The spectrum here ranges from hard-core scientists who would consider *any* astrology to be a ridiculous example of human gullibility, all the way on to some truly fuzzy people of our own. Astrology is often spoken of as being a "Uranian" discipline, but Neptune would seem to figure into it quite heavily as well. This is not necessarily bad by any means, but we need to keep this in mind as we uncover some truths that need to be looked at, if astrology is to ever regain its position as a subject of mainstream study. Some wouldn't even like that, of course: there are mixed viewpoints here. And the scientists, to beat a dead horse, are often as limited by their skepticism in seeing things accurately as are some of us in our own occasionally indiscriminate acceptance and beliefs.

One way to tell lasting astrology is simply time: looking back at years of old journals, some techniques are simply not as much in evidence these days as they once were, having been subject to a sort of winnowing out process, which presumably shows at least some vague correlation between popularity and effectiveness. (Though it must be said, there is a "flavor of the month" component to much of this as well. "Vedic" astrology for Westerners seems to be filling some of this niche at the moment.) As an example, while Uranian astrology is still around, it is not nearly as well-supported or mainstream as it once was years ago, although for some it is still the go-to technique. Some of its tenets, such as planetary pictures and midpoints—which have a history dating back to Guido Bonati and the Arabic Parts—have simply become, to an extent, absorbed into the mainstream. At the same time, the "hypothetical planets" component of the system has not been part of many popular astrology discussions for a while now. This is not to pass judgment on the overall effectiveness of Uranian astrology; it is simply to pull in one example of what seems to be a sifting process over time.

So we see that those ideas that seem to have the most validity for the most people last, while those that don't often become marginalized. This is a process that mainstream science is very familiar with as well. Another example of this process in astrology is that of AstoCartoGraphy™, which, when it appeared several decades ago, could easily have turned out to be just another off-the-wall idea which appeared out of nowhere, and went nowhere. It was basically invented out of whole cloth by astrologer Jim Lewis, and in fact he received a patent for it (!) in 1981. Since then, it has proven its merit and is used very widely in the field, demonstrating that there are indeed new ideas under the sun. It may be contrasted with the alternative local space techniques that never really caught on. Astrodynes (or Cosmodynes) are a technique that seemed to have promise (and still do, to this writer), but they, too, have languished away from popular acceptance. Other ideas will continue to appear: Rick Levine's concept of the planets as particle/wave dualities analogous to other forms of matter and energy, and differentiated only by their extremely long wavelengths, is one of these that is certainly very intriguing. There are many others.

The *most* interesting thing here is that the evolution of these sorts of new concepts demonstrates that, contrary to what skeptics would like to believe, astrology is actually alive and well, growing and changing, and stumbling forward in its own erratic way. It is doing so through the same processes that science uses: speculative theories, which are then tested by empirical observation and verification, albeit in a somewhat more casual and haphazard fashion. Astrology started with earlier peoples observing the skies nightly, and attempting to make correlations to life here on earth; and it continues to this day using the exact same process. This process came to be used throughout history in various other fields, and was later formalized as something we call the "scientific method"—but astrologers were there from the beginning.

***

That said, there are some real issues in using or talking about astrology, and they are frequently the ones that are used to attack the discipline. For example: it may certainly be very true that a position of the Sun in the tropical zodiac in the sign of Cancer may make one emotional and nurturing, but it is also certainly the case that if I am doing a reading for you and tell you that you're emotional and nurturing (at least if you are a woman), you may be very likely to agree with that, no matter what sign you are. Who isn't emotional and nurturing, at least to some extent? This is one of the chief criticisms of astrology; and while astrologers can readily discern a difference in the *quality* and *type* of emotion and nurturance exhibited by a Cancer vs. another sign, this is very difficult to comprehend for outside observers. But we need to understand some of these issues ourselves to stay on track, and to be honest about where we are with our art and science.

Wikipedia enumerates nearly 100 entries under the heading "List of Cognitive Biases." (Google them: it's *very* revealing, not only for our study of astrology, but for pretty much any issue in our lives.) Many of these we share with scientists, as well as with historians and housewives. They are human tendencies, built into our consciousness and nature. The best that we can do is to recognize and minimize them. Let's talk about several of them that are frequently mentioned regarding astrology (although, again, they often apply to science as well). These are inaccuracies and biases that we are often accused of, and in some cases are certainly guilty of. An honest and critical appraisal of our ideas is always in order. Sometimes this takes place; often it doesn't. Often we don't have the knowledge or tools for effective evaluation; sometimes we don't have the desire for an honest appraisal. Here, one might think of the geologist in a former section who didn't want to support Wegener because it would mean cleaning out a lot of ideas that were already in place, convenient, and had the force of inertia. In that context, we were talking about new ideas, but biases often have the same force of inertia, and the same temptation to put on blinders.

The chief criticism of astrology may be that of the Forer effect (after a 1948 study by psychologist Bertram Forer), which is more commonly known as the "Barnum effect"; a slang and intentionally derogatory term, derived from the circus impresario. This alludes, as shown in the example above, to the idea that a very generic sounding list of personality traits "about you" (as is often seen in newspaper horoscopes) could easily apply to anyone; and indeed, that most people will find that these generic descriptions "sound like me." This is a far cry from personalized horoscope readings derived from accurate birth information, using many factors, and done in collaboration with the subjects themselves. These tend to produce, of course, much more accurate and meaningful results. There *is* a large difference between someone who is primarily Cancerian and someone who is primarily Arian, for example, and these are the things that will come out in a "real" astrological reading—not just "sometimes you are very social, and at other times you like some time alone," which are the type of statements targeted by the Barnum Effect. (Although both the Cancer and the Arian would probably agree with that statement if they saw it in a newspaper or magazine; that's why this whole thing is a bit slippery.)

The problem with the Barnum effect is that it leads to incorrect ways of seeing things, or thinking about things, for those who know little about astrology *on both sides:* either people who take newspaper columns to *be* astrology, and have only a very superficial and casual interest in the subject; or scientific types with an equal lack of knowledge who are "investigating" astrology—which usually means trying to fit it into their own cognitive biases—and who also have little, or more commonly, *no* interest in the subject. Often, they simply want to prove to their wives or friends that it's a pile of nonsense. It's such a pile of nonsense, in fact, that they can't be bothered to actually learn something about it. For those who take the time and effort to delve deeper, as the multitude of various factors are learned and observed in practice, the superficiality of these sorts of statements quickly fades to irrelevance. It is true that glib and generic statements will appeal to many people. It's also true that this will give those who don't like astrology a shallow and easily digestible way to write the subject off without further inquiry. So what's the point?

Another cognitive bias that may better apply to those involved in astrology is what is called "hindsight bias." Most of us learned as children that "hindsight is 20/20." Here, although events that happen may not have been foreseen by astrologers, after the fact analysis *always* reveals an "of course!" analysis that shows a correlation—even if an asteroid or two must be pressed into service. A good example here is that of the 2007-2008 financial meltdown that triggered the "Great Recession." There were a few astrologers who correctly hinted at this sort of event, but by and large it took the astrological community (and of course the world at large) by surprise. Everyone seemed at the time to have been waiting for drama connected with the (then) upcoming outer planets' cardinal squares.

And if we do want to talk hindsight, of note perhaps is that at the moment of the meltdown, Pluto, the power planet, was on the verge of entering the sign of Capricorn, a sign associated with (in its more negative manifestations) money, elitism—and power. Power conjoining power. (Capricorn, of course, also has plenty of admirable qualities as well that are more usually expressed.) Since the meltdown (as of this writing in 2015), the world has become more and more of a *plutocracy*, and income inequality is increasingly becoming a topic of conversation. (As hard as it is to believe, about 85 specific, individual people in the world apparently have as much combined wealth as the bottom 50% of the entire planet. And it's getting worse.)

Pluto doesn't leave Capricorn until 2024, and there are many interesting possibilities for planetary alignments before then, so perhaps there will be some reactionary force that will take place. Occupy Wall Street's feeble protestations of a few years back seemed to go nowhere, but following Uranus' square to Pluto in 2015/2016, there seems to be a bit more unrest regarding inequality issues, which is partially driving the U.S. pre-election political circus of 2016. It is always interesting to watch the planetary ballet and its coordination with puny human affairs. The times they were a-changin' in the 1960's, and many of the larger planet configurations in the mid 2010's echo those placements. In addition, it will be interesting to see just what occurs when Saturn enters Capricorn and conjoins Pluto in 2020 (Jupiter will also be in Capricorn). That 2020 may produce a lot of future hindsight.

All of this, however, may simply go to demonstrate that astrology's hindsight bias or missed predictions may not necessarily show flaws in astrology, but simply demonstrate how difficult it is to predict events, given a multitude of often contradictory astrological factors, in addition to quantum uncertainty, which hangs over everything. These are indeed some interesting astrological times: what do *you* predict will happen? Be prepared to be surprised, as we always are. The *character* of events, however, is always in keeping with the archetypal energies involved, even in hindsight.

(An interesting historical aside featuring a steely eye to realism, as well as a combination of several biases, is provided in the second paragraph of Johannes Kepler's short treatise "Concerning the More Certain Fundamentals of Astrology," published in 1602. Kepler was the last of the astronomers who also accepted astrology as part of the package. In this brief monograph, he attempts to put astrology on more secure astronomical/scientific footing—starting the tradition of that frustrating task that continues to this day. He writes: "In these booklets some things will be said which time will prove, but many things will be refuted by time and experience as vain and worthless: as is customary with the people, the latter will be committed to the winds, and the former, entirely to memory.)

***

Confirmation bias and expectation bias often work in tandem in any field where one is trying to demonstrate something, whether that be science or astrology. In "gray" areas, they can run rampant. For example, since as of this writing global warming is accepted by only 97% of scientists, those who are disbelievers cling mightily to the other 3%, and find evidence for this viewpoint wherever they look. If you "know" that something is true, then you will find evidence to support that. Believing is seeing. However, if you *really* think that you know something, then you will often treat any evidence at all as superfluous. (In the 1933 Marx Brothers movie *Duck Soup,* Chico Marx says, "Who are you gonna believe, me or your own eyes?") If you are a scientist, you quite simply "know" that astrology is ridiculous; you don't need to waste time with any silly investigations to demonstrate that. If you are an astrologer, it's as plain as the nose on your face that astrology is not only valid, but pretty much woven through every nook and cranny of life, and something as minor as ridicule from the scientific establishment is not going to deter you. (Of note here is that, by definition, astrologers have investigated astrology, and most scientists have not. Take that for what it's worth.) So who's right? That's what confirmation bias is about. We search for, and find, things that "confirm" our particular pet positions, and ignore and discount those that don't.

Expectation, or experimenter's bias is defined by Wikipedia as "The tendency for experimenters to believe, certify, and publish data that agree with their expectations for the outcome of an experiment, and to disbelieve, discard, or downgrade the corresponding weightings for data that appear to conflict with those expectations." It may be thought of as a more action-oriented version of confirmation bias; they go hand in hand. Amateur investigators may be especially prone to this, partly because they can get away with it more, and partly because they can at times delude *themselves* more easily in isolation. There is, however, an unending trove of stories regarding professionals caught up in this bias on a regular basis; particularly those funded by corporations or organizations with a certain agenda or product to sell. (Cigarettes are good for you: here's the evidence.)

If we have the noblest of intentions, and accept that astrology is a real and valid part of the world, we still have to be watchful for our own biases in this regard as to the details. We will often "find what we're looking for" when evaluating data; preconceived notions are a real danger. Moving back towards confirmation bias, more than one person has had the experience of finding out that someone they thought they knew about astrologically turns out to have a different time of birth, or even a different birth month or year, than was originally thought. Louis Armstrong was thought to have a birthday of July 4th for decades, until it was discovered that his true birthday was August 4th—he had simply publicized the July 4th date to make him seem more "American." But for those reading his chart, the July 4th planets no doubt "confirmed" his personality, as then did the August 4th date.

There are other biases to watch out for, the observer-expectancy effect and illusory correlation among them. These can be associated with the more popularly named "cherry picking" for the former, and Michael Shermer's idea of "patternicity," or pattern-seeking, for the latter, which has also been called "apophenia" by Klaus Conrad. (Which is, for example, the tendency for Jesus to appear to people on a slice of toast, to be later sold on Ebay.) The former also figures prominently for both sides in many debated astrological studies. Astrologers, it must be admitted, often have a great temptation to cherry-pick things in order to prove a point, and oftentimes don't understand that they are doing so. So do scientists, by the way; and usually with a bit less naivity. And so we are back to the experimenter's bias: many of these biases are very similar, dovetail together, and go hand in hand with each other. For those who want an example of bias in the real world, Edward Snow's examination of the "Carlson Study" in Astrology News Service's wonderful book *Astrology Considered* is a practical and intriguing analysis of the subject in a particular astrological experiment. The important thing for most of us is to simply try and recognize them when they are occurring.

(A personal favorite of this author, which is really something that is only second cousin to biases, is what is known as the Dunning-Kruger effect. Wikipedia explains it succinctly: "An effect in which incompetent people fail to realize they are incompetent because they lack the skill to distinguish between competence and incompetence. Actual competence may weaken self-confidence, as competent individuals may falsely assume that others have an equivalent understanding." In other words, humility is a distinguishing characteristic of those who really know what they're talking about. It's worthwhile for all of us to meditate on that for a moment!)

***

In addition to cognitive biases (and there are plenty more that we haven't talked about), we often additionally fall prey to various "research errors." Even if we are just casually explaining an insight to a colleague, we are actually relaying informal research that we have done. If we are noting a particular correlation that we have found, for example, then that's our own individual and small-scale research project. An example would be having an unusual and creative friend, who we note has Mercury trine Uranus. A-ha! We latch onto this as an explanation. *Of course* she's unusual: she has a strong Uranus aspect. However, let's consider this: how many personal planets, in addition to the Ascendant and Midheaven, might Uranus aspect? Five? And how many "major" aspects count?

Five again? And what are our orbs? Four to eight degrees or more each way, depending on the aspect? One might wonder whether there is anyone who *doesn't* have a Uranus aspect of some sort that could be called upon. (The answer, according to a random sampling of my own saved charts, is mostly "no.")

So this could likely fall within the general concept of research errors. On the other hand, when we run across a trait that marries to an archetype (Uranus = Unusual), it may be entirely proper to separate it and "pull it out" of the rest of the chart to explain that particular *fragment* of a person, keeping in mind that it is only a piece of the whole person. She may also have Mercury trine Saturn. So, the Mercury trine Uranus aspect would not perhaps statistically differentiate this person as being more unusual than other people who may have Uranus aspects of their own (although perhaps a lot of Uranus aspects might), but this person might be seen to be *expressing* that particular aspect or energy more than someone else, or more than other, different energies in her own chart. (And how do you test for that "scientifically"?) Again, in many ways astrology is more akin to other such "soft" disciplines as psychology, than to hard science. We are people, after all, not electrons. Weightings of this sort are the art part of the art/science, and there are always individual factors that elude us. Good, reproducible rules are hard to come by here. No wonder chart reading takes so much effort and skill!

Without the rules and algorithms that are available to those in the mathematical or scientific fields, the art of astrology lies in the intuitive synthesis of chart factors. How will the various components actually play out in a life? Richard Feynman was one of the best-known physicists of the 20th century. He did indeed have a strong Uranus: square both his Sun and Moon, and sextile his Mercury, it gave him the potential for genius and/or nuttiness, as any astrologer would note. (Einstein did not have these strong Uranus aspects, except to Jupiter.) Let's agree that it is doubtful that Feynman knew astrology, and so in living his life, he wasn't consciously trying to fulfill some notion of what his chart was like, or "act out" his astrological signatures. Nonetheless, even scientists live and demonstrate their charts. Feynman was known for being unusual—for being *very* unusual, in fact, amongst the physicist crowd. Although a Taurus (a traditionally conservative sign), he played the bongos (music, but a rather unusual form), and hung out with strippers in night clubs (Venusian hedonism). One of his most enduring legacies are his "Feynman diagrams," which are visual representations (art) of subatomic physical processes. He additionally loved camping (earthy), and took his family regularly on wilderness expeditions in a van with his diagrams painted on the side (you may find pictures online). So we see here how the native Taurean traits are expressed, when joined to the energies of Uranus. That is the art of chart synthesis. And in reviewing the above, we also see that it is not a matter of "believing" in astrology: it's a matter that we all simply live our charts, whether scientist or seamstress.

So whether we are astrologers, scientists, or members of any other field, humility and open-mindedness are always called for, as well as a critical sense which remains attentive towards biases in cognitive interpretation. We must watch out for prejudices and temptations to fudge, and we must evaluate our own preferences and beliefs carefully. Astrology is by tradition a Uranian field, but it also contains the Neptunian; both positively, as well as less so. Balance and critical thinking are the key. We must temper intuition with common sense. In many ways, as astrologers, we have been given the Keys to the Kingdom; we need to use them wisely.

Addendum:

Gratitude is love made visible. It's important to say here, that although certain issues with astrology have been brought up in this multi-segment section of the book as points of discussion, this is in no way meant to disparage any particular astrologer, or even school of astrology. In my own life, astrology sits right up at the top with my recovery from alcoholism as one of the two most important influences that have brought me endless joy, as well as at least a modicum (hopefully) of growth over the years. I admire, and am grateful for, all of the astrologers out there who have fought misunderstanding and prejudice to bring this archetypal message to so many people throughout the centuries. Kudos to all, and thank you, each and every one!

Which Came First, the Chicken or the Egg?

As astrologers, we are taught that the horoscopic circle is everything: that everything in life can be placed under the jurisdiction of one or more archetypes, one or more segments of the wheel, one or more keywords. Physics itself is simply placed under the generic heading of "earth," as if it were as easy as putting a can of beans in its proper place on the shelf. Science? Just an example of Mercury doing its analytical thing, just another part of the circle. Conversely, physicists, in *their* sphere, are taught that everything may ultimately be explained by physics, even if some of those things must be tagged at the end with the word "eventually." Science itself, in *all* of its spreading and proliferating facets, eventually boils down to physics: if there were no atomic stability or molecular bonds, there would be no chemistry or biology (or psychology or sociology) to talk about.

Metaphysicians would look at both of these and chuckle. It's pretty obvious that they are simply examples of different ways of looking at reality: alternate ontological speculations that may or may not be the way things really are. So what *does* best describe reality? Might all of reality be placed into the grouping of physics or astrology or metaphysics? If so, then which one would be "primary?" One so inclined could make an argument that physics is a subset of invisible astrological archetypes which determine all of reality, or that astrology is an as-yet undiscovered special case of physics. Or perhaps everything ultimately *is* metaphysics, and is thus driven by some overriding philosophic or spiritual principle that gives birth to both physics *and* astrology. Much has been written in recent decades about the path of convergence that physics is on with Eastern spirituality. Astrology here waits by the mailbox for its invitation to join the party.

And what of other solar systems, galaxies, universes? Astrology as we know it (meaning the archetypes that we use) pretty much is tied to our own solar system, and even to our own psyches and cultures; which is not to say that the principles of correspondence and synchronicity that drive our version might not apply in some fashion to other stellar systems or locales. Similarly, there has been more than one physicist who has speculated that the "laws" of physics that we know and use may be applicable only to our particular corner of spacetime; it is widely thought that the current laws of physics, for example, "broke down" or weren't yet in place at the moment of the Big Bang, or of any singularity. No one knows what laws may have applied at that time. They may additionally not apply elsewhere in the universe, or in other universes. How is one to sort through all of this?

The chicken and the egg analogy is actually very apropos here. So is the Mobius strip, or the Klein bottle. One side of the Mobius strip is astrology, psi, synchronicity; and the other is physics. Perhaps the whole strip is metaphysics. Whatever Whole is out there must include both astrology *and* physics; it must include everything. One perhaps doesn't "lead to" the other, or act in a primary fashion; only the Whole is primary. One may find astrology by searching through physics (the physics of the future, anyway), and one may find physics by searching through astrology (physical, mental, emotional, spiritual). The chicken and the egg are a yin-yang system, as is the Mobius strip. Travel the strip, and you will not know whether you are travelling the path of astrology or physics. The whole is greater than the sum of the parts.

Astrology and Quantum Physics Parallels

How might modern astrology be similar in many ways to modern physics? Here's a quick summary. These are similarities by analogy or metaphor, and are not meant to be taken literally:

FATE AND FREE WILL: Science itself has the same problem here as astrology: are things in our lives, in our universe, ultimately determined by fate or by free will? In science, it is the clockwork, general relativistic, block universe vs. quantum possibilities and probabilities. In astrology, it is a mechanistic horoscope, one that is simply awaiting better rules of interpretation to bring out its fatalistic potential, vs. a more modern and humanistic approach, pioneered by Dane Rudhyar. (Geoffrey Cornelius and the divination crowd add to the indeterminacy side of this as well.) Likely for both astrology and physics, the answer may lie in an undiscovered level of reality that makes this dichotomy as useless as arguing whether light is a particle or a wave.

(Some people here may take the line of reasoning that "well, if free will and fate have the same results, or are the same thing, then it must mean that things are actually fated, and what seems like free will is only an illusion." That's not what we're talking about. That's similar to saying that light must really be a wave, and it only seems like a particle. No, it *really is* a particle *and* a wave. Fate *and* free will likely both exist as expressions of some higher principle.)

SIGNS AS ENERGY SHELLS, PAULI EXCLUSION PRINCIPLE: In physics and chemistry, an atom has energy shells, or orbits, associated with it. The electrons occupy these shells, surrounding the nucleus (protons and neutrons). Electrons can't be found with any energy values that do not correspond with these shells. Many of us who have taken basic physics and chemistry have a lasting image of this imprinted on us, although the visualization is simplistic. Moving from one shell to another is associated with an electron making a "jump" in energy, up or down. These jumps and their associated energy packets in or out of the atom are known as "quanta"; thus quantum mechanics. This idea was pioneered by Niels Bohr. It has a very digital, on/off flavor. The movement is not continuous, but discrete.

In astrology, the movement of energy around the circle is also not continuous, but jumps from one type of energy to the next very abruptly. There are 12 energy "levels" or shells, although this is best described more as quality than quantity. One is either in one of these or the other, but never in two at the same time, and never in between. The cusps here are fairly sharp. Any perceived blending is more likely due to other planets or influences from the neighboring sign than cuspal influences. The exception to this is the Great Ages, which have significant bleed-over.

ELECTRON CLOUDS: In physics, the above model of the atom is complicated by the very quantum theory that it generated. Once indeterminacy was added in by Heisenberg, the exact position of the electrons within the shells were found to be better represented by density (of probability) clouds, since the exact location was only probabilistic until "collapsed" by measurement or interactions. In astrology, one may visualize the future in terms of "event clouds." Future events remain as archetype-associated possibilities or probabilities until they are manifested, until they are collapsed into a current real-world actualization. Nonetheless, like electron clouds, they have some predictability and may exhibit a density cloud of lesser or greater probabilistic outcomes. Sun/Saturn events rarely have to do with new romances, for example, and Sun/Venus events rarely have to do with life overhauls.

RELATIVITY OF OBSERVER: Einstein's observation that there is no ultimate and fixed frame of reference, but only that specific to the observer, is echoed in astrology's idea that we see the world through chart-colored glasses: we can never have ultimate knowledge about the world, but only the knowledge that we are permitted to see, filtered through our own chart biases. All reality is local to us, although through theory and imagination we may see farther. Synchronicity is similar in that, due to the personal and emotional component, synchronicities that seem very large to us may appear very small or insignificant to others.

CONSCIOUSNESS AS A CO-CREATOR OF REALITY: Again, here we are choosing the consciousness-mediated collapse version of the Copenhagen interpretation of quantum mechanics, which permits this possibility. Here, conscious interaction, possibly through measurement, *can* (although this may not be required) be instrumental in helping to collapse the probabilities of the wave function into gross material reality. In astrology, our consciousness helps to collapse the possibilities of our transits, or even our natal chart factors, into actualities. For example, it is widely accepted in astrology that, facing a transit, if we are receptive and flexible, the changes may be more likely to be interior—but we if we are stiff, fearful, and resistive, they may be more likely to manifest as external events, which then *force* us to make the necessary interior adjustments. Our consciousness, the physical world, quantum possibilities, and synchronicity are all team-mates here in a complicated web of interactions that we have not yet begun to understand.

THE UNCERTAINTY PRINCIPLE: Heisenberg showed that for paired variables, the more we know about one, the less that we will know about the other. They can never both be known exactly at the same time. Again, our consciousness seems to play a role here, in that we get to choose which variable to narrow down our focus on, or to measure. By focusing more and more on a particular variable, we force the other variable to become more and more indeterminate and unknown. In astrology, there often seems to be an inverse correlation between how much we try and "worry" the results of a particular transit (for example), and the predictability of that transit. The more we speculate about, try to guess, focus on, manipulate, and generally put energy into constant thought about a particular transit, the more often we seem to be surprised at the actual event, which is often completely unexpected. As we try to become more certain in our expectations, the actual event itself becomes more uncertain, the cloud becomes hazier. After the fact, of course, it all makes sense. Hindsight, the collapsing of the wave possibilities, is always 20/20.

CYCLES, WAVES, ENERGY, MATH, AND FIELDS. For physics, everything is cycles, waves, energy, math, and fields. For astrology? The same. 'Nuff said. Thanks again to Rick Levine for the interesting idea that the planetary orbits themselves may form cycles of electromagnetic waves (or possibly waves of *meaning*?) that influence us, although with extremely long wavelengths by physics standards. That would not be the only strange thing in the universe.

Astrology on the Ropes

I "came of age" in the astrology world in the 1970's. At that time, on the heels of the fabled 60's, astrology was everywhere. It was the Dawning of the Age of Aquarius. Popular culture, experimentation, research, new concepts: all manifestations of astrology were to some extent accepted and part of the cultural gestalt. Seemingly, everyone had at least a passing interest in the subject. Bookstores always had a large and well-browsed astrology section. A few short years later it was revealed that even the president (Reagan) and his wife were barely making the journey from the kitchen to the bathroom without consulting their astrologer, Joan Quigley.

Fast forward to now. I browse the few remaining bookstores and note that there is section after section of "New Age" books which contain a mishmash of occultism, vampires, religiosity, dowsing, self-help, and so on. Hundreds of books. But astrology, these days, occupies only a lonely little corner of this large section. Usually a dozen or two books might be there, poorly curated, an afterthought. The same is true in the dedicated New Age bookstores, amongst the crystals and incense. Nothing against crystals and incense (I'm burning some right now; the smell and smoke help my mind to drift), but what has happened to astrology?

I've attended astrology conferences in recent years, and it's a bit dispiriting to note the seeming lack of new blood coming into the field. This is not to ignore or disparage those young astrologers who actually ARE moving their careers forward in this profession (good for *you*!), or to ignore those established astrologers who are busy teaching, forming schools, doing research, and trying to advance the discipline forward; but simply to note that the attendees at these conferences skew towards the folks with more than one gray hair, many of whom are the same folks that I noted back at conferences in the 70's or 80's. Where is the vibrant new blood?

I live in a fairly large, and fairly trendy, metro area. I attend a couple of astrology groups each month. There are typically maybe 10-20 folks who show up at these gatherings, maybe a bit more if there is a "marquee" guest speaker. Out of curiosity, I decided to attend another group recently which bills itself as a "paranormal" interest group. The first thing that I noticed was that doing a quick internet search yielded about 10 paranormal research or support groups in my metro area, vs. 3 for astrology. The second thing that I noticed was that, at the particular group I attended, there were about 70 or so attentive and enthusiastic people.

The paranormal group was interested in such alternative topics as aliens, Bigfeet, ghosts, and the like. Speaker after speaker got up and talked about how they had "heard" about someone seeing aliens at a grocery store in some rural area. (Why do aliens always haunt the rural, uneducated areas? One would think that advanced intelligences would be more interested in talking with scientists or astronomers. But they seem to prefer folks living in trailers on the outskirts of dusty towns.) I began to feel somewhat as if I were back playing "telephone" in elementary school: he said, that she had said, that so and so saw... At any rate, there were very few first-person accounts; most were stories of how someone else had heard or seen something. There were ghosts in bedrooms, vortexes from which to view events from a hundred years ago, and secret alien cities underground that were breeding with humans to produce "hybrids," which (reportedly) had their DNA verified by someone somewhere as being only half human. There were lots of UFOs, of course.

It made me sad. How might one who is interested in astrology think about all of this? It's a shame that the proud art/science of astrology, practiced for thousands of years by some very respectable minds, has come to be lumped in together with Bigfoot and secret half-breed aliens in underground cities in rural areas. But more to the point, and even sadder: why are the alien cities and Bigfeet seemingly more popular? What has happened to astrology? The most recent Gallup poll that appeared by search (2005) showed that about 25% of Americans "believe" in astrology, notably trailing ghosts (32%) and demonic possession (42%). ESP clocked in at 41% and telepathy at 31%. Astrology was, in fact, not far ahead of witches, at 21%.

What has happened? Could it simply be a "fad" thing, such that astrology in recent years has had its day in the sun, and is now crowded out by other odd or paranormal trends? Could it be that fickle people who never really took the time to learn astrology, but just latched onto it for being "cool" have moved on? Perusing the bookstore shelves would certainly lend credence to this. Could it be that those who more supported astrology in the past simply enjoy fantastical and difficult to prove stories, and astrology was just too dry and boring—aliens and vampires were found to be more exciting? Could it be that the great promise connected to research (scientific validation of astrology is just around the corner!) hasn't panned out to date, and those on the fence simply lost interest and drifted away?

Whatever it is, it is sad. Although astrology continues more as a day-to-day part of life in India, in the West it has been pushed to the side and marginalized. (It is waning in India also.) It would certainly be tempting for those of a scientific bent to say that we're simply more "advanced" and have moved away from superstition, but the continuing prevalence of ghosts, aliens, and certain religious traditions show that this is simply not the case. Neptune is baked into the system and is not going away. (Neither is Uranus, for that matter.) And the ongoing and bizarre mysteries of science itself (quantum mechanics, etc.) show that there is more to reality than we may dream, and thus hold out at least the possibility that astrology may yet again have its day in the sun, and a resurrection in academia. So it's difficult to tell what's going on. Whatever it is, astrology needs a new injection of energy and creativity. Who will be called upon to perform this? If you are young and smart and creative, and have a scientific bent as well as a curiosity and open-mindedness about astrology, perhaps it may be *you*.

***

Since writing the above, I attended a traveling "Body, Mind, and Spirit" show that rotates around the U.S., and which, judging from the volume of attendees, is quite popular. Thousands of attendees were milling around the exposition center where it was held. Besides the usual gypsy garb mixed in with pirates, Renaissance merchandise, crystals and bumper stickers, it featured a variety of "readers." Lots and lots of readers. Probably fifty to a hundred readers, most of which had clients. There was only one legitimate-appearing astrologer there with a computer, but I didn't get a chance to talk with him, as he also had a client. There really weren't even very many Tarot readers. Astrology and Tarot both require many years of training, diligent work, and experience: and so an understanding of what was going on with all of this stuff began to form in my mind. The readers, by and large, were advertising skills involving telepathy, "intuitive" readings, past life readings, holism, mediumship, deep healing, spirit healing, Native American healing, hypnotic healing, angel channeling, body field energy reading, and more other similar New Age skills than I can remember. In other words, skills that required no training, and of which no one would really be able to tell if they were "proficient" or not. Perhaps people today don't really have as much interest in an astrology reading and consequently don't know what the skill set involves; or perhaps, conversely, learning astrology may seem like simply too much trouble for most of these folks, or they themselves aren't interested. The gift of gab certainly seemed to be in better supply.

An Invitation to the Young Astrologer Learning the Field

Astrology has existed for as long as humans have looked up at the heavens and wondered at the bodies moving slowly to and fro above them. It has moved with man, both in time and geographically, and has adapted and grown. It has evolved and matured, and yet anyone in the field would agree that there is always room for the new; we are always searching. Astrology started out tied to the gods, acting as their messenger, or giving divinatory clues as to the leanings of the universe's will. But at this time, the more overtly spiritual approach has settled in to become simply another branch of modern astrology, an optional icing that appeals to some more than others: astrology has by and large gone secular. Astrology started out largely deterministic, and indeed that remains a popular misconception for those not in the field. The deterministic aura seemed for a time as if it would be able to link hands sympathetically with the advance of science, as the Enlightenment took hold: what could be more compatible with Newton's newly laid out clockwork universe than the orderly motion of the planets, as observed in astrology, and applied to human affairs?

But alas, it was not to be. Science divorced itself from *all* of its philosophical attachments, including astrology, and moved further towards empiricism, reproducibility, and materialism. The word "scientist" was coined in 1833. The former friends grew apart. Even the death of predictability, the rise of probability, the growing fascination with correlation rather than causation, and the bald fact that things as nebulous as observation and measurement affected the material world could not heal the rift. Open-mindedness was accorded to quarks and galaxies, but not to how the objects in our own solar system might influence or correlate with the humans living there. Astrology had too much baggage. Astrology meant superstition, and superstition had no place in the modern world.

We live in a materialistic age, and one dominated by physical science. For astrology to ever be taken seriously by the scientific thinkers of our age, it must at minimum be compatible with materialistic science. Indeed, for astrology to be valid for anyone, it must be compatible with the material world, as well as with the world of the spirit, synchronicity, and the realm of human emotions and thoughts. Quite a large order! Reality must ultimately be a Whole, and not fragmented. How might this be accomplished? What sort of paradigm shift is needed? What sort of new knowledge is needed, either on the part of astrology, or on the part of science?

The current paradigm, realistically, is unlikely to change soon: views this thoroughly imbedded in the societal gestalt run deep, and ships this large take a long time to turn around. Prejudice stacks the deck. Science no doubt feels that astrology has "had its chance" to prove itself, and failed by the rules that it (science) set up. No wonder that most astrologers are weary and gun-shy about interfacing with science, feeling that the uphill battle is pointless and not worth the effort. Forget that those rules, thrown like a gauntlet at astrology, are based on scientific paradigms centuries old, and are obsolete in light of the changing models of science itself. Einstein overthrew Newton and quantum overthrew Einstein as the latest and most prominent Keeper of the Secrets. Who knows what the next tectonic shift in science might be: might an opening appear at last, at some point, for astrology? Jupiter opposes Saturn. Optimism opposes pessimism. The glass is *always* half empty, and yet is always half full. Stories are always works in progress. R always=K+1.

If you are a young, smart, and energetic astrologer who doesn't mind swimming upstream a bit, consider having another go at the astrology/science challenge. Get some training to afford credibility. There's something there, it's guaranteed. The right key just hasn't been found yet. The map of the world sits there with Africa looking like it should fit into South America, but... nah. Couldn't be. There's no way the continents could be drifting all over the world. There's no mechanism by which that could happen. Just a coincidence. Not worth investigating...

It is paradoxically more possible that we are waiting for science itself to come around: it may be more likely that science will come to astrology at some point sooner than astrology will come to science in its current incarnation. There's simply one or more pieces of the puzzle missing. They will be found at some point. Why not help advance that? We know only a little: more will always be revealed.

Metaphysics

A Curious Thing

The first chapter of this book opened with a Curious Thing involving my alcoholism, a nearly fatal auto accident, and its aftermath. It seems fitting, then, that this last section should open with a more positive synchronistic event concerning the same issue.

After a couple of decades plus of hard binge drinking, which included a long series of changing and frequently meaningless, jobs, I had decided to go to nursing school. The original field of study for my first college degree had been pre-med, but I was far too restless and interested in partying to follow through with this; I eventually took a psychology degree somewhat by default. However, much later, during a compressed and rapidly changing period in my life, which included a big move and much soul-searching (Uranus conjunct my Moon, Saturn conjunct my Midheaven, Jupiter conjunct my Saturn, and Pluto opposite my Sun: all of these aspects exact over a fairly short period of time), I decided to completely change my career direction—not that there had *been* much of a direction up to that point, it must be acknowledged. It was another very electric and accelerated period in my life, and, although still heavily binge drinking, I managed to graduate with honors from nursing school, and began looking for my first nursing job. The spotlight was on high, as my family was excited to see me finally moving away from "black sheep" status into something more mainstream. Everyone was cheering me on and backslapping me for the wise move towards respectability.

As I made my applications, I knew that I would have to pass a urine drug screen to get hired, and so I started paying more attention to my binging and other drugs (which had actually been very minimal for many years), so that I would have time to clear anything out of my system prior to a test. To decide what period of time that might be, I used the "guess" method. I did eventually get a good interview,

I did my urine test, and I was hired to start work at a hospital a couple of weeks later. Excitement ran high for both myself and my family. My first nursing job! Atta-boys increased.

I showed up for my first day of orientation, and was seated at a long wooden table in a conference room with probably ten or twelve other new employees, waiting for our training to begin. It was a bit before 8:00 in the morning. Suddenly, prior to our orientation, the door opened, and a woman poked her head in. "Is there a Doug Egan in here?" she asked. My heart sank, felt like it had stopped, and then began pounding. I didn't know what this was about, but I had a crushing intuition that something bad was about to happen. As if in a daze, the room became indistinct and dark around me, and I slowly moved towards the door like a zombie.

I was right. The woman pulled me aside in the hallway, told me that I had produced a "dirty" urine sample a couple of weeks earlier, and regretfully informed me that I couldn't start work. She was so sorry. As to why they had waited for that particular moment to tell me, I have no idea. Perhaps it was just bureaucratic miscommunication, maybe it was policy, perhaps it was the timing that the universe had chosen. Who knows? But there it was. The disappointment of my family lurked in the back of my terrified mind, waiting to hear how the first day of my new career had gone. I was paralyzed. I had no idea what to do. I was completely frozen, dumb, unable to even put a thought together. The worst event of my life had just happened.

***

Bike riding has always been a great stress reliever for me, and so in a daze I drove home on autopilot, numb, and eventually decided to go for a bike ride to try and sort things out. I needed to try and figure out what had just happened; to come up with *something* that I could do, something that I could think of to tell people, something to somehow salvage the situation. I got on my bike and rode for two hours, all around the city, although my surroundings were far more interior than exterior. After the biggest bomb in my life had gone off and seemingly filled me with shrapnel, it was appropriate that this bike ride also proved to be the most important one of my life.

I hadn't really been in full-blown denial about my alcohol problems for years, but I had never really looked at them very clearly either. I fudged my misadventures quite a bit, making up stories and excuses for myself. My understanding of my drinking had existed in a sort of dimly lit corner of my mind, never really fully acknowledged or examined in the light of day. Now it was. The bright sun on the bike ride seemed to dry up my minimizing, my confusion about this issue, the secret crannies of my life that it had lurked in. It came to me quite clearly and suddenly: my whole life, I realized, was about drinking; drinking was *the* problem in my life, and this recent misadventure was only the most recent symptom. There would be more, and very possibly worse, if I didn't do something to change. The jig was up. The war was over: I had lost. I began reciting pleading, desperate, and feverish 911 "foxhole" prayers for salvation. I bargained with whatever God might be out there that if He would help me out of this, I would never, ever, drink again. I was an alcoholic, and I knew it. I discovered that I could literally connect everything in my entire life somehow with my drinking: my choices of jobs, of relationships, of hobbies, of travel, of *everything*. The balloon of denial had been punctured, and had flown away in a crazy spiral. It was gone. My life as a drunk ended on that bike ride. What was my new life to be?

***

I'm happy to report that, as of this writing, I have been clean and sober for over 20 years, and very gratefully so. I'm thankful that my years of drinking didn't ruin either my mind or body, and that I've been able to enjoy a wonderful new life, a gift, a second chance. I have a wonderful career, a wonderful wife and partner, and I love learning about science, astrology, philosophy, and spirituality: what a marvelous and exciting journey this new life has become! I also love giving back, and helping other alcoholics who are suffering from this life-destroying illness, many of them not even realizing it;

it's nice to know that my own battlefield scars and experience might aid someone else.

(In a related and additionally odd curiosity, as a nurse, I later ended up working in *the exact same room* in the hospital ED where I once was brought and revived after my Volkswagen van crash in 1976. In my sobriety, I often looked around at the walls, trying to perceive perhaps the ghost of that lost, lonely, and alcoholic youth who had visited there at that time. Who says that life is not strange, and does not contain circles within circles?)

We can never finally divine the Will of God, the Mind of the Universe, the Collapsing of Quantum Possibilities, or the inscrutable path of the Tao. We think that we know what's best for us, but so often we don't. We focus on the yang, but it is the yin that we need to listen to, to make ourselves receptive. Things that seem like the greatest setbacks frequently turn out to be our greatest assets or opportunities. We fixate on, fear, and resist Saturn, clinging to the structures that we have built; but while our attention is incorrectly placed, other planets can sometimes sweep Saturn out of the way as if it were made of ashes. Our past turns to dust, and our future arises from the mortar made of the dust. We must have faith and trust the Flow. That dark day, the sun was shining bright, but I could not see it at first. I see it now.

***

In astrology, Saturn represents the status quo, our own paradigms, and the structures that we have built up and sit upon. It traps us in the illusion of permanence. It represents the building process itself, but it can also represent where we are complacent or resistant to progress; where we are "stuck." It can speak of our dark side, our shadow, our fears, our limitations, our burdens, our lessons. It lurks outside of our consciousness, but prods us—seemingly taunts us at times—if we do not make the effort for correct understanding. Saturn can be our greatest ally, but is just as often our temporary undoing, stripping us of the old and outdated, teaching us lessons that we didn't even know that we needed to learn, and challenging us to build new and more appropriate structures.

In contrast to Saturn, the Sun in astrology represents light in every form: physical, mental, emotional, and spiritual. It shines and illuminates, and is generous to all. It's not cold and penurious, as Saturn sometimes may be, but magnanimous and warm. Its nature is to bring light and life to whatever it touches. Like Jupiter, it may be seen as an opposing and complementing force to Saturn. Saturn is hard and cold; the Sun is warm and fiery, and melts away any negative energy or situations in its path. It illuminates and eliminates the dark cubbies that Saturn has created. The Sun's transits are rarely followed in astrology, because it moves so quickly; a day's influence and it is gone, moving on. And, in keeping with the other mysteries in astrology, most of the time there is nothing of note that happens during the Sun's transits—they are too fast, and pass by unnoticed. But sometimes, something of note *does* happen, and the Sun in these rare situations is a very large force indeed.

Saturn sits in my natal chart at 8 degrees and 50 minutes of Libra. The Sun in the past had made many laps across this point without much of anything happening as it traced its circles over the years. But on October 2, 1995 at 7:30 in the morning local time, the Sun's rays were exactly at 8 degrees and 50 minutes of Libra. Odds of it being at that identical place in the zodiac: 1 in 21,600 (360 degrees times 60 minutes per degree). In astrology, the meaning of the Sun conjoining and shining on Saturn might be very literally read as "bringing light to the darkness." I woke up that morning in chains; I went to bed a free man. It was the most important day of my life.

Going Deep

> "...among the advancing hosts of the forces of knowledge, metaphysics is the vanguard, establishing the forward outposts in an unknown hostile territory..."—Erwin Schrödinger

Metaphysics simply and literally means beyond physics. The word itself implies that there is something more to the world than merely math, physics, or materialism. The idea is not for everyone. It has come to be associated with a certain quest for meaning in things, in life. For some, the excruciating beauty of the universe as described by current science is more than enough: the intricacies of nature are adequate in and of themselves. Carl Sagan felt that way. He sums up many persons' views when he writes (in *The Demon-Haunted World*) "Plainly there is no way back. Like it or not, we are stuck with science. We had better make the best of it. When we finally come to terms with it and fully recognize its beauty and its power, we will find, in spiritual as well as in practical matters, that we have made a bargain strongly in our favor."

For some that is enough; for others it leaves them still wondering or thirsting for more. It is human to question. It is human to question in a scientific way, and it is human to question whether science is all. Our brains are built to look for patterns, and our brains are built to understand that patterns often confer meaning. Meaning is a central concept to human life: the quizzical meaning that we may ponder as to why a particular situation seems to synchronistically pop up in our life, or the meaning of life itself. In the search for the larger meaning of life and how to live it, we naturally turn to patterns, just as we do in smaller and less significant matters.

Merriam-Webster defines metaphysics as "a division of philosophy that is concerned with the fundamental nature of reality and being and that includes ontology, cosmology, and often epistemology," and "a study of what is outside objective experience." It is abstract rather than concrete. Physics is the purview of the body; metaphysics is the realm of the mind and the spirit. Measuring spoons and calculators cannot corral these, although there are those who would dream that they can. Metaphysics is speculative and hard to define, as opposed to empirically verifiable and settled. It has to do with the relationship between mind and matter, between being and meaning, and much more; it deals with knowing and speculating, fact and value, and the nature of reality. It contains science, religion, and philosophy; as well as other ways of looking at the world. If physics is the left brain, then metaphysics is the right brain, although these popular divisions are proving to be much more artificial than real. It has, in fact, occupied the minds of some of the greatest names of history, and brought us some of our most thought-provoking literature.

This chapter is not intended to be a rigorous or scholarly study of metaphysics by any means—it is meant to be nothing more than a collection of short thoughts involving only a small portion of the metaphysical field. Ontology has to do with being, and epistemology has to do with knowing. In a sense, this whole book has had metaphysical overtones. Here, we will not get even more weighty, but will instead ease up some, using this chapter as an excuse for a grab bag of further miscellaneous discussions. Some of them will be asking questions, and some of them may simply be sharing some freely passed-on insights as to how one might best live the examined life, a quest that has caught the attention of everyone from Greek philosophers and Indian Sages to more modern interpreters.

Spirituality may be seen as second cousin to metaphysics, with considerable overlap. It may be defined as an attempt to *experience* metaphysical issues, including meaning and the nature of reality. Along with the physical, the mental, and the emotional, it completes the key components of human experience. It may generously range from the very secular and humanistic, to the more explicitly numinous. It is distinct from religion in its openness to differing interpretations and points of view, although both are searching for, like metaphysics, a larger or ultimate view of reality. Spirituality includes religions, but is not limited to them. Spirituality does not require the immaterial, but it is happy to incorporate it. Wikipedia states, "Modern spirituality is centered on the 'deepest values and meanings by which people live.' It embraces the idea of an ultimate or an alleged immaterial reality. It envisions an inner path enabling a person to discover the essence of his/her being." Spirituality will thus be considered to be part of the metaphysical search, at least as far as the present book is concerned.

It should be no secret by now that this book is attracted towards the idea of spirituality (of whatever sort) being a journey back to Wholeness, a journey away from duality and fragmentation. Modern physics, as well as ancient spiritual traditions and astrology, confirm a connectedness to the world, an undivided and shared commonality. It may be the "butterfly effect"; it may be myself finding my own humanness in you. We are together. A journey of this sort points towards an understanding of the Ground of Being that we all arise from, and that, if we are ever to make further progress as humans, needs to increasingly inform our view of connections with our fellows, and with the world around us.

It has always seemed that, behind everything, there is something else which informs it, and which leads to larger principles; this expansion or reduction (as one wishes) continues infinitely until we reach that Oneness. The Oneness may be secular, or more traditionally spiritual. Behind lightning, there is electricity; behind electricity there is atomic theory; behind atomic theory, there is quantum. Behind quantum, what might there be? Energy underlies everything. Each level includes more of the world in it. In the search for connections and unifying principles, it does not seem illogical that there may at some point, and in some fashion, be a principle lurking behind and linking together both physics and synchronicity/psi/astrology (for those who have found those meaningful); a principle that would unify, and be found in the shadows behind matter and archetypes, and behind materialism and consciousness—simply because they all exist together in our world. They must be manifesting from some place of connection. Everything that rises must converge. Fate and free will, subject and object must dissolve in the layers beneath, until we see that there is no difference. Thou art that, and that art thou, as is said in the Upanishads. There is work to do in these discoveries, but the mystics have taken for themselves a more direct approach: the intuitive spirit at times may grasp more than the mind can process logically. That is true for scientists, it is true for astrologers, and it is true for the rest of us as well. The parts by definition must come from some whole.

Our world is likely, then, to be one of layers, only one of which is visible; just as our universe is mainly dark matter and dark energy. We can see only the smallest portion. There is so much left to discover. It imaginably consists of the physical, supported by an underlying layer of consciousness, of whatever sort, with whatever implications that may engender. The physical layer, at least the macro portion that we can see, is seemingly fragmented, disjointed, discontinuous, and dualistic. The deeper micro layer hints at a more undivided source, although its character remains elusive from a materialistic perspective. The layer of consciousness below this is finer still, more refined, more difficult to discern, but worth the effort of the search. Below this, conceivably lies yet an even more mysterious ground of energy from whence all the above arise; it is one that we may *never* know. It is continuous, non-fragmented, connected, and of a single fabric. We are its nodes.

Lord of the Dance

The figure of Nataraja on the cover of this book is an iconic one in the Hindu world, and one that is known to many Westerners as well. Nataraja is the dancing form (or avatar) of the god Shiva, part of the Indian Trimurti; the other two being Brahma and Vishnu, the three making up the Whole, the One of existence. In fact, a 6 foot tall Nataraja figure stands outside the CERN Large Hadron Collider in Geneva, Switzerland; it was a gift from the Indian government in 2004. It features quotes from Fritjof Capra, who most popularly wrote *The Tao of Physics*, and who first wrote of the symbolic connection between Shiva and modern subatomic physics in "The Dance of Shiva: The Hindu View of Matter in the Light of Modern Physics," published in *Main Currents in Modern Thought* in 1972. He writes "Modern physics has shown that the rhythm of creation and destruction is not only manifest in the turn of the seasons and in the birth and death of all living creatures, but is also the very essence of inorganic matter," and that "For the modern physicists, then, Shiva's dance is the dance of subatomic matter."

CERN, in their research into subatomic particles (it was here that the so-called "God particle"—the Higgs boson—was discovered to great fanfare in 2012), deals with creation and destruction on a split-second, sub-nuclear level. We all deal with the same energy in our lives every day. Things are born, and they die. They come into existence and they disappear from our lives, or from the universe. Ideas, people, events, material objects. All follow a predictable pattern; all obey the same cosmic laws. (For a further discussion on this, see the section titled "AUM." Buddhism, which grew out of Hinduism, is another discipline that attempts to deal philosophically with this flux.)

Nataraja celebrates that cosmic cyclical force of continuous creation and destruction, both material and otherwise. The only constant is change: our world is being constructed and destroyed at every moment. Heraclites in Greece, a contemporary of the Buddha, observed that "no man ever steps in the same river twice, for it is not the same river, and he is not the same man." Nataraja wears a dispassionate expression, for it is not his job to play favorites, to judge, or to be emotionally involved; it is simply his duty to carry the message and effect the change. This is the same message that astrology carries, without prejudice or preference, simply according to the laws of the universe, both physical and spiritual. Try as we might, plead as we may: we, too, with our petty schemes must comply with these universal laws. Atom, quark, boson, mountain, hill, or human, we all must obey. To attempt resistance is to be out of touch with the cosmos, with the Tao, with the Flow. To understand is to join the Dance.

Nataraja dances within a ring of fire, which represents the cosmos. The circle is the Whole; it contains everything. Everything is energy; this is represented on earth by fire. Fire is always in motion; it flickers and fades, flares and blazes. It turns matter into energy, and energy into matter. Things appear and disappear. We have limited input into this creation; our primary job is that of understanding and acceptance. We may add creative input only if it is in harmony with the Dance. Hindu gods often have more than two arms; this is to signify or represent their association with power, energy, and a force of manifestation greater than that which humans can muster.

Nataraja in his upper left hand holds fire: this is the fire of destruction, the burning of the universe, minute by minute. The old, the used up, the unneeded, must be destroyed, must pass away to create space for the new. In his right hand he holds a drum: concurrently with the destruction of the old, he is drumming into existence the new, the created, the as yet unseen and unmanifested. It is a continual cycle, creation and destruction. He is tireless, and without passion in his duties. Although his affect is blank, the cycles are not arbitrary or meaningless, and in fact are infused with meaning at every turn. Nataraja's job is simply to produce the cycles, to take part in, and to exemplify the great rhythm. Returning to CERN: significance in life may not popularly be thought of as arising from the mundane physical and atomic cycles found there, and yet even from these we can draw great meaning and speculation, for it is here that the universe comes into being.

The lower right hand shows the *Abhaya Mudra* hand gesture; this is also seen frequently in figures of the Buddha, and of Jesus. It is a gesture of strength and fearlessness: a gesture of assurance that, although the world is in flux around us, it is *going to be OK*. It counsels faith as the antidote to fear, and gives us assurance that things will always work out as they are meant to be. There is meaning within the seemingly random cycles. The lower left hand points towards the raised left foot, which Shiva/Nataraja has lifted in the dance. This indicates that true wisdom is to be found not on the mundane, physical, dualistic, earthly plane, but in an elevated and higher understanding of a reality that is larger and more complete. The right foot stands on the earth, and specifically holds at bay a figure that represents the chains of materialism, the personal ego, attachment, and ignorance. The seemingly violent resistance from the figure speaks to how difficult it is to let these go. It is Nataraja's job to show that this illusory view of existence must be overcome, and true awareness put into place, in order to join the Dance.

It is a beautiful image, and the crowning visual achievement of Indian spirituality. For those who wish to investigate further, there is far more symbolism to the figure than is given here. It is, at the same time, entirely compatible with both Western culture and with modern science, as well as with Eastern spiritual traditions. It is the way of the universe; how could it not be? It seems to lend itself especially well to astrology. Physics is all about cycles and energy, as is astrology. The electron circles the atom; the planets circle the sun, and the themes of our lives circle us in patterns mysterious and elusive. All of life is cycles. In our quest for understanding them, Nataraja offers us clues.

A-U-M

If the undifferentiated energy of the universe is formless, then what is the origination of form, the development and course of energy and action in the universe? That is, what is the path that energy takes as we become aware of it, or as it produces its effects? (Or as it becomes aware of us?) Energy may be condensed and manifested, as in a state of matter, or it may remain as non-material energy. As we have seen, energy itself, apart from the material, may be manifested in many ways, some of which interact with matter, some of which may not. There are the more familiar forms of chemical, mechanical, atomic energy, etc. There are also the more esoteric forms of energy that may manifest as spirit or consciousness. There is in fact, energy associated with each of the four familiar elements: earth, air, fire and water. Earth of course being physical energy, air being mental energy, water being emotional energy, and fire being spiritual energy. All forms of energy, as they manifest, take a similar course. Matter, as a form of energy, arises and passes away; as do situations, emotions, thoughts, and enthusiasms. All are impermanent, as the Buddhists teach: all arise, manifest, and subside. The recognition of this is ancient, and spans cultures.

Energy manifestation of any sort follows a predictable path, and is divided into three parts: arising, continuing, and subsiding. In astrology, these are known as the modes or quadruplicities: cardinal, fixed, and mutable. Each has their function in the dance of energy. They correspond exactly to Nataraja's dance, and in Hinduism are symbolized by the primordial cosmic sound of AUM. (Sound waves of course being a form of energy themselves.) This is often incorrectly shortened to "OM," as the intonation is often slurred together and sounds closer to this syllable. But the more correct form is that of three syllables, that of AUM. This is visually represented by the popular Hindu characters that have become known in the West as a symbol for yoga. A-U-M corresponds to the three phases of any energy manifestation: creation, maintenance, and destruction. Since energy is dynamic, however, these states really have no true beginning or end: destruction may be more correctly thought of as resolution, reorganization, and the continuance of energy simply in a different form or path. Each AUM event, whether a photon event, the temper tantrum of a child, or the history of a universe, is merely an artificial slice in a larger continuum.

AUM in Hinduism corresponds to the three principal gods of the pantheon: Brahma, Vishnu, and Shiva. Together, these are known as the Trimurti, and are themselves part of a greater whole known as Brahman, the ultimate Ground of Being. Brahma is known as the Creator; Vishnu, the Maintainer; and Shiva, the Destroyer. Most Hindu gods can be thought of as avatars or variations of these three primary gods, just as each of the twelve signs of the zodiac can be assigned to one of these three principles. Nataraja is an avatar of Shiva, but his existence also corresponds to whatever brief static state of balance exists between the one hand holding fire, destroying existing manifestations, and the other holding a drum, bringing into being the next manifestation of energy through the primordial sound.

So it is in astrology. Aries, Cancer, Libra, and Capricorn initiate and bring new energy systems into being; Taurus, Leo, Scorpio, and Aquarius continue, consolidate, and refine the manifestation; and Gemini, Virgo, Sagittarius, and Pisces either adapt and analyze, or dissolve the system, clearing the way for new manifestations. In addition, the polarities (masculine/feminine signs, the yin-yang sine wave cycle) may be thought of as being either that of potential or kinetic energy that also takes part in the dance in a rotating fashion, formless to formed, and back. The wheel continually turns. The cycle of all energy that has moved from formless into form follows this predictable sequence.

The schema then is: formless energy > form (creation, maintenance, destruction) > formless energy > form (creation, maintenance, destruction), etc. All forms of energy are vibrating cycles, which can create fields. We live in fields of various types that manifest in conjunction with the energy cycles. Some energy fields are known and mapped (for example electromagnetic, gravitational, etc.), and some may be sensed but are more speculative (consciousness, archetypes, astrology, etc.). It's all part of the dance. We live in an ever-churning soup of vibrating, interacting, cosmic energy. Nothing is static, all is in motion. All is becoming.

As Above, So In Between

"As above, so below." Macrocosm and microcosm. These words, which every astrologer is familiar with, are paraphrased from the Emerald Tablet of Hermes Trismegistus, the mythic originator of the Hermetic tradition, which straddles an odd gray area between Western dualistic and Eastern non-dualistic thinking. A modern visual correlation of the idea is that of fractals: extremely simple mathematical equations that produce endless self-mirroring and self-reproducing forms. Yet there is an adjustment of scale needed for these concepts in the modern world.

Although as far back as the Greeks, Democritus had proposed an atomic theory of the world, the prevailing thought for most of history was simply that the earth and its inhabitants (us!) were a microcosm that reflected God's heavens, the macrocosm. But with the advent of serious inquiry into the atomic structure of matter in modern times, it became evident that we are actually caught in the middle somewhere between the atomic or subatomic scale at one end, and the cosmic scale at the other. Rick Levine likes to use the term "mesocosm," which is defined by Wiktionary simply as "Any system larger than a microcosm but smaller than a macrocosm"; a pretty straightforward explanation.

So it seems more appropriate that we live in the mesocosm, suspended in scale between two extremes. No one knows if these extremes go on forever, or if there are boundaries. It seems likely, according to current science, that there may be fundamental building blocks at the lower end (quarks, etc.) that make up reality: but, like all of science, that is simply the best idea that we have at this point. No one knows. We are talking of sizes here that exist at what is known as the Planck scale. For length, this is in the range of 10^{-35} of a meter. It is the range that not only includes electrons, quarks, and theoretical strings, but also quantum foam, possibly the very fabricator of reality itself. And what might lie below *that*, with even more zeros added on? *Is* there a limit? We also must remember here that what we are calling "building blocks" or "particles" is somewhat of a misnomer, because these seemingly solid items, at this scale, actually are nothing more than patterns of vibrating and interlocking energy. This is one of the ideas behind string theory, although the idea of strings is somewhat arbitrary; there may be other visualizations or explanations of the energy makeup of these subatomic energy patterns. (String theory itself seems on a bit shakier ground than it did several years ago.) But there *is* a growing consensus that as we go further and further down, eventually we will find nothing but pure energy or potential.

On the upper scale: walking outside at night, we can look out from our mesocosm and behold the next scale up in all of its sparkly glory. We are to the universe, as atoms are to us: infinitesimally small. And amidst the talk of the expanding universe and the size of the universe, one question is so insoluble and unknown that it is normally not even asked: where or what is the boundary of the universe itself, and what is outside of that? Leaving aside valid topological speculations (everything is possible here) that would have us returning to the same spot if we walked an infinite straight line into the universe—if the universe is taken to mean simply everything that there is, then there is perhaps no boundary at all. Perhaps the very idea of a boundary is meaningless, and perhaps the simple but not-so-simple idea of infinity rules; here we may reference the famous (and variously attributed) quote that "God (or the universe) is a circle whose center is everywhere and whose circumference is nowhere." But if we talk about the universe as scientists often do, as the "known" universe, the one whose sparkly stars we see, then what lies outside of this known universe? Is our entire universe perhaps just an atom in an incalculably larger universe, one so far away that we may never even know about it? And what of *that* "metaverse?" Where does *it* end? What larger whole is *it* a part of? The visualization here is that of Russian nesting dolls. Ultimately, "what's outside of the universe?" or "what is the boundary of the universe?" are more Zen koans than answerable questions.

One often hears that there are around 100 billion galaxies in the known universe, and that each galaxy contains around 100 billion stars. The very roundness of these numbers should be a clue that we really don't have a very accurate idea, but let's assume that they are in the ballpark. Neil deGrasse Tyson additionally points out that, on the opposite end of the scale, "there's as many atoms in a single molecule of your DNA as there are stars in the typical galaxy. We are, each of us, a little universe." On top of that, he goes on to note that there are more atoms in the tip of one of our little fingers than there are stars in the *entire universe*. Wow. Take a look right now. Talk about perspective! *That's* macrocosm and microcosm.

***

So here we are, stuck in the middle, so to speak. For fun, and to further the efforts at perspective, let's take a brief trip in our imagination. Pretend in your mind that you are riding a bicycle down a country lane, dirt road. The bicycle, maybe, is not state of the art; it's just an old one-speed with balloon tires—pink, I think—a little rusty, with a white stripe along the center frame tube. The seat has a small tear on the rear back corner. There is some old dried grease on the sprockets. The rubber of the tires is absorbing the small shocks of the road as you go over pebbles and holes in the road, making quick and constant adjustments in an attempt to obtain a smoother ride. There is a nice breeze, the weather's fine, and the trees along the road are in full leaf, throwing dappled shadows over you as you ride. The air smells fresh with an organic, flowery hint to it. In the distance, there is an old farm with a silo. Cows are lazily grazing in the fields to your left. The bright sun is winking down on you and warming your shoulders as you look ahead, daydreaming and enjoying the day.

So let's go down, and then up. Imagine now that you are just the atoms of your body, *in the shape of you*, on an amalgam of atoms shaped like a bicycle, riding through a turning world, in a universe of atoms, all connecting and interacting through energy. We know that atoms are 99.9999999999996% empty space, which means that you are actually 99.9999999999996% empty space as well. This is very hard to visualize. "You" are now just a ghostly apparition, a nearly absent shadowy flicker of untold points of energy, flying about in their little orbits at the speed of light, all temporarily in the shape of yourself, all communicating and interfacing. In the timeline of the universe the arrangement won't last long, just the blink of an eye. It is in constant motion and flux. No two moments are the same. Who *are* you? Less than a trillionth of "you" is even solid, and that is on loan from, and part of, the universe around you. The rest is space. "You" are nowhere: you exist in your mind, in your consciousness; a mind somehow arising from this phantom collection of energetic interactions. *Your consciousness is more real than your body.* Your atoms, in their temporary configuration, sit on the atoms of the temporary bicycle, also a ghostly apparition, wheels of energy turning in the sun: the sun of hydrogen fusing into helium in violent nuclear reactions millions of miles away, sharing its energy with your spectral bicycle system on its country road.

Going down the road, then, is a sparkling, phantom whirling of invisible energy that is somehow you, hovering above a collection of atoms gathered in metallic molecules, gravitationally tied to the larger collections of atoms that are the ground, the dirt, the oceans, the planet. There is no separation—the atoms are all linked and interacting: form is temporary, arbitrary, and illusory. The mostly empty space planetary collection of energy packets we call earth is whirling on its axis at 1,000 miles per hour, suspended in space, and traveling around the sun at 67,000 miles per hour. The sun, also mostly empty space containing its tiny hydrogen and helium packets of fusing atomic energy, is moving around the galaxy at 514,000 miles per hour. The galaxy itself is moving at a large and increasing rate of speed away from the other galaxies in the universe, and amazingly, this is not due to actual motion, but to space itself expanding.

If a pink photon (of course there are actually no "pink" photons) were to fly from your bicycle and head out into space, it would take 4.24 years *at the speed of light* to reach the nearest star to us, Proxima Centauri. And that is still in our own galaxy, the Milky Way. The nearest galaxy to ours is the Andromeda Galaxy, which would take our photon 2.2 *million* light-years to arrive at. And with its estimated 1 *trillion* stars (it's a large galaxy, and the most distant object that can be seen with the naked eye), the Andromeda galaxy is, again, only one of about 100 billion other galaxies in the known universe. Each is interacting with each other through gravitational and other forces, continuing the swirling mix of cosmic energies. From the invisible empty space atoms in our fingertips, to the Andromeda galaxy, all is part of the One; all is connected and interacting.

This is the dance that astrology is part of, and that we are part of. It is the dance of the universe. It is physics' dance. It is Shiva's dance. It is our dance. It has levels upon levels, dimensions upon dimensions. It reveals itself slowly. The quest for understanding it is a pool with no bottom. Its purpose and parameters are unknown, its course unclear. But that does not mean that it cannot have meaning, or cannot be connected to meaning.

Our consciousness in appreciating this story is not tangible like the fairy atoms; but the fairy atoms themselves are barely tangible, snippets of cooled energy, nearly lost in empty space, blipping in and out of existence. How does our intangible consciousness seem to hover over and within this energy field, apparently existing separately, and yet by necessity a part of? *Why does our consciousness, when presented with an analogy* (itself a non-existent will-o'-the-wisp) *such as this one, actually seem more real to us than the material world itself?*

> "All we know is still infinitely less than all that remains unknown."—William Harvey (still as true today as it was in 1600)

"Isn't that wonderful? That feeling of not knowing too much about something... Incomplete information... Endless possibilities... When you don't know much about something, it's the most exciting sensation."—Erol Ozan

"There are things known and there are things unknown, and in between are the doors of perception."—Aldous Huxley

Big Minds Think Big

Prior to 1833, the word "science" or "scientist"' simply did not exist; it was coined at that time by a polymath named William Whewell, a Gemini who was good with words, and who also coined the term "physicist" (Wikipedia). This seems surprising today, considering the dominance of the scientific model in our modern world with all of the precise, clinical associations that this implies. Science is *science*, and scientists are... *scientists*. The very words themselves seem to call out for italics, or bold, or caps, or all three. Scientists are *important*.

And so they are! It wasn't always the case, however, that they were so narrowly focused and specialized. Perhaps the invention of the word itself, and the invention of subspecialties such as physics made them take their profession more seriously, and taught them to see themselves as limited to a particular category. A large part of the specialization, of course, was simply due to an increasing level of required knowledge and complexity in the various fields. At any rate, walls and boundaries went up; an element of self-imposed exile started to set in. Prior to this time, one who studied anatomy, or planets, or gravity, or botany, or anything else in the natural world was simply called a "*natural philosopher*." That included such giant names as Aristotle and Newton. Not only was it "allowed" for these early scientists to study and speculate on philosophical matters, it was in fact expected.

Aristotle, for example, while intensely curious about the physical world around him, and while putting into place many elements of the scientific method, would yet have considered himself first and foremost a philosopher. For him, as for his contemporaries, the information gathered about the physical world around him was subservient to, and simply grist for, larger philosophical speculations regarding what life and the world were about. What was the point of observations or experiments if they didn't tell us something larger about human life, about the way the world worked on a grander scale? It would have never occurred to him to limit himself to one field, or to simply tally the results of various experiments. His mind was too big, too curious.

Newton, the greatest figure in the world of science since Aristotle and prior to Einstein, also did not confine himself solely to the physical world. While laying the foundation for the scientific revolution that followed him, Newton avidly pursued Bible studies, as well as alchemy and occultism. Although he actually cautioned against seeing the universe as a giant clock set in motion by God, this idea ironically came to be associated with Newton, for it naturally follows from the predictable mathematical and physical world that Newton's studies gave birth to. In the time of the Greeks, science often followed (and was subservient to) philosophy; but by Newton's time philosophy was becoming the poorer stepchild of the pair. The point here is simply to note that Newton, in addition to his remarkable insights into the physical world, had an interest in the spiritual, the unseen, and the philosophical.

So, one might imagine, since these folks were from more primitive times (while serving to advance those times), surely in the modern world scientists would have moved on from these philosophical and speculative subjects to purely "scientific" matters, based on objective evidence connected to the observable, material world. Surely they wouldn't be distracted by these side issues. Surely, in fact, they would discourage philosophical speculations, and work to erase them and shut them down. Unfortunately, some of them, of course, do.

Like Aristotle and Newton, however, Big Minds think Big; you can't quite keep them between the rails. They don't necessarily conform to what's expected. They don't always color within the lines. Some in the scientific community might consider this an embarrassment or an aberration. However, it is precisely this willingness to think outside the box, to be curious about implications, that has served to move human knowledge forward. Typically (one might particularly examine the cycles of Uranus and Pluto here), there is at certain moments in history a great leap forward in human knowledge, a "breakthrough" of some sort; and then as the years go by, the particular breakthrough that seemed so revolutionary becomes accepted, and then becomes paradigm. Saturn takes over, things become solidified and turn to concrete and dogma. "You can't think otherwise!" the technicians, the mechanics, cry as this hardening takes place. Or, more precisely, "You can think about new things, but only if they conform to our ideas of what we think new things should be about": a self-limiting stance, and one out of spirit with the innovators that they profess to admire. As with the previous segment on AUM, we see again the tripartite rhythm of creation, solidification, and dissolution or overthrow, leading to new cycles of knowledge and energy. The middle phase is a difficult one to move on from; it carries the force of inertia.

So philosophy and the non-material are not in danger of dying any time soon. It is man's nature to wonder and speculate about origins, dispositions, meaning, and ultimate truth. Niels Bohr, who was one of the chief architects of quantum physics, ended up constructing a family coat of arms that featured the Taoist yin-yang symbol as its centerpiece. He perceived complementarity as not just a force in physics, but in a larger sense as a force in the universe itself. Odd that he was a Libra. And shame on him for stepping outside the calculations to look for larger significations! The implications of quantum for reality, to him, were huge. How could he *not* speculate on what these exciting discoveries might "mean" for our understanding of the world? It was Bohr, again, who developed the most popular interpretation of quantum mechanics, known as the Copenhagen interpretation. It is this one that leaves the door open for consciousness to influence the material world (should one be so inclined). How can one *not* speculate about *that*? A couple of Bohr quotes:

"Anyone who is not shocked by quantum theory has not understood it," and

"Everything we call real is made of things which cannot be regarded as real."

***

So much for "Shut up and compute." Big Minds think Big. The purpose here is not to give the impression that Bohr himself was particularly interested in the connection between consciousness and the material world. He respectfully stayed away from most of those discussions. But his experiments, and those of others, showed that humans operating measuring devices could change the behavior of the "material" world in the double slit and other experiments. Other researchers have explored the various possibilities here, and there is no definitive answer as yet, although much of the direction of modern physics makes less room for such speculations. Moreover, more than one person besides Einstein has been dissatisfied with the Copenhagen interpretation, as along with Heisenberg, it strips our reality of any possible predictive "clockwork" interpretation of things, although it remains the most popular one. But what does it *mean*?

Bohr belonged to a group of physicists that were taking part in what was arguably the greatest single period in the history of the discipline. As pointed out by Richard Tarnas in *Prometheus the Awakener*, the period beginning around 1900 with Jupiter conjunct Uranus saw Max Planck figuring out that energy at the atomic scale was not continuous, but only transmitted in certain discrete packets that he called quanta. Bohr later expanded on this and came up with the electron shell "planetary" model of the atom which most of us are familiar with from grade school (and which has been superseded). Quantum theory was born. Planck's idea was followed by Einstein's "miracle year," 1905, in which he published four papers that revolutionized our ideas about space, time, mass, and energy. In one, he discovered the photoelectric effect, which ultimately pointed to the dual nature of light (particle and wave at the same time), and eventually of matter. In another, he laid out his theory of relativity, which not only stated that everything is relative and dependent on the particular observer, but made the startling prediction that the speed of light was constant for every observer, no matter what their own particular speed or orientation. A very difficult one to grasp! Finally, he came to the amazing conclusion that matter and energy were equivalent, and thus could be thought of as different versions of one principle. This was his famous $E=mc^2$. If you run the numbers, you will see just why atomic and hydrogen bombs are so powerful. Neptune at the time was sextile to its natal position in Einstein's chart, which was also conjoined by Jupiter; and Uranus was trine to its natal position in his chart, which was trined by Jupiter and opposed by Saturn.

In 1927, Jupiter was again exactly conjunct Uranus, and the Solvay physics conference of that year in Brussels not only featured 17 of the 29 attendees going on to win Nobel prizes, but also served as a culmination of the hectic, productive, and incredible years in physics that had begun in 1900, two Jupiter cycles earlier. Attendees included Einstein, Bohr, Heisenberg, Schrödinger, Pauli, Dirac, de Broglie, Max Born, Max Planck, and Marie Curie. If you are not familiar with physics history, these names may mean little to you, but they are the people who moved our world from Newtonian to quantum, from a predictable clockwork cosmos to one of probability, the equivalence of matter and energy, and the full range of quantum weirdness that we are still trying to sort through. The world at that moment was upended as surely, or more so, as when Copernicus proposed that the earth was not at the center of the universe.

Like it or not, philosophy attaches to science, and to physics. Our world *is* a whole, and a disturbance in the knowledge of one part of it ripples out to the other parts. Besides gravitational waves, there are philosophy waves. Philosophically, there is a huge difference as to whether the universe is centered on the earth, on us, or whether we are just another microscopic speck in an infinite collection of anonymous galaxies. This was a strong factor in the movement away from a Church-based society towards a more secular and science-based one in the Enlightenment. Similarly, it is useless to pretend a disconnect between physics and philosophy when less than a hundred years ago, in many living people's lifetimes, the world changed from one of stability and predictability to one of hydrogen bombs and electrons being in two places at once, or possibly in no place at all: mathematical descriptions of energy only brought into existence by measurement or observation.

Big Minds think Big. They will always be prone to speculate, to drift towards philosophy, because that is what we as humans do. Of the names mentioned above at the Solvay conference, most of them have, in addition to their work in physics, written books or taken part in other written endeavors that expressly address philosophical issues. Bohr wrote *Atomic Physics and Human Knowledge*, which includes a wonderful first-person account of the ongoing philosophical and physics arguments that he was having with Einstein. Einstein wrote *The Evolution of Physics* which includes the sections "The Rise of the Mechanical View" and "The Decline of the Mechanical View"; in addition, he waxed philosophic regarding a number of subjects in another book called *The World as I See It.* Pauli became quite involved for a time with the psychologist Carl Jung, and their discussions are laid out in a book titled *The Interpretation of Nature and the Psyche*. Schrödinger wrote *My View of the World*, which was a somewhat garbled version of Hindu philosophy, although for some odd publishing reason an Egyptian Eye of Horus appears on the front cover; apparently the publishers knew even less of Indian philosophy than he did. Max Planck wrote *The Philosophy of Physics*, and Heisenberg jumped in with *Physics and Philosophy: The Revolution in Modern Science*.

You can't keep a Big Mind down, or confine it only to mathematics: the world is too large, too curious, too strange, too tempting, too unknown. It's begging to be turned around and over and examined in every way, to be looked at from every angle. It's hard for the creative mind to play by the rules set by others. Below are a few quotes from those 1927 Solvay attendees, so long ago. They speak to a moment in scientific history when there was a turning of the paradigms, a time of questioning without constraints, which opened all possibilities up for examination. What *did* these new discoveries mean? The quotes below can be an instructive beacon perhaps for us today in their open-mindedness—or at least teach us that science and philosophy can not only coexist, but by nature *must* do so. Here are the Big Minds in their own words:

EINSTEIN:

> Nature shows us only the tail of the lion. But there is no doubt in my mind that the lion belongs with it even if he cannot reveal himself to the eye all at once because of his huge dimension.
>
> Whether you can observe a thing or not depends on the theory which you use. It is the theory which decides what can be observed.
>
> Try and penetrate with our limited means the secrets of nature and you will find that, behind all the discernible concatenations, there remains something subtle, intangible and inexplicable. Veneration for this force beyond anything that we can comprehend is my religion. To that extent I am, in point of fact, religious.
>
> I see a clock, but I cannot envision the clockmaker. The human mind is unable to conceive of the four dimensions, so how can it conceive of a God, before whom a thousand years and a thousand dimensions are as one?
>
> It has often been said, and certainly not without justification, that the man of science is a poor philosopher. Why then should it not be the right thing for the physicist to let the philosopher do the philosophizing? Such might indeed be the right thing to do at a time when the physicist believes he has at his disposal a rigid system of fundamental

laws which are so well established that waves of doubt can't reach them; but it cannot be right at a time when the very foundations of physics itself have become problematic as they are now. At a time like the present, when experience forces us to seek a newer and more solid foundation, the physicist cannot simply surrender to the philosopher the critical contemplation of theoretical foundations; for he himself knows best and feels more surely where the shoe pinches. In looking for a new foundation, he must try to make clear in his own mind just how far the concepts which he uses are justified, and are necessities.

Great spirits have always encountered violent opposition from mediocre minds. The mediocre mind is incapable of understanding the man who refuses to bow blindly to conventional prejudices and chooses instead to express his opinions courageously and honestly.

Perfection of means and confusion of goals seem—in my opinion—to characterize our age.

So many people today—and even professional scientists—seem to me like someone who has seen thousands of trees but has never seen a forest. A knowledge of the historic and philosophical background gives that kind of independence from prejudices of his generation from which most scientists are suffering. This independence created by philosophical insight is—in my opinion—the mark of distinction between a mere artisan or specialist and a real seeker after truth.

I prefer an attitude of humility corresponding to the weakness of our intellectual understanding of nature and of our own being.

Imagination is more important than knowledge.

Only a life lived for others is a life worthwhile.

BOHR:

Opposites are complementary.

For a parallel to the lesson of atomic theory regarding the limited applicability of such customary idealizations, we must in fact turn to quite other branches of science, such as psychology, or even to that kind of epistemological problems with which already thinkers like Buddha and Lao Tzu have been confronted, when trying to harmonize our position as spectators and actors in the great drama of existence.

There is no quantum world. There is only an abstract quantum physical description. It is wrong to think that the task of physics is to find out how nature is. Physics concerns what we can say about nature...

Every valuable human being must be a radical and a rebel, for what he must aim at is to make things better than they are.

The fact that religions through the ages have spoken in images, parables, and paradoxes means simply that there are no other ways of grasping the reality to which they refer. But that does not mean that it is not a genuine reality.

Every sentence I utter must be understood not as an affirmation, but as a question.

Never express yourself more clearly than you are able to think.

SCHRÖDINGER:

Nirvana is a state of pure blissful knowledge... It has nothing to do with the individual. The ego or its separation is an illusion.

The world is given to me only once, not one existing and one perceived. Subject and object are only one.

Although I think that life may be the result of an accident, I do not think that of consciousness. Consciousness cannot be accounted for in physical terms. For consciousness is absolutely fundamental. It cannot be accounted for in terms of anything else.

The multiplicity is only apparent. This is the doctrine of the Upanishads. And not of the Upanishads only. The mystical experience of the union with God regularly leads to this view, unless strong prejudices stand in the way... Multiplicity is only apparent, in truth, there is only one mind... The plurality that we perceive is only an appearance; it is not real.

We must therefore not be discouraged by the difficulty of interpreting life by the ordinary laws of physics. For that is just what is to be expected from the knowledge we have gained of the structure of living matter. We must also be prepared to find a new type of physical law prevailing in it. Or are we to term it a non-physical, not to say a super-physical, law?

It seems plain and self-evident, yet it needs to be said: the isolated knowledge obtained by a group of specialists in a narrow field has in itself no value whatsoever, but only in its synthesis with all the rest of knowledge and only inasmuch as it really contributes in this synthesis toward answering the demand, "Who are we?"

DE BROGLIE:

The history of science shows that the progress of science has constantly been hampered by the tyrannical influence of certain conceptions that finally came to be considered as dogma. For this reason, it is proper to submit periodically to a very searching examination, principles that we have come to assume without any more discussion.

Two seemingly incompatible conceptions can each represent an aspect of the truth.

The actual state of our knowledge is always provisional and ... there must be, beyond what is actually known, immense new regions to discover.

MAX BORN:

Can we call something with which the concepts of position and motion cannot be associated in the usual way, a thing, or a particle? And if not, what is the reality which our theory has been invented to describe?

The answer to this is no longer physics, but philosophy

I am now convinced that theoretical physics is actually philosophy. It has revolutionized fundamental concepts, e.g., about space and time (relativity), about causality (quantum theory), and about substance and matter (atomistics). It has taught us new methods of thinking (complementarity), which are applicable far beyond physics.

It is true that many scientists are not philosophically minded and have hitherto shown much skill and ingenuity but little wisdom.

The belief that there is only one truth and that oneself is in possession of it, seems to me the deepest root of all that is evil in the world.

There are metaphysical problems, which cannot be disposed of by declaring them meaningless. For, as I have repeatedly said, they are "beyond physics" indeed and demand an act of faith. We have to accept this fact to be honest.

MAX PLANCK:

> I regard consciousness as fundamental. I regard matter as derivative from consciousness. We cannot get behind consciousness. Everything that we talk about, everything that we regard as existing, postulates consciousness.

PAULI:

> Later, however, I came to recognize the objective nature of these dreams or fantasies ... Thus it was that I gradually came to acknowledge that such fantasies or dreams are neither meaningless nor purely arbitrary but rather convey a sort of "second meaning" of the terms applied.
>
> The layman always means, when he says "reality," that he is speaking of something self-evidently known; whereas to me it seems the most important and exceedingly difficult task of our time is to work on the construction of a new idea of reality.
>
> What now is the answer to the question as to the bridge between the perception of the senses and the concepts, which is now reduced to the question as to the bridge between the outer perceptions and those inner image-like representations. It seems to me one has to postulate a cosmic order of nature—outside of our arbitrariness—to which the outer material objects are subjected as are the inner images... The organizing and regulating has to be posited beyond the differentiation of physical and

psychical... I am all for it to call this "organizing and regulating" "archetypes." It would then be inadmissible to define these as psychic contents. Rather, the above-mentioned inner pictures are the psychic manifestations of the archetypes, but which would have to produce and condition all nature laws belonging to the world of matter. The nature laws of matter would then be the physical manifestation of the archetypes.

In the new pattern of thought we do not assume any longer the detached observer, occurring in the idealizations of this classical type of theory, but an observer who by his indeterminable effects creates a new situation, theoretically described as a new state of the observed system.

The best that most of us can hope to achieve in physics is simply to misunderstand at a deeper level.

HEISENBERG:

There is a fundamental error in separating the parts from the whole, the mistake of atomizing what should not be atomized. Unity and complementarity constitute reality.

I think that modern physics has definitely decided in favor of Plato. In fact the smallest units of matter are not physical objects in the ordinary sense; they are forms, ideas which can be expressed unambiguously only in mathematical language.

We have to remember that what we observe is not nature herself, but nature exposed to our method of questioning.

The existing scientific concepts cover always only a very limited part of reality, and the other part that has not yet been understood is infinite.

Big minds think Big.

Wisdom Is a Pyramid

In 1963, Bob Dylan released his second album, *The Freewheelin' Bob Dylan*, and Uranus moved into orb for its conjunction with Pluto: the 60s were on. Turbulent, explosive, and transformative years were the template for the decade to follow, and the news seemed continuously full of excitement and change, though often of a mixed nature. On November 22nd of that same year, the Beatles also released their second album, *With the Beatles*, apparently laying in munitions for their North American invasion. That same November 22nd, two people passed away within hours of each other who, though leaving prior to the party getting into full swing, left their mark on the years to follow. President John F. Kennedy was assassinated in Dallas, Texas, and Aldous Huxley, a close friend of the Indian sage Krishnamurti, died in Los Angeles (he was originally from England). On his deathbed, unable to speak due to laryngeal cancer, Huxley passed a note to his wife asking her to administer him LSD intramuscularly, which she did. He passed away a short while later.

Aldous Huxley became one of the many inspirations for the counterculture to follow (as did John F. Kennedy, for his youthful idealism). Although best known for his novel *Brave New World*, he also experimented heavily with psychedelics, and penned *The Doors of Perception* (inspiring the rock band The Doors) about his experiences with mescaline; it was originally published, far ahead of its time, in 1954. Further back still, in 1945, he had published a book about comparative mysticism called *The Perennial Philosophy*, cementing early on his interest in the spiritual and in transformative experiences. In fact, as far back as 1931, in *Brave New World*, he name-checks William James' 1902 *The Varieties of Religious Experience*, an even earlier exploration into man's search for the numinous. *The Perennial Philosophy* draws parallels by using readings from various mystical traditions through history, and shows them to be equivalent in their search.

Huxley was born on July 26, as was Carl Jung (although in different years); they both had Sun in Leo as well as both having Moon in Taurus. They additionally shared Mercury and Venus in Cancer, Mars in fire, Jupiter and Saturn in air, and tight Moon/Uranus aspects. Both men were fascinated with seekers' efforts to understand and transcend their normal levels of being: the Quest, the Hero's journey. Jung's *Man and His Symbols*, in fact, could almost stand as a companion piece to Huxley's *Perennial Philosophy*. It is more psychological, although with wonderful visuals, but covers some of the same territory. The quest, the journey, the reaching beyond: science covers this terrain, as does mysticism. Occasionally they converge, as in the great Einstein, who had an almost esoteric sense of how physics could lead to a larger reality; one accompanied by an overriding sense of unity, of Oneness. He lamented, however, that "The intuitive mind is a sacred gift and the rational mind is a faithful servant. We have created a society that honors the servant and has forgotten the gift."

***

Many these days will not remember what was called a slide projector: a white hot incandescent bulb which shone through a series of celluloid transparencies, and projected pictures onto a screen; basically the stationary version of traditional movie reels. It's a shame, as it forms a great analogy as to how we might understand the various cultures on earth, and their versions of common human myths, Gods, and accumulated wisdom. Each culture in such an analogy would have its own slide projected onto the screen, while the Ground of Being, the roots of reality, remained the constant white light behind the changing images. God, or whatever Ultimate Reality, would then be a slide show of infinite dimensions and variations, enclosing all, containing all, and showing slides to each culture as appropriate to them, to the receptiveness of their own sensibilities. All slides *in aggregate* would be the reflected truth, or projected truth, or the analogous truth. We never directly or fully perceive the Ground of Being, just as we don't see the white light behind the slides: we see only the projections, the secondary manifestations from which we draw clues. Our search for reality resembles drawing inferences about a distant galaxy by poring over its spectrogram. Projected on the screen might be our varied ways of understanding the truth: Jehovah, Physics, Krishna, Jesus, Science, Plato, Allah, Math, Shiva, Quetzalcoatl, Philosophy, Zeus, Buddha, or possibly only ourselves, in a lonely little slide. Too often, we mistake the slide shown to us for the white light behind it, and are ever ready to argue and fight when our slide picture does not match that of others. Our slide, we think, is the only way of understanding things. But the slides change, the colors move, the cultural icons vary: the light itself does not change; it is eternal and constant. It is truth.

The truth does not necessarily have to be seen as something spiritual, although throughout human cultural history it more often is than not: or at least has spirituality as a component. Spirituality may be all, or it may even be a byproduct: an emotion of curiosity, wonder, and awe found through contemplating the other pieces. Math is a component; fables, proverbs, and secular stories are components. Human nature, cosmology, myths, astrology, physics, religions: all are components. The White Light is made up of all of these, and more; it contains the entire spectrum. The list is as varied as we can conceive of, as it is inclusive of all. Humans cannot conceive of the bulb, the Ground of Being; we see only its colorful and varied manifestations on the screen. Awe is the proper response to understanding that what we see projected is nothing but an image; the Ground lies beyond our vision, or possibly beyond the ability of our vision.

***

A current trend in psychotherapy and associated groups as of this writing is the increasing use of what are called "mindfulness" techniques. Upon closer examination, these are revealed to be little more than basic Buddhist meditation practices, cloaked in new language in order to avoid scaring off the more closed-minded folks, who might be threatened by the very word Buddhism. The aura of quiet detachment and contemplation is the same. The same detachment and yet presence of awareness also permeates other far-flung traditions, both temporally and spatially. The goal of mindfulness is that of the "Wise Mind," which occurs at the intersection of analysis and intuition. Again, we see the yin-yang play that governs the universe. It is a great seat from which to view the slideshow.

The Greeks (the Stoics) had a view of reality that revolved around the idea of what they termed "mind-fire." They believed that the universe was a single ever-present, living being, a combination of consciousness and energy; and that all we see and experience was a manifestation of this "mind-fire." Intelligent energy was primary. Material objects came from this energy; the four elements (earth, air, fire, and water) came from this energy, and yet all were ultimately connected and traceable back to the single One. This is so similar in conception to that of ancient Hindu teachings, that it is unlikely to be a coincidence. As it turns out, the Stoic school in Athens was preceded only a short time prior by Alexander's great armies' failed attempts to invade India; trade routes predate even this contact, and there is no doubt that ideas as well as spices were carried and shared throughout the ancient world. Interestingly, those trade routes went both ways: "Vedic" astrology actually developed through Indian astrologers adopting Hellenistic techniques, imported from Greece. Aesop's fables from Greece bear a striking resemblance to the Panchatantra animal folk tales of India. Both echo the Southern U.S.' collection of Uncle Remus tales, black folklore transcribed by Joel Chandler Harris in the 1800s. Using anthropomorphized animal tales as a disguise for passing down human folk wisdom may thus even be traced back to Africa, the cradle of humanity, and be lost in the distant mists of our common antiquity.

Wisdom is both secular and spiritual, and has been ever so throughout human history. The philosophers of today rehash debates that people in Athens, or Kenya, or Paris have argued since human intelligence began to flower. There are no answers, and there are the same answers: the Ultimate is finally unknowable in its fullness, and is thus always the subject of conjecture. Who can know the Mind of God? Who can know the ways of the universe? Who can say that we have reached the end result of our explorations in physics? In their basest forms, religions seem to be quite different, and have little to agree on. However, as one moves forward in spiritual understanding, things start to appear more and more similar (not that differences will disappear entirely). But at the mystical level, things start to blur together completely. Christian mystics such as St. Augustine, Meister Eckhart, and Ignatius of Loyola might have a lot to share in conversation with Indian sadhus, Muslim Sufis, and even Jewish kabbalists, not to mention Bohr and Einstein. At the level of the Ultimate, science and spirituality may finally talk. *True* spirituality (as opposed to divisive and separatist religions) must, joining in with true secular wisdom and true science, reach a global point of understanding, and be shown to be universal.

All science must be agreed upon by anyone investigating it. All folk wisdom, in order to truly be wisdom, must apply to anyone sharing our human lineage. Brer Rabbit is as surely Swedish as he is African. And all spirituality, to be genuine, must transcend the petty squabbles of different cultures, sects, and religions, which often serve more as exclusive entities than inclusive ones. We need to recognize that our colorful and compelling slide is only one of many, and that all are ultimately only partial, limited, and watered-down versions of something that is greater and more universal.

As one gathers up the bits of wisdom strewn throughout human time and geography, one cannot help but be amazed in following the trail of breadcrumbs to and from their various sources. Aphorisms, stories, folk wisdoms, priestly pronouncements, direct experience—all are seen to flow upwards, leading to a single elevation. The name of that mount is humanity. It is only as we get out of the woods on the lower slopes and proceed above the clouds to the barren clear air of the more rocky highlands that we notice there are other trails on the mountain, some coming from seemingly far away, progressing through their own woods, through jungles and dense underbrush; all leading also and ever upwards, converging here in the clearer light of dawn with our own trail. All are leading inexorably towards the top as we are, all are converging at the summit. Here, there are no separate trails: there is only the enduring wisdom of humanity, agreement, commonality, spirituality, and Oneness. Here is our real home, our home in truth.

Dharma

The Eagle and the Tortoise (adapted from Aesop's Fables):

A Tortoise, sunning herself on some rocks one day, began to complain about her lot to an Eagle resting nearby, bemoaning the fact that Eagles could fly and that she could not. "What will you give me if I take you to soar above the clouds?" asked the Eagle. "All of the riches that lie here on the ground with me," answered the Tortoise. So the Eagle latched on to the Tortoise, and swung her up into the sky. However, as the Eagle flew over some mountains, its talons lost their grip and the Tortoise fell hundreds of feet to her death, smashing her shell on the rocks below. As she lay dying, she muttered, "Why did I think that I was meant for flying, when I can barely move about here on the earth?"

> "Be yourself: everyone else is already taken"—Oscar Wilde

Scholar J. A. B. van Buitenen, in a 1957 article in the journal *Philosophy East and West*, states that dharma is "...a kind of natural law on all existent beings in the universe... an innate characteristic, that which makes a being what it is, assigning the part it is to play in concert. It is the dharma of the sun to shine, of the rivers to flow, of the cow to yield milk..." Rasamandala Das, in his excellent book *The Illustrated Encyclopedia of Hinduism* echoes this by explaining that "A further connotation is 'that which is integral to an object', hence the dharma of fire is to be hot, of sugar to be sweet. For humans, dharma consists of duties that sustain them according to their innate characteristics." Dharma, then, is our essential nature and path as it relates to the larger forces of existence; an Eastern concept which dovetails nicely with the subject of astrology, and is deserving of study by anyone interested in that practice. It is the dharma of the Capricorn to rise, of the Taurus to accumulate, and of the Virgo to analyze. It is the dharma of *all* humans, however, not to be limited solely by these lesser specialized characteristics, but to also live in harmony with the larger celestial laws; this is also an expression of our nature. Astrological dharma is contained within, and subservient to, a more universal and cosmic dharma that all humans take part in.

Dharma is often thought of as a system of laws or teachings that one must follow in order to be in harmony with the cosmos, but as seen in the quotes above, dharma is also specific to a particular entity, and their particular role to fill in the grand scheme. Bees buzz, humans... human. Aries, "Aries." There are components of dharma which apply to all humans, but each also has his own particular role to play, and has his own specific dharma, which may be thought of as a "fine-tuning" of the more universal principles. This is known as sva-dharma. However, it is important that one should not violate the tenets of the more universal dharma in their personal quests and expressions. It is the dharma of all to recognize the illusion of the personal ego and to honor connectedness, for example. The expression of this in real life is that of helping other humans, and being respectful of the earth and nature. This is similar in idea to the Tao, and appears again in Buddhism. In the Mahabharata of the Hindus, it is cautioned that the understanding of dharma is complex, and "should be performed conscientiously, with foresight and the ability to juggle conflicting needs." (Rasamandala Das again.) A particular person's dharma is based on that individual's "unique context and disposition."

Dharma is a concept best thought of as part of a triad which includes rita and karma. It is found in nearly every Eastern tradition in different variants, and has evolved and changed slightly in meaning over the years; it is difficult to define exactly. According to Wikipedia, rita (from early Hinduism) likely was the more original and central concept of natural law or cosmic order, while dharma had more to do with the effective carrying out of this infinite and comprehensive template of existence; a more "instructional" component, focused on duty. (In Buddhism, dharma often refers to the Buddha's teachings.) However, dharma in popular usage has often come to combine these two, with dharma standing in for both the cosmic order and the carrying out of the same. The person and the path are one; to speak of either is to speak of the other.

Thus, astrologically, it might be one's dharma to be a Sixth House person, meaning that it is both one's place or assignment in life, *and* the duty to fulfill that assignment. To do otherwise would be to throw the cosmos out of balance. In addition, (for those into reincarnation, anyway) dharma can be thought of for many people as being inseparable from karma, which is the sum of one's actions, currently or in the past. "Dharma carries out the karma." That is, one's actions may determine one's future dharma, just as one's dharma will hopefully produce certain actions (karma) in accordance with that dharma. The system is a whole, and does allow a measure of free will. The successful expression of dharma, being who we are meant to be, can lessen any future karma. Living our destiny is in harmony with the cosmic order, and thus freeing. This may again, for those interested in reincarnation, carry on from one lifetime to the next, or it may be seen to operate simply within a lifetime. So if one were to commit a crime and go to jail, the questions may arise: is this a case of free will and "instant karma" (thanks, John Lennon), an aberration of an underlying karma/dharma system, or is this in itself an expression of fate, and the fruition of a more enduring karma/dharma system?

These questions harken back to questions of fate vs. free will, and again, the best way to approach this is likely as a holistic system, with the various parts simply sides of a single coin. Karma connotes both the action and its results; dharma pairs both one's essential self and the path associated with expressing that self. Nothing causes anything: everything is connected, part of an intertwined order, synchronistic, an expression of the Whole. The cat doesn't cause the tail, although the tail follows the cat. The universe is everywhere connected and energetic. Regardless of whether reincarnation exists or not, we are still born with a certain dharma, and the willing and effective carrying out of this template puts us in tune with harmony, happiness, and the cosmic order.

So how does this combine with astrology? It is perhaps best to think of the horoscope simply as a map of one's dharma, one's lot and journey in life. As such, it is potentially the most powerful tool that we will ever have available to us in our wanderings. It is one's assignment in life, and it is one's task and pilgrimage to carry out that assignment. In addition, it contains the roadmap and guidelines for doing so. That is the way of integration, of true understanding, and of serenity. An old saying goes "cobbler, stick to thy last," what one is best at. It is the way of disappointment and stress to fight one's dharma, to try and be something that one is not meant to be, to allow oneself to be pushed in inappropriate directions by family or society that are not according to one's blueprint; or to push oneself in these directions due to an imperfect understanding. It's unfortunate that many lives are not lived to their full potential, or otherwise produce episodes of unhappiness due to delusions or poor insight in this area. It is extremely difficult to see ourselves clearly at times, and objective questions, reflections, and opinions are always in order, although they must be tempered with perceptive self-analysis. Skillful astrologers can be of immeasurable assistance in helping their clients understand this.

So the biggest asset that we may possess in life is to understand our dharma, so that we can effectively work *within* it, rather than at scattered cross-purposes. If we are a hare, we can never be a wolf, exciting though that may sound. However, if we are a wolf, we will always be in danger of being killed by hunters; that is our place and our dharma, and we must *be* a wolf and accept all of the consequences that come with that also, good and bad. If we are a Cancer, we are not *meant* to be a Leo, even if we secretly feel that this might be a more glamorous place that we would like to be. We have our own admirable strengths. If we have Moon in Gemini, the life of a hermit, cut off from communication, is likely not for us. Acceptance of our dharma, of our own path in life, is the secret to happiness: want what you have, be who you are.

The biggest danger that we face in life is to misinterpret our dharma. To feel that we are supposed to be a wolf, when in fact we are not. Disillusionment, disappointment, resentment, and tension are sure to follow. In fact, these are a few clues that we need to reexamine who we are "supposed" to be, or what we are "destined" to be doing. Conversely, a nearly equal danger is to sell ourselves short; to minimize talents and skills that we might have success with, in lieu of pursuing those things that we are ill-suited for. To pursue romantic interests or job opportunities that are "not in our stars." Quite often, we may have tremendous talents to maximize the potentialities that are shown in our charts or our dharma, but we are choosing someone else's chart, and simply fumbling at their particular path or talents. The problem is often the willfulness of the easily-confused ego in not being able to see what actually quiets the seas in our life, what brings us contentment and serenity, and what might put us in synch with the cosmic plan for us... with our dharma.

***

Dharma is not completely set in stone, however, if one does not buy into abject determinism. Here is Jung's or Rudhyar's individuation in the chart. Dharma shows guidelines and strong tendencies; the carrying out of dharma is exactly as free as the universe is free and unfettered. (The exact extent of that, of course, remains to be determined.) Dharma, again, is like astrology: it impels but it does not compel. It is not set in stone, but only in moderately firm clay; it may be molded to a certain extent, often with great effort, and then only within certain parameters. If you were meant to be an actor, you may learn to be a public relations person, but you will never be either effective or happy as an engineer. The skill is in learning these invisible limits.

And dharma must also answer to our lives as they move: the transits and progressions of our lives affect our dharma, and produce changes and adjustments in its course. At one point we are meant to play out our inner knight, slaying dragons and rescuing maidens, while at another, perhaps, our Moon is accented and we are meant to raise a child, or to take care of an elderly parent. Cycles loop, intertwine, move on, and carry us along: "We cannot direct the wind, we can only adjust our sails." Acceptance is the key to everything in life, as it keeps us in touch with reality, and staves off wishful thinking. It guides us in our dharma, and in particular our dharma as it may be playing out at this moment. Many are aware of the Serenity Prayer:

> God, grant me the Serenity to accept the things I cannot change;
> Courage to change the things I can,
> And Wisdom to know the difference.

The search to understand our dharma is the most beautiful quest in life. More than 2,000 years ago, Socrates counseled "know thyself." It's still good advice. Socrates additionally noted that "wonder is the beginning of wisdom," and nowhere else can we get such a sense of wonder as in contemplating the subject of our dharma, how it is expressed through our astrological charts, and what this all may intimate about the universe at large. A lifetime of awe and meditation lies here for anyone willing to take on the task. To see our children, our spouses, our friends, and ourselves act out the personas and dharma foretold in their horoscopes is an amazing thing. To fully regard the implications to our normal understanding of reality is chilling.

Life Is a Hungry Thing

> "It's amazing how quickly nature consumes human places after we turn our backs on them. Life is a hungry thing."—Scott Westerfeld

"Life is a hungry thing." I love that. Life will not be denied. Life is kudzu in the Deep South where I spent most of my life. Kudzu will not be denied: it blankets the South with lush green foliage, crawling over fences and telephone poles and trees; chemicals slow it down, but do not keep it at bay. Dusty roads throughout Alabama, Mississippi, Louisiana are lined with it. Life is also Formosan termites in New Orleans, which will not be denied: they gnaw day and night at the wood of the French Quarter, their nests buried deep in the ground or high up in the rafters near the rain gutters, providing water and shelter. Pick up a floorboard and their antennas are waving at you; fell a rotting oak tree and they come swarming out: they are relentless. There is a force that is with them, that they take part in, that moves them ever forward, unstoppable. The lotus blooms, the termites eat. Vitalism as a scientific idea has fallen out of favor in modern times. And yet...

My dad passed away a few years ago, the first of my parents to do so. He was 89 years old, and had enjoyed a wonderful life; his last day, he ate a good Creole meal in a New Orleans neighborhood restaurant with some friends, and died later that afternoon of a heart attack after feeling poorly in his office at home. The ambulance came, but he died while on the journey to the hospital; with Mars in Sagittarius, he was always a traveler. I was living elsewhere, and flew in as soon as I could.

Life is a hungry thing, but what thing *is* it? What *is* life? By the time I got down to New Orleans the next day, my dad was at the funeral home and being prepared for cremation. The rest of my family had seen him recently, but I had not—I wanted to see him one last time. They declined to accompany me, but I went to the mortuary, and the employees there allowed me private time in a room with him. I wanted to get a lock of his hair to give to my mother. It was a strange experience: those who have lost loved ones will know what I'm talking about. My dad lay stretched out, mostly covered by a sheet with his only head uncovered. He had a peaceful expression on his face, and in fact looked almost alive, but wasn't. His skin felt cool but not cold. A lot of emotion came over me as I bid him goodbye, but I also had the overwhelming thought and feeling that *the life force had left him.* Just that simple, just that sudden, just like that. The force of Life, whatever it is, had been in him, and now had taken its leave. One day, he was alive, and it was as if a switch had been turned off. He was gone. The force which will not be denied, which is a hungry thing, was gone from him.

The force of life is biochemical processes, is consciousness, is quantum interactions, is possibly whatever we may conceive of God to be. It is the Chinese chi, the Hindu prana, the Greek pneuma. It is the manifestation of the force of creation in the universe, which will not be denied, the great and eternal unfolding. Ultimately, no one knows what it is. It is a Mystery; it is *the* Mystery. The Latin "spiritus" means breathing, soul, spirit, vigor. It is most commonly identified with the breath in spiritual traditions, as that is the most visible sign of life, but the life-force goes far beyond simple breath.

The life-force is scientifically incorrect, and yet it is present and real for those who contemplate the living and the dead. It exists, and we are a part of it, and expressions of it. The wind blows across the land and signifies its life, and our individual breaths join in. Life is the question, as well as the answer. Its force is here with us and our loved ones, and then it is gone. It is a phase, it is a wave, and no one knows what happens in the off or dark phase of the wave. We have only our own parts to play, and our own efforts to understand in this brief lifetime of our own.

Bye, Dad. I miss you.

Haven't I Been Here Before?

There are countless world visions of what happens after we die. Three of the most popular are (a) nothing (the least popular), b) heaven (or its evil twin, hell), and c) reincarnation. Two of these three are based on the idea of a personal and identifiable soul that endures after death in one form or another. There is a direct and virtually unchanged version of this soul after death in (b), and a more difficult to trace form in (c), due to transmigratory processes. Whether coincidental or not, the religions that subscribe to these two have the enviable position of having a sword to hang over their members during their lives here on earth: if you don't act right, you will either go to hell for all of eternity (quite a long time), or you will be reincarnated as a toad. At least (c) is not so all-or-nothing; if you strike out, at least the game isn't over. You still get a chance to bat again, although from a somewhat handicapped position. If you are a gambling sort of person, you will seriously have to weigh the odds here, as putting your money on black and having red come up in this matter isn't the same as playing poker for pennies.

This book is interested in physics and spirituality, in astrology and synchronicity, and in psi and science. So how might one reconcile these varied subjects in regards to the weighty issues above? Sad to say, but most of them of course probably won't be, at least not anytime soon; but some thoughts do occur. Science of course makes no room for any sort of soul, let alone its continuance after death; but then again, science barely makes room for consciousness itself, and then only on a physically produced, reductionist basis. Science *does* make room for an odd sort of "reincarnation," but again keeps it shackled to the material plane. Our bodies are made up of an untold number of atoms and molecules, themselves "products of stardust," a concept that Carl Sagan popularized. That is to say, all elements and their associated atoms, except for hydrogen and helium (which were produced in the original Big Bang), were formed in the hearts of stars across space and time and dispersed through the explosions of those very same stars, through supernovas. Thus, in a physical sense, we are indeed "stardust"; little more than the recyclings of those elements that existed perhaps millions or billions of light years away in some unknown galaxy, and which were thrown across the universe during violent explosions, to subsequently take part in the formation of the earth. Pretty humbling thought, that. In a more immediate, local, and prosaic sense, we are the recyclings of atoms and molecules here on earth that may have once been Neanderthal men and women, bees and trees, mountains and streams, and have now ended up in us, in the fingernail that we may be looking at. William Blake wrote:

> "To see a World in a Grain of Sand
> And a Heaven in a Wild Flower,
> Hold Infinity in the palm of your hand
> And Eternity in an hour."

So science itself is inspiring enough, with its physical connectedness, continuity, and molecular reorganization and redistribution. But what if we venture beyond the physical, and question the realms of the spirit and of consciousness? What then lies ahead? Assuming that Consciousness is a force of some sort in the universe, and that it is not constrained by time or space, or local to our craniums, what possibilities could then arise?

If Consciousness exists apart from our own nodes that we perceive to be inside our heads, and transcends the limitations that we can conceive of, then what is our portion, and what is its longevity? Are we confusing our consciousness with our ego, which may be only temporarily on loan to us? Is Consciousness and/or Spirit in this larger sense the manifestation of an old man with a white beard, separate from us, the God of Moses and those who have followed behind? Or is it the manifestations of the Hindu Godhead with their various and endless permutations, all taking part in the game of Lila, of which we are active but tiny participants? Or is it a more impersonal and amorphous thing, a Presence with no face, yet immanent throughout the universe, and everywhere?

Or might Consciousness be a secular thing, more psychological and Buddhist-like (although the Buddhists, normally fairly secular folks, but originating out of Hinduism, interestingly cling to the reincarnation portion of that faith)? Or is it scientific but non-local; a type of force that exists as electromagnetism exists, but as yet undiscovered? Or *is* it just the byproduct of evolutionary biochemical processes within the brain? We all get to make our own choices here. But it is guaranteed that there will always be more to it than we know: the secrets of the universe, and of consciousness and spirituality, are not laid bare so easily. Einstein said, "The most beautiful experience that we can have is the mysterious. It is the fundamental emotion which stands at the cradle of art and true science." I don't know precisely what it is that I don't know; I can stand in wonder only, and in awe and modesty.

It's also possible that, just as our bodies are collections of elements that will one day dissolve back into the lagoon, to be reissued again as another body; that our consciousness is correspondingly a temporary drop from a larger ocean that is on loan to us. Here, our personal slivers (along with the illusion of our personal egos) would ultimately dissolve back into some universal pool, to be distributed again to others, unbeknownst to us personally just as our chemical elements are unbeknownst to us. Our nodules of the Universal Consciousness are not so special: we are only the foam thrown up by the Ocean. We are only the fluctuations of zero-point energy, shivering for a moment in the manifestation of What Is. The world and its underlying Consciousness may be aptly captured by the metaphor of the lotus blossom so prevalent throughout the East: an ever-blossoming, unfolding, engulfing and illuminating, constant and yet ever-changing flower whose bloom signals the cyclical and paradoxically forward-moving flow of things. I have been here before, and I shall be here again; yet there is no me.

It's Out of Control!

"Relax. Everything is out of control."

Where *does* the drive, universal to humans at various moments, to control situations and people around us come from? Most of us have been accused of this at certain intervals; all of us have been guilty on occasion, to whatever degree. And if we *are* trying feverishly to control things, the old joke is that we must think that they are completely out of control. But are they really? Well, of course they are!

Efforts at control mainly arise from fear, although this fear is very shy and likes to hide from us, making it difficult to recognize. In astrological terms, Saturn is often lurking in the wings, and Saturn is associated with the Shadow, those parts of our personality and life that are off-limits to our conscious mind. Clues towards uncovering our hidden fears may be found by analyzing under what circumstances our efforts at control seem to arise. This is often easier said than done, however, as fear protects itself, just as the ego does. The Saturnian structures of ego and fear are very vigilant and defensive. Others that we trust in our lives may be able to see beyond our blind spots and be of assistance here, as may dreams, therapy, and astrological chart-work.

Fear usually falls into one of two categories: either we have the fear of losing something that we already have, or else we have the fear that we will not get something that we really, really, want. Both of these forms of fear show the face of Saturn, if we can muster the courage to look at them directly. Either we have built up a structure that we are attached to and are afraid will crumble, or we have emotionally sensitive and tender hopes and wishes (often connected with Saturn's natal placement in our chart) for a new structure that we would like to build, but that we are fearful we are inadequate to construct. It seems too much for our capabilities, or forever beyond our reach, or not in our destiny. We consequently and frequently blunder about, ineffectively trying to control things without much skill in knowing what we are doing, and then feeling impotent and helpless; or resentful. In Eastern terms, this may be thought of as being out of synch with the Tao. In Western (religious) terms, it is arguing with God's will for us. In scientific terms, it ignores the simple fact that things will be what they will be, and that the universe is larger than us. In astrology, it is being out of touch with the greater chart as a whole, its meaning and course, and our understanding of how Saturn works. We need to step back and learn to let things flow more, to listen to the universe instead of trying to teach it: "don't push the river," as the saying goes. And, it *is* true, some things simply are *not* meant to be for us:

> "If God shuts a door, stop banging on it. Whatever is behind it is not for you."—Anonymous

Why do we do this? What's the solution? What's the alternative? Let's break things down a bit. All fear is fear of the unknown, so let's change tack and look at that particular angle. The unknown *is* often scary: we don't know what is going to happen. We often double our attempts at control in the face of the unknown, or else give up and fall apart in a quivering jelly-like mass, becoming depressed. The unknown is the Dark. It may be Death. It is Change. It is Pluto. It is (gasp!) often Beyond Our Control, try as we might to fight this fact. It is Scary. So what can we do? How can we handle fear? How can we tame the monster?

What we don't see is that *everything* is the unknown; it's just that we are more attached to the results of some things than others. So let's do a simple and practical analysis here. Fear is the unknown: it is more specifically the *unknown outcome of a particular situation*. So what might the outcome turn out to be? The outcome of any situation can take only one of two paths. Either the outcome will be something to our liking, or the outcome will be not to our liking. If it is the former, there is no problem: it's easy to accept outcomes that play out as we had hoped. If, however, things go awry and veer off the road, don't go according to our hopes and wishes, what happens then? Let's think this through.

If something doesn't go our way, we may gnash or moan, we may double down with our already-proved-ineffective control tactics, or we may even go into blunt denial; but the end result, whether it's fifteen minutes or a lifetime later, is that *we have to accept the results*. They have happened. We have no choice here. Reality moves on, and we must move with it whether we like it or not. The only alternative is a life of delusion; not a very satisfying one for most people. And as most of us have learned, life frequently *isn't* fair; that's just part of the deal. (But sometimes it is. Sometimes, in fact, life is *more* than fair and we get things we don't actually deserve. One rarely hears complaints about that particular situation.)

But the bottom line is this: life moves on from whatever fearful, traumatic situation we were sweating over, and we are forced to accept the results, whether they are to our liking or not. We have no choice. This is the equivalence of quantum collapse: the results are now known, they have been delivered. The possibilities have turned into actualities. Things are what they are. This is not in any way meant to imply that being passive, or giving into discouragement at trying to achieve things is the way to go: the healthy approach here is to give it our best shot, but not to be attached to the results. We swing the bat, we hit the ball, and our job is done; we must be ready to accept where it lands. Buddhism teaches this. Our efforts are not directed towards trying to control others, or the situation. Our efforts are directed towards putting forth our best strivings with good intentions, and being ready for any outcome with equanimity. Regardless, it will either be our time, or it won't. Efforts that come from a place of love will increase our odds. We can't know the mind of the universe, or of chance. All that we really have control over is our own efforts, and our attitudes as to how we accept results.

Knowing this, let's back up through the path. I have fear, which is causing desperate and thrashing attempts at control. The fear is of the unknown, the unknown results of a situation. The situation is either that I may lose something that I want to keep, or that I may not get something that I want to have. The situation will result in one of two ways: to my liking or not to my liking. Either one of these will ultimately demand acceptance. The final result of both is thus acceptance.

Therefore, if looked at correctly, the whole subject of fear, and thus of control, is completely moot, useless, and irrelevant. The end result of any fearful situation that I'm trying to control is acceptance. So why not cut out the middlemen (fear and control), and move straight towards acceptance? By quantum law, the possibilistic and uncertain mechanism of the universe, we can never know the results in advance anyway. Everything prior to acceptance, then, becomes pointless and unimportant: no more stress hormones, angry shouting matches, devious plotting, sleepless nights, or self-pity. Much easier said than done, of course; but acceptance connected to flow *is* the answer to getting rid of all of our fear and control issues.

***

Acceptance is also the answer to another particularly nasty problem that is frequently associated with attempts at control: that of resentments. Quite often, we have an expectation of the way that we feel things should turn out, or the results that our efforts at control should have wrested from reality. When they don't turn out the way that we had envisioned, we either turn depressive or become filled with resentments, our blood pressures rising, rightful indignation clouding our vision: how dare life not be fair to *me!*

Resentments can be delicious: some of us nourish, feed, and cherish them for many years. They give us a certain dysfunctional salve for our bruised and angry egos, because, even though we're feeling miserable, by God we're *right*. "Would you rather be right, or be happy?" goes a popular question. Some of us fail this every time, flushing happiness and serenity down the toilet in the service of being "right." Forget that half of the time, our "right" doesn't even have the slightest basis in objective reality. It is all in our minds. And for those who really have been wronged: it's OK. We still have to let it go. The universe will take care of righting things, we don't need to. Or possibly there were lessons, or simply things that we needed to learn (as difficult as that may sometimes seem), and we can find meaning in that. Whatever the case may be, we need to recognize first and foremost that holding on is ruining *our* life, not theirs.

For those who finally get tired of lugging their resentments around, the clue to relief here is the word *expectations*. As difficult as it may be to believe, it is our own expectations that actually produce resentments. We are the source. We are only resentful because a particular situation or person didn't turn out *as we expected*: those expectations, in fact, often being little more than a projection of our own wishes and fantasies. If we had no expectations of situations, or of other people, we would have no resentments. It really is as simple as that, although again far from easy. No expectations means acceptance. Acceptance and letting go of expectations come from being *willing* to do so. The single greatest barrier to letting go of resentment is the unwillingness to do so. Resentments come from expecting people or situations to be different than they actually are. We never get to control that. Letting other people be who they are, letting situations develop as they want to, is the whole secret here.

We also need to watch that we are not tempted into another vicious cycle: one where we attempt to control things, things aren't amenable to our control, and we then double down and try even harder to take control. This can go around and around in pretty tight circles, especially with other people who are willing to play the game with us. Do these things ever end well? How do *we* feel in these cases? Good about ourselves or others? What would happen if we just let go? Let go of control, let go of fear, and allow to wash over us the reality that *everything* in the future is unknown, it always will be, it's out of our control, and that's OK. It will be known shortly, and we will be obliged to accept it. Would the world end? Would the floor fall out from underneath us? The path of acceptance and flow seems counter-intuitive to many of us, but it always proves ultimately to be the path of serenity and contentment. We don't always get what we want, but we get understanding and peace of mind; *the actual outcomes will be the same regardless*. Only our outlook on them will have changed.

Let's make one more move, and take a more spiritual view of things. Here, we are looking at spirituality in a larger sense: it may or may not include formal religion. Here, we are again saying that control issues arise from fear, and that acceptance is the key. But now we are adding in a new element: faith. Faith here may be that of a traditional religion; faith that God will carry us through, that all will work out through God. But faith doesn't necessarily have to have that particular association. For those who are non-religious in any established format, faith can simply mean the idea that things will work out the way that they're supposed to work out.

How are they supposed to work out? Things work out the way that God wants them to work out, or they simply work out the way that they work out. Importantly, either way gives the same results, since we can never be sure if we are seeing God's will or the results of more secular forces. This is similar to the fate vs. free will quandary. Things are as they are. All that we can see are the results. Faith is the opposing force to the fear that things won't work out "our way." They never do. They work out the way they work out, and that is sometimes to our liking, and sometimes it is not. Faith is the feeling that however things work out, it is going to be OK. Faith holds hands with acceptance. Faith is always the answer to fear; in fact they are opposite sides of the same coin. Again, it is a zero-sum game. One cannot be completely full of fear and have any faith at all, just as one cannot be completely filled with faith and be full of fear. Faith in God, or in the flow of life, will bring us through.

The requirement here is in getting outside of our personal egos, and feeling connected with the flow of life, either through our personal version of God, or through our other unique and personal spiritual understandings. The ego here is finally revealed to be the source of attachment to results. It is the ego that blocks the flow, that balks at acceptance, that confronts situations with fear and control. Faith lets the ego go, lets the ego soften and see itself as merely the speck in the universe that it really is. The importance of micro-managing fades away. It's OK. Life is seen to march along at its own rhythm and pace, and we can only wonder at the spectacle, and be grateful for being able to take part. Our only real choices here are to go with the flow of life, or to resist it. The first is acceptance, the second is control. The first is faith, the second is fear.

> "The graveyards are full of people the world could not do without."—Elbert Hubbard

In the Year 2525

Science in the 1500s: To avoid the Church making his life miserable, Copernicus wisely publishes *De Revolutionibus Orbium Coelestium* on his deathbed. It states that the earth goes around the sun, rather than the other way around. Intriguing, but... massive controversy ensues. Too weird. Can't be. Unnatural. Against God's will. Attracts very few adherents at first.

Science in the 1600s: Galileo is the first to put forth a theory of relativity, speculating that physical laws are the same for separate observers that are in different settings of movement and space. Thus, there is no constant and enduring frame of reference. Intriguing, but... nah. Too weird. Doesn't make sense. Chaos would rule the universe.

Science in the 1700s: Georges Cuvier becomes the "father of paleontology" by postulating that species can arise and become extinct, leaving behind fossil records. Intriguing, but... really? Pretty absurd, frankly. Not really even worth considering. The earth was created 6,000 years ago. Anything else is blasphemy. Read Genesis and do the math.

Science in the 1800s: Alfred Wegener and others have noted that the continents, if pushed together, would interlock like a giant jigsaw puzzle. Intriguing, but... forget it. Too weird. No mechanism. Can't be. He finally presents his paper in 1912 to ridicule and ostracism.

Science in the 1900s: Eugene Wigner and others note that consciousness seems to be somehow involved in determining the results of physical experiments. Other free-thinking physicists dip their toes in the water. Intriguing, but... c'mon. We'd look pretty ridiculous if we went down that path. They're quickly overridden by the more sensible members of the profession. Too weird. No mechanism. Can't be. Shut up and compute.

Science in the (late) 2000s: Those watching the fledgling science of consciousness (after it was determined that observers did indeed influence the material universe) speculate that perhaps the ancient science/art of astrology may also be somehow tied into both consciousness and matter. Hey, if we've just solved the earth's power needs forever with the recent advances in cold fusion, then maybe *anything* is possible! But... nah. Too weird. No mechanism. Can't be.

And in the year 2525?

What Is Math?

"As far as the laws of mathematics refer to reality, they are not certain, and as far as they are certain, they do not refer to reality."—Albert Einstein

"The map is not the territory"—Alfred Korzybski

There was recently published a book titled *Our Mathematical Universe* by a well-credentialed cosmologist which, while speculative, was mostly well received in the scientific community. In it, the author puts forth a theory that math is Everything: that is, the entire universe can be understood to be nothing more than the expression of mathematical formulas, that indeed nothing really exists *except* math. Matter is math, and energy is math. Consciousness itself is in fact math. Specifically, it is a particular state of matter known as Perceptronium, per the author.

So let's talk about that. If you are at all interested in the subjects presented in this book, you will have come into contact with math; it is indeed everywhere. Physics is of course math, but astrology is also: in fact, astrology can be understood to be nothing *but* math and archetypes. Orbital mechanics drive a continual process of interacting cycles which trigger various archetypes. Math here is most obviously seen as a tool, as a way of understanding the planetary motions. But is it more? What *is* math?

Math may seem to be more properly understood as a language. In fact, although math took on notational aspects fairly early, it also used to be a much more verbally-inflected way of talking about things. Some samples of early mathematical treatises are in fact mainly descriptive; the efficient notation of today developed more slowly. Mathematics could actually be entirely explained verbally; its notation is simply a convenience, a shortcut to convey certain ideas. That gives us a clue that it is simply another language, although more universally understood, more precise, and less subject to interpretation and continual change than French, Hindi, or English. Math itself, by needs, has an underpinning of reality. Maxwell's equations were not just math, but described something real underlying the math. We are in touch with this "something" any time we turn a light on, or check our email; it is manifested most commonly in our world as electricity and light.

Reality exists, reality is what *is*; language, whether verbal or mathematical, simply attempts to describe it. Each of these two have their own purpose and specialty in regards to this description. This is a point worth making. If I look out of my window in the morning and see a robin in the yard, how might I best describe it? I may describe it from the standpoint of math and physics: it is this measurement in length, weighs that much. It reflects a certain portion of the electromagnetic spectrum. It is made of fleshy tissue which in turn is organized into certain biological systems that have evolved for maximum efficiency. The tissue is made of molecules that interact with each other. The molecules are constructed of atoms which in turn are composed of sub-atomic structures that obey certain laws in their energies and interactions. There—you have a robin!

From a more verbally descriptive standpoint, one might speak of the way that the bird (shiny coat of black and orange, pointed yellow beak, odd-shaped nostrils, skinny little stick legs) tips its head quizzically, eyes darting about, and then in a brief swoop, pecks downward and comes up empty-handed, piece of green grass still in its mouth, dew drop clinging and then falling. Comically, it hops a couple of paces and repeats the show again and again, cocking its head, looking about as if embarrassed that it has proven to be such a poor hunter this morning. Finally, it spots something and flies off, above the split rail fence into the egg-blue morning sky, with dark thunderheads beginning to appear low on the horizon.

So which description of the robin is the "best"? Which describes reality more accurately? Hopefully one will note that neither is better, but that each contributes to the overall description. One key point is that both descriptions are second-hand. They attempt to describe through words or numbers what might be better apprehended by direct experience. Things exist. Things are what they are. Everything else is an attempt to capture them and pin them down using limited tools. And in appraising a description of something, it's well to keep in mind that each person approaches reality from their own biases: if you are a mathematician, then everything is math. If you are a poet, then everything is poetry. If you are a lumberjack, then everything is lumber. Abraham Maslow said in 1966, "I suppose it is tempting, if the only tool you have is a hammer, to treat everything as if it were a nail." Again, believing is seeing. Our view of reality is always limited and self-reinforcing.

So math is the servant and not the master, as are words. Reality contains them both, and is at the same time beyond them both. Reality exists; we are a subset. Math is a subset, and words are a subset. We try in our feeble way to "get at" reality, but it ultimately remains forever just slightly beyond our reach. R = K+1.

***

We run into a somewhat parallel problem when talking about astrology, and especially when trying to explain astrology to an "outsider." The problem is that of how best to convey an *experience* to another who has no commonality, understanding, or point of reference. Hence, the outsider is often unable to effectively connect the subject being studied with the language used to describe that subject or experience. To the uninitiated, there doesn't seem to be a subject at all, and the description therefore is just so many words, few of which make any sense. This is where the seeds of doubt or derision come from: "Are they just making all of this up? What are they even *talking* about?" (One also runs into this with math: mathematicians may wax eloquent about a particular formula or theorem as if it were an exquisite jewel, while the untutored bystander will stand there with a glazed and dumb look on their face. Experiences are hard to convey.)

Astrology is perhaps similar in its somewhat arcane and acquired knowledge to being a connoisseur of something: wine, Baroque painting, math, whatever. The untutored eye may look at a painting such as Caravaggio's "The Lute Player," and not see much more than a young man holding an instrument of some sort: pleasing to look at, perhaps, but not much beyond that. The connoisseur or expert, however, fairly breathes the painting in as a sommelier might: senses alive, details reminding him or her of other places, other times. Details spring to life: the pattern of the brush strokes, the area that looks as if it may have been overpainted.

Knowledge is what really makes the difference: knowledge of Caravaggio, knowledge of period Italian painting, knowledge of the madrigal sheet music laid out before the young man, knowledge of his costume, perhaps knowledge of lute tuning, how a lute sounds, how a madrigal sounds. The skillful use of light and shadow, and how its use may have developed in certain guilds of the time speak their own sub-dialect. How can one effectively convey this to another? There is a depth and an *experience* here that must ultimately reside only with the connoisseur. The appreciation is built up over years, over thousands of minute notations and correlations. The subtleties must be focused on and nurtured. Others may read a description, but the painting will not live for them as it does for the cognoscente.

Astrology is not nearly so rarified, and yet the point is: to truly love something, whether it may be math, painting, or astrology, one has to *know* it, one has to have an *experience* of it. Love without knowledge is not love at all, but infatuation, a projected image, superficial and hollow. Love must get to know the hair, the smell, the short temper and snoring of math or astrology.

Try to describe something that you love to another who has no interest, and your enthusiasm will fall not so much on deaf ears, as on senses that simply haven't been trained to see. And to see, one must of course at minimum have an interest, a desire, to do so, again whether in math or astrology. Prejudice blocks this ability completely. If you "aren't good at math" or "don't like math," you will probably never see the jeweled kaleidoscope that they are talking about. If astrology is "superstitious bunk for the gullible," then you will never see that, either. Believing *is* seeing.

So when one says, "I can see this person's Scorpio Moon stifling their Leo Venus, but progressed Sun going into Libra is likely to open things up a bit," what is an outsider to think? It's as if someone just told us about differential equations, and we are supposed to therefore and somehow be in awe at their beauty. If one spends time getting involved in math (assuming a native interest), the beauty of the experience will come through, difficult though it may be to communicate to others. It is the same with astrology: it is rare for someone to really delve into astrology without noticing that maybe, just maybe, there might be something there. I *do* seem to fit the description of my Sun sign that I just read. Reading the sign next to it, I can see that they *are* different, not simply generic, and that I fit mine more than my neighbor's. Wow: can that be? Like math, the deeper one gets into astrology, the more it opens up: here, too, is the exquisite jewel; here, too, are the secrets to the universe. But there has to be interest. No interest will mean no experience and no perception or understanding of why someone could develop a fascination with the subject. Conveying the excitement of astrology to the mathematician may have the same success as the mathematician getting the astrologer fired up about calculus, although the points of commonality may be missed. Astrology uses math intensely; it is again nothing but math and archetypes. Math doesn't use astrology, but uses symmetries, correspondences, and cycles, which are of the realm where astrology dwells.

Outsiders (especially those not interested) often come at astrology from the wrong direction. They (often belligerently) ask to be shown "proof" that there is something there prior to investigation. Unfortunately, whatever astrology is, it hasn't shown an aptitude thus far for being particularly friendly with the clockwork, Newtonian, cause-and-effect, predictable and verifiable modes of investigation that others are looking for. It's coy; it's subtle. What the outsiders don't understand is that this *doesn't* mean that there's "nothing there." There's plenty there: a rich lode of amazing synchronistic and archetypal wisdom that goes back thousands of years, and is there to be experienced by anyone, if one were but to open their vision. It's there for the viewing; but then again, so is math, and many people turn away from that also. Affection for any subject requires interest, time, and knowledge; but, above all, it requires hands on experience of the subject. That is as true for sewing as it is for math or astrology.

So reality is what it is. It contains math, and astrology, and Caravaggio, and a million other things. The direct experience of something is the ideal. It is as close as we may stand to raw manifestation. Everything else is just description: mathematical, verbal, musical, visual, or other. The world is not math, nor is it astrology. Those are descriptors. Astrology is itself nothing but a language. It is a language describing the experience of "seeing" certain archetypal energies at work, and coordinated meaningfully in time at some deeper level than we are normally used to operating at. These energies may be experienced, defined, and delineated. Like other things in life, they sit in front of us, to be seen by some, and yet not by others. Such is the way things are.

Where the Heck Am I?

Where am I? Who am I? This book has been infused with the idea that All is One, part of a Whole, and that we are but drops of space/physics/Godhead/astrological archetypes in a sea of energy, whatever that energy may ultimately turn out to be. So how do we think about this on an everyday basis? How do we handle this in our daily lives of jobs, kids, society, broken cars needing fixing, tragedies across the ocean? How are we to digest this and make use of it? Where is the personal "I" in relation to the universal "One" in all of this?

There are several clues. Much can be learned from the Zen traditions, as epitomized by the saying "Before enlightenment: chop wood, carry water. After enlightenment: chop wood, carry water." Similar to this is another Zen sentiment: "At first, I saw mountains as mountains and rivers as rivers. Then, I saw that mountains were not mountains and rivers were not rivers. Finally, I see mountains again as mountains, and rivers again as rivers." The "Ten Ox-Herding Pictures" show this progression visually. But what realization has been attained?

The Hindu traditions have the concept of Lila, wherein the Godhead in its infinite manifestations has a sense of play, using our forms as well as others to engage in a sort of "hide and seek" with itself. (Thank you, Alan Watts.) Here we find enlightenment popping in and out of our personal consciousness like the bubbles on a pot of soup. Also, like the bubbles, the One appears in various momentary manifestations that appear unique, but are not. Are we the bubbles, or are we the soup?

F. Scott Fitzgerald said "The test of a first-rate intelligence is the ability to hold two opposing ideas in mind at the same time and still retain the ability to function." And so we must retain this dichotomy in our minds: we are unique, personal egos floating like bubbles in the Grand Soup, and at the same time, we are the Soup itself: our bubbles are continually appearing and disappearing, manifesting and ceasing to exist, and finally being absorbed back into the Soup. This is the same analogy as that of being foam on the ocean. It is entirely compatible with the connections shown by physics, which are missing only the spiritual component; but since everything *is* One, this is actually a moot point, as ultimately Lila and quarks all dissolve into the mysterious aggregate Soup, whatever that may be. All else is fragmentation, maya, categorizing, and duality.

So in our everyday lives, the best that we can do is to hold onto this dichotomy: we are expressions of the One, and yet we are frequently lost in our own personal thoughts and egos. Our consciousness is an oftentimes isolated backwater of the universal stream. Perhaps some rare sages in caves can spend most of their daily time in blissful awareness of the One, but the best that most of us can hope for is to retain some recognition of this as we chop wood and carry water. That in itself is enlightenment of a degree, and will manifest outwardly, if so experienced, as a changed perspective towards life around us, towards ourselves, and towards our relationships with the world--as well as with our fellow "soup bubbles" churning away together in the pot. Commonality and connection will appear, and the view around us will expand.

***

The Self and the ego:

The ego is a good servant, but a poor master. Placing too much importance on the ego is the equivalence of the *Lankavatara Sutra* analogy involving a finger pointing at the moon. Many mistakenly look at the finger pointing at the moon (teachings) instead of the moon itself (reality), and end up missing both. Similarly, the ego is a *function* of the Self, it is not the Self. The two are very often confused. If we are looking at the ego and mistaking it for the Self, we are destined to stay stuck in limited awareness. The self (as opposed to the larger and more connected Self), confused by the ego, is often subject to the illusion of separateness, the identity of the bubble in a pot of soup: it does not see that it is part of the Whole, does not see that it is not independent or detached. The beginning of "enlightenment" (which is partly about discovering the proper place and function of the ego) is the realization of this. The Self that is real is the Self that is connected to the Soup, and through the Soup, to other Selves, other co-bubbles. Separateness is illusion. The ego's function, as laid out by psychologists and spiritual teachers, is that of mediary: the ego mediates between the (illusory) separate self and the world around it, between the personal "I" and the larger and truer Self. The ego's job is to come to an understanding of this. If it gets stuck in worldly things, it remains confused. It comes from the Self, but unlike the Self, its tenure is temporary. It is a *functional* entity. This may be psychological, spiritual, or even physical for those so inclined. It veers away from functionality when it embraces division, selfishness, and grandiosity—the *dys*functions of the ego.

We are, after all, only tourists in this world: poor compositions of chemicals, molecules, and electrical bonds; psychological entities interacting with other psychological entities; tiny nodes of consciousness on the outskirts of the ocean, humbled and small before the Mind of God, before the physics of connection, before What Is. Our egos are not our true Selves, and those that confuse this issue are triply lost: lost to themselves, lost to others, and lost to the Whole. Piles of cash or power (or other ego salves) will never replace piles of understanding. "Happy is the man that findeth wisdom, and the man that getteth understanding." (Proverbs 3:13)

The ego may never be gotten rid of: it is part of us in this life, and it is necessary. But it must remain tamed, and must be made to understand its correct function. The ego is often called our sense of self. It is our choice as to whether it is our sense of self or our sense of Self. It is at its noblest when it functions, with humility, to tie our illusory and temporary selves to the larger That-Which-Is. The ego as mediary serves best when it draws us *towards* a feeling of connectedness and commonality with others and the larger world, never away. Then, we find our true Selves.

***

For those studying astrology, where might one find the ego? Is it somewhere in the chart that can be identified? In this context, we are often talking about the self, rather than the Self. One hears that the Sun is the basic overarching self, and that the Moon is the coloring of the personality, with the Ascendant being a filter through which we see and are seen. Some alternately consider the Rising Sign to be primary, and would say (for example) that a person is a "Libra with Sun in Pisces." Whatever the scheme, these three factors are always foremost, but there are a host of others that follow closely behind. Together, they *all* contribute to the ego, and to the self. The terms self, personality, and ego blur together, and are an interacting synthesis. Only the Self rises out of and above this stew. This search for the "self" will, in fact, quickly point up the limitations of seeing the chart as a group of separate elements vs. seeing it as a whole (which remains, for most people, a very difficult task, of course: the multiplicity of factors can be daunting).

In the study of the self as ego (on its way towards becoming Self), we can again turn to Joseph Campbell and the concept of the "Hero's Journey." This journey implies energy, movement, effort, and an upwards spiral through trials and difficulties towards a hard-won denouement. The steps may be smooth, or, for most people, lurching and discontinuous. It is not difficult to see the ring of 12 Houses as a parallel "Ego's Journey" towards Wholeness. An Odyssey, a Pilgrim's Progress. The Houses are conditions, temptations, and components that the ego must work through; the final stage of Wholeness being where the ego may finally find rest. Perhaps that journey is the very purpose of life, if there must be one.

One can imagine the ego starting out with the 1st House self: me, myself, and I. Here I am! In the very first House, things are infantile in consciousness: the self *is* the ego, the ego is the self. The ego here is innocent discovery, and eager to learn. The full awareness of others is simply lacking at this point. The more sophisticated or duplicitous forms of self-seeking are several houses away. The Self in its larger form is an entire circle away. Here the self and the ego are a package which has just come into being, with limited awareness, as a seemingly separate entity apart from the booming, buzzing world around it, and the people therein. The bubble has just risen up from the Soup. Duality reigns. We are early in the journey here, at birth in fact, and the true connections to others and to the larger pot are far in the distance. The discovery of the self, of the ego, is the theme here. It's fun to linger, but the world awaits. Leaving this house to continue its journey around the wheel, it is an enjoyable exercise to imagine the ego's progress as it "learns" the various archetypes, and their relationships to life. The ego finally finds, after completing the circumnavigation of the circle, a sense of internal wholeness, as well as an understanding of its relation to the larger Whole.

Astrological cookbooks will take us the rest of the way around the circle, through the complete circuit. The ego initially starts out, even prior to the journey, as one with the self and the Self, but crosses the Ascendant counter-clockwise in a primordial differentiation process that takes it initially in reverse from Oneness to duality. It will eventually return back again: this is one of the sacred oscillating cycles of the universe: Oneness to duality and back to Oneness again. Everything is energy, and nothing stays static. The wheel never stops turning. This is the play of Lila. The self and the ego slowly work their way around the circle, as in the Hero's journey: many are the experiences had, many are the lessons learned, many are the connections made, and many are the difficulties overcome. The complete panoply of human experiences will be made available to us, will be laid out before us, whether or not we take part in them. Our lives are often as rich as we let them be, and the inner is as important here as the outer. The journey for each particular person is not always an obvious one.

So the soul/self/ego/soup bubble treks the Hero's Journey around the zodiac, through the houses and experiences, and eventually arrives at Neptune's home, the 12th, the last in the cycle, the last house on the block. Ego and all illusory and dualistic boundaries dissolve here, and must be left at the door. They become meaningless and useless, and all again is divulged to be manifestations of the One. The ego has found respite from its travails. It is revealed here that the ego—that which we have clung to, placated, fought over, dominated others with, felt hurt by, and bathed in ermine—is now useless and unimportant. The only *real* task that it has had now seems puny; that of leading the self around the circle to be at rest here, to join its Self. The soup bubble now bursts and sinks back into the pot with its fellows: it is home.

***

Again, it would be nice if one could elucidate a particular point, or set of points, in the chart which constitute the self, but that does not seem to be the case. Is it the Sun, the Moon, the Rising Sign? Planets in the first house, planets in the 10th, aspects to the Sun or other particular planets? It seems to be more slippery than that. As for the ego, it is simply a *function*, an illusory entity bridging self to Self that only *seems* real, just as the separate self seems real. It *is* likely, however, that the Sun may be the most significant contributor to the self. That's why Sun signs "work." It is also likely that the Moon plays a role in being an important component of the ego, as one often thinks of the ego in its less useful forms as either gleefully imposing itself upon others, or being hurt and disappointed in interactions that don't go well (a "bruised ego"). Both are emotional reactions, the provenance of the Moon, and both of course are false alleys leading away from the true Self. The Moon reflects back from others and mediates the emotions; this may in dysfunctional cases be similar to the stereotype of an ego-centered person who is seen as shallow, and at the mercy of the opinions of others. The best Moons serve the self with an awareness of true connections. The authentic Self, which is not at the mercy of the ego, has no need or interest in feeling better than, or less than, others: it is calm and secure in its particular expression of the universal and inclusive. There are, in fact, no "others." Commonality and connection rule the day. We celebrate together. The self on its higher journey understands its particular node, its assigned dharma, and its connection with the Self.

Gimme That Ole Time Religion

"God is too big for one religion"—Bumper Sticker

"Faith and doubt are (both) needed, not as antagonists, but working side by side to take us around the unknown curve"—Lillian Smith

As of this writing, according to Pew research, the death of religion is vastly overrated, the Age of Aquarius notwithstanding. In fact, speculative projections show that the current population of the world, (7.2 billion as of 2015) is projected to grow to about 9.6 billion by the year 2050. (Yikes!) That number is projected to include 2.92 billion Christians, 2.76 billion Muslims, 1.38 billion Hindus, 1.23 billion "unaffiliated," and 4.9 million Buddhists. The "unaffiliated" group includes atheists, agnostics, and what are called the "spiritual but not religious" folks. This group looms larger in the educated West, with their numbers in the U.S. projected to increase from 16% to 26%, but will show declines in the rest of the world, along with Christianity, as Islam continues its march amongst the poorer and developing countries. This trend also shows that the rise of dualistic religions (mainly Christianity and Islam) will continue to gain, while non-dualistic groups (mainly Buddhists and Hindus) will either be completely flat (Buddhists), or show only very modest gains (Hindus).

So the question is: what role does religion play in people's lives? What function does it serve? Is it necessary, unnecessary, beneficial, benign, or harmful? Prior to answering those questions, let's try to take apart some of the straw men put forth by those who would get rid of religion, who feel that the world would be better without it. One idea advanced by those who don't like religion is that religion keeps people mired in ignorance and superstition. Karl Marx, for example, famously stated that "religion is the opium of the people."

There are many others in the scientific world and various secular sectors who would also venture an opinion that religion is one of the great curses upon the world. All of the evils throughout history, they maintain - ignorance, intolerance, and wars mainly - are directly traceable to mankind's historic associations with religion. Without religion, we would live in an enlightened world of peace and harmony. They simply can find no reason to think kindly of that portion of human culture.

However, independent of any religious affiliation, there will always be some people more questioning or curious than others, and some people more motivated to learn and stretch their minds. This is not a religious issue, but a human issue. In the year 0, or 1000, or 2000, there was always a smaller group of people exploring the world around them, and a much larger group not very interested in moving their understanding forward at all, but simply content to hang out at the well sharing gossip, or to lie on their sofas watching TV. That's OK, and it's not a judgement; it is simply the way things are, a bell curve type of thing, and is not likely to change anytime soon. As to whether various "religious leaders" sometimes exploit this fact, it's probably true. Religion only requires passive belief rather than active investigation, after all. But the root problem here doesn't seem to be religion at all, but human nature.

On April 22, 2015 a grim anniversary was celebrated: the 100th anniversary of the use of chemical warfare by humans. Chlorine gas was first opened and allowed to drift with the wind across Flanders Field in Belgium on that date in 1915, holding low to the ground like an evil cloud, engulfing the unsuspecting French troops dug into their trenches. Few survived. My own grandfather was gassed in WWI, and died early of lung complications. Ultimately, over one million were gassed on both sides; 90,000 died directly, and many more had complications and premature mortalities. There was no religious flag anywhere to be seen.

That was not the only secular threat to mankind's peace and harmony. One may consider, a couple of short decades later, Hitler's attempted extermination of the Jews. Hitler was not religious and this was not any sort of religious pogrom. It was cultural. He just didn't like something about them, about their ethnic group or culture. Perhaps he felt threatened by them; they violated his delusional aspirations for a master Aryan race. In addition to Hitler's side project to eliminate the Jews, we might consider his general aspirations and attempts to take over Europe (and possibly the world). We might consider Napoleon's conquests, or Britain's relentless and often ruthless drive to form an empire, or the decimation of natives in America and Australia as the "new" continents were "discovered" and conquered. The crosses that were carried by the priests that he dragged along with him for justification likely meant little to Cortez as he slashed his way through both jungle and inhabitants in his search for gold.

One may consider Mao Tse Tung or Stalin as they attempted to move their countries towards societies that would be too advanced for superstitious religious thought. Mao, using the most conservative estimates, killed about 45 million people in 4 years; Stalin clocks in at 23 million. Eradicating religion was a core part of their plans. More contemporarily, we have Kim Jong-un in North Korea, purging his uncle and other family members by machine gun simply because of their ties to his dad. He has stated that he wants to be "his own person."

One may consider Alexander's conquest of most of the known world in his time. The Greeks were renowned for their enlightened thought at the time, but their society was not free of religion, although Alexander's conquests were. Of course, both Ancient Greece and Rome were enabled to live their elevated lifestyles and think deep thoughts partly in debt to slavery, something frowned upon today. And speaking of Rome, and conquest... And speaking of the New World and slaves...

The truth is, the vast majority of human deaths that were caused by other humans throughout history have had nothing to do with religion; most of the ones which ostensibly have, such as those caused by Islami radicals, or during the Christian Crusades, have turned out to be not so much religious as political, or simply power grabs. Religion has often been the smoke screen put out to legitimize bad behavior. The participants in these cases will be found upon examination to be violating the principles of the very religions that they ostensibly adhere to. The problem isn't religion; the problem, it turns out, is people. And specifically, human nature, genetics.

***

Moving into whether religion makes people "intolerant," we stub our toe again on the same problem, namely that annoying human nature. We can hold up the Christian Crusades or the Inquisition, or the Islamic beheadings as examples of intolerance, but what's behind those, besides thinly veiled grabs for power and territory? Studies with monkeys show that they have great intolerance towards "outsiders" entering their groups, with violent opposition used in attempting to drive off anyone perceived as being foreign. The apple is not falling far from the tree here. After WWII, U.S. relations with Germany improved at a much more rapid pace than those with Japan; within a few short years we were buying Volkswagens and celebrating Oktoberfests, My dad, however, who was in the Pacific in WWII, wouldn't go near a sushi restaurant until he was about 70 years old. The difference? The Germans looked like us; the Japanese didn't (as a gross generalization). He himself never put it that way; it was coming from a place far too deep and instinctual. There's some good, although controversial, science on this one: human nature, completely distinct from any religious layer added on top, is partially programmed to be intolerant; the rest is completed by culture, an additional human-nature based factor. Religion often simply gives us an excuse for the behavior that we would be exhibiting anyway. We are social animals. We follow our pack, and look askance at those who might smell differently. (Watch scientists going after New Agers; watch Richard Dawkins or Christopher Hitchens going after anyone who attempts to find greater meaning in the universe.) To overcome this, we must work at it. It's obviously a worthwhile endeavor, and both people and animals may, with effort, overcome a natural mistrust of each other to forge new bonds and accords. It happens every day.

It's also very important to make the point that religions themselves are by and large cultural: you believe in the same God as your mother, father, friends, and neighbors. It doesn't mean that spirituality isn't a real force in the universe; it simply means that if you are in the Bible Belt of the U.S., you simply *know* that Jesus will be your savior, and if you are in Calcutta, you *know* that Shiva or Krishna expresses the fullness of God as much as human understanding may grasp. So the problem is not just human nature, but human culture, which in turn expresses human nature. And around we go. It's already been pointed out that subcultures bragging of no ties to religion can be as intolerant as any religious person may ever be, if not more so. These aren't issues that are often deeply discussed; at most times, we tend to coast above all of this brain-tiring examination by simply falling back on autopilot and mindless blame, yet another favorite tactic of human nature.

So those darn humans seem to have a rather nasty streak at times; videos of some of our genetic cousins, chimp societies, again show disturbing parallels. Chimps frequently hunt down and kill "outsiders" encroaching on their tribe's territory. In fact, it would likely be not too far off base to state simply that the portion of "human nature" that we are really talking about here basically boils down to testosterone. Chimp wars cut to the chase. In these wars, chimps are likely not trying to prove to each other that their beliefs are correct; they are simple and instinctual expressions of the desire for dominance and territory so that their genes may be passed on, and Darwinian procreation ensured. The chimps don't know that. Humans don't know that, either: because they fancy themselves as being more advanced, they normally have to invent some quasi-logical "reason" for their misadventures. Of note here is that, not excusing the abhorrence of the practice, the Italian Castrati of years gone by rarely started wars.

***

What role then *does* religion play in societies? It would perhaps be nice (per some) if societies were run by enlightened scientists who went strictly by evidence-based research. But really, what are the chances of that actually happening in the real world? (And how would you prevent one scientist from arguing with another that *his* research was superior, and should therefore be the guiding force?) What are the chances that the average person is going to move away from the water cooler, TV remote, or funny videos on social media to sign on to this more enlightened view of the world? Politics is emotional. Anyone who has watched the process closely knows that it's not built on logic, or at least not entirely. Perhaps there will be some progress in this regard, but the chances of whole societies moving into this Spockian realm, realistically, are minimal. People by nature aren't that rational, and in fact, don't want to be.

So if religion *hasn't* in fact caused all of the nastiness in human history, and we may better chalk it up to human nature, then what might be religion's more genuine role in various human cultures across time? One might make an argument that religions fulfill two important functions in society, and in human history. First, they likely serve to actually *prevent* even worse intolerance and bad behavior in those same nasty humans by at least *offering* a series of moral principles and aspirations to guide one's life by; the fact that *people* often fall short need not be a criticism of the religions themselves, but may more properly be placed upon the individuals. (This becomes obvious when we unsentimentally examine human nature stripped of religion, and again consider Hitler, Mao, Stalin, and the whole rest of the gang: it's a very long list. Those humans seem to need all the help they can get to keep themselves in line.) And while a strictly reason-based scientific approach with exemplary and well-researched principles might seem to suffice, at least as an ideal, there is a second function of religion that is important for most people who *do* consider themselves religious.

Religions, besides providing a moral code, also provide not only a sense of community, but an existing structure and accessible way to answer the call of the numinous or the spiritual for many people. Astrology is not the only model that has considered humans as mental, emotional, physical, and spiritual beings. Your doctor most likely learned that exact same idea in medical school: the march towards holism continues, albeit slowly. Most people do seem prone to accenting one or more of these characteristics over the others, so it is not surprising that certain people are more drawn to the spiritual realm than others may be. Some people seem to be naturally more emotional, or more practical, or more cerebral than other people, and some seem more in synch with the metaphysical. We are all nonetheless constructed of all four. There is no "right" mix here: the mix that each of us has is the correct one *for us*. But knowledge and acceptance of the others can lead to a greater tolerance and understanding, which is always a good thing.

The Pew studies noted at the beginning of this section may or may not turn out to be correct. A telling moment may be the transition of Pluto from Capricorn into Aquarius in 2023. Pluto in Sagittarius (1995-2008) seemed to coincide with the rise of certain ideological and extremist religious groups, ones who would (while using cell phones and the internet to do so) take us back to a medieval version of their religion. This was during the period in the U.S. when the 9/11 attacks on the World Trade Center occurred, and showed the willingness of these groups (using religion to cloak and excuse their anarchic destruction) to use terrorism as a way to force their beliefs on others or to achieve political aims. The transition of Pluto into Capricorn in 2008 coincided not only with the near collapse of Wall Street and the rise of the plutocratic "one percent" in the U.S., but also with the more obvious, organized, and energetic drive for power of these same groups. Will Pluto in Aquarius be their last gasp? *Are* these groups just the most extreme example of a clinging to the old and fading Piscean religious order while the "secular humanism" of the Aquarian age continues to gain ground? Stay tuned; it will be interesting to find out. And regardless of the outcome of their aspirations, these more modern groups still pale in comparison to the secular bad guys of history noted above. And of course, there is ultimately nothing religious about their behaviors: once again, we see the smoke screen being used.

As we do move further into the Aquarian Age, however, it will be a shame if religion or spirituality takes as much of a back seat to humanism as self-discovery (Aries) did to religion in the peak of the Piscean Age, Europe's Dark Ages. Too much of anything is not healthy, and leaves the cosmos unbalanced. The lesson for humanity is to see the larger picture; to understand that these shifts of the Great Ages, although long, are simply massive expressions of the same astrological principles that continually cycle in our day-to-day lives. As in all of life, we need to remember that the parts are only that: parts. Only together do they make up the whole.

The spiritual instinct is large, and ultimately universal. It, too, is part of human nature. It is the drive for transcendence, wholeness, and meaning. We are all familiar with the more common religious expressions of spirituality. But spirituality may also include scientists or atheists who find the metaphysical in the universe itself with its amazing manifestations and laws, in simple human altruism, or in other more idiosyncratic ways. But to try and strip the spiritual away from humans is like trying to strip away the mental, the physical, or the emotional. Trying to "get rid" of a particular component leaves us with a hollow spot, lopsided. Finding satisfaction and completeness in life, in fact, ultimately has a lot to do with the correct proportioning and integration of these four components into our journeys. There are, fortunately, many roads to spirituality, and if one is interested, there will be an appropriate path waiting for them. On balance, finally, it would seem that religion and spirituality, of whatever variety, have more likely been a positive force in human history than a negative one. Religion is not the problem: human nature has been the problem. And what are we doing about *that*?

Spokes in a Wheel that's Turning

Not many people would peg Mardi Gras in New Orleans as being a particularly spiritual holiday, even though its date is determined by the Catholic Church, through being tied to the Christian Lenten season. Mardi Gras in French translates as "Fat Tuesday," and it is always the day before Ash Wednesday, the beginning of Lent. Traditionally, however, it ends up being more of a season than a day; for the folks in New Orleans, a single day seems just a bit too miserly for a party. It's alternate name is Carnival, which comes from the Latin *carne vale*, meaning "farewell to meat," or "farewell to the flesh." A daunting prospect indeed in the land of eat, drink, and be merry.

The interesting thing is how similar from a distance Mardi Gras seems to many Indian Hindu festivals, especially that of Holi, the Festival of Colors. Viewing a long shot of the crowds of both, one can barely tell them apart. Color, laughter, packed humanity, floats, and revelry tie them together. They both evolved from primitive celebrations of spring, and they both take place at that time of year. Both feature people letting loose and "getting out of themselves" for a day; either through costumes, or through throwing colored powders on each other. In letting people get away from their normal personas, both festivals celebrate the communal, the coming together in distraction and diversion to blend with and reflect off of each other, to merge with the crowd. The parts become a whole.

Both feature the bending of consciousness: the color, noise, and jostling is enough in itself to knock one out of their normal frames of reference, but there is additional assistance. Mardi Gras is famous for its drinking, and Holi, while also tolerating drinking, is better known for the use of bhang, or cannabis, in various forms. Interestingly, while etymological dictionaries do not list any cross influence between the Indian word Holi and the Western word Holy, it seems amazingly synchronistic that they should describe concepts related to the spiritual in cultures so widely scattered. Mardi Gras, of course (at least in Louisiana), is listed as a "holiday."

We have talked in this book about the ego, and the transformation or overcoming of the ego. Let's look at these holidays, and especially at Mardi Gras. For many, the idea of spirituality is aligned with visions of quiet, solitary, and peaceful thought and meditation, or prayer; the idea of raucous celebrations would seem to be the furthest thing from spiritual. And yet, both of these experiences have to do with the overcoming of the personal self. How can we reconcile the diverging notions of the monk's cave and the festival's chaos? One clue is this: if we ask ourselves what class of zodiac signs would be most likely to be aligned with these festivals, what would spring to mind? Most likely the fire signs: Aries, Leo, and Sagittarius. Energy, color, and movement. And as astrologers, we learn that the fire signs are associated not only with energy, but with spirit.

In the East, the austerity of most branches of Buddhism contrasts with the sometimes flamboyance of Hinduism. In the West, the austerity of Islam or Judaism contrasts with the more colorful and ostentatious (at times) Catholic Church. (We are exaggerating these for stereotypical effect.) They are all expressions of spirituality. They have in common the challenging attempt to minimize the personal ego and find something higher. Curiously, alcohol, the dissolver of the self at Mardi Gras, is also sometimes casually known as "spirits." Both crowds and alcohol at times allow us to move outside of our egos, to attempt to join a greater collective, a greater One than ourselves. The long-term effectiveness is rather shaky in the case of alcohol, of course. But tribes and groups of humans throughout history have, in fact, frequently used chemicals of one sort or another to try and reach larger and less personal states of consciousness.

Jung, in his studies of cultures and archetypes, touched upon the spiritual many times. In treating alcoholics in his practice, his advice was for them to try and find a "conversion experience," a way to completely move into a transformation of the personality, using spirituality to achieve this. Here, he was probably thinking of, and possibly acquainted with, people who had undergone just such experiences of one sort or another with successful results. William James had written of these experiences also, years earlier. Jung's formula was "Spiritum contra Spiritus"; the use of a truer spirituality to overcome the false, limited, and addictive spirituality of alcohol. He saw the connection clearly between spirituality and alcohol, as well as its connection with other mystical or magical substances. All fall under the realm of Neptune and the 12th House.

The loss of self in a crowd, the changing of consciousness, *does* allow us to take part in something greater than ourselves. It "points us in the right direction" so to speak, although there are obviously limitations to this approach. One fascinating thing in regards to Mardi Gras and the ego is this: the casual observer might think that all of the people wearing their elaborate, expensive, and time-consuming costumes might be full of ego, enjoying the ultimate celebration of the personal self. Quite the opposite is actually true, however. There is no doubt that the wearer has a true and humble pride when their costume is recognized by others. But that is not the intent: the purpose in the wearing of costumes is actually to entertain *others*, to lose the self in communal celebration. This is a difficult concept for some to grasp that haven't actually been down in the streets on Mardi Gras day. By doing their best to come up with a costume that will add to the enjoyment of the day for all (and frequently of a nature satirical to themselves or others), they are saying "we're all in this together to celebrate the spirit of humanity, and the God-given gift to have fun and relish life." The Saturn of the workaday world has its limits: today is for Jupiter. My costume, in pleasing you, has achieved its aim: it is the collective that matters. Joie de vivre is the real King for the day, reigning over all. Those caught up in Holi would voice similar sentiments. Jupiter (Jove) was the primary Roman god until Christianity took over; again we see the Saturn (Christian Original Sin and penance, Hindu karma) versus Jupiter duality play out on culture's stage.

***

This book is primarily written from a 12th House perspective. We live and share what we know, we follow and express our dharma. But there is so much more to life than whatever circumscribed corner of the archetypes it is that we presently occupy. Our own positions and experiences are by definition limited, and usually quite a bit more so than we are willing to admit. The twelve houses or signs in their visual display form a wheel: wheels imply movement and wholeness, each part depending on the other parts for strength and completeness. There is no segment of a wheel that is "better," or more important, than the other parts. Furthermore, the spare appearance of the astrological circle contains only the barest hint of the abundance that is to be found hidden within its thin spokes and odd glyphs. The astrological wheel is one of infinite variety and inclusiveness:

Babies, old folks, rich folks, poor folks, wise folks, dim folks, love, hate, jealousy, kindness, empathy, and humor are all there. Holi, Mardi Gras, circuses, monasteries, nurseries, skateboarding, sewing machines, academic awards, palaces, caves in the hills, actors and actresses, thieves, therapists, businessmen, scholars, gravediggers, kings and queens, doctors, lawyers, Indian chiefs, travelers and nannies all figure heavily. Walt Whitman is there: "I contain multitudes." The incense and dark cubby of the monk are there, alongside the ecstasy and color of the reveler. Introverts, extroverts, ambiverts, the skeptical, the gullible, the caring, and the self-centered are all found. Those who fear God, and those who celebrate physics. Those who hate materialism are caught buying the latest consumer gadget. Those who love materialism are caught up in karmic undertows or synchronistic experiences that point to that position's futility. All march together, all are spokes of the wheel.

None is better than the other. All make up the Whole. In this book, we talk about the dissolution or illusion of the physical, and the meaning, consciousness, or spirit that may lie beyond, or beneath: provinces of the 12th house. But this corner of life is no more important than the secretary or the servant, the titan of business or the committee member. 1,2,3,4,5, and all the rest play their assigned roles. All are spokes that must support the wheel, and all must join together in this with each other. The mystic points at one portion of the circle, the accountant at another. Stepping back, we can see the whole.

Astrology is beautiful in its structure and manifestations, and in its implications. It is the most accessible and brightest glittering jewel of metaphysics. It incorporates all, it contains all. It is a tesseract, a crystalline structure looking into other dimensions. Regarding in wonder the completeness of the circle is exquisite and dazzling; seeing our part of the circle and how it supports the others is even more amazing. Understanding and *accepting* the other spokes of the wheel, and how we all fit together, is wisdom.

Shhh...

"I have noticed that a man is usually about as happy as he has made up his mind to be."

This quote is traditionally attributed to Abraham Lincoln, but the sourcing for this is dubious. Lincoln was of a melancholy disposition (he had Moon in Capricorn), and his wife was clinically depressed, so this rather upbeat take on things seems a bit incongruous. He was certainly more Saturnian than Jupiterian. That doesn't take away from the fact that, barring a biochemical depression (which is unfortunately fairly common), it remains true for most people in most situations. It speaks to the interaction between mind and emotions, a specialty of Cognitive Behavioral Therapy. CBT has, like "mindfulness," mined some ancient Buddhist teachings, in conjunction with such diverse figures as Epictetus and Albert Ellis, to show the close connections between our thinking, our emotions, and the general tenor of our lives: how things "show up" for us. The common view for many people is that we drift through life at the mercy of our emotions, and that our emotions then drag our thoughts along with them to their angry, fearful, or depressed corner of the world. However, the above historical figures have demonstrated that the reverse is actually true, and that we can "train" our thoughts to take primacy over our emotions, so that we are not at their whim, beck, and call. By choosing our thoughts, or the way that we think about things, we can have control over our emotions, and thereby manifest a different life.

***

The problem with many "New Age" or motivational books and speakers is not so much that they're wrong; it's typically more common that they are incomplete, or half-true, or oversimplified, or over-sold. A half-pound of truth is wrapped in a pound of miracle packaging. In 2006, Australian Rhonda Byrne ignited a global phenomenon with her book (and DVD) *The Secret*. Let's make it clear up front that the book IS worth reading (or the DVD worth watching), as many people have not previously been exposed to these techniques or lines of thinking. It contains important concepts, but it must also be taken with a certain grain of salt, as the saying goes. Its main premise is second cousin to the CBT idea mentioned above, which, for those who have not been let in on *that* particular "secret," is an equally awakening revelation. *The Secret* sits as the latest in a long history of "positive thinking" books. Byrne herself has credited Charles Haanel's 1912 book *The Master Key System*, which was preceded by Wallace Wattles' 1910 *The Science of Getting Rich*. Apparently, the early 20th century, with its immigration, robber barons, and self-made men, was fertile ground for these sorts of books. Later, we had Napoleon Hill's *Think and Grow Rich*, and Dr. Norman Vincent Peale's *The Power of Positive Thinking*. In between these groups, and focusing less on the financial, and more on the general New Thought movement (which itself owed a large debt to Hinduism, mixed with American practicality and can-do spirit), was Ernest Holmes' *The Science of Mind*, which provided a more non-denominational spiritual slant to many of these concepts. It appeared in 1926, and still has a devoted following. Going further back, we have such "secret societies" as the Rosicrucians (which also figure prominently in astrological history) and others, drawing from history in a fashion similar to the paragraph on CBT above.

Byrne's ideas carry on much of this lineage. Again, a key difference is in the emphasis on more contemporary packaging and marketing. She also mixes in some more modern concepts (some of which will already be familiar to readers of this book), but shies away from anything other than somewhat superficial sound bites. This isn't a necessarily a criticism, as more in-depth examinations simply wouldn't be in keeping with the general audience target of the book.

But it can gloss over some important things. For example, she states that "Quantum physicists tell us that the entire universe emerged from thought." Well, *some* quantum physicists may say that, but as made clear earlier, that is far from the mainstream interpretation. It is, in fact, an exciting *non*-mainstream interpretation; but that clarification doesn't lend itself easily to a sound bite. It is actually mystics or Hindu holy men who are more likely to be saying that. Interestingly, Sandra Anne Taylor published a book titled *Quantum Success: The Astounding Science of Wealth and Happiness* in the same year as *The Secret*, and containing basically the same ideas; but it didn't seem to catch the media frenzy that Byrne's book did. Other authors, including Esther Hicks, have also trod the same path; to her credit, Byrne doesn't minimize her lineage. All of these books (with the exception of Ernest Holmes) concentrate on the Big Four: wealth, relationships, health, and weight loss. Most (including *The Secret*) lean heavily towards the manifesting wealth end of the spectrum. It certainly worked for Byrne: she listed her home in Montecito, California for sale in 2014 at $23.5 million. In keeping with this theme, she also mentions in her book the series *Millionaires of the Bible* by Catharine Ponder, where "you will discover that Abraham, Isaac, Jacob, Joseph, Moses, and Jesus were not only prosperity teachers, but also millionaires themselves, with more affluent lifestyles than many present-day millionaires could conceive of." Really?

But again, this is just quibbling about the packaging of the message, and we don't want to throw out the baby with the bathwater. The message itself, the "law of attraction," has a lot going for it. It *does* seem to be one of the universal truths, and is also kin to "believing is seeing." All of these sorts of concepts are built on the idea that we *do* construct the reality around us from our own minds, and that, to a large extent, we get to choose the reality that we are constructing. We've all known "sad sacks" who seem to wrest poor-me woe from the most ordinary of situations, and on the flip side, those who remain remarkably stoic, upbeat, philosophical, and optimistic in the face of surprisingly difficult circumstances. Perhaps, as the non-Lincoln quote above states, happiness really *is* a choice: perhaps mental attitude *is* incredibly important.

We are really talking about creating two different realities here: the physical and the psychological. The physical is up for grabs: perhaps we create our physical reality, perhaps we don't. Perhaps we partially do, or do so under certain conditions, or do so in certain ways. It seems certainly possible from a hundred years of discussion in modern physics that consciousness has *some* interaction of *some* sort with the physical world, but that is not yet finalized. What *is* guaranteed is that, psychologically, we assuredly *do* create our reality in endless and myriad ways. Again, this is similar to the "believing is seeing" riff that has appeared here several times. There is a tight cluster of related concepts: CBT, the law of attraction, believing is seeing. If we are angry people, amazingly, we will continually find ourselves in angry situations. If we are peaceful and loving people, then those sorts will find their way to us. If we hold success in our minds, we are more likely to find achievement than if we hold the feeling of failure in our minds. To a large extent, we *do* attract to us what we are holding in our minds; so we *do* need to be careful as to what that is. Thus, ultimately, there *is* likely some mysterious connection between the psychological and the physical.

But there are limits, and this is not foolproof. Byrne talks about there being no exceptions to the immutable law that "your current reality or your current life is a result of the thoughts that you have been thinking." In an online essay titled "The Immorality of the *The Secret*," Massimo Pigliucci questions whether the problem with the six million Jews gassed in Nazi Germany was that they just weren't thinking positively enough to manifest another outcome. The implication of *The Secret* is that if we completely create our own reality, then we are completely responsible for it, and if it is an unfortunate reality, then it is our fault for not trying hard enough. The Puritan work ethic meets the New Age. If someone is rich, or "saved," it is simply evidence that they are God's chosen person, or that they are working the law of attraction much better than we are. Bummer. I was trying so hard. Or perhaps we haven't manifested enough Jupiter in our natal charts. And what of all those folks who have biochemical imbalances: depression, bipolar, others? All of this does not negate the law of attraction, but it qualifies it, and requires philosophical discussion. In addition, the universe is larger than us, and it's always possible that what we want is not what the universe wants for us.

So we *do* create our reality, but we do not do so alone. That is solipsism. We create our reality in conjunction with other consciousnesses also creating their own realities. The world is a stew of overlapping and interacting consciousnesses, of which we are but a participatory node. The overall effect on the larger reality is synergistic, and we do not know the weighting, or the reason for the weighting. Why was Hitler's consciousness at the time creating more of reality than that of the Jews? The same question arises in astrology: did all of the Jews have death in their horoscopes at that moment? Then why did Hitler's horoscope overrule theirs? This need not be evidence that astrology or the law of attraction doesn't work. That's simplistic, either/or thinking. It *is* evidence that we have a long way to go towards understanding these things in general: bad news for those who want overly simplified, black and white explanations or justifications for things, pro or con. That's the way it's always been, and the way it always will be. The world is far more nuanced than our favorite blogs or pontificators would suggest. Byrne doesn't give her date of birth, but perhaps her horoscope is one that shows a propensity for wealth. That would add a new wrinkle to the breezy personal will manifestation vs. dharmic potentiality aspect of the law of attraction. The universe is an unbroken fabric, but we are only able to see a small portion of the pattern.

In addition to these issues involving the law of attraction, there are others. If we are talking about large and universal spiritual laws (which this would seem to take part in), then how does this particular law do when it interacts with the quests and desires of personal egos? Byrne states that "We are all connected, and we are all One." That would seem to argue for a humble awareness and appreciation of the commonality of humans, and yet most of these books seem aimed at people wanting to satisfy their separate and self-serving personal egos, mainly through the acquisition of wealth. All over the world, there are people concentrating on a vacant spot in their driveway and trying to manifest a BMW there. Unsurprisingly, most are disappointed, leading to a disillusionment that the law of attraction doesn't work. It *does* work; it's just that in this realm, as in other realms, life is a bit more mysterious and cryptic than we are able to decipher.

Byrne states that "It is impossible to feel bad and at the same time have good thoughts." Alternate metaphysical traditions state this as "it's impossible to be grateful and miserable at the same time." These two phrases seem very similar, and yet there is a subtle difference. Gratitude has a spiritual component to it; "good thoughts" may easily be interpreted by readers of *The Secret* as Positive Thoughts, which may turn into "I really, really, really, *really* want and deserve that BMW!", which is obviously a bit less spiritual. Byrne does recommend gratitude, but tellingly, not so much as a spiritual exercise in itself, but as just another technique to get what one wants.

***

Since the law of attraction ultimately *is* a spiritual or metaphysical law, in that it connects us to realities outside ourselves and to larger truths about the world, there is a paradox here: the more spiritual that we are, the more connected to the One spoken of by Byrne, the deeper our understanding and experience will be regarding the law of attraction. But at the same time, the more spiritual that we are, and the closer that we are to the Whole, the more likely it is that we will also move towards humility and concern for others, and the less likely we are to be found trying to manifest money for a BMW.

But that's perhaps overly deep. For most of us, in most situations, it IS true that what we keep in our consciousness, or even in our unconscious, attracts mirrored reflections back to us. As we sow, so shall we reap. That's karma, and that's attraction. What we hold in our minds determines the people and events that appear in our lives. Byrne correctly points out that even negative thoughts attract their energy towards us, and so we must be careful and aware of what exactly we *are* holding onto, and the energy that we are putting out into the world. Generosity comes back to us, as does the reverse. Fear, suspicion, mistrust, anger, and discouragement have their results, as do faith, trust and goodwill. Battles for control attract more confrontations, and lead to further battles for control; acceptance and understanding attract serenity, but don't negate the need for limits and boundaries. Love will attract love; if it doesn't seem to be, then we are simply not understanding something properly. What we are calling love likely has a missing component; it is missing some understanding of the other person, and what they actually need. Or we may be expecting romantic love when the universe is offering something else. It is not in our own projections, desires, or wishful thinking that we show love, but through answering another's' needs. Then love can attract love. We may claim that we don't like strife or drama, but if these are continually showing up in our lives, then that requires a bit of soul-searching. Karma, believing is seeing, trust, faith, and love: all of the laws of the universe converge here.

Like attracts like; resonance induces sympathetic response. Who we are, and what we put energy into, is what shows up in our lives; this is often more easily perceived by those around us than by ourselves. Feedback from others is always valuable. But we *can* adjust our courses: *Change Your Thoughts—Change Your Life*, as the Dr. Wayne Dyer book title states. Other people we find in our lives, and situations surrounding us, are merely reflections of who we ourselves are, and of our own energies. Finally, Byrne also correctly brings up the action component of attraction, although in her book this often gets lost in the overwhelming stress on visualization. Pure visualization seems easier. Intention without action, however, is often toothless. Faith without works is dead. The law of attraction is magnetic, but we must work the magnet.

> "Once you make a decision, the universe conspires
> to make it happen."—Ralph Waldo Emerson

"The law of attraction is this: you don't attract what you want. You attract what you are."—Dr. Wayne Dyer

"A grateful mind is a great mind, which eventually attracts to itself great things."—Plato

"Right now you are looking at the results of your past creations. And right now how you feel is creating your future."—Odille Rault

"Everything begins on a mental level before it manifests in physical results."—Anonymous

"Whatever you hold in your mind on a consistent basis is exactly what you will experience in your life."—Anthony Robbins

"Your thoughts are the architects of your destiny."—David O. McKay

"Your perception of me is a reflection of you. My reaction to you is an awareness of me."—Coach Bobbi

"We become what we think about. Energy flows where attention goes."—Rhonda Byrne

"Start telling the universe what you want instead of what you don't want."
(good or bad thoughts are both magnets: they attract that energy into our lives)
—Anonymous

"Whether you think you can, or think you can't... you're right."—Henry Ford

"A man is but the product of his thoughts. What he thinks, he becomes."—Gandhi

"Our thoughts are most important. All that we are is the result of what we have thought."—The Buddha

Who Can Know the Mind of God?

> "I distrust those people who know so well what God wants them to do, because I notice it always coincides with their own desires."—Susan B. Anthony

Humans are frail and fallible in the face of the unknown, the ultimate, the moving energy of the universe. We are always looking for the reason, the meaning, the explanation, the ways in which the seas might heave during the voyages of our flimsy and fleeting little boats. That explains science, as well as astrology and religion. We have progressed in every field due simply to the depth of our inquisitiveness, our fear at times (should we be honest), and our desire to Know; and yet we lie awake at night, worry stealing our peace.

But with all of our knowledge and strivings for certainty, who among us can really know the Mind of God, whatever we might conceive of God to be: bearded old man, or secular physics energy? Who can ascertain which way the wind will blow, which way the cards might fall this hand? The word *divination* itself comes from the word *divine*. Many people long, more than anything, to know the Mind of the Divine: life seems so capricious and fickle—it is often disheartening. We think that God, or life, will feint left; and yet it veers right, again. What should we do? Who can we turn to? Who can track or understand the Seers of the Olmec, of CERN, of Babylon; the Oracles of Delphi, Didyma, Delos? Who can follow the prophets of the Old Testament, the prophets of the New? What of Nostradamus, Cassandra, Cayce? Who can second-guess before the fact the diviners of the horoscope, the I Ching, the cards, the calculations? Hindsight will be 20/20, and will arrive soon enough.

Who is privy to the seemingly arbitrary and erratic Mind of God, or of Fate?

For the atheist, the world moves along in its own way, at its own speed. It may be partially understandable and partially predictable in accordance with our current scientific abilities, but much remains in the hands of chance, or simply the not-yet-known. For the believer, the world moves in accordance with God's will; we as humans are left with haphazard and quirky navigational efforts entailing the use of prayer, hope, desperation, and pleading. But this leaves much left unexplained, and unsatisfying. Yahweh, Allah, Jesus, Shiva, Krishna, Apollo, Jupiter, Imhotep, Marduk, Quetzalcoatl, Obatala, Woden, Zeus, and a thousand more may all be called upon; *which one has the power?* Our choices, in the majority of cases, seem determined by our ethnography. Why are things not moving along in accordance with the way that we had envisioned? Are we doing something incorrectly? Perhaps we are calling upon the wrong God or gods, or in the wrong way. How are we to know? Our culture (university laboratory, or worn Baptist pew) determines our God. But how do we know that we are on the right track?

The world *does* move. And it moves the same whether it is God's will, astrology, or physics. Things are the way they are, they manifest continually, and in ways that we are not fully privy to. Quantum Laws = God's Inscrutable Ways = astrological cycles. Fate = Free Will. The best that we can do is to try and move *with* things, with the Tao. The point here to stress is that *things move the way that they move*, regardless of our choices or pleadings, which may or may not have an effect. We can never know if our pleadings have actually changed things, or if things were going to be that way anyway. We can never know the Mind of God. To understand the Mind of God is to figure out the flow of the river; to follow the Will of God is to move downstream. Effortlessness is the expression of being in harmony with God's will, with the transits, with the universe, with the Flow. We instinctively and oftentimes know when we are in conformity with where we're supposed to be; we just as frequently don't want to accept that particular outcome or set of circumstances, and so begins the pleading. The problem then is not God's will or the divination of that; the problem is us.

Ultimately, there can be only one Reality, and we conform to *it*, it does not conform to us. It doesn't so much matter if we're Christian, Muslim, Jewish, atheist, Buddhist, Hindu, "spiritual but not religious," or other. All are ultimately One. Everything is an expression of the One. Things seem separate only because we are living one dimension below the vision that we need. Everything is connected: God, the universe, the Way Things Are. The Mind of God *is* the Flow, *is* fate, *is* karma, *is* the Tao, *is* quantum physics, *is* what *is*. They are all identical, being simply different ways of saying the same thing. We *are* co-creators, through our consciousness, but our parts are small. The drop in the ocean is part of the ocean, but is not a large part. Humility and acceptance are the beginnings of wisdom. The world is a larger mystery than we will ever solve.

The very first lines of the Tao Te Ching begin:

> The Tao that can be spoken of is not the enduring and unchanging Tao.
>
> The name that can be named is not the enduring and unchanging name.

We are the Mind of God, we are the universe expressing itself. "That art thou."

> "The eye with which I see God is the same eye with which God sees me." —Meister Eckhart

Om Namah Shivaya.

Rules for Being Human

When I was younger and kicking around from apartment to apartment in the 1980's, someone passed on to me a yellowed, typewritten sheet that had obviously been copied more than a few times; this was evidently a later generation. On it was the headline: "Notes Found on a Refrigerator Door." Below this was the odd subtitle, "Rules For Being Human." It seemed wonderful, like some transmitted, secret knowledge. Where had it originated from? Who had written it? I posted it on my own refrigerator using a black and white magnet that showed a jazz trumpeter in full swing.

Thanks to the internet, we can all know now that the originator of this cryptic set of rules was Chérie Carter-Scott, who, besides being quoted anonymously (in error) in Jack Canfield's original *Chicken Soup for the Soul*, wrote her own book in 1998 explaining the Rules, with the self-explanatory title of *If Life is a Game, These are the Rules*. There are few more succinct or wiser takes on how to find a bit of spiritual progress in life than these. Enjoy them if you haven't seen them before, and read Carter-Scott's book for more clarification.

THE RULES FOR BEING HUMAN:

When you were born, you didn't come with an owner's manual; these guidelines make life work better.

1) You will receive a body. You may love it or hate it, but it will be yours for the duration of your life on Earth.

2) You will be presented with lessons. You are enrolled in a full-time informal school called 'life.' Each day in this school you will

have the opportunity to learn lessons. You may like the lessons or hate them, but you have designed them as part of your curriculum.

3) There are no mistakes, only lessons. Growth is a process of experimentation, a series of trials, errors, and occasional victories. The failed experiments are as much a part of the process as the experiments that work.

4) A lesson is repeated until learned. Lessons will be repeated to you in various forms until you have learned them. When you have learned them, you can then go on to the next lesson.

5) Learning does not end. There is no part of life that does not contain lessons. If you are alive, there are lessons to be learned.

6) 'There' is no better than 'here'. When your 'there' has become a 'here,' you will simply obtain a 'there' that will look better to you than your present 'here'.

7) Others are only mirrors of you. You cannot love or hate something about another person unless it reflects something you love or hate about yourself.

8) What you make of your life is up to you. You have all the tools and resources you need. What you do with them is up to you.

9) Your answers lie inside of you. All you need to do is look, listen, and trust.

10) You will forget all of this at birth. You can remember if you want.

(From the book "If Life is a Game, These are the Rules" by Cherie Carter-Scott, copyright 1998)

More on Fate and Free Will

Q: Are our lives determined by fate or free will?

A: Yes.

There is good evidence that the question of fate vs. free will is a meaningless one, and that ultimately both are in play. We must here refer back to Bohr's law of complementarity, which he derived from physics, but which is also symbolized by the Taoist yin-yang symbol on Bohr's family crest. Those who are even minimally familiar with Eastern thought will immediately understand this concept. We can't know black except as it contrasts with white: if the entire world were black, we would not know black as a separate thing - it would just be "what is," and we wouldn't be able to pick it out or recognize it. In the same fashion, a world that is all white, or all good, or all up, or all down is impossible. It is only in contrast and connection to an opposite or differentiated duality that things take on meaning. Jesus needs the Devil, and the Devil needs Jesus. If black exists, it *reveals* the existence of white: *both* must therefore have manifestation and meaning. ALL opposites fall into this recognizable pattern. Good and bad, up and down, ad infinitum.

Of note here is that the "Oneness" of the universe, although we may recognize it on a conceptual level, and occasionally obtain a taste or experience of it at times, is not an easy thing to describe or get a handle on, simply because it is the unrecognized and underlying framework of existence. As such, it is nearly invisible. There is nothing to contrast it against, although philosophically we may set it in opposition to the general term "duality." However, since duality, or separateness, also seems to be a taken-for-granted "what is" in our everyday world, these are seeming opposites that take some practice to see. In addition, we have a somewhat different situation here, in that duality *itself* has its origins in the primordial One: the One is beyond duality; it is an unbroken and infinitely connected foundation. It is the strata from which black and white, fate and free will themselves arise. It is like water to a fish; water is the unrecognized milieu in which the fish swims. The fish no doubt never thinks about "water." (Of course, the fish probably doesn't think about much at all.) We rarely think about air, although it would come into sharper focus for us were it suddenly to be taken away, shown to be in contrast to the lack of air. Oneness, however, is the source of all dualities, includes and contains all dualities, and is above and beyond them. It is the undifferentiated ground of things, prior to their differentiation and naming. There are parallels in many religions for this process, including the Judeo-Christian-Islamic ones. Separateness arises from the recognition, distinction, and naming of subsets of the One, which brings things into being. This is the dawning of duality. This is how things are "created" from the Void in the Bible. (Although, unlike Eastern traditions, God himself here is dualistic, and remains separate from man and his other creations.) Thus, to bring ourselves back around to our discussion, we would not know fate or free will if either one was all that existed. We know them only because they are complementary: they exist together, they are part of a larger whole, and they define each other.

***

So what would it be like if there were only fate? A good example might be the "block universe" mentioned earlier. Everything, all events for all of time, would be stuck in a four dimensional aspic, unchanging and solidified. Events would be raisins in a loaf of raisin bread that we "came upon" as we worked our way through the loaf. But now there would be no quantum uncertainty; here the raisin events would be completely determined in advance. Except that even the idea of "coming upon" would be an incorrect terminology: all things would exist at once in space and time. Any movement would be illusory, although it would be difficult to explain how our consciousness itself moved within this static realm. (How can a universe without movement have movement of consciousness? If all is One, then presumably consciousness is part of the One - it would be difficult to envision that our thoughts don't move, or that they are perhaps completely predetermined.) And could the block universe really have locked in the results of *every* single wave function collapse for every single electron or other variable that existed throughout all of time across the entire universe? It seems a bit of a stretch.

It would also cause moral problems: morals and ethics are products of the idea that we have a choice in things. If all is fated, then morals and ethics become meaningless: there are no alternatives to choose from. Responsibility makes no sense. There is nothing to be responsible *for*: there are no "consequences" of our actions; only fixed events in spacetime. Why get mad about, or even feel sorry for, that crack mom on welfare who allows her worthless drug-dealer boyfriend to sexually abuse her 3 year old? It's simply part of the aspic. She can't change it, and your outrage can't change it. It's therefore not even worth getting upset about. This view could quickly lead to nihilism: a vacant pointlessness would hover over human life.

Conversely, what would it be like if only free will existed? It's difficult to even speculate here, as mountains of anecdotal as well as scientific research shows that this is so unlikely as to be a negligible possibility. The evidence is all around us: I have my dad's bad knees, or my mom's dark eyes. I am of a certain race, culture, and socio-economic status. My life has been determined for me in myriad ways that intertwine their tendrils in an endlessly complex and personal butterfly effect that reaches from my past to my future. And we haven't even gotten to my astrological chart yet. More impressively, experiments by the American physiologist Benjamin Libet show a disturbing mismatch between free-will volitional acts and body processes that he calls "readiness potentials." In his experiments, he asked volunteers sitting at a table and hooked up to an EEG machine to simply move their hands whenever they wanted to, and note on an accurate clock at what second they *decided* to do this. Amazingly, the EEGs showed that a full 1/5 second before they "made a decision" of a free-will volitional nature to move their hand, the electrodes showed that this movement was already in process. Our poorly-understood unconscious mind and other factors play a much larger role than we would like to admit in all of the lofty, well-thought-out decisions that we make in our lives. Freud, of course, knew this a hundred years ago.

One can continue to go even deeper here, and talk about the *extremely* odd "delayed choice" experiments in quantum physics. Or, to mix in a wild card, the basic indeterminacy of quantum mechanics itself, and experiments such as the double slit, show that we *cannot* predict the future with certainty, and thus cannot determine it through pure free will *or* through a better understanding of fate: randomness itself plays a real and concrete role in reality.

What does it all mean? No one knows, but modern astrologers seem to have the best approach in their day to day workings. To recap the analogy from the last chapter, we come across "raisins" of only a vague nature in the loaf (or block universe) as we (yes) actually move through the slices. It is the (often unconsciously, or at least connected to the unconscious) exercising of our free will *within the probability curve that is allotted to us* that "collapses" the vague raisin events into actualities and moves our lives forward. The future is murky but not completely unknown; our choices are undetermined but not completely free. It is a partnership, fate and free will, working together in conjunction with both the universe and with our own consciousness that "determines" what will happen in our lives. As the particle and wave duality of matter hint that there is a deeper level to physics than we have yet discovered, so too does the seemingly incompatible duality of fate and free will in our lives hint that there is a deeper level to reality itself, beyond physics, than we are used to considering.

Limitations Will Set Us Free

> "A happy person is not a person in a certain set of circumstances, but rather a person with a certain set of attitudes"—Hugh Downs

> "I seldom think about my limitations, and they never make me sad. Perhaps there is just a touch of yearning at times; but it is vague, like a breeze among flowers."—Helen Keller

Let's take an imaginary journey. Suppose that we are born blind. Suppose further, for the sake of analogy, that we are living alone on the top of a very large column, perhaps a quarter mile in diameter, but that we don't have any idea where on this space that we actually are. No one has shown us the extent or boundaries of this column; all that we know is that it is very high, is circular, and to fall off would mean certain death. What would be our lot? Most likely, we would be paralyzed with fear by not knowing where our boundaries (limitations) were, and afraid to take a step in any direction, lest we should discover the edge inadvertently and fall off, plunging to our death. This is, by the way, not an unreasonable position to take. We might discover, therefore, that we have unfortunately ended up with very diminished lives, and very stuck ones: not knowing our limits, and being afraid to move in any direction, we are constricted and trapped.

Now suppose that there actually ARE people available that we didn't notice before, who can help us navigate this landscape; but in our fear and isolation, it has never occurred to us to open our mouths, and ask if anyone else were out there. But maybe one day, this does dawn on us, and we realize that help was actually waiting there all the time, just for the asking. Someone appears who takes our hand and walks us around and through our space on the top of the column, someone who is able to show us where the edges are and help us develop a mental roadmap that we can use in the future. Aha! Now our life has opened up: we still have limitations (blindness and living on a column), but *within our limitations*, we are as unfettered and mobile now as a woman or man can be. The feeling of freedom is indeed overwhelming: we can dance, waltz, cartwheel —nearly fly!— as long as we stay within the parameters which have been laid out for us, which we now know. Our life has opened up; we are released from our previous, and partially self-imposed, limitations.

Human freedom always exists within parameters and boundaries. There are more self-imposed ones than external ones. We all have scotomas, blind spots in our vision that limit our direct perception of the world. None of us can fully "see" the edges of our possibilities. None of us has ultimate freedom; all of us have our circumscribed limits. Part of the search for wisdom is the process of discovering where those limitations and boundaries are, *accepting them*, and then finding meaning, movement, and freedom within them. No one is above this universal law, no one has it "better" than us: we are all part of the human condition. Some may seem to have more of a particular "thing" than others, but that is because we are training our vision on only one part of the picture, and not seeing the whole. That, too, is part of the human condition. We can look to Helen Keller and Stephen Hawking for the antidote to this type of skewed thinking: both of them were and are in their own ways happy, joyous, and free. They *made* it so. They didn't waste time bemoaning their fate, but discovered the edges of their worlds, and maximized *their* territory on the column. The happy and free people that we see are not happy and free because they don't have limitations: they are happy and free because they know what those limitations are. They accept their constraints, and work within the territory given to *them*. The *I Ching* (Hexagram 30) states:

> "Human life on earth is conditioned and unfree, and when man recognizes this limitation and makes himself dependent upon the harmonious

> and beneficent forces of the cosmos, he achieves success."

Acceptance of our constraints, and gratitude for what we *do* have, are not only the answer to the problems of our limitations, but are also the key to finding their perimeters. We are fortunate in astrology in that we have a tangible roadmap that shows us not only our encumbrances, but our talents and gifts as well. We have been shown the edges of our personal territories, and have found that they are as vast or as constricted as we allow them to be. We cannot directly venture beyond; much of life we have to simply assume, or accept through the testimony of others. But we can find, once the boundaries have been shown to us, that our particular circle contains a lifetime of learning, exploration, satisfaction, and joy.

There IS No End

Peter Russell has said that "we are the universe's way of looking at itself." Amit Goswami has a book called *The Self-Aware Universe*, and Dean Radin chimes in with *The Conscious Universe*. Buddhism talks of the primacy of consciousness, and Hinduism extends that to the idea that Consciousness consists not just of that which is between our own ears, but is of a more universal and connected form, ourselves being nodes. God, material manifestation, humans, and Consciousness are One. Plato talked about the Forms, Jung about the Archetypes. Astrology has its own set of archetypes. All are recognition that there is *something* to the universe beyond simple mechanics, quantum or otherwise. Materialism has been on the rise, along with humanism, in the Age of Aquarius. It would be a shame if it were to completely erase our memories of the other astrological archetypes, as happened in the "Dark Ages" in Europe, when religion for a time became all, during the peak of the Age of Pisces. Perhaps that is the way that things are meant to unfold, however. We forget the past, and we are invited to repeat it, both personally and societally. We express the play of Lila. The Ages themselves are but mere spokes in another wheel, albeit one that takes 26,000 years to turn. Even that is a drop in the cosmic bucket. Wheels turn within wheels, cycles oscillate within cycles, inside and outside are a Mobius strip.

The universe as we find it, then, has no choice but to exist, and we within it; it is the yang portion of yet another cycle. Form follows function, and we are part of the function, in both a mathematical and spiritual sense. We surely manifest the universe as much as it manifests us. Not personally, in our imaginary and temporary ego-shells, but as nodes of the collective, as parts of the Whole. Physics describes a part of the Oneness, and astrology as well weaves its threads through the warp and weft. But the Whole is beyond both of these, and includes them, and more. It includes all. Its limits will never be reached; R will always equal K+1. It is a cyclical, and yet ever-changing and evolving thing, a kaleidoscope that is always turning. We are part of the dance: physics, consciousness, spirituality, synchronicity, and astrology are all part of the dance. We intertwine and move together, waltzing across the cosmic floor; leader and follower blur together, fate and free lose their meaning. The music continues, the song of the universe plays on...

Additional Reading

Feedback is, of course, always welcome. Email the author at danceofastrology@outlook.com.

If you have particularly enjoyed one or more sections in this book, you may be interested in further reading related to a particular topic. During the course of writing this book, I have had the great privilege of becoming aware of many, many other books that were intriguing, thought-provoking, and enjoyable, involving all of these subjects. I am more than happy to pass them along to readers, who, like myself, may not have been aware of some of them. Again, the idea here is not to hoard a proprietary set of ideas, but to take part in the sharing of knowledge that we all may access. That's how growth in human understanding will take place in the current Age of Aquarius. There are also hundreds of interesting websites, YouTube videos, podcasts, and a lesser number of DVDs out there. We will limit ourselves here to published books. Be aware, however, that while metaphysics changes very little, as it intends to deal with universal truths, science changes practically day by day. Thus, for the latest thinking in science, one really does need to keep up the many excellent websites and newsfeeds available.

There is quite a long list below. Please don't get the impression that I've read all of these: most of them I haven't. They do include a fair amount of books that I've actually read (especially in the astrology, metaphysics, and new physics categories), but also far more that I've gotten from the library and skimmed through, or purchased for future reading. (I'll need at least another couple of lifetimes.) A few of them simply looked intriguing on Amazon. In light of the space that the list might take, and in view of the fact that information is so easily obtained these days online, we will confine ourselves simply to author and title.

Some categories have more entries than others, and even so the list does not contain all of the books that it could have. The astrology group, in particular, contains simply some of my favorites; my own fairly typical library contains many more titles. If you are not on the list, please don't feel slighted; there are literally thousands of astrology books out there, and the line had to be arbitrarily drawn somewhere. I *would* like to give a word of thanks at this point to the increasing number of astrologers who are specifically talking about synchronicity and even delving into quantum ideas in their writings, as well as to those brave physicists and science writers who are willing to risk the scorn of their colleagues to voice new and fresh theories, opinions, and ideas. Some of them will bear fruit and point us towards the next leap forward; perhaps one that *will* have a place in it for the consideration of astrology once again.

Finally, for those who may have read this book but not come to it from an astrological point of view: I invite you to investigate the subject yourselves rather than just getting others' opinions on it second-hand, especially others who have not themselves obtained any knowledge of its workings. Astrology is one of the most amazing tools for self-discovery and wonder at the mysteries of the universe that anyone could ever be privy to. It's been a blessing and a joy to have had it as a part of my own particular journey, and I thank all who have contributed to its tenacious flourishing in the face of skeptical paradigms. I hope that, if you haven't already, you will consider making it part of your own journey. Namaste.

Physics and Astronomy

Al-Khalili, Jim
Quantum, A Guide For the Perplexed
Black Holes, Wormholes, and Time Machines
Paradox, the Nine Greatest Enigmas in Physics

Baker, Joanne
50 Physics Ideas You Really Need To Know
50 Quantum Physics Ideas You Really Need To Know
50 Ideas You Really Need To Know, Universe

Brennan, Richard P.
Heisenberg Probably Slept Here (physicist bios)

Callender, Craig, and Ralph Edney
Introducing Time, A Graphic Guide

Clegg, Brian (editor)
30-Second Quantum Theory

Cox, Brian, and Jeff Forshaw
The Quantum Universe (And Why Anything That Can Happen, Does)

Crease, Robert P., and Alfred Scharff Goldhaber
The Quantum Moment (historical view)

Davies, Paul
About Time, Einstein's Unfinished Revolution

Dickinson, Terence
Hubble's Universe, Greatest Discoveries and Latest Images

Einstein, Albert

The Collected Papers, Vol. 2, 1900-1909 (Anna Beck, translator)

The Evolution of Physics (with Leopold Infeld)

Epstein, Lewis Carroll

Relativity Visualized

Feynman, Richard (with Ralph Leighton and Edward Hutchings)

Surely, You're Joking, Mr. Feynman!

Flitcroft, Ian, and Britt Spencer

Journey By Starlight

Ford, Kenneth W.

The Quantum World: Quantum Physics For Everyone

Gamow, George

One, Two, Three, Infinity..., Facts and Speculations of Science

Gefter, Amanda

Trespassing on Einstein's Lawn

Gilmore, Robert

Alice in Quantumland

Goswami, Amit

Quantum Mechanics (textbook)

Greene, Brian

The Fabric of the Cosmos: Space, Time, and the Texture of Reality

Hart-Davis, Adam

DK Science, the Definitive Visual Guide

Hawking, Stephen

The Illustrated Brief History of Time
The Universe in a Nutshell

Jackson, Tom
Physics, An Illustrated History of the Foundations of Science

Jones, Roger S.
Physics for the Rest of Us: Ten Basic Ideas of 20th Century Physics
(one of the few physics book that speaks open-mindedly, at least in a historical sense, about astrology and other alternative or philosophical ideas)

Kastner, Ruth E.
Understanding Our Unseen Reality: Solving Quantum Riddles

Koupelis, Theo, and Karl F Kuhn
In Quest of the Universe, 5th Edition

Kumar, Manjit
Quantum: Einstein, Bohr, and the Great Debate about the Nature of Reality (science history)

Lederman, Leon
The God Particle: If the Universe is the Answer, What is the Question?

Lindley, David
Uncertainty: Einstein, Heisenberg, Bohr, and the Struggle For the Soul of Science (science history)

Manly, Steven L., and Steven Fournier
Relativity and Quantum Physics For Beginners

Marshall, Ian, and F. David Peat

Who's Afraid of Schrödinger's Cat?: All the New Science Ideas You Need to Keep Up With the New Thinking

McEvoy, J.P., and Oscar Zarate
Introducing Quantum Theory, A Graphic Guide

Morrison, Philip, and Phylis Morrison
Powers of Ten

Pickover, Clifford A.
Sex, Drugs, Einstein, & Elves
The Physics Book
Fractal 3D Magic (see the back cover of this book)

Rucker, Rudolf v.B.
Geometry, Relativity, and the Fourth Dimension

Sagan, Carl
Cosmos
The Demon-Haunted World: Science as a Candle in the Dark

Schwartz, Joseph, and Michael McGuinness
Introducing Einstein: A Graphic Guide

Schumacher, Benjamin (Great Courses book and DVD set)
Quantum Mechanics: The Physics of the Microscopic World

Southwell, Gareth
50 Philosophy of Science Ideas You Really Need To Know

Sparrow, Giles
Cosmos

Suplee, Curt
Physics in the 20th Century

Whyntie, Tom, and Oliver Pugh
Introducing Particle Physics, A Graphic Guide

Wheeler, John Archibald, Wojciech Hubert Zurek, editors
Quantum Theory and Measurement

Wolfson, Richard (Great Courses book and DVD set)
Einstein's Relativity and the Quantum Revolution

Alternative Physics

Abbott, Edwin A. (foreword by Isaac Asimov)
Flatland, A Romance in Many Dimensions

Bohm, David
The Essential David Bohm (edited by Lee Nichol)
Thought as a System

Bohr, Niels
Atomic Physics and Human Knowledge

Capra, Fritjof
The Tao of Physics: An Exploration of the Parallels Between Modern Physics and Eastern Mysticism

Carroll, Sean
From Eternity to Here: The Quest For the Ultimate Theory of Time

Chopra, Deepak, and Leonard Mlodinow
War of the Worldviews: Science vs. Spirituality

Davies, Paul
The Mind of God: The Scientific Basis For a Rational World
*The Matter Myt*h (with John Gribbin)

Elvee, Richard Q., editor
Mind in Nature (Papers delivered at the 1981 Nobel Conference)

Gleiser, Marcelo
The Island of Knowledge: The Limits of Science and the Search For Meaning

The Dancing Universe: From Creation Myths to the Big Bang

Goldberg, Dave
The Universe in the Rearview Mirror: How Hidden Symmetries Shape Reality

Goswami, Amit
The Self-Aware Universe: How Consciousness Creates the Material World

Heisenberg, Werner
Physics and Philosophy: The Revolution in Modern Science
Physics and Beyond: Encounters and Conversations

Herbert, Nick
Quantum Reality: Beyond the New Physics

Jahn, Robert G., and Brenda Dunne
Margins of Reality: The Role of Consciousness in the Physical World

Jones, Roger S.
Physics as Metaphor

Kaiser, David
How the Hippies Saved Physics: Science, Counterculture, and the Quantum Revival (science history)

Lanza, Robert (with Bob Berman)
Biocentrism: How Life and Consciousness are the Keys to Understanding the True Nature of the Universe

Nadeau, Robert, and Medas Kafatos
The Non-Local Universe

Planck, Max

The Philosophy of Physics

Poe, Edgar Allan

Eureka: A Prose Poem

Rosenblum, Bruce, and Fred Kuttner

Quantum Enigma: Physics Encounters Consciousness

Schild, Rudolph (editor in chief)

Cosmology of Consciousness: Quantum Physics and the Neuroscience of Mind

Schirmacher, Wolfgang (editor)

German Essays on Science in the 20th Century

Schrödinger, Erwin

My View of the World

Stapp, Henry P.

The Mindful Universe: Quantum Mechanics and the Participating Observer

Talbot, Michael

The Holographic Universe

Beyond the Quantum

Mysticism and the New Physics

Toben, Bob, and Fred Alan Wolf

Space-Time and Beyond: Toward an Explanation of the Unexplainable

Tulku, Tarthang

Time, Space, & Knowledge: A New Vision of Reality

Walker, Evan Harris

The Physics of Consciousness

Wilber, Ken (editor, with Ann Niehaus)
Quantum Questions: Mystical Writings of the World's Greatest Physicists

Wolf, Fred Alan
Taking the Quantum Leap: The New Physics For Non-Scientists

Wolfe, Robert
Science of the Sages: Scientists Encountering Nonduality from Quantum Physics to Cosmology

Zukav, Gary
The Dancing Wu Li Masters: An Overview of the New Physics

Consciousness

Blackmore, Susan
Consciousness: An Introduction
Conversations on Consciousness

Chalmers, David J.
The Conscious Mind: In Search of a Fundamental Theory

Chandler, Keith
The Mind Paradigm: A Unified Model of Mental and Physical Reality

Dossey, Larry
One Mind: How Our Individual Mind is Part Of a Greater Consciousness and Why It Matters

Fontana, David
The Secret Language of Dreams

Hameroff, Stuart; Alfred W. Kaszniak; and Alwyn C. Scott (editors)
Toward a Science of Consciousness: The First Tucson Discussions and Debates

Herr, Eva
Consciousness: Bridging the Gap Between Conventional Science and The New Super Science of Quantum Mechanics

Hofstadter, Douglas R., and Daniel C. Dennett (composed and arranged by)
The Mind's I: Fantasies and Reflections on Self and Soul

Horgan, John
Rational Mysticism: Spirituality Meets Science in the Search For Enlightenment

Papineau, David, and Daniel C. Selina
Introducing Consciousness: A Graphic Guide

Pelletier, Kenneth R.
Toward a Science of Consciousness

Robinson, Daniel N.
Consciousness and its Implications (Great Courses book and DVD set)

Russell, Peter
From Science to God

Ryle, Gilbert
The Concept of Mind

Searle, John R.
The Mystery of Consciousness

Shear, Jonathan (editor)
Explaining Consciousness: The Hard Problem

Wilber, Ken
The Essential Ken Wilbur: An Introductory Reader

Wolf, Fred Alan
The Dreaming Universe: A Mind-Expanding Journey Into the Realm Where Psyche and Physics Meet

Synchronicity and Psi

Carter, Chris
Science and Psychic Phenomena

Chandler, Keith
Psi: What it is and How it Works

Hayward, Jeremy W.
Perceiving Ordinary Magic: Science and Intuitive Wisdom

Hyde, Maggie
Jung and Astrology
Introducing Jung (with Michael McGuinness)

Jung, C.G.
Synchronicity, an Acausal Connecting Principle

Koestler, Arthur
The Roots of Coincidence

Mansfield, Victor
Synchronicity, Science, and Soul-Making

Mitchell, Edgar D. (with John White, editor)
Psychic Exploration, A Challenge For Science

Peat, F. David
Synchronicity, The Bridge Between Matter and Mind

Progoff, Ira
Jung, Synchronicity, and Human Destiny

Radin, Dean
Entangled Minds
The Conscious Universe

Rhine, J.B.
Extra-Sensory Perception

Tart, Charles T.
The End of Materialism: How Evidence of the Paranormal is Bringing Science and Spirit Together

Astrology

Arroyo, Stephen

Astrology, Psychology, and the Four Elements: An Energy Approach to Astrology and Its Use in the Counseling Arts

Astrology, Karma & Transformation: The Inner Dimensions of the Birth Chart

Chart Interpretation Handbook: Guidelines for Understanding the Essentials of the Birth Chart

Relationships and Life Cycles: Astrological Patterns of Personal Experience

Bobrick, Benson

The Fated Sky: Astrology in History

Brady, Bernadette

Cosmos, Chaosmos, and Astrology: Rethinking the Nature of Astrology

Braha, James

How to be a Great Astrologer: The Planetary Aspects Explained

How to Predict Your Future: Secrets of Eastern and Western Astrology

Carter, Charles (C.E.O.)

An Encyclopedia of Psychological Astrology

Clifford, Frank C.
Getting to the Heart of Your Chart: Playing Astrological Detective

Cochrane, David
Astrology for the 21st Century

Cornelius, Geoffrey
The Moment of Astrology

Cunningham, Donna
How to Read Your Astrological Chart: Aspects of the Cosmic Puzzle
An Astrological Guide to Self-Awareness

Damiani, Anthony
Astronoesis

Davidson, Ronald
Synastry

Dean, Geoffrey (with Arthur Mather)
Recent Advances in Natal Astrology—A Critical Review 1900-1976
(see note elsewhere in this book regarding Dean lying about his birthdate)

Diaz, Armand M.
Integral Astrology: Understanding the Ancient Discipline in the Contemporary World

Doane, Doris Chase
Astrology: 30 Years Research
(interesting in that it points up both the informal empirical investigations that separates astrology from "superstition," and the typical layperson nature of those investigations)

Elwell, Dennis

Cosmic Loom: The New Science of Astrology

Eysenck, H. J., and D. K. Nias

Astrology, Science or Superstition?

Falvey, Tom

Principles of Astrology

Forrest, Steven

The Inner Sky

The Changing Sky

Gauquelin, Michel

The Cosmic Clocks

Cosmic Influences on Human Behavior: The Planetary Factors in Personality

(he has many more books than these, all focusing on his original research studies)

Geary, Nan

Astrology: The New Generation

(essays by up-and-comers, including Frank C. Clifford and many more)

Grasse, Ray

The Waking Dream

Signs of the Times

Greene, Liz

Saturn: A New Look at an Old Devil

Relating: An Astrological Guide to Living With Others on a Small Planet

The Outer Planets and Their Cycles

The Jupiter/Saturn Conference Lectures

(with Steven Arroyo)

(This writer had the pleasure of attending.)

Hand, Robert
Planets in Transit: Life Cycles for Living
Essays on Astrology
Horoscope Symbols

Holden, James Herschel
A History of Horoscopic Astrology

Hone, Margaret E.
The Modern Textbook of Astrology
(The very first "real" astrology book that I read, in my 1st class, along with McCaffery's "Graphic Astrology." An antique now!)

Howell, Alice O.
Jungian Symbolism in Astrology
Jungian Synchronicity in the Astrological Signs and Ages

Hyde, Maggie (see synchronicity section)

Kochunas, Brad Hiljanen
The Astrological Imagination, Where Psyche and Cosmos Meet

Leinbach, Esther .
Degrees of the Zodiac

Lewis, James R.
The Astrology Encyclopedia

Lutin, Michael
SunShines: The Astrology of Being Happy

Mann, A. T.
The Round Art of Astrology

Michelsen, Neil F. (with Rique Pottenger)
The American Ephemeris for the 21st Century, 2000-2050 at Noon
The American Ephemeris for the 20th Century: 1900 to 2000 at Noon
(what can you say; the standards. Although if you have an Iphone, check out the Iphemeris app)

Moore, Marcia with Mark Douglas
Astrology, The Divine Science

Nassar, Rafael
Under One Sky

Oken, Alan
Alan Oken's Complete Astrology: The Classic Guide to Modern Astrology

Omarr, Sidney
My World of Astrology (the "astrologer to the stars" of his day, and a pivotal figure in popularizing astrology for the masses)

Parker, Derek and Julia
The Compleat Astrologer
(the ultimate coffee table book; first edition is still the best, used)

Perry, Glenn
An Introduction to AstroPsychology: A Synthesis of Modern Astrology & Depth Psychology

Phillipson, Gary
Astrology in the Year Zero

Pottenger, Mark
Astrological Research Methods, Vol. I

Ptolemy (translated by F.E. Robbins)
Tetrabiblos

Rogers-Gallagher, Kim
Astrology for the Light Side of the Brain

Rudhyar, Dane
The Astrology of Personality: A Re-Formulation of Astrological Concepts and Ideals, in Terms of Contemporary Psychology and Philosophy

Sakoian, Frances, and Louis S Acker
The Astrologer's Handbook (the cookbook for a generation!)
The Astrology of Human Relationships
Predictive Astrology: Understanding Transits as the Key to the Future

Sasportas, Howard
The Twelve Houses, Exploring the Houses of the Horoscope

Seymour, Percy
The Scientific Basis of Astrology: Tuning to the Music of the Planets
(interesting search for physical "causes")

Snow, Edward (editor, Astrology News Service)
Astrology Considered: A Thinking Person's Guide
(and his excellent ANS website)

Tarnas, Richard
Cosmos and Psyche
Prometheus the Awakener

Tompkins, Sue
Aspects in Astrology

Vaughn, Richard
Astrology in Modern Language

Weaver, Helen (editor, with Jean-Louis Brau, Allan Edmands, and others)
Larousse Encyclopedia of Astrology

West, John Anthony and Jan Gerhard Toonder
The Case for Astrology (West has produced subsequent editions on his own)

Metaphysics and Spirituality

Anand, Sudhir
The Essence of the Hindu Religion

Aurelius, Marcus
Meditations (with Martin Stanforth intro)

Bhaktivedanta, A. C., Swami Prabhupada
Bhagavad Gita, As it Is

Bello, J. (Julio)
Prisoners of Space and Time: Our Bondage to a Counterfeit Reality

Blofeld, John (translator)
The Zen Teachings of Huang Po: On the Transmission of Mind

Bronowski, J.
The Ascent of Man

Byrne, Rhonda
The Secret

Bucke, Richard Maurics
Cosmic Consciousness

Campbell, Joseph
A Joseph Campbell companion (edited by Diane K. Osbon)

Carter-Scott, Cherie
If Life is a Game, These are the Rules

Coogan, Michael D. (editor)
The New Oxford Annotated Bible, Third Edition

Das, Rasamandala
The Illustrated Encyclopedia of Hinduism

Davis, Leesa S.
Advaita Vedanta and Zen Buddhism: Deconstructive modes of Spiritual Inquiry

Dupre, Ben
50 Philosophy Ideas You Really Need To Know

Easwaran, Eknath (translator)
The Dhammapada
The Bhagavad Gita
The Upanishads

Eckhart, Meister
Selected Writings
Meister Eckhart, From Whom God Hid Nothing: Sermons, Writings, & Sayings (edited by David O'Neal)
Meister Eckhart, An Introduction to the Study of His Works, With an Anthology of His Sermons (with James M. Clark)

Farrer-Halls, Gill
The Illustrated Encyclopedia of Buddhist Wisdom

Furuya, Mitsutoshi
Basic Buddhism Through Comics

Goldberg, Philip
American Veda: How Indian Spirituality Changed The West (history)

Graves, Robert (introduction)
The New Larousse Encyclopedia of Mythology

Hanson, V., Stewart, R., and Nicholson, S.
Karma: Rhythmic Return to Harmony

Huxley, Aldous
The Perennial Philosophy

James, William
The Varieties of Religious Experience

Jung, C. G.
Man and His Symbols
The Viking Portable Jung (edited by Joseph Campbell)

Kim, Jaegwon, Ernest Sosa, and Gary S.Rosenkrantz,
A Companion to Metaphysics, 2nd Edition

Krishnamurti
The First and Last Freedom
The Krishnamurti Reader

Kurtz, Ernest, and Katherine Ketcham
The Spirituality of Imperfection

Lash, John
The Seeker's Handbook: The Complete Guide to Spiritual Pathfinding

Law, Stephen
Philosophy (Visual Reference Guides)

Lao Tzu
The Tao Te Ching (Derek Lin, translator)

Magid, Barry
Ending the Pursuit of Happiness: A Zen Guide

Maharshi, Ramana
The Spiritual Teaching of Ramana Maharshi (foreword by C.G. Jung)

McGreal, Ian P. (editor)
Great Thinkers of the Western World
Great Thinkers of the Eastern World

Miller, Timothy
Want What You Have: Discovering the Magic and Grandeur of Ordinary Existence

Millman, Dan
Living On Purpose: Straight Answers to Life's Tough Questions

Muller, Max (translator) with Jack Maguire (annotator)
Dhammapada Annotated and Explained

Ney, Alyssa
Metaphysics: An Introduction

Osborne, Richard, and Borin Van Loon
Introducing Eastern Philosophy

Plato
The Republic
The Dialogs

Ram Das
Be Here Now

Rahula, Walpola
What the Buddha Taught

Reagan, Michael
The Hand of God
Inside the Mind of God

(two books of quotes bridging science and spirituality, both with introductions by Sharon Begley)

Red Pine (translator)
The Lankavatara Sutra

Reps, Paul and Nyogen Senzaki (compilers)
Zen Flesh, Zen Bones

Ricard, Matthieu, and Trinh Xuan Thuan
The Quantum and the Lotus

Robinson, Dave, and Judy Groves
Introducing Philosophy, a Graphic Guide

Rosenberg, Donna
World Mythology, an Anthology of the Great Myths and Epics

Ross, Nancy Wilson
Three Ways of Asian Wisdom
The World of Zen (editor)

Shearer, Alistair
The Upanishads (with Peter Russell, translators)
Effortless Being, The Yoga Sutras of Patanjali (translator)

Smith, Huston
The World's Religions
The Illustrated World's Religions

Sinetar, Marsha
Ordinary People as Monks and Mystics: Lifestyles for Self-Discovery
Sri Nisargadatta Maharaj
I am That

Suzuki, D. T.
On Indian Mahayana Buddhism
An Introduction to Zen Buddhism
Zen Mind, Beginner's Mind
Zen Buddhism, Selected Writings (edited by William Barrett)

Swami Nikhilananda
The Upanishads

Terhart, Franjo, and Schulze, Janina
World Religions: Origins, History, Practices, Beliefs, Worldviews

Underhill, Evelyn
Mysticism

Watts, Alan
The Book: On the Taboo Against Knowing Who You Are
The Way of Zen
Does It Matter?
This is It
The Two Hands of God
Myth and Religion
The Essence of Alan Watts
Tao, The Watercourse Way
Become What You Are

Wheeler, John (not the physicist)
You Were Never Born
The Light Behind Consciousness

Wilhelm, Richard, translated by Cary F Baynes
The I Ching, or Book of Changes

Wilkinson, Phillip
The (DK) Illustrated Dictionary of Religions
Mythology (Visual Reference Guide) (with Neil, Philip)

Made in the USA
Charleston, SC
12 June 2016